Hay Day
Country Market Cookbook

HayDay
Country
Market
Cookbook

by Kim Rizk

with Maggie Stearns

New Illustrations by Peter Siu

WORKMAN PUBLISHING, NEW YORK

Copyright © 1998 by Sallie Van Rensselaer and Alex Van Rensselaer
New illustrations copyright © 1998 by Peter Siu

Library of Congress Cataloging-in-Publication Data

Rizk, Kim.
Hay Day country market cookbook / by Kim Rizk; illustrations by Peter Siu
p. cm.
Includes index.
ISBN 0-7611-1429-7. —ISBN 0-7611-0025-3 (pbk.)
1. Cookery. 2. Farm produce. I. Hay Day (Firm) II. Title.
TX714.R575 1998
641.5—dc21   98-37983
CIP

Cover and book design by Paul Hanson
Front cover photograph by Kindra Clineff
Back cover photograph by Hugh Smith

Workman books are available at special discounts when purchased in bulk for
premiums and sales promotions as well as for fund-raising or educational use.
Special editions or book excerpts can be created to specification.
For details, contact the Special Sales Director at the address below.

Workman Publishing Company, Inc.
708 Broadway
New York, NY 10003-9555

First printing October 1998
10 9 8 7 6 5 4 3 2 1

Dedication

Hay Day has flourished over the years because of the spirit and imagination of the people who work here. Whether they knead the bread, scrub the kitchen, drive the trucks, or greet customers at the registers, their ideas, loyalty, and enthusiasm have made Hay Day a very special place.

Some are new, some arrived when we joined forces with Sutton Place Gourmet, some have been here since biking over after school years ago; they all have a love for the business that transcends hours or job descriptions. They invent recipes and bake pies; they build spectacular produce displays; they stand in the snow selling Christmas trees or drive to the market at three in the morning. They are wonderful people and this book is dedicated to them.

Thanks

Maggie Stearns has been the voice of *The Hay Day Rural Times* and has forged much of the style and spirit of the company newsletter over the last decade. This book would not have been possible without her candor, imagination, and endless willingness to pick up the phone.

Christina Baxter's energy and flair is reflected every day in all our stores, and on every page of this book. Hay Day and Sutton Place Gourmet owe much of their style and spirit to her creativity; her support and insight have have been invaluable in writing this book.

Thanks also to: Varick Niles for her charming *Rural Times* illustrations, fabulous artistic style, and devoted service; Sallie Williams for consistently delicious and inspirational menus; Tom Johnston for his continued support and enthusiasm; executive chef Steven Roberts for recipes and concepts; Pascal Jubault for technical baking advice; Jennifer Clement and Chris Snell for their enthusiasm and imagination; Bill McGowan for support, information, and time on the phone; Connor Usowski, Tim Schlenz, Omar Shilleh, and Hector Heredia for invaluable produce information; Susan Dolan for sound advice on cheeses and other specialty ingredients; Claude Mallinger for culinary advice and wisdom on a wide range of subjects; Nancy Davis for steadfast recipe testing; Dawn McLaughlin for inspirational ideas and technical advice; Betsy Garside for enthusiastic recipe testing and constructive suggestions; Amin, Natalie, and Katherine Rizk for devoted sampling and support; Susan Testa for continued enthusiasm and support of the Hay Day philosophy; Karl and Sallie Strand, David Hamilton, Jack Seeno, and Randi Brawley for inspiration, technical advice, and recipe testing; Lorraine, Denise, and Rosie for answering all my requests from the commissary; Lisa Simenauer and Neil Oldford for their help with the Hay Day product line; Marianne Jeffries and Augusta Olmedo for packing and shipping sample gift packages all across the U.S.; Graham Whitney for his cheerful smile and seventeen years of Hay Day heritage; George Pantzis for delicious biscuits and baking wisdom.

And thanks as well to the many farmers, suppliers, and producers who have provided Hay Day with an endless wealth of great products, services, and information over the years—including Ed Weiss, Vernon Gray, Rob Bildner, John Minard, Jimmy Belta, Paul Heintz, Dick Rogers, Miles and Lillian Cahn, Peter Mohn, Ann Wilder, Nancy Radke, Bob Giambalvo, Jim Lampman, Ariane Daguin, and the members of the American Cheese Society and the American Institute of Wine and Food for inspiring us all.

Special thanks to Suzanne Rafer and to Katherine Ness for their editorial skill, keen eyes, and unfailing support, and to the whole Workman Publishing team—Andrea Glickson, Ellen Morganstern, Jackie Mills, Paul Hanson, Paul Gamarello, Barbara Balch, and the entire art department for putting together such an elegant package, and Peter Workman for believing in us.

And to Alex and Sallie Van Rensselaer, without whose marketing genius, insight, enthusiasm, style, and spirit Hay Day and the *Hay Day Country Market Cookbook* would not exist at all.

Contents

Great Beginnings

These are the recipes that give any day an inspired start. There's no better way to kick off the morning than with warm Banana-Berry Muffins or Plum Breakfast Cobbler, fragrant Citrus-Steamed Pears with Honey Yogurt or a light Summer Fruit Ambrosia.

Small Pleasures

Easy dips, spreads, salsas, and toasts are the irresistible way to welcome friends. Bowls of Oven-Baked Sweet Potato Chips, Obsessive Olives, Avocado and Jicama Salsa, Tapas Skewers, or Roasted Eggplant Caviar make any get-together all the more successful.

Soups—and a Few of Our Favorite Breads

Soup simmering on the stove while bread bakes in the oven—it's a classic homey picture. Accompany Mediterranean Bean Soup, Sweet Corn and Lobster Chowder, Golden Tomato Gazpacho, or Curried Chicken and Basmati Rice Soup with Cheddar-Chive Biscuits, Hay Day's Best-Ever Potato Bread, or Ham and Cheddar Scones. Make that picture a year-round reality.

Salads for All Seasons 105

What could be more versatile than a salad? It travels well to picnics and pot lucks. It can be tossed or composed. It can be cool and crunchy or warm and wilted. Buy the freshest produce and prepare a Mozzarella, Tomato, and Grilled Fennel Salad, Peppered Peach and Vidalia Onion Salad, B.L.T. Pasta Salad, and crisp Creamy Mustard Coleslaw made light by a yogurt dressing.

The Main Attraction 129

An inventive and full-range collection of dishes that make your table the one to be at when dinner is served. *Meat (page 130)* includes well-seared Kona-Crusted Beef, a savory Mexican Meat Loaf, and a spicy Pork and Apple Chili; *Poultry (139)* serves up Lemon-Chèvre Chicken, Chicken Pies with a Puff Pastry Lid, and finger-licking Southern Pulled Chicken Barbecue; *Seafood (page 156)* offerings include an East Coast Fisherman's Stew, a Jamaican Spiced Snapper with Rum-Glazed Plantains, and a Creole/Cajun-inspired Low-Country Shrimp; look to *Vegetable Entrées (page 178)* for a Summer Vegetable Risotto, a Wild Mushroom, Spinach, and Goat Cheese Lasagne, and a time-honored Cornbread-Crusted Chili.

A Harvest of Vegetables and Grains 191

Oven-Roasted Beets, Red Onions, and Oranges, Spring Pea Medley, Buttermilk-Chive Mashed Potatoes, Grilled Ratatouille Vegetables—all easy to prepare, all with sensational flavor, and all with a touch of glamour.

Sweet Endings 211

Good meals should come to great endings and these endings are exceptional. When serving Strawberry-Apple Pie, Mixed-Fruit Summer Pudding, Fresh Apricot Coulis, Cranberry-Almond Biscotti, and Maple Cashew Crisps, be prepared to dish out plenty of second helpings.

The Pantry 249

Here are the basics, the recipes that helped make Hay Day's reputation. Dan's Mustard, Aunt Maud's Apple Cider Applesauce, Black Peppercorn Dressing, and Helen's Honey Barbecue, plus good solid stocks and perfect pie pastries. You now know our treasured secrets. Enjoy!

The Story of Hay Day

People still have a hard time believing that any normal couple would drop off the corporate ladder to open a vegetable stand on a major highway in Connecticut—but in short, that's just what we did.

The story, of course, is more complicated than that. After ten years of frustration with corporate bureaucracy, we had gone into the then very new field of hydroponics, growing beautiful tomatoes in greenhouses in Cincinnati. We loved the business, but found it incredibly hard to develop any volume; this was in the early 1970s, and as far as supermarkets were concerned, fresh tomatoes grew in little cellophane packages. Their customers were eager for our samples—they would buy them right out of the box—but we were constantly stymied when the chains wouldn't even allow a red-ripe tomato on their loading docks. We had no problem selling to specialty food stores, but that volume was hopelessly small at the time; there was no way around the fact that we needed the supermarkets in order to survive.

We struggled for several years and finally in frustration decided to take our products directly to the customer. The idea was to start with a test store, then gradually open a series of small farm stands off I-95 between Washington and Boston. We loved the Westport area, and somehow sensed that a farm stand with a rural, old-fashioned image (by now we were calling it Hay Day) would flourish there.

The fact that we loved the area turned out to be more significant than we realized. In a way, we embodied our own customers—people who had made plenty of cake mix cakes and soup mix dips but were now being led by Julia Child into a whole new world. Just when we were ready to sell fresh local produce, the neighborhood was ready to buy it.

As we began to branch out, adding local homemade bread and pies and farmstead cheeses to our wares, Hay Day grew in a direction that made us decide to phase out of hydroponics completely and put all our energies into developing the store. It was a watershed moment in the food world, and things were happening fast—we had to be quick learners to stay ahead of the business. While one of us (Sallie) studied at La Varenne in Paris, the other (Alex) went all over Europe learning about cheeses.

Friends like Helen Brody and Mimi Boyd joined us to develop recipes like Obsessive Olives and Peasant Bread that pretty much put us on the map in Fairfield County. We started the mail-order department that placed Hay Day gift boxes under Christmas trees from Connecticut to California. We published *The Hay Day Cookbook* and brought in well-known chefs to spread the gospel of fresh seasonal cooking through the Hay Day Cooking School.

Wanting to do things the old-fashioned way accidentally put us on the side of the angels. We just liked to cook with fresh vegetables and fruits and other top-of-the-line ingredients and thought even additives as natural as pectin somehow cheapened our products. Fortunately, we were out there on a surfboard when the great wave of interest in fresh healthy cooking curled onto the shores of the U.S.

So Hay Day grew from one store to five, and when an alliance with Sutton Place Gourmet (same age, similar philosophy) seemed the most natural thing in the world, we joined forces with them. We're still doing what we set out to do, but on a larger scale than we dared to envision (fourteen stores and growing); we're reaching out to customers from Washington, D.C., to Connecticut, the way we dreamed so long ago.

So with this new *Hay Day Country Market Cookbook*, we throw open the doors to Hay Day! It's not a little farm stand anymore, but the spirit is very much the same. We hope you like it.

—Alex and Sallie Van Rensselaer

The Little Farm Stand That Could

Welcome to Hay Day! Whether or not you actually know our stores, you'll discover a lot about them in these pages—not just the recipes for the things we sell, but the style and spirit of Hay Day as well.

Although Hay Day started as a country farm stand in Westport, Connecticut, almost right from the beginning it grew to more than that. The stand soon became a shop, offering homemade breads, glorious imported and domestic cheeses, and an abundant array of pastas, oils, grains, and charcuterie. And because we couldn't resist cooking with these museum-quality ingredients, we began developing products inspired by them: Black Peppercorn Dressing to go with sweet local high-summer tomatoes; Lemon Dressing to complement bright spring asparagus and fiddlehead ferns. One idea led to another until gradually our kitchens were turning out a whole range of prepared hors d'oeuvres, soups, main courses, and desserts.

Giving Away Hay Day Secrets

Our first book, *The Hay Day Cookbook*, was published in 1986 and was a compendium of ideas for things to do with fresh produce. Many of its recipes were developed by our good friend Sallie Williams and first appeared in our monthly newsletter, *The Hay Day Rural Times*.

Hay Day Country Market Cookbook, on the other hand, gives away the store. Are the recipes included here really *the*

Hay Day recipes? Yes, they are. They're reduced in quantity, of course—the store recipe for Dan's Mustard calls for 153 eggs and 19 pounds of dry English mustard—but they are the real thing, the Hay Day All-Stars, presented in these pages for the first time ever. The dishes are contemporary American, prepared with a great deal of care and flair. They are rich in flavor but not in fat; they are easy and quick to make, and they're great to serve at both family meals and weekend parties.

We've always enjoyed saying that we sell everything from soup to nuts. And we do—breads, muffins, and pastries, salads, entrées, stocks, and sauces—all reflecting our fresh-is-best philosophy: Roasted Vegetable Couscous, Chunky Tomato and Bacon Soup, Kona-Crusted Beef with Sweet Onion Jam, Peppered Peach and Vidalia Onion Salad, Curried Chicken and Basmati Rice Soup, Summer Vegetable Bruschetta. And for a finish with a flourish, how about Gingerbread Peach Upside-Down Cake or a Buttermilk Wild-Berry Cobbler or a Mixed-Fruit Summer Pudding or a batch of Old-Fashioned Peanut Butter Cookies?

Since customers come to us not just for food, but for advice as well, we've included a whole spectrum of helpful tips that we've been giving out over the counters for years. And you'll also find dozens of "Bright Ideas" for adapting dishes so that you'll be inspired to transform leftover Asparagus Soup into a sauce for sea bass or to dress a chicken salad with Black Bean Salsa.

Coming into the kitchen should be a voyage of discovery, a revelation of all the potential available with the right ingredients. When you come right down to it, Hay Day is as much a mindset as it is a market, as much lifestyle and attitude as it is groceries. We hope you'll take some of that home with this book.

—Kim Rizk

Great Beginnings

This is the chapter that starts the day. Whether it's fruit, pancakes, oatmeal, or something divine from the oven, these recipes make the sun shine even on a dreary winter morning. Although our muffins, biscuits, and coffee cakes are stars at the breakfast table, most do just as well for coffee breaks, brunch, afternoon tea—the moments in life when people sit down long enough to have an actual conversation.

Many of the recipes—like Jam-Filled Corn Muffins and Banana-Pecan Coffee Cake—are great year-round. Some, like Apricot-Blueberry Cornbread Coffee Cake and Cranberry-Applesauce Crumb Cake, showcase seasonal fruits. But given a well-stocked pantry, all of them will adapt to even the most harried schedule, because, most importantly, they are not difficult to prepare.

So stock up on dried fruits, stone-ground cornmeal, and unbleached flour, and keep a few blueberries in the freezer. Then when the time comes, all you need is the bowl, the spoon, and the inspiration—which we hope you will get from us.

1

Pumpkin-Raisin Muffins

MAKES 12 MUFFINS

Savvy mothers sometimes soft-pedal the word "pumpkin." So call these Halloween Muffins if you like, but whatever you call them, they are always a huge success with the sandbox crowd as well as their parents. Serve them for breakfast or tea, with apple butter or with sweet butter or cream cheese blended with a little orange zest.

◆◆◆◆◆◆

*8 tablespoons (1 stick) unsalted
  butter, at room temperature
¾ cup (firmly packed) light
  brown sugar
1 egg
¾ cup pumpkin purée (see About
  Pumpkin Purée, facing page)
⅓ cup fresh orange juice
2 cups unbleached all-purpose flour
1 teaspoon salt
2 teaspoons baking powder
1 teaspoon baking soda
1 tablespoon pumpkin pie spice
  (see Note)
Generous ½ cup golden raisins
½ cup walnuts, preferably toasted
  (see Toasting Nuts, page 55),
  coarsely chopped*

◆◆◆◆◆◆

1. Preheat the oven to 350°F. Lightly butter 12 muffin cups.

2. Using an electric mixer, cream the butter and brown sugar together in a large mixing bowl until light and fluffy. Blend in the egg, pumpkin purée, and orange juice. (The mixture will appear curdled, but it will pull together once the dry ingredients are added.)

3. In another mixing bowl, stir together the flour, salt, baking powder, baking soda, and pumpkin pie spice. Toss in the raisins, separating any clumps, along with the walnuts. Make a well in the center and add the pumpkin mixture. Blend until all the dry ingredients are moistened.

4. Spoon the batter into the prepared muffin cups, filling them three-quarters full, and bake until nicely colored and risen (a toothpick inserted in the center should come out clean), 18 to 20 minutes. Remove from the oven, and cool in the muffin cups for 5 minutes. Then turn the muffins out onto a wire rack to cool for a few minutes more before serving.

Note: The blend of aromatic spices referred to as pumpkin pie spice traditionally is sold for pies made with winter squash, pumpkin, and sweet potatoes. Formulas vary, but you can make your own by combining equal parts of ground nutmeg, cinnamon, and allspice, and half as much ground cloves.

Jam-Filled Corn Muffins

MAKES 12 MUFFINS

Plain, these corn muffins are great, but filled with jam, they're a real event. We've made them at Hay Day forever. Lightly sweetened cornbread combines naturally with many fruits; we've used raspberry here, but strawberry,

ABOUT PUMPKIN PURÉE

For us, fall really starts with the first bright heap of pumpkins for sale by the side of the road. We sell literally tons of pumpkins in October, and while most of the big ones end up carved into jack-o'-lanterns, the smaller sugar pumpkins are also classic table fare in New England. Sweet, fine-textured sugar pumpkins make fabulous breads, cakes, pies, muffins . . . even a delicious savory purée to serve with roast game.

The easiest way to cook a sugar pumpkin is to set it on its side and slice off the top, then quarter the pumpkin and remove the seeds. Place the quarters in a baking pan and add water to a depth of about an inch. Cover with aluminum foil or a tight-fitting lid, and bake in a 400°F oven until fork-tender, about 1 hour. Drain, cool, then scoop out the pumpkin flesh and purée it in a food processor or run it through a food mill. Pumpkin can be substituted in any recipe that calls for winter squash, and the purée freezes beautifully.

currant, blueberry, or blackberry jam would be just fine. These muffins are great served warm, but remember that the sugary jam gets very hot—so be sure to cool them sufficiently before serving. Well wrapped, they keep for a day or two in the refrigerator, and they perk up nicely with a quick oven toasting.

◆◆◆◆◆◆

1 cup medium-grain stone-ground
  cornmeal (see Stone-Ground
  Cornmeal, page 4)
2 cups unbleached all-purpose flour
¼ cup sugar
1½ teaspoons baking powder
2 teaspoons baking soda
2 eggs
1 cup buttermilk
8 tablespoons (1 stick) unsalted
  butter, melted and cooled
12 generous teaspoons raspberry jam
Sugar, for sprinkling (optional)

◆◆◆◆◆◆

1. Preheat the oven to 375°F. Lightly butter 12 muffin cups.

2. In a large mixing bowl, whisk together the cornmeal, flour, sugar, baking powder, and baking soda.

3. In another mixing bowl, whisk the eggs with the buttermilk and melted butter. (The mixture will appear slightly curdled, but it will pull together when combined with the dry ingredients.)

4. Make a well in the center of the dry ingredients, and add the wet ingredients. Stir with a few swift strokes until all the dry ingredients are moistened.

5. Fill the prepared muffin cups one-third full. Top each with a teaspoon of the jam, placing it directly in the middle of the batter and away from the edges. Then add a large spoonful of the remaining batter, completely covering the jam and dividing the batter evenly among the muffin cups. Sprinkle the tops with a little sugar if desired.

6. Bake until the muffins are nicely risen and browned on top, 12 to 15 minutes.

Remove from the oven and cool in the muffin cups for 5 minutes. Then turn the muffins out onto a wire rack, and allow them to cool for a few more minutes before serving.

Variations

◆ Skip the jam. Instead stir the finely grated zest of 1 orange and 1¼ cups blueberries, preferably the tiny wild Maine variety, into the batter, and proceed with the recipe.

◆ Use this recipe (plain or with blueberries) to make cornbread: divide the batter among four mini-loaf pans and bake for 18 to 20 minutes, or two regular loaf pans and bake for 25 to 30 minutes.

STONE-GROUND CORNMEAL

The label "stone-ground" can't always be taken literally these days, but it does mean that the cornmeal will have a nice coarse texture. Stone-ground cornmeal is milled without the heat that strips the germ from the grains, thus preserving more of its original nutrients, and it is therefore more perishable. It keeps well in the refrigerator, though, and we always have a supply on hand at home for making bread, muffins, and pie crusts.

Cornmeal is ground into a variety of textures, ranging from as fine as bread flour to as coarse as cracked wheat. We prefer to use a medium-grain stone-ground cornmeal in all our baked goods. Slipping through your fingers, it has more or less the texture of coarse beach sand.

Banana-Berry Muffins

MAKES 18 MUFFINS

The combination of ripe banana and fresh berry flavors is a big hit with children, and the yogurt here provides not only moisture but a nice credibility for parents riven with Nutrition Guilt. These muffins are very moist and keep well in an airtight container for two to three days. The batter itself keeps well in the refrigerator for a couple of days, which means you can scoop out enough for a few fresh muffins each morning.

◆◆◆◆◆◆

8 tablespoons (1 stick) unsalted
    butter, at room temperature
1 cup sugar
2 eggs
1½ cups mashed ripe banana
    (about 3 large bananas)
1 teaspoon pure vanilla extract
3 cups unbleached all-purpose flour
2 teaspoons baking soda
1 teaspoon baking powder
½ teaspoon salt
1 cup plain yogurt
1 heaping cup fresh raspberries,
    stemmed blueberries, or blackberries,
    gently rinsed and drained

◆◆◆◆◆◆

1. Preheat the oven to 375°F. Lightly butter 18 muffin cups.

2. Using an electric mixer, cream the butter and sugar together in a large mixing bowl. Add the eggs one at a time, blending well after each addition and scraping down the sides of the bowl as needed.

Add the mashed banana and vanilla, and blend in. (The mixture will look slightly curdled, but it will pull together once the dry ingredients are added.)

3. In another bowl, whisk together the flour, baking soda, baking powder, and salt. Add the dry ingredients to the creamed mixture in batches, alternating with the yogurt. Mix until all the dry ingredients are moistened. Stir in the berries.

4. Fill the prepared muffin cups two-thirds full, and bake until the muffins have risen and are nicely colored (a toothpick inserted in the center should come out clean), 20 to 25 minutes. Remove from the oven and cool in the muffin cups for about 2 minutes. Then turn the muffins out onto a wire rack so they're bottom side up, and allow them to cool for a few minutes more before serving.

Note: When you're baking an odd number of muffins, avoid overbaking the muffins and protect the empty muffin cups by filling the empty cups halfway with water.

Variation

◆ **Banana-Mango Muffins:** Substitute the diced flesh of 1 ripe mango for the berries.

Summer
Breakfast Buffet

Everybody's coming to your place for graduation day. Greet them with a summery breakfast set out on the porch, and all the logistics ("Who's taking the car?" "Who's got the camera?") will magically take care of themselves.

Orange-Carrot-Pineapple Cooler

Summer Fruit Ambrosia

Banana-Mango Muffins
Zucchini-Pineapple
Corn Muffins

Apricot-Blueberry
Cornbread Coffee Cake

Zucchini-
Pineapple
Corn Muffins

MAKES 12 LARGE MUFFINS

Pineapple adds moisture and a light, uncloying sweetness to these corn muffins and gives the zucchini a wonderful new flavor. We put out a basket on the barbecue buffet in the summer, and they disappear in seconds.

◆◆◆◆◆◆

*1 cup medium-grain stone-ground
   cornmeal (see Stone-Ground
   Cornmeal, page 4)*
2 cups unbleached all-purpose flour
¾ cup sugar
½ teaspoon salt
2 teaspoons baking soda
½ teaspoon freshly grated nutmeg
2 eggs, lightly beaten
*1½ cups crushed or chopped
   pineapple, with juices*
*8 tablespoons (1 stick) unsalted
   butter, melted and cooled*
*2 cups (lightly packed) shredded
   zucchini (about 1 medium zucchini)*
⅓ cup sunflower seeds

◆◆◆◆◆◆

1. Preheat the oven to 375°F. Lightly butter 12 large muffin cups.

2. In a large mixing bowl, whisk together the cornmeal, flour, sugar, salt, baking soda, and nutmeg. Create a well in the center and add the eggs, pineapple and juices, melted butter, and grated zucchini. Stir together with large swift strokes until all the dry ingredients are moistened.

3. Fill the prepared cups three-quarters full. Top each one with a sprinkling of sunflower seeds, and bake until the muffins have risen and are golden (a toothpick inserted in the center should come out with moist crumbs attached), 15 to 18 minutes.

4. Remove from the oven and cool in the muffin cups for 2 minutes. Then turn the muffins out onto a wire rack so they're bottom side up and allow to cool for a few minutes more before serving.

Maple-Glazed Cranberry-Walnut Muffins

MAKES 12 MUFFINS

This great tart-sweet muffin recipe can be made as a quick bread, too; it is wonderful for a fall brunch or breakfast, or even for a holiday dinner with roast turkey, ham, or game.

◆◆◆◆◆◆

2 cups unbleached all-purpose flour
1½ teaspoons baking powder
½ teaspoon baking soda
1 teaspoon salt
*6 tablespoons (¾ stick) unsalted
   butter, at room temperature*
1 cup sugar
1 egg
*Finely grated zest of 1 orange
   (see About Zest, page 229)*
¾ cup fresh orange juice
*1½ cups fresh cranberries, coarsely
   chopped (see Note)*
*1 cup walnuts, preferably toasted
   (see Toasting Nuts, page 55), coarsely
   chopped*
2 tablespoons pure maple syrup

◆◆◆◆◆◆

1. Preheat the oven to 375°F. Lightly butter 12 muffin cups.

2. Whisk together the flour, baking powder, baking soda, and salt in a mixing bowl.

3. Using an electric mixer, cream the butter and sugar together in a large bowl until light and fluffy. Blend in the egg and orange zest, scraping down the sides of the bowl as needed. Add the dry ingredients in batches, alternating with the orange juice, and mix to form a smooth batter. Fold in the cranberries and half of the walnuts.

4. Spoon the batter into the prepared muffin cups, filling them two-thirds full. Sprinkle the tops with the remaining walnuts, and bake until the muffins have risen and are lightly browned (a toothpick inserted in the center should come out clean), 18 to 20 minutes. Meanwhile, warm the maple syrup in a small saucepan over low heat.

5. Remove the muffins from the oven and immediately brush the syrup over them. Cool the muffins in the muffin cups for 5 minutes. Then turn them out onto a wire rack and allow to cool for a few minutes more before serving.

Note: It can be tedious, chasing bouncy cranberries around a cutting board. Instead, chop them in a food processor: Just pulse the whole cranberries once or twice—so they're coarsely chopped, not puréed.

Raspberry-Ginger Scones

MAKES 8 SCONES

One of the wizards in our bakery developed this technique for baking scones with a ribbon of jam inside—which makes them particularly appealing at teatime. Using cream instead of shortening makes the scones extra-tender and flaky.

While it is not crucial to the success of this recipe, lining the baking sheet with parchment paper is a huge help with cleanup. In general, parchment is a good idea whenever spillover is likely; a bit of jam may ooze from the sides of these scones, and the natural sugar in a milk glaze tends to fuse itself onto the pan.

ABOUT CRYSTALLIZED GINGER

Crystallized ginger—peppery-sweet slices of ginger cooked in sugar syrup and coated with coarse sugar crystals—has been eaten as candy for centuries. It has a wonderfully palliative effect after an indulgent meal. Minced crystallized ginger is lovely in cakes and pies or sprinkled over fresh fruit or ice cream; look for it in small jars on the spice or condiment shelves at your favorite market.

WHY CHILLED BUTTER?

Like croissants, biscuits, and pie crusts, most scones get their light, flaky texture from tiny chunks of ice-cold butter or shortening that are cut in quickly enough to stay cold until they melt in the oven, leaving air pockets behind—which is why recipes like the one for Whole-Wheat Currant Scones (facing page) call for chilled butter. Refrigerator-cold is fine, but if you're cutting it in using a food processor, by all means use butter straight from the freezer if you have some stored there.

We've specified a food processor for incorporating chilled butter into the dry ingredients because it's the quickest way to do it and keeps the butter ice cold. You don't need a machine, however. People have been "cutting in" shortening to tenderize pie crusts and biscuits for centuries, using just a fork, two knives, or a pastry cutter. Just keep your hands light, as grandmother used to say, and do it quickly.

◆◆◆◆◆◆

2 cups unbleached all-purpose flour
1 teaspoon salt
1 tablespoon baking powder
2 ounces (¼ cup) chopped crystallized ginger (see About Crystallized Ginger, page 7)
1 cup heavy (whipping) cream
¼ cup raspberry or strawberry all-fruit spread
1 tablespoon milk or heavy (whipping) cream

◆◆◆◆◆◆

1. Preheat the oven to 400°F.

2. Whisk together the flour, salt, and baking powder in a large bowl. Add the crystallized ginger, and stir to distribute it evenly. Stir in the cream to form a soft dough.

3. Turn the dough out onto a lightly floured work surface, and roll it out to form a ¼-inch-thick rectangle, roughly 14 × 9 inches. Spread the fruit spread lengthwise (14 inches) over the bottom two thirds of the dough. Using a large floured spatula or dough cutter, fold the top third down over the center portion of the dough. Then fold the bottom third up and over the other two layers, forming an envelope-style package that measures about 14 × 3 inches.

4. Square off any jagged ends, and using a sharp knife or dough cutter, cut the rectangle into four pieces, each about 3½ × 3 inches. Cut each piece in half diagonally, making eight triangles.

5. Transfer the scones to a parchment-lined or plain ungreased baking sheet, and sparingly brush the tops with the tablespoon of milk.

6. Bake until the scones have risen and are golden brown on top, 12 to 15 minutes. Remove them from the oven and cool for 5 minutes on the baking sheet. Then transfer to a wire rack to cool further.

Variations

◆ We sometimes make these with ⅓ cup chopped nuts in place of the ginger. Pecans make a nice combination with sour cherry fruit spread; chopped walnuts are excellent with peach and apricot.

Whole-Wheat Currant Scones

MAKES 8 SCONES

The whole-wheat flour and orange zest in these nourishing scones give them a nice autumnal quality, and the coarse, tawny crystals of turbinado sugar add crunch and a delicate molasses flavor. Like biscuits, scones should be mixed and handled gently for the lightest, most delicate texture.

◆◆◆◆◆◆

1 cup whole-wheat or whole-grain
    pastry flour
³/₄ cup unbleached all-purpose flour
¹/₂ teaspoon salt
2 tablespoons granulated sugar
2 teaspoons baking powder
¹/₂ teaspoon baking soda
8 tablespoons (1 stick) unsalted butter,
    chilled, cut into several chunks
¹/₂ cup dried currants
Finely grated zest of 1 orange
    (see About Zest, page 229)
1 egg
¹/₂ cup plus 1 tablespoon buttermilk
1¹/₂ teaspoons turbinado sugar (see
    About Turbinado Sugar, page 10)

◆◆◆◆◆◆

1. Preheat the oven to 400°F.

2. Combine the flours, salt, sugar, baking powder, and baking soda in a food processor and pulse several times to mix.

3. Add the chilled butter and pulse several times, until the bits of butter are no larger than small grains of rice. Transfer the mixture to a large bowl, and stir in the currants and orange zest.

4. In another bowl, whisk the egg with the ¹/₂ cup buttermilk. Add this to the dry ingredients, and stir just until a soft, slightly crumbly dough forms. With lightly floured hands, gather the dough together and, using the palm of your hand, press it out on a parchment-lined or ungreased baking sheet to form a 7-inch round.

WHOLE-WHEAT PASTRY FLOUR

Pastry flour is a fine-textured, soft wheat flour that is high in starch and low in gluten—and therefore makes wonderfully tender pastries. It should be used, however, only in recipes that specifically call for pastry or cake flour, because its moisture content and absorption qualities are very different from those of all-purpose or bread flour. Pastry flour is often hard to find in supermarkets, but it is readily available in health-food and specialty stores. It should be stored in the refrigerator. Whole-wheat pastry flour is unbleached and therefore has more flavor and nutritional value.

5. If you like your scones to have crisp edges, use a sharp knife or a dough cutter to divide the dough into eight wedges; pull the wedges apart. If you prefer tender edges, leave the round intact and simply score the divisions.

6. Brush the dough with the remaining 1 tablespoon buttermilk and sprinkle with the turbinado sugar. Bake until nicely browned and nearly doubled in height, 12 to 15 minutes. Remove from the oven and cool for 5 minutes on the baking sheet. Then transfer to a wire rack to cool further.

Variation

◆ Use ½ cup dried blueberries in place of the currants.

ABOUT TURBINADO SUGAR

Turbinado is a popular form of natural "raw" sugar. Harvested from 100 percent sugar cane, it is coarse-textured and golden brown because of a natural coating of sweet golden molasses that remains on the crystals. It makes a delicious and interesting topping for pastries; sprinkle it on muffins, scones, or sugar cookies just before baking. Or use it to add rich flavor to a bowl of granola, yogurt, or sliced fresh fruit. "Sugar in the Raw" is one brand you can find in the supermarket.

Gingered Gingerbread

MAKES 1 CAKE OR 12 MUFFINS

Dark, fragrant gingerbread is usually served for dessert, but it's great for breakfast too. The presence of both fresh and crystallized ginger gives this one a particularly rich flavor; it is truly spectacular served warm with a dollop of crème fraîche and some sliced plums or peaches alongside.

◆◆◆◆◆◆

2 eggs
½ cup buttermilk or
   sour cream
½ cup unsulfured molasses
8 tablespoons (1 stick) unsalted
   butter, melted and cooled
½ cup (firmly packed) dark
   brown sugar
1 tablespoon grated or finely
   minced fresh ginger
1½ cups unbleached all-purpose flour
1 teaspoon baking soda
¼ teaspoon ground cloves
¼ teaspoon freshly grated nutmeg
½ teaspoon salt
2 ounces crystallized ginger,
   chopped into small bits
   (½ cup chopped; see About
   Crystallized Ginger, page 7)
Sliced fresh plums or peaches,
   for serving (optional)
Crème Fraîche (page 255), for serving
   (optional)

◆◆◆◆◆◆

1. Preheat the oven to 350°F. Lightly butter an 8-inch square cake pan or 12 muffin cups.

2. Beat the eggs in a large mixing bowl with a wire whisk or an electric mixer on medium speed. Stir in the buttermilk, molasses, butter, brown sugar, and minced ginger. Mix until blended and smooth.

3. In another mixing bowl, whisk together the flour, baking soda, cloves, nutmeg, and salt. Add the dry ingredients to the wet ingredients, and mix to incorporate. Stir in the crystallized ginger, and pour the batter into the prepared cake pan or muffin cups (filling the muffin cups two-thirds full). Bake until the gingerbread springs back lightly and a toothpick inserted in the center comes out clean, 25 to 30 minutes for the cake, 20 minutes for muffins.

4. Remove from the oven and cool in the pan for 10 minutes. Then turn out the cake and cut it into squares, or empty the muffin cups. Arrange on individual plates, topping each serving with the sliced fruit and a spoonful of crème fraîche if desired.

Variation

◆ For a fabulous dessert, substitute an equal amount of chopped bittersweet chocolate for the crystallized ginger and serve the cake warm, topping each serving with a generous spoonful of lightly sweetened crème fraîche.

Cranberry-Applesauce Crumb Cake

MAKES 12 SQUARES

A luscious topping of cranberry-jeweled applesauce makes this delicious tart-sweet breakfast cake a perfect choice for autumn entertaining—ideal for holiday breakfasts and brunch buffets. It remains so moist and tender that you can bake it the day before the company arrives.

◆◆◆◆◆◆

Fruit Sauce
½ cup Aunt Mauds Apple Cider
    Applesauce (page 255) or other
    chunky applesauce
1 bag (12 ounces) fresh cranberries
¾ cup sugar
½ teaspoon ground cinnamon

Topping
⅓ cup unbleached all-purpose flour
⅔ cup (firmly packed) light brown
    sugar
4 tablespoons (½ stick) unsalted butter,
    at room temperature

Cake
12 tablespoons (1½ sticks) unsalted
    butter
1 cup granulated sugar
2 eggs
2 teaspoons pure vanilla extract
2⅔ cups unbleached all-purpose flour
3 teaspoons baking powder
1 teaspoon salt
1 cup milk

◆◆◆◆◆◆

STORING BAKED GOODS

Always allow baked goods to cool completely (preferably on a wire rack) before wrapping and storing. (If they're wrapped before they're thoroughly cooled, pastries will steam, turning their nice crisp surfaces soggy and limp.) The texture and flavor of most baked goods fare best when stored, well wrapped, in a cool dry location for a couple of days. However, those that are particularly high in moisture will be safest stored in the refrigerator. The recipes will note when that's the case.

1. Preheat the oven to 350°F. Lightly butter and flour a 13 × 9-inch baking pan.

2. Prepare the fruit sauce: Combine the applesauce, cranberries, sugar, and cinnamon in a saucepan and bring to a simmer over medium-high heat. Simmer, stirring frequently, just until the cranberries begin to pop open, about 5 minutes. Remove from the heat and set aside to cool.

3. Prepare the topping: In a mixing bowl, stir the flour with the brown sugar. Using your fingertips or the tines of a fork, quickly work in the butter to form coarse crumbs. Set aside.

4. Prepare the cake batter: In a large mixing bowl, cream the butter and sugar together with an electric mixer on high speed until light and fluffy. Add the eggs one at a time, beating well after each addition and scraping down the sides of the bowl as needed. Stir in the vanilla.

5. In another bowl, whisk together the flour, baking powder, and salt. Add this to the creamed mixture in batches, alternating with the milk, and blend until smooth.

6. Spread the batter in the prepared pan, and spread the cooled cranberry applesauce evenly on top. Sprinkle with the topping, and bake until it is bubbling hot and crisp, 40 to 45 minutes. Remove the cake from the oven and cool completely in the pan. Shortly before serving, cut it into squares. If you are preparing it a day ahead, wrap the cooled cake well and refrigerate it.

Banana-Pecan Coffee Cake

SERVES 12

This gorgeous, moist sour cream coffee cake gets extra flavor and nutrients from mashed bananas and crunch from a topping made with wheat germ and chopped pecans. If it is well wrapped in an airtight container, it will keep for two to three days. Serve it with coffee at a committee meeting, and the members will vote any way you want them to.

◆◆◆◆◆◆

Pecan Crumb Topping

½ cup unbleached all-purpose flour
⅔ cup (firmly packed) light
brown sugar
2 teaspoons ground cinnamon
8 tablespoons (1 stick) unsalted
butter, chilled, cut into large chunks
⅔ cup toasted wheat germ
(see Note, page 26)
2 cups pecans, preferably toasted (see
Toasting Nuts, page 55), coarsely
chopped

Cake

12 tablespoons (1½ sticks) unsalted
butter, at room temperature
1 cup granulated sugar
2 eggs
1 teaspoon pure vanilla extract
2 cups unbleached all-purpose flour
2 teaspoons baking soda
2 teaspoons baking powder
¾ teaspoon salt
1½ cups mashed ripe bananas
(about 3 large bananas)
½ cup sour cream

◆◆◆◆◆◆

1. Preheat the oven to 350°F. Lightly butter and flour a 13 × 9-inch baking pan.

2. Prepare the topping: Combine the flour, brown sugar, and cinnamon in a food processor, and pulse to blend. Add the butter to the processor, and pulse until the mixture forms a coarse meal. Stir in the wheat germ and pecans by hand, cover, and set aside.

3. Prepare the cake batter: In a large mixing bowl, cream the butter and sugar together with an electric mixer on high

speed until light and fluffy. Add the eggs one at a time, beating well after each addition and scraping down the sides of the bowl as needed. Add the vanilla and blend in.

4. In another bowl, whisk together the flour, baking soda, baking powder, and salt. Add this to the creamed mixture in batches, alternating with the mashed bananas and sour cream. Blend until smooth.

5. Spread a little less than half of the batter in the prepared pan. Sprinkle with half of the crumb topping, and top with the remaining batter. Scatter the remaining topping over the batter. Bake until the cake has risen and browned and a toothpick inserted in the center comes out clean, 25 to 30 minutes. Remove from the oven and cool for at least 10 minutes in the pan. Then cut into 12 squares and serve.

FREEZING BANANAS

Those of us of a certain age were trained never to put bananas in the refrigerator—but nobody said anything about the freezer. Store slightly overripe peeled bananas in a plastic bag in the freezer; then toss them, still frozen, into the blender to enrich a smoothie, or thaw and mash them to add to muffin and quick bread batter.

Blueberry Streusel Coffee Cake

SERVES 10 TO 12

Streusel, a German word meaning "sprinkled," usually refers to a crumb topping of nuts and cinnamon. Here the streusel goes in the middle of a rich, moist buttermilk coffee cake made with fresh summer blueberries (or with the supply you kept stored in the freezer). The cake is generous enough for company, or for roommates visiting for the weekend, and it's a great stimulant for business meetings. It is moist enough to keep well for two to three days in a cool, dry place as long as it's in an airtight container.

◆◆◆◆◆◆

Almond Streusel
½ cup old-fashioned rolled oats
½ cup sliced almonds
½ cup (firmly packed) light brown sugar
1 teaspoon ground cinnamon
4 tablespoons (½ stick) unsalted
    butter, chilled

Cake
8 tablespoons (1 stick) unsalted
    butter, at room temperature
1 cup sugar
2 eggs
1 teaspoon pure vanilla extract
3 cups unbleached all-purpose flour
2 teaspoons baking soda
1½ teaspoons baking powder
1 teaspoon salt
1¼ cups buttermilk
2 cups fresh or frozen blueberries
    (stemmed, gently rinsed, and
    drained, if fresh)
1½ teaspoons finely grated lemon zest
    (see About Zest, page 229)
Confectioners' sugar, for dusting

◆◆◆◆◆◆

FREEZING BERRIES

The season for sweet summer berries always seems to come and go far too quickly. So when the fields and produce stands are brimming with perfectly ripe sweet local blueberries, raspberries, strawberries, and blackberries, enjoy them in as many ways as conceivably possible. Then just before the season comes to a halt, buy up several extra pints to tuck away in the freezer for adding to cakes and muffins or for puréeing into sauces and smoothies—it's a great way to add a bit of summer sunshine to dreary winter days.

To do this, rinse the berries judiciously, pat them dry, and pick through them for stems; then scatter them in a single layer on a sheet pan or pie plate and freeze completely. Once they are frozen, transfer the berries to plastic bags or containers for freezer storage. This way you'll have individually frozen berries for puréeing or for stirring into batters. The only trick is to keep them frozen. Don't let them thaw out, and stir them in at the last minute so their juices won't bleed into the batter.

1. Preheat the oven to 350°F. Lightly butter and flour a 10-inch bundt pan.

2. Prepare the streusel: Combine the oats, almonds, brown sugar, and cinnamon in a food processor and pulse several times to blend. Add the butter and pulse to cut in and form a crumbly mixture. Cover and set aside.

3. Prepare the cake batter: In a mixing bowl, cream the butter and sugar together with an electric mixer on high speed until light and fluffy. Add the eggs one at a time, beating well after each addition and scraping down the sides of the bowl as needed. Blend in the vanilla.

4. In another mixing bowl, whisk together the flour, baking soda, baking powder, and salt. Add this to the creamed mixture in batches, alternating with the buttermilk, and mix until smooth. The batter will be thick. Stir in the blueberries and lemon zest.

5. Spread one-third of the batter in the prepared pan, then sprinkle the streusel evenly over the batter. Spread the remaining batter evenly over the streusel layer. Bake until the cake has risen and browned and a toothpick inserted in the center comes out clean, 45 to 55 minutes.

6. Remove the cake from the oven and cool for at least 10 minutes in the pan. Then turn out onto a serving platter. Sprinkle with the confectioners' sugar just before slicing and serving.

Apricot-Blueberry Cornbread Coffee Cake

SERVES 6

The peak seasons for apricots and blueberries coincide briefly in July and August; seize the moment and make this upside-down cornbread coffee cake with its beautiful caramelized topping.

◆◆◆◆◆◆

Fruit Topping
3 tablespoons unsalted butter
¼ cup sugar
2 tablespoons fresh orange juice
½ teaspoon ground cinnamon
3 or 4 ripe fresh apricots
⅔ cup fresh blueberries, stemmed,
*   gently rinsed, and drained*

Cornbread
4 tablespoons (½ stick) unsalted butter
⅓ cup sugar
1 egg
⅔ cup medium-grain stone-ground
*   cornmeal (see Stone-Ground*
*   Cornmeal, page 4)*
½ cup unbleached all-purpose flour
2 teaspoons baking powder
½ teaspoon salt
⅔ cup milk

◆◆◆◆◆◆

1. Preheat the oven to 375°F.

2. Prepare the topping: Melt the butter in an 8-inch ovenproof skillet (preferably *not* cast iron) over medium-high heat. Gently whisk in the sugar, orange juice, and cinnamon. Bring to a simmer and cook until slightly thickened, about 1 minute. Remove the skillet from the heat and set it aside to cool for about 5 minutes.

3. Slice the apricots in half and remove the pits. Slice each half into thirds, and arrange them in a large overlapping circle in the skillet. Pile the blueberries in the middle and scatter some between the apricot slices.

4. Prepare the cornbread batter: In a large bowl, cream the butter and sugar together with an electric mixer on high speed until light and fluffy. Add the egg and blend in. In another bowl, stir together the cornmeal, flour, baking powder, and salt. Add this to the creamed butter mixture in batches, alternating with the milk. Blend until smooth.

5. Spoon the batter gently over the fruit so as not to disturb the arrangement, and spread evenly. Bake until the cornbread is set and a toothpick inserted in the center comes out clean, 30 to 35 minutes. Remove the skillet from the oven and cool for 5 minutes. Then invert the coffee cake onto a serving platter. Serve warm or at room temperature.

Variation

◆ When fresh apricots are unavailable, substitute thinly sliced unpeeled nectarines or peaches—the flavor will still be terrific.

Plum Breakfast Cobbler

SERVES 4 TO 6

Cobblers are frequently made with the fruit on the bottom; here the batter puffs up to surround the plums like a light version of a torte or a kuchen. The whole assemblage is topped with cinnamon-scented brown sugar and wheat germ. It is divine with a spoonful of plain yogurt on top.

◆◆◆◆◆◆

1 cup unbleached all-purpose flour
2 teaspoons baking powder
½ teaspoon salt
1¼ teaspoons ground cinnamon
4 tablespoons (½ stick) unsalted
  butter, chilled
¼ cup honey, at room temperature
  or slightly warmed
½ cup milk
1 pound ripe sweet plums (Italian
  prune plums or another small
  variety), split in half and pitted
3 tablespoons light brown sugar
3 tablespoons wheat germ
Plain yogurt, for serving
  (optional)

◆◆◆◆◆◆

1. Preheat the oven to 375°F. Lightly butter and flour an 8-inch round cake pan.

2. Whisk together the flour, baking powder, salt, and 1 teaspoon of the cinnamon in a large bowl. Using a hand-held pastry blender or two knives, cut 3 tablespoons of the butter into the mixture until it resembles coarse meal.

3. In a small bowl, whisk the honey and milk together; add all at once to the dry ingredients. Stir to combine all of the dry ingredients. Then spread the batter in the prepared pan.

4. Using a small paring knife, score an X through the skin of each plum half. Arrange the plums, skin side up, in a single layer over the batter.

5. Mix the brown sugar, wheat germ, and remaining ¼ teaspoon cinnamon in a small bowl. Cut in the remaining 1 tablespoon butter to form a crumbly topping. Sprinkle the topping over the plums, and bake until the center of the cobbler is set and the topping is nicely browned, 25 to 30 minutes.

6. Remove the cobbler from the oven and cool in the pan for 10 minutes. Then slice it into wedges and serve, topped with yogurt if desired.

Double Corn Waffles

MAKES 8 TO 10 LARGE WAFFLES

These buttermilk-cornmeal waffles are lovely on a summer Sunday for brunch, slathered with a spoonful of Maple Strawberry Butter. Or you can top them with maple syrup and fresh berries.

◆◆◆◆◆◆

1 cup unbleached all-purpose flour
1 cup medium-grain stone-ground
*   cornmeal (see Stone-Ground*
*   Cornmeal, page 4)*
1½ teaspoons baking powder
1 teaspoon baking soda
¼ cup sugar
¼ teaspoon salt
2 eggs
2 cups buttermilk
4 tablespoons (½ stick) unsalted
*   butter, melted and cooled*
1 cup fresh corn kernels (see Note)
Maple-Strawberry Butter
*   (recipe follows), for serving*

◆◆◆◆◆◆

1. Preheat a waffle iron.

2. In a large mixing bowl, whisk together the flour, cornmeal, baking powder, baking soda, sugar, and salt.

3. In another bowl, whisk the eggs with the buttermilk. Add the melted butter and whisk to combine (the mixture may look a bit curdled). Add this all at once to the dry ingredients, and stir with a few swift strokes until all the dry ingredients are moistened and combined. Stir in the corn kernels.

4. Pour the batter, a spoonful at a time, onto the hot waffle iron and cook until the waffles are well browned and very crisp, 3 to 5 minutes. Serve warm, topped with Maple Strawberry Butter.

Note: You can also use leftover steamed or grilled corn in these waffles with excellent results.

Maple-Strawberry Butter

MAKES ¾ CUP

O nce you've tried dipping strawberries in pure maple syrup, there's no looking back. That mix of flavors inspires this fresh-fruit butter, which is spectacular with hot corn waffles. It also turns crumpets, toast, muffins, and scones into something really superb.

◆◆◆◆◆◆

8 tablespoons (1 stick) unsalted
    butter, at room temperature
3 tablespoons pure maple syrup
5 or 6 large fresh ripe strawberries,
    rinsed and hulled
2 teaspoons confectioners' sugar
    (if needed)
Sliced strawberries, for garnish

◆◆◆◆◆◆

1. Using an electric mixer or a food processor, whip the butter with the maple syrup on high speed in a small bowl until light and fluffy.

2. In another bowl, use a fork to mash the whole strawberries. Add, one spoonful at

a time, to the butter, blending well to incorporate. If the moisture of the berries causes the butter to separate, add the confectioners' sugar to bind the mixture.

3. Mound the strawberry butter in a small serving dish, garnish with the sliced strawberries, and serve immediately, or cover and refrigerate until ready to serve.

Oven-Puffed Pancake with Berries and Orange Sauce

SERVES 4 TO 6

T his puffy Dutch pancake is like a sweet Yorkshire pudding, and is particularly dramatic when brought to the table straight from the oven. It deflates quickly, and the result is a berry-filled pancake with crisp edges and a warm custardy center. We serve it here with honeyed orange sections decked with fresh mint for a summer breakfast, but you could just as easily cut it in wedges and serve it with maple syrup or warm honey, or just dust it with powdered sugar and serve it for dessert.

HAY DAY'S OWN MAPLE SYRUP

Our friend Vernon Gray moved farther north a while ago, and now he sends back beautiful Grade A medium-amber syrup from his spectacular Maple Ridge Farm in East Burke, Vermont.

Maple syrup is a uniquely North American product, made by reducing the orange sap of the sugar maple to a rich syrup. The process is incredibly labor-intensive (35 gallons of sap for every 1 gallon of syrup), but happily Vernon has been able to keep pace with the demand at Hay Day.

Uses for maple syrup go far beyond pancakes. Try it on ice cream, or on plain yogurt with a little crunchy granola, or substitute it for sugar in salad dressings, dips, and fruit salads. It took us a while to accept Vernon's suggestion that we put maple syrup on our morning grapefruit, but now it's a winter standby: Put 2 teaspoons of syrup on each grapefruit half, and watch the sun come out.

Maple syrup keeps well in the refrigerator after opening; if crystals develop, just melt them by heating the syrup very gently over low heat.

◆◆◆◆◆◆

Simple Fresh Orange Sauce
3 juicy seedless oranges
¼ cup honey
¼ cup fresh orange juice

Pancake
3 tablespoons unsalted butter
¾ cup unbleached all-purpose flour
½ teaspoon salt
3 eggs
1 cup milk
1 teaspoon pure vanilla extract
1 cup fresh stemmed blueberries,
  blackberries, or raspberries, gently
  rinsed and drained

◆◆◆◆◆◆

1. Preheat the oven to 450°F.

2. Prepare the sauce: Slice the skin from the oranges, removing all the white pith. Combine the honey and orange juice in a small saucepan; whisk together and place over low heat. Then, working over the saucepan to catch the juices, cut out the orange segments and drop them into the pan. Keep warm over low heat while you cook the pancake.

3. Place the butter in a 10-inch oven-proof skillet (preferably cast iron), and put it in the oven.

4. Combine the flour and salt in a large mixing bowl. In another bowl, whisk together the eggs, milk, and vanilla. Add this to the dry ingredients, and whisk until combined and smooth.

5. Wearing an oven mitt, remove the hot skillet from the oven (the butter should be bubbling), and pour in the batter all at once. Sprinkle the berries evenly on top, and return the skillet to the oven. Bake until the pancake is nicely browned and puffed around the edges, 12 to 15 minutes.

6. Remove the pancake from the oven. Bring it to the table, then carefully lift it out of the skillet with a large spatula and transfer it to a serving platter. Cut it into wedges and serve it immediately on plates or in shallow bowls, topped with the orange sauce.

Pecan-Date Pancakes

SERVES 4 TO 6

You could double or triple the quantities of dry ingredients in this recipe (including the dates and pecans) and store the mix in a jar in a cool pantry—or in a brown paper bag to take on a ski weekend. Then when you need it, just add 2 eggs, 1½ cups milk, and 3 tablespoons melted butter to every 2 cups of dry mix. The pancakes are very light—they're lovely just served with maple syrup—and they're even good if you skip the dates and nuts.

◆◆◆◆◆◆

⅓ cup old-fashioned rolled oats
1¼ cups unbleached all-purpose flour
¼ cup buckwheat flour (see
   right)
2 tablespoons sugar
1 tablespoon baking powder
¾ teaspoon salt
⅓ cup chopped pitted dates
⅓ cup coarsely chopped pecans
2 eggs
1½ cups whole milk
3 tablespoons unsalted butter,
   melted and cooled
Vegetable oil, for oiling the griddle
Maple syrup or Maple-Glazed
   Bananas (recipe follows),
   for serving

◆◆◆◆◆◆

1. Place the oats in a food processor and pulse to form a coarse meal. Combine the oats with the flours, sugar, baking powder, and salt in a large mixing bowl. Toss, then add the dates and pecans, breaking up any lumps as needed.

2. In another bowl, whisk the eggs with the milk and butter. Add this to the dry ingredients all at once, and stir with a few swift strokes until all the dry ingredients have been incorporated.

3. Lightly oil a griddle with the vegetable oil and place it over medium-high heat. Ladle the pancake batter, about ¼ cup at a time, onto the griddle, in batches, and cook until small bubbles cover the surface and the pancakes are golden brown on both sides, about 1 minute per side. Keep warm in a low oven while you cook the remaining pancakes. Serve the warm pancakes topped with maple syrup or with slices of Maple-Glazed Bananas. Pass additional maple syrup if desired.

BUCKWHEAT FLOUR

Traditionally used for pancakes and essential in Russian blini, buckwheat flour has a robust, earthy flavor that is great in muffins and whole-grain breads. We like it best in combination with other flours, such as in our Pecan-Date Pancakes. It's easy to find in health-food and specialty stores, and like cornmeal, it keeps well, tightly covered, in the refrigerator.

Maple-Glazed Bananas

SERVES 4 TO 6

When we served our buckwheat pancakes with glazed bananas in the late, great café at our Ridgefield store, they always got raves. Use small red finger bananas if you can find them; their tiny size is ideal (just slice them lengthwise), and their texture holds up well in baking.

◆◆◆◆◆◆

6 small red finger bananas, or
    3 medium-size yellow bananas,
    slightly unripe
1 tablespoon unsalted butter,
    melted
2 tablespoons maple sugar or
    maple syrup

◆◆◆◆◆◆

1. Preheat the oven to 375°F.

2. Peel the bananas and slice them in half lengthwise. If using yellow bananas, cut each half on the diagonal into two 3-inch-long pieces. Place the bananas, cut side up, in a baking dish that's large enough to hold them in a single layer. Drizzle the butter on top, sprinkle with the maple sugar, and bake until the bananas are nicely glazed, 10 to 12 minutes.

Best-Ever Oatmeal with Raisins and Maple Cream

SERVES 4

Steel-cut oats are the secret ingredient for the nubbliest best-ever oatmeal. A bowlful served with maple syrup, cream, and plump raisins can be a real event. No wonder the Three Bears were so crabby when they came home to find their dishes empty.

◆◆◆◆◆◆

3½ cups water
1 cup heavy (whipping) cream,
    at room temperature
½ cup pure maple syrup
1 cup steel-cut oats (see About
    Steel-Cut Oats, page 22)
⅓ cup raisins
2 tablespoons light brown sugar
½ teaspoon ground cinnamon

◆◆◆◆◆◆

1. Bring the water to a boil in a small saucepan.

2. Combine the cream and maple syrup in a small pitcher, and set aside at room temperature.

3. Briskly stir the oats into the boiling water, and return to a boil. Reduce the heat and simmer, stirring occasionally, until the water is absorbed and the oats are tender, 30 minutes.

4. Meanwhile, put the raisins in a small bowl, cover with warm water, and set

aside until plumped, about 15 minutes. Then pat the raisins dry and toss them with the brown sugar until coated.

5. When the oatmeal is ready, stir in the cinnamon and half of the maple cream. Ladle the oatmeal into individual bowls, top each with a small handful of the sugared raisins, and serve with a bit of the remaining maple cream swirled on top.

ABOUT STEEL-CUT OATS

Commonly referred to as Irish or Scottish, oats in this form are highly nutritious, no matter whether you buy the fancy can with the royal seal or just pick up a plain bag of steel-cut oats at the market or health-food store. They take a bit longer to cook than rolled oats, but the quality is worth the wait—they cook up into a porridge with an irresistible flavor and a chewy texture.

The cooking time can be cut in half by soaking the oats overnight in water to cover. Before cooking, drain the oats, and proceed with the recipe.

Citrus-Steamed Pears with Honey Yogurt

SERVES 6

Think of airy, latticed Moorish pavilions brushed by palm leaves. In this lazy-weekend breakfast dish, pears and yogurt take on the fragrance of orange-blossom water to make the kind of concoction they bring you in a really good seraglio. Although Boscs hold their shape particularly well, any fresh pears will be fine (see A Note on Pears, page 24). And don't worry—orange-blossom water is readily available in specialty, ethnic, and Middle Eastern markets.

◆◆◆◆◆◆

1 tablespoon orange-blossom water
1 tablespoon fresh lemon juice
⅓ cup water
1 tablespoon superfine sugar
3 large pears, slightly underripe,
   cut in half, peeled, and cored
⅔ cup plain yogurt
2 tablespoons honey
½ teaspoon freshly grated nutmeg,
   plus additional for garnish

◆◆◆◆◆◆

1. Combine the orange-blossom water, lemon juice, and water in a wide (10-inch) shallow saucepan or skillet. Place over medium heat and bring to a simmer. Add the sugar, stirring until it has dissolved.

2. Arrange the pear halves, cut side down, in the liquid. Cover and simmer gently, occasionally spooning the juices over the pears, until they are very tender, 15 to 20 minutes.

3. Meanwhile, stir the yogurt, honey, and ½ teaspoon nutmeg together in a small bowl.

4. When the pears are ready, use a slotted spoon or spatula to remove them from the pan. Slice the pears and serve them warm or at room temperature, topped with a generous tablespoon of the yogurt mixture and a sprinkling of nutmeg.

Spring Strawberries in Papaya Purée

SERVES 1

During the spring, when papayas are in season, enjoy their delicate flavor as you would summer melons. This easy recipe is for one serving, but you can multiply it by however many you're expecting for breakfast. How about surprising Mom on Mother's Day—this is easy and fun for the kids to prepare.

DID YOU KNOW . . .

Papaya contains a natural tenderizing enzyme. Add the puréed flesh to marinades for meat and see the effect.

◆◆◆◆◆◆

1 small ripe papaya
1½ tablespoons fresh lime juice
1 generous teaspoon minced fresh
  ginger
Honey to taste
2 small lime wedges
6 large fresh ripe strawberries, rinsed,
  hulled, and quartered

◆◆◆◆◆◆

1. Slice the papaya in half from stem to blossom end. Using a spoon, remove and discard the black seeds. Scoop the flesh from one half of the papaya into a food processor or blender. Add the lime juice and ginger, and purée until smooth. Taste, and sweeten with a small drizzle of honey as desired.

2. Cut a ¼-inch slice from the bottom of the remaining papaya half (or just enough so it will rest steadily), and place the papaya half on a plate. Squeeze one of the lime wedges on top. Toss the strawberries in the papaya purée, and then spoon them into the hollow of the papaya. Garnish with the remaining lime wedge and serve.

Variation

◆ Turn this into a brunch dish by serving it alongside thinly sliced prosciutto.

Summer Fruit Ambrosia

SERVES 8 TO 10

This updated '60s classic is a mélange of ripe summer fruits that's given a tropical spin with a dressing of honey, coconut, lime, and ginger. We've included it with the breakfast recipes because there's no better way to begin the day, but it defies categories—ambrosia is indeed the food of the gods, and it is fabulous any time.

◆◆◆◆◆◆

Flesh of 1 large ripe honeydew
    melon, cut into 1-inch cubes
4 ripe nectarines, rinsed,
    halved, pitted, and sliced
    into thin crescents
6 ripe plums (assorted varieties),
    halved, pitted, and sliced
    into thin crescents
1 pint fresh blueberries,
    stemmed, rinsed, and drained
Juice of 3 limes
¼ cup honey
1 cup unsweetened flaked coconut
2 tablespoons sugar
2 tablespoons finely minced
    crystallized ginger (see About
    Crystallized ginger, page 7)
2 teaspoons minced lime zest
    (see About Zest, page 229)

◆◆◆◆◆◆

1. Pile the melon, nectarines, plums, and blueberries in a large glass serving bowl. Whisk the lime juice and honey together in a small bowl, and pour over the fruit. Toss gently, cover, and refrigerate until serving time or for up to 2 hours.

2. Preheat the oven to 300°F.

3. Spread the coconut out on a small baking sheet, and toast it in the oven until golden brown and crisp, 5 to 10 minutes. While it is still warm, toss the coconut with the sugar. Allow to cool briefly, then toss in the ginger and lime zest.

4. When ready to serve, sprinkle the coconut topping over the fruit.

A NOTE ON PEARS

It's weird, but pears do not ripen well on the tree; they turn to mealy mush. So, unlike every other fruit except avocados and bananas, pears must be picked green and ripened separately (brown paper bags work well; see page 26). Pears ripen from the inside out, too, so don't wait until they're soft all over—just look for a nice pear fragrance and some softness at the stem end. (At home, you can make a tiny cut with a sharp knife; the cut will heal if the pear isn't ripe, but if it is, you'll see drops of juice.) The prince of eating pears is the Comice, with its very fine textured, sweet, juicy flesh, but they're all good. Seckel, Packham, Bartlett, and Bosc pears all hold up well for cooking, especially if they're slightly underripe.

Orange-Carrot-Pineapple Cooler

SERVES 4

We all know that fresh carrot juice is incredibly nourishing, but sometimes it's a hard sell. Mixed with orange and pineapple, though, it makes a fresh breakfast drink that somehow seems more familiar. If you have a juicer, you already know how easy it is to make carrot juice, but it's also increasingly easy to find in stores—and not just health-food stores, either.

◆◆◆◆◆◆

Crushed ice
1 cup fresh carrot juice
1 cup fresh orange juice
2 cups fresh pineapple chunks
4 large fresh pineapple spears,
  for garnish

◆◆◆◆◆◆

Fill four tall glasses with crushed ice. Combine the carrot juice, orange juice, and pineapple chunks in a large blender. Blend at high speed until smooth, and pour into the glasses. Garnish each glass with a pineapple spear, and serve right away.

Orange-Banana Smoothie

SERVES 2

A blend of frozen ripe bananas and orange juice makes a nutritious breakfast drink that is just

"EXCUSE ME, IS THIS MELON RIPE?"

There's no question that we're asked more often. People thump and shake melons all over the store, but the seeds of a perfectly ripe melon won't necessarily rattle. Ripe melons will smell very slightly fragrant and will yield to gentle pressure at the stem end. Store personnel will often pick them out for you, or even cut them open.

as creamy and satisfying as a milkshake. Top it with wheat germ and you will automatically be a better person. Keep a couple of ripe bananas in the freezer to toss in the blender on harried mornings.

◆◆◆◆◆◆

2 ripe peeled bananas, frozen
  (see Freezing Bananas, page 13)
1/3 cup fresh orange juice
2/3 cup plain yogurt
2 tablespoons honey, preferably clover
1/4 teaspoon freshly grated nutmeg
2 teaspoons toasted wheat germ
  (see Note)
2 orange slices, for garnish

◆◆◆◆◆◆

25

Combine the bananas, orange juice, yogurt, honey, and nutmeg in a blender and purée to form a thick smooth shake. Pour the shake into two tall glasses, and top each with a sprinkling of wheat germ. Garnish with a fresh orange slice, and serve.

Note: To toast wheat germ, preheat the oven to 325°F. Spread the wheat germ in a small cake pan or rimmed baking sheet and bake, stirring occasionally, until lightly browned, 8 to 10 minutes.

Variation

◆ Add a couple of pitted Medjool dates to the blender, in place of the honey, to make a smoothie with sweet chunks.

BROWN-BAGGING IT

Refrigeration slows down the natural metabolic ripening process in most fruit—which is why we leave underripe fruit, like pears, plums, peaches, and apricots, out on the kitchen counter. At room temperature, fruit naturally produces ethylene, a gas that triggers ripening. If you wrap an underripe fruit inside a brown grocery bag and leave it at room temperature, the bag will capture the ethylene and speed the ripening process. Once the fruit is soft to the touch, serve it or refrigerate it in order to preserve the texture and flavor.

Triple Berry Smoothie

SERVES 4

Not only is this a completely virtuous (and quick) summer breakfast, but it can be frozen into completely virtuous Popsicles! The sweet blueberries and strawberries get a dash of tartness from the cranberries, and the whole thing just goes in the blender. Divine.

◆◆◆◆◆◆

1 cup fresh blueberries, stemmed, rinsed, and drained
1 generous cup sliced ripe fresh strawberries
1 cup frozen cranberries
1½ cups plain yogurt
1 large ripe banana, peeled and sliced
1 cup fresh orange juice
Whole strawberries and orange slices, for garnish

◆◆◆◆◆◆

Pile the blueberries, sliced strawberries, cranberries, yogurt, banana, and orange juice into a large blender—or do it in batches—and blend at high speed until smooth. Pour into tall glasses, garnish with the whole strawberries and orange slices, and serve right away.

Hot Chocolate for a Crowd

SERVES 8

When the troops gather for skating or bobsledding, warm them afterward with creamy hot chocolate. You can use powdered cocoa (see Hot Cocoa, right), but you can also get fabulous results by melting whatever good eating chocolate comes to hand. Whether it's a package of Belgian chocolate, a bar of Toblerone, or even an Easter bunny, it all makes great hot chocolate. (Milk chocolate will make the cocoa a little sweeter; semisweet will give it a darker color and deeper flavor.) One year at Hay Day, we overstocked on solid chocolate Santas and proceeded to delight our customers at the coffee bar clear through February!

◆◆◆◆◆◆

8 cups milk
8 ounces best-quality semisweet or
* milk chocolate, coarsely chopped*
⅛ teaspoon salt
2 teaspoons pure vanilla extract
Crème Fraîche (page 255) or whipped
* cream, for topping*
Cinnamon sticks, for serving

◆◆◆◆◆◆

Combine the milk, chocolate, and salt in a heavy saucepan over low heat. Cook, stirring continuously, until the chocolate has melted. Whisk until foamy, then stir in the vanilla. Immediately pour the hot chocolate into mugs, top each one with a spoonful of crème fraîche, swirl with a cinnamon stick, and serve.

MENU

Winter Weekend Warmer

The gang has been out on the mountain since early morning. Here's what they're hoping to find when they clomp cheerfully into the kitchen, getting snow all over the floor. Make the crumb cake a day ahead, and just add a few more pears to the pan if there are more than six people.

Hot Chocolate for a Crowd

*Citrus-Steamed Pears with
Honey Yogurt*

Cranberry-Applesauce Crumb Cake

Hot Cocoa

SERVES 1

Dutch-process cocoa makes the richest hot cocoa; simple additions like cinnamon and vanilla make it almost irresistibly fragrant. By all means use skim or 1 percent milk if you prefer, but don't use water—you'll end up with a thin and unrewarding gruel, a waste of good cocoa.

◆◆◆◆◆◆

1 cup milk

2 teaspoons unsweetened cocoa powder,
   preferably Dutch-process

2 rounded teaspoons sugar

⅛ teaspoon ground cinnamon

⅛ teaspoon pure vanilla extract

◆◆◆◆◆◆

1. Heat the milk in a small heavy saucepan until it is steaming hot but not boiling.

2. Stir the cocoa, sugar, and cinnamon together in a serving mug; then add just a splash of the hot milk. Using a spoon, work this into a smooth paste. Then stir in the remaining milk and the vanilla, and serve immediately.

Variations

◆ Add a splash of brewed dark-roast coffee, ⅛ teaspoon pure almond or peppermint extract, or a sprinkling of finely grated orange zest.

◆ Add a couple of crushed cardamom pods to the milk while it is heating. Strain the milk into a mug.

Small Pleasures

Some people enjoy getting out the linens and polishing the silver, while others of us can't even remember where the silver *is*. Whichever camp you're in, welcoming friends to your house should be comfortable, relaxed, and fun.

These pages highlight some Hay Day inventions that have been party centerpieces since we opened the store. Old friends include Marvelous Mushroom Dip and Roasted Eggplant Caviar, Vidalia Onion Dip and Obsessive Olives. We also offer newer creations like Polenta Crostini, Summer Vegetable Bruschetta, and Avocado and Jicama Salsa—which might once have seemed exotic, but are now among the favorites for casual entertaining. Accompany them with our popular Blueberry Lemonade or Fresh Ginger Beer— and transform a simple gathering into a real event.

The majority of these "small pleasures" can be made ahead of time and stashed in the fridge; few of them require more equipment than a sharp knife and a cutting board. So call up some friends, push the newspapers off the coffee table, and put out an easy combination—Tapenade and Chèvre on Spears of Fresh Fennel and maybe some Cumin-and-Orange-Glazed Almonds and a Walnut-Crusted Camembert— and just lean back and enjoy one another.

Obsessive Olives

MAKES 1½ CUPS

There was a time when we were inventing so many new items at Hay Day that naming them became a lunchtime preoccupation. When Helen Brody (creator of many of the products we sell to this day) brought these out to the picnic table behind the store, they disappeared before the discussion could even get started! So the name was obvious, and Obsessive Olives have been an irresistible Hay Day institution since then. When we make them at home, we sometimes add button mushrooms, cubes of aged provolone, or Spanish manchego cheese to the marinade. Serving them beside a bowl of roasted or glazed nuts like the Cumin-and-Orange-Glazed Almonds (facing page) is a great way to get the conversation off politics and golf handicaps.

◆◆◆◆◆◆

7 ounces (1½ cups) small green olives (Spanish manzanilla if possible), pits removed
1 large clove garlic, peeled and finely minced
½ cup red wine vinegar
½ cup light vegetable oil
¼ teaspoon red pepper flakes
2 tablespoons finely minced onion
1 teaspoon minced fresh parsley
¼ teaspoon dried oregano

◆◆◆◆◆◆

Combine all the ingredients in a small bowl, cover, and set aside to marinate at room temperature overnight, stirring occasionally to distribute the flavors. Stored in the refrigerator, the marinated olives will keep well for several weeks; stir just before serving.

Bright Ideas

❦ Add a little tuna and mince in a blender for a green olive tapenade.

❦ Chop and toss with diced summer tomatoes and basil for a spicy bruschetta topping.

❦ Pop an Obsessive Olive into a cold martini.

❦ Add to a favorite caponata recipe.

❦ Chop and blend into softened cream cheese for a tangy bagel spread.

Meringue Pecans

MAKES 2 CUPS

These sweet, spicy nuts are irresistible all by themselves, but you can gild the lily at Christmastime by mixing them with dried cherries or cranberries for extra color.

◆◆◆◆◆◆

2 large egg whites
¾ cup sugar
2 teaspoons ground cinnamon
½ teaspoon ground cardamom
¼ teaspoon cayenne pepper
1 teaspoon Worcestershire sauce
1½ teaspoons coarse (kosher) salt
8 ounces (2 cups) pecan halves

◆◆◆◆◆◆

1. Preheat the oven to 350°F.

2. Line a large baking sheet with parchment paper.

3. Using an electric mixer, whip the egg whites in a large bowl until soft peaks form. With the mixer running on medium speed, add the sugar in a slow, thin stream. Stir in the spices, Worcestershire, and salt.

4. Add the pecans to the seasoned egg whites and toss to coat evenly. Scrape the contents of the bowl onto the prepared pan and spread the nuts out in a single even layer. Place in the oven and bake for 10 minutes. Stir the nuts together, spread them out again in a single layer, and continue baking until the meringue is browned, crisp, and nearly dry, about 10 minutes longer. Remove the pan from the oven and allow the nuts to cool for 10 minutes. Then break the nuts apart and serve. Or store them in an airtight container for up to 1 week.

Bright Ideas

❦ Use to accent a plate of Roquefort cheese, offered as an hors d'oeuvre or as a cheese course.

❦ Toss with crumbled blue cheese and scatter over mixed greens for a holiday salad.

❦ Crumble and serve as a luxury topping on ice cream.

❦ Mix into the crumb topping for a baked fruit crisp.

A Toast to the Holidays

Yes, Virginia, you *can* entertain during the holidays. A pretty assortment of sweet and savory nibbles makes for a lively gathering. Prepare almost everything ahead of time, and toast the season with elegant kir royales brightened with cranberry.

❦   ❦   ❦

Cranberry Kir Royales

Mushroom and Prosciutto Rolls
Lady Apples Filled with
Chicken Liver Pâté
Cumin-and-Orange-Glazed Almonds

Gingered Pear Torte
Cranberry-Almond Biscotti

❦   ❦   ❦

Cumin-and-Orange-Glazed Almonds

MAKES 2 GENEROUS CUPS

These almost take longer to describe than they do to make; you just toast the almonds and toss them gradually with sugared spices to add a chunky glaze. Another plus: They'll keep well in an airtight container for several days. Why both raw and blanched nuts? Simply because the combination is more interesting visually.

◆◆◆◆◆◆
½ cup sugar
1 teaspoon coarse (kosher) salt
1½ teaspoons whole cumin seeds
1 teaspoon red pepper flakes
Finely grated zest of 1 large orange
1 teaspoon vegetable oil
1 cup whole raw almonds
1 cup whole blanched almonds
◆◆◆◆◆◆

1. Combine the sugar, salt, cumin, red pepper flakes, and orange zest in a small bowl. Stir, using the back of a spoon to blend the zest in thoroughly, until the mixture resembles coarse meal. Set aside.

STUFFED MEDJOOL DATES

Big fresh Medjool dates are delicious when filled with a savory stuffing to balance their powerful sweetness; the combination of sweet and savory makes an outstanding hors d'oeuvre for holiday entertaining. Just slice them open with a sharp knife, remove the long thin pit to create a 1-inch pocket, and fill with:

◆ A thin slice of Roquefort and a toasted walnut half

◆ A sliver of creamy Camembert and a smoked almond

◆ Thin shards of Parmigiano-Reggiano cheese

◆ A wedge of crystallized ginger and a little Curried Chutney Spread (page 53)

2. Heat the vegetable oil in a large heavy-bottomed skillet. When it is very hot, add all the nuts and sauté over high heat, stirring constantly, until they are lightly toasted and sizzling hot, 3 to 5 minutes. Sprinkle 1 tablespoon of the seasonings over the nuts, and stir over high heat until it caramelizes and forms a glaze. Continue to stir over medium-high heat, adding the remaining seasonings 1 tablespoon at a time to build up a chunky glaze over all the nuts. Spill the nuts out onto a large baking sheet to cool, breaking up any large clumps.

3. Place the nuts in small bowls for serving. Or store them in an airtight container (plastic tub or bag). The nuts will stay fresh and crisp for 2 to 3 days.

Hummus with Herb-Toasted Pita Chips

MAKES 2 CUPS

This great, healthful (relatively low-fat) dip is a natural with triangles of pita bread and with crisp spears of fresh vegetables like fennel, celery, cucumber, and endive, or whole radishes. Reserve a few whole chickpeas for garnishing the bowl, or finish with a handful of sesame seeds and a little parsley. In the Middle East it's traditional to make a small well in the top and pour in some good fruity olive oil to give the dip a nice silky texture.

◆◆◆◆◆◆

1 can (16 ounces) or 2 cups cooked
  chickpeas, drained
1 large clove garlic, peeled
¼ cup sesame tahini
Juice of 1 large lemon (3 generous
  tablespoons)
½ teaspoon coarse (kosher) salt
1 tablespoon coarsely chopped fresh
  parsley or cilantro
¼ to ⅓ cup water or reserved bean
  cooking liquid
Sesame seeds or fresh parsley sprigs,
  for garnish
Herb-Toasted Pita Chips
  (recipe follows)

◆◆◆◆◆◆

1. Put the chickpeas in a food processor or blender, setting a few aside for garnish if you like. Add the garlic, tahini, lemon juice, salt, and parsley and purée until smooth.

2. Blend in the water, 1 tablespoon at a time, until the hummus reaches the desired consistency (thick for a spread, slightly thinner for a dip). Spoon the hummus into a shallow serving bowl, garnish with whole chickpeas, sesame seeds, or parsley, and surround with pita chips.

Bright Ideas

❦ Serve as a condiment for grilled chicken or lamb kebabs.

❦ Spread on lavash or slices of a coarse country bread, and top with fresh sprouts and sliced tomatoes for a great vegetarian sandwich.

❦ Spread thickly on small toasted bread rounds and serve as a crostini appetizer, garnished with a chickpea or two and a sprinkling of sweet paprika.

ABOUT SESAME TAHINI

A thick paste made from ground sesame seeds, tahini (like natural peanut butter) keeps well even at room temperature. Good-quality sesame tahini should be thin and fluid; if it has separated, just stir the oil back into the paste.

Herb-Toasted Pita Chips
MAKES 48 CHIPS

Seasoned pita chips come in bags, of course, but they'll never be as fresh and appealing as these. Making pita chips at home is a real no-brainer (there's a sort of childish satisfaction in cutting up pitas with scissors), and the parsley, thyme, and sesame seeds make them perfect dipping partners for creamy hummus.

◆◆◆◆◆◆

2 teaspoons dried thyme
1 tablespoon finely minced
  fresh parsley
2 teaspoons sesame seeds
¼ teaspoon coarse (kosher) salt
¼ cup olive oil
3 round pita breads (6-inch size)

◆◆◆◆◆◆

1. Preheat the oven to 350°F.

2. Stir the thyme, parsley, sesame seeds, salt, and oil together in a small bowl.

3. Using clean kitchen shears, snip the pita breads in half, then cut each half into four triangles. Tear each triangle in half at the seam, and brush the rough sides generously with the herb mixture. Place on a large baking sheet, herb side up, and bake until lightly browned and crisp, 12 to 15 minutes. These will keep for 3 to 4 days in an airtight plastic bag.

Oriental Dip with Daikon Chips

MAKES 1½ CUPS

O riental Dip is the great Hay Day invention for crisp vegetable crudités. We especially like it with daikon, but it's also wonderful with carrots, cucumbers, jicama, garden radishes, snap peas, and broccoli florets. You'll get high marks for imagination if you serve it in an "organic" bowl—such as a hollowed-out red or green bell pepper or small head of cabbage.

◆◆◆◆◆◆

6 ounces cream cheese, cut into chunks
2 tablespoons sour cream
2 tablespoons mayonnaise
1 small clove garlic, peeled and minced
¼ cup coarsely chopped onion
1 tablespoon tamari
1 red bell pepper, roasted (see How to Roast Peppers, page 80),
 peeled, seeded, and cut into strips
Tabasco or other hot pepper sauce
Coarse (kosher) salt
Daikon Chips (recipe follows)

◆◆◆◆◆◆

Combine the cream cheese, sour cream, mayonnaise, garlic, onion, and tamari in a food processor or blender, and pulse five or six times to create a chunky purée. Add three-fourths of bell pepper strips and blend until the mixture just begins to turn pink, with small chunks of pepper still visible. Season to taste with hot sauce and salt. Garnish the dip with the remaining pepper strips. This will keep for several days in the refrigerator.

Note: For extra bite, substitute roasted Spanish-style piquillo peppers for the bell pepper.

Bright Ideas

❦ Serve as a sauce for shrimp cocktail.

❦ Use as a spread for roast beef or grilled chicken sandwiches.

❦ Smear a tablespoonful over a fish steak hot from the grill.

❦ Use for a dressing with shredded roast chicken and fresh bean sprouts for a delicious Asian chicken salad.

ABOUT DAIKON

R aw daikon also adds a nice crunch to stir-fries and salads. Its high moisture content makes it more perishable than other root vegetables, however, so buy only what you need right away and keep it well wrapped in plastic wrap in the refrigerator's vegetable bin. It should be as firm as a carrot when you buy it, and not too big—excessively large roots can sometimes be dry and spongy at the center.

Daikon Chips

SERVES 8

Westerners discovered the virtues of daikon not too long ago. This sweet, peppery white Asian radish is a cousin of our own garden radishes; it's bigger, has a mellower flavor, and makes wonderful chips for serving with dip. And it takes a lot of guilt out of hors d'oeuvres! Just peel and slice it (not too thin), and arrange the slices around the dip on a bed of sturdy greenery, such as chicory, frisée, or kale.

◆◆◆◆◆◆

*1 piece (12 ounces) daikon root
(no larger than 3 inches in diameter)*

◆◆◆◆◆◆

Peel off the thin outer layer of the daikon root with a sharp swivel peeler, and cut the daikon into ¼-inch-thick diagonal slices. Keep the slices in ice water in the refrigerator until serving time so they'll stay crisp and white. Arrange them around the dip bowl on a tray or platter lined with sturdy greens.

Roasted Eggplant Caviar

MAKES 2 CUPS

Everyone loves this creamy eggplant purée for its rich flavor—and also because it contains very little fat. Serve it in a "bowl" made from a hollowed eggplant, and surround it with crackers or toast points and freshly cut

MENU

A Wintry Dipping Platter

❧ ❧ ❧

*Brussels sprouts
Cauliflower florets
Endive spears
Daikon Chips*

Complementary dips
*Hummus
Marvelous Mushroom Dip
Oriental Dip
Hay Day's Roquefort Dressing
Cranberry Vinaigrette*

❧ ❧ ❧

vegetables. It's great with Herb-Toasted Pita Chips (page 33), too. You'll get the richest flavor if the eggplant is thoroughly roasted, with its skin blackened and its flesh very soft—and you'll get even more flavor if you cook it on the grill over a charcoal fire.

◆◆◆◆◆◆

*1 large eggplant (about 1 pound)
2 large cloves garlic
2 tablespoons fresh lemon juice
1 small handful fresh Italian
   (flat-leaf) parsley leaves
3 scallions, white and light green parts
   coarsely chopped
2 tablespoons olive oil
Coarse (kosher) salt*

◆◆◆◆◆◆

1. Preheat the oven to 400°F and line a baking sheet with parchment paper. Or simply preheat the grill.

2. Pierce the eggplant in several places with the tines of a fork, and place it on the baking sheet or directly on the grill. Enclose the garlic cloves in a small piece of aluminum foil and place them beside the eggplant. Roast or grill, turning the eggplant once, until it is softened and collapsed, with blackened skin, 35 to 45 minutes. The garlic will roast into a paste within its skin at the same time.

3. Remove from the heat and set aside to cool.

4. Once the eggplant is cool enough to handle, slice it in half and scrape the soft cooked flesh into the work bowl of a blender or food processor. Be sure to incorporate any bits of roasted flesh clinging to the skin, as they are full of flavor. Squeeze the roasted garlic from its papery skin into the work bowl. Add the lemon juice, parsley, scallions, and oil. Blend to form a creamy spread. Season to taste with salt, and transfer to a serving bowl. Serve at room temperature. The dip will keep nicely in the refrigerator for several days. For the fullest flavor, allow it to come to room temperature before serving.

Bright Ideas

❧ Use as a spread for summer tomato and basil sandwiches.

❧ Serve as a condiment with grilled fish.

❧ Blend with a little tahini for a creamier dip.

❧ Spread on sole fillets, roll, and top with a little olive oil and chopped tomato. Cover with aluminum foil and bake at 375°F until the fish is white and flaky throughout, 20 to 30 minutes.

Cherry Tomatoes Filled with Eggplant Caviar

SERVES 8 TO 12

Hollowed red and yellow cherry tomatoes make easy, pretty summer hors d'oeuvres when they're filled with dips, spreads, or soft cheeses. (For speed and neatness, use a pastry bag fitted with a large star tip.) Fill them with Roasted Eggplant Caviar and pretend you're on a balcony looking out over the Mediterranean.

◆◆◆◆◆◆

24 cherry tomatoes, preferably assorted red and yellow
1 cup Roasted Eggplant Caviar (page 35)
1 large bunch fresh Italian (flat-leaf) parsley

◆◆◆◆◆◆

1. Slice just the tops off the tomatoes, using a sharp paring or serrated knife. Hollow the interiors with a small melon baller, taking care not to rip the side walls. Lightly salt the interior of the shells and place them, cut sides down, on paper towels to drain for about 30 minutes.

2. Fill a pastry bag fitted with a ½-inch tip with the Eggplant Caviar and pipe it into the tomato shells, mounding it up high (or use a teaspoon). Garnish each with a leaf of parsley, and arrange the tomatoes on a platter lined with parsley.

Note: To avoid runaway tomatoes, use a sharp paring knife or a serrated knife to slice a tiny sliver off the bottom of each.

Marvelous Mushroom Dip

MAKES 2 GENEROUS CUPS

This is a real Hay Day original—we can't imagine the stores without it. It's thick, more like a spread, and glorious on roast beef sandwiches. For casual fall entertaining we just serve it alone on squares of whole-grain bread, but for dress-ups we cut the bread into stars, moons, and hearts with a cookie cutter and top the mushroom spread with chopped walnuts, orange zest, and dried cranberries plumped in red wine.

◆◆◆◆◆◆

¼ ounce dried porcini mushrooms
About ¼ cup hot water
2 tablespoons olive oil
¼ cup minced fresh shallots
8 ounces fresh cremini mushrooms, wiped clean, caps and stems coarsely chopped
1 tablespoon brandy
1 teaspoon fresh lemon juice
8 ounces cream cheese
1 tablespoon minced fresh chives
Coarse (kosher) salt
Freshly ground black pepper

◆◆◆◆◆◆

1. Place the porcini mushrooms in a small bowl, add the hot water (it should cover the mushrooms), and set aside until softened, 10 to 15 minutes.

2. Heat the oil in a large heavy-bottomed saucepan. Add the shallots and sauté over medium heat until very lightly colored, about 3 minutes. Stir in the cremini mushrooms and sauté until very soft and richly colored, about 5 minutes. Add the brandy, lemon juice, and porcini mushrooms along with their soaking liquid. Stir and simmer until most of the liquid has been absorbed, about 1 minute. Remove from the heat and spoon the mushroom mixture into a food processor or blender. Pulse the machine on and off to finely mince.

MENU

A Full-Color Summer Array

❦ ❦ ❦

Miniature pattypan squash
Red and yellow cherry tomatoes
Green beans
Zucchini slices
Garden radishes
A rainbow of bell pepper strips

Complementary dips

Marvelous Mushroom Dip
Roasted Eggplant Caviar
Southwestern Tomato Salsa
Chunky Clam and Bacon Dip
Roasted Garlic Mayonnaise
Tomato-Pesto Mayonnaise

❦ ❦ ❦

3. Combine the cream cheese and chives in a bowl, and blend together with an electric mixer on high speed. Blend in the mushroom mixture and season to taste with salt and pepper. Refrigerate, covered, until ready to serve. Well wrapped, the dip will keep for several days.

Bright Ideas

❦ Pipe or spoon Marvelous Mushroom Dip into mushroom caps, hollowed-out cherry tomatoes, or cucumber cups.

❦ Use the dip as a filling for roasted boneless chicken breasts, and serve on a bed of sautéed wild mushrooms.

❦ Serve Marvelous Mushroom Dip as a condiment with hot grilled filet mignon.

Mushroom and Prosciutto Rolls

SERVES 16 TO 24

Mushroom Dip makes an easy, elegant hors d'oeuvre when you combine it with crunchy enoki mushrooms and savory prosciutto.

◆◆◆◆◆◆

1 cup Marvelous Mushroom Dip (page 37)
12 large thin slices prosciutto, each cut into four 2 × 4-inch pieces
8 ounces fresh enoki mushrooms, trimmed
Sprigs of fresh parsley, for garnish

◆◆◆◆◆◆

Spread a thin layer (1 scant teaspoon) of Mushroom Dip on each piece of prosciutto. Lay a small cluster of enoki mushrooms (about 6) crosswise on the prosciutto so they peek out of each side. Roll up tightly and arrange on a serving platter decorated with enoki mushrooms and parsley sprigs.

Hay Day's Roquefort Dressing

MAKES 1½ CUPS

Whipped until it's creamy, this tangy masterpiece is a lovely dip for all kinds of fresh vegetables. Left a bit chunky, it's the king of dressings for rich greens like arugula, spinach, watercress, and mesclun, especially when they're accented with seasonal fruit like sliced pears, apples, grapes, or figs.

◆◆◆◆◆◆

1 egg
2 tablespoons red wine vinegar
Freshly ground black pepper
¼ teaspoon salt
¾ cup light vegetable oil (preferably safflower or canola)
1 tablespoon coarsely chopped fresh parsley
1 tablespoon coarsely chopped scallions
¼ cup heavy (whipping) cream
2 ounces Roquefort cheese, crumbled (about ⅓ cup crumbled)

◆◆◆◆◆◆

1. Blend the egg, 1 tablespoon of the vinegar, a dash of pepper, and the salt in a food processor or blender until pale and foamy, about 1 minute.

2. With the machine running, slowly add the oil in a thin steady stream, and blend to form a thick mayonnaise. Add the parsley, scallions, cream, and remaining 1 tablespoon vinegar. Pulse five or six times to combine.

3. For a thick chunky dressing, stir in the crumbled cheese. For a thinner, creamy dressing or dip, use the processor to blend in the cheese. Season to taste with additional pepper as desired.

ABOUT ROQUEFORT

Made only in the hallowed limestone *caves* of Mont Cambalou, near the village of Roquefort in southwestern France, the production of this magnificent, creamy blue sheep's-milk cheese is strictly controlled by the French government (look for the trademark red sheep on the wrapper). And woe to anyone who attaches the name "Roquefort" to a dip or dressing made with anything else. With its intense flavor and crumbly texture, it is truly one of the great cheeses of the world, grand at the end of a meal with a glass of port or Sauternes.

Tomato-Pesto Mayonnaise

MAKES 1¼ CUPS

Glorious as a dip for crudités—especially cherry tomatoes, zucchini, and baby potatoes—this is also a superb sandwich spread. Smear it on toasted Everybody's Favorite Peasant Bread (page 100), add thick slices of ripe tomatoes, really good bacon, and sliced roast chicken, and you have a club sandwich that is glamorous enough for the Côte d'Azur.

◆◆◆◆◆◆

1 ounce dry-packed sun-dried tomatoes (about 5 whole tomatoes)
⅓ cup dry white wine
2 tablespoons Pesto (page 250)
¾ cup mayonnaise, preferably homemade

◆◆◆◆◆◆

Combine the tomatoes and the wine in a small bowl and soak until the tomatoes are softened, about 30 minutes. Drain the tomatoes, coarsely chop them, and place them in a food processor or blender. Add the pesto and blend to form a fine paste, stopping to push the ingredients down into the work bowl as needed. Stir the paste into the mayonnaise, cover tightly, and refrigerate until ready to use. The mayonnaise will keep for a week in the refrigerator.

Bright Ideas

❦ Serve as a dipping sauce for snow-crab claws or lobster cocktail.

❦ Use as a dressing for potato, pasta, chicken, or shrimp salad.

❦ Spread sparingly over fish fillets, wrap in parchment, and bake at 350°F until flaky, 20 to 30 minutes.

❦ Serve as a finishing condiment for grilled tuna or swordfish steaks.

A Summer Vegetable Aïoli with Roasted Garlic Mayonnaise

In France, aïoli isn't just the mayonnaise. It's a summer event in villages all across Provence. The whole town gathers at long tables out in the square, where they dip chunks of vegetables and cooked whitefish into pungent garlicky mayonnaise and wash it all down with generous quantities of the local red wine.

You needn't go as far as France, though, to create this celebration of the high-summer harvest. Surround rich Roasted Garlic Mayonnaise with an abundance of bright vegetables and a few hard-cooked eggs, decorate the arrangement with fresh green herbs and whole bulbs of raw or roasted garlic, and invite the neighborhood to join you—it would be a wonderful way to celebrate Bastille Day (July 14).

◆◆◆◆◆◆

Green beans, stem ends trimmed
Zucchini, sliced at an angle into
  ¼-inch-thick rounds
Medley of bite-size tomatoes
  (red and yellow cherry, red and
  yellow teardrop, clusters of Sweet
  100's), rinsed, stems intact
Hard-cooked eggs, peeled and halved
  lengthwise
Roasted Garlic Mayonnaise
  (recipe follows)
Whole garlic bulbs, roasted or raw,
  for garnish
Small clusters of fresh herbs,
  for garnish

◆◆◆◆◆◆

1. Fill a large bowl or sink with ice water.

2. Bring a large pot of water to a boil. Salt the water, return it to a boil, and add the beans and zucchini. Stir, and blanch just until bright green and crisp, no more than 1 minute. Quickly drain and transfer the vegetables to the ice water to stop the cooking and set their color. Allow to cool for several minutes. Then drain and pat dry with paper towels.

3. Spoon the Roasted Garlic Mayonnaise into a ceramic serving bowl. Place the bowl in a large open basket or on a platter, and surround it with the tomatoes, beans, zucchini, and eggs. Garnish with garlic and herbs if desired, and serve right away or cover and chill until serving time.

Roasted Garlic Mayonnaise

MAKES 1 CUP

Traditional aïoli is made with fresh raw garlic that is pulverized in a mortar with a pestle. We've mellowed the flavor by roasting the garlic first. Use a garlic roaster if you have one, but a tight wrapping in aluminum foil is just as effective.

◆◆◆◆◆◆

1 head garlic
1 teaspoon olive oil
1 tablespoon minced fresh chives
1 cup mayonnaise, preferably
   homemade
Freshly ground black pepper

◆◆◆◆◆◆

1. Preheat the oven to 350°F.

2. Remove the outer papery skin from the garlic without separating the cloves. Place the whole bulb on a large sheet of aluminum foil, and drizzle the olive oil over it. Wrap the bulb tightly in the foil and bake until the garlic is softened and nearly liquid inside, about 1 hour. Remove from the oven, open the foil, and allow to cool for 15 minutes.

3. Separate the cloves and squeeze the roasted garlic from its skin onto a cutting board. Finely chop any large bits of garlic with a sharp knife.

4. Add the roasted garlic and the chives to the mayonnaise, and stir thoroughly. Season to taste with a few grindings of

GOOD OLD GARLIC

For years just two varieties of garlic ("early" and "late") were grown in California, but now a whole range of varieties is appearing in farmers' markets: Celaya Purple, a strong garlic from Mexico; Creole Red, a hot and peppery American original; Inchelium Red, a mild, sweet white garlic discovered on an Indian reservation, excellent raw; Red Toch, a good keeper from Russia, mild and sweet when roasted; and Spanish Rioja, abundant in the Northwest, robustly flavored and easy to peel.

The two compounds, allin and allinase, that make garlic pungent are separated by membranes; as soon as the garlic clove is cut, the two combine to form a sulfur compound called allicin. The more you crush the cells (in a garlic press, for instance), the hotter the results. The volatile sulfur is dissipated by heat, however, so garlic is easily tamed.

Finely chopped or pressed raw garlic is the hottest of all, and is used in salad dressings and traditional aïoli. Briefly cooked chopped garlic is still a major presence, great in stir-fries and cooked sauces. Whole cloves that are simmered until they are soft and tender are almost tame enough to be eaten plain. And roasted unpeeled heads and cloves are the mildest and sweetest of all. Just remember never to scorch garlic in cooking, or it will become horribly bitter.

Just like onions, garlic bulbs should be kept in a cool, dry place away from heat and sunlight. The bulbs should be crisp and firm, with no green shoots. Remove any green sprouts you find inside the cloves—they'll be bitter and indigestible.

black pepper. Cover, and refrigerate until serving time. Wrapped and tucked away in the refrigerator, the mayonnaise will keep nicely for a couple of weeks.

Bright Ideas

❦ Use as a spread on roast beef and B.L.T. sandwiches.

❦ Serve as a condiment with warm grilled or broiled fish steaks.

❦ Use as a dressing for chicken, pasta, or potato salad.

Tapenade and Chèvre on Spears of Fresh Fennel

SERVES 8 TO 12

Crisp, aromatic fennel has a very gentle anise flavor. It is wonderful on its own in crudités or as a base for this simple hors d'oeuvre, which balances the intense richness of black olive tapenade with creamy goat cheese.

◆◆◆◆◆◆

*1 large bulb fresh fennel, rinsed
    and trimmed of feathery tops
    and stalks
8 ounces fresh creamy chèvre
Tapenade (recipe follows)
Sprigs of fresh thyme, for garnish
Small black olives, for garnish*

◆◆◆◆◆◆

Split the fennel bulb in half lengthwise and cut out the V-shaped core. Separate the sections and slice into generous ½-inch-wide strips. Trim off any tough strings, as you would with celery. On each strip spread first a small teaspoonful of goat cheese, then an equal amount of Tapenade. Arrange on a decorative ceramic platter, garnished with thyme sprigs and olives.

Tapenade

MAKES 1 CUP

It's lunchtime in Provence, and in the green shade of a grape arbor the waiter has brought some fresh chèvre, a carafe of Bandol, and a pottery bowl of dark, rich olive paste to spread on sliced baguettes. Life doesn't get much better . . .

ABOUT CAPERS

Pungent capers, frequently used in Mediterranean cooking, are actually flower buds plucked from a shrub. Available in sizes from the tiny French nonpareil (about the size of peppercorns) to the oversize stemmed Spanish caperberries (which can run as large as a cherry), they are fully edible and add rich tart flavor to dips, spreads, salads, and sauces. Most capers are packed in brine or preserved in salt and should be rinsed thoroughly before using.

OLIVES FOR TAPENADE

The intense flavor of tapenade very much depends on the quality of the olives that go into it, and since excellent tree-ripened and cured olives are easily available these days, there's no need to settle for canned ones. It's good to balance the sharp flavor of brine-cured Niçoise or Kalamata olives (the plump kind, packed in juice) with some more intense, earthy dry- or oil-cured Moroccan or Nyons olives (wrinkled and dry-packed).

If you don't have a hand-held pitter, the quickest way to remove the pits from a quantity of olives is to press down on them with either your thumb or the flat side of a large knife until they split in half and the pits can be discarded. The good news is that most markets now sell good olives with the pits already removed.

◆◆◆◆◆◆

*½ cup brine-cured black olives
(such as Kalamata or Niçoise),
pits removed*
*½ cup dry-cured black olives
(such as Italian, Moroccan, or
Nyons), pits removed*
*1 small clove garlic, peeled and
crushed*
2 anchovy fillets, rinsed
*¼ cup nonpareil capers, drained and
rinsed (see About Capers, facing page)*
1 teaspoon Dijon mustard
*2 tablespoons extra-virgin olive oil,
plus additional for topping*
*1 tablespoon fresh thyme or chopped
fresh basil leaves*

◆◆◆◆◆◆

1. Combine the olives, garlic, and anchovies in a food processor and pulse to finely chop.

2. Add the capers, mustard, 2 tablespoons oil, and thyme, and pulse several times to work into a uniform chunky paste. Transfer to a serving bowl. Topped with a thin layer of olive oil, Tapenade will keep for several days in a sealed container.

Bright Ideas

❧ Toss into hot pasta along with a little olive oil and some crumbled aged goat cheese.

❧ For an easy appetizer, arrange medallions of fresh goat cheese on a bed of lightly dressed mesclun greens, and spoon Tapenade on top.

❧ Use as a grilling paste for fresh tuna or swordfish steaks or vegetable brochettes.

❧ Thin with additional olive oil and a little red wine vinegar and use as a dressing for warm potato salad.

❧ Use as a sandwich spread (delicious with sliced tomatoes, tuna salad, or grilled vegetables).

❧ Spread thinly on toast points and serve with a bowl of hearty soup, such as Oven-Charred Vegetable (page 94) or Mediterranean Bean (page 71).

TAPENADE YOGURT

Simply stir together equal portions of Tapenade and plain yogurt for a creamy olive-rich dip that's great with fresh fennel spears, celery, cucumber, radishes, daikon, zucchini, and tomatoes. Garnish the bowl with a sprig of fresh thyme and a scattering of sliced or chopped black olives.

Roasted Chile Peppers con Queso

SERVES 6 TO 8

The classic balance of spicy peppers and rich cheese is not a new idea, but this version gives the peppers center stage, cloaking them lightly with cheese instead of floating them in a sea of creamy cheese dip. A wonderful idea for fall football weekends.

◆◆◆◆◆◆

2 fresh poblano chile peppers
2 red bell peppers
Juice of 1 lime
¼ cup finely minced red onion
⅓ cup fromage blanc or sour cream
½ teaspoon coarse (kosher) salt
1 fresh jalapeño pepper, sliced in half, seeded, and deveined
1 tomato, coarsely chopped
4 ounces Monterey Jack cheese, grated (1 cup grated)
Thick-cut unsalted corn chips

◆◆◆◆◆◆

1. Preheat the broiler.

2. Place the poblano and bell peppers on a large baking sheet and roast under the broiler, turning occasionally, until the skins are blackened on all sides and the flesh is softened, 8 to 10 minutes. When the peppers are done, toss them in a paper bag, roll the top down to close it tightly, and set it aside to cool.

3. In a large bowl, stir together the lime juice, onion, fromage blanc, and salt.

4. As soon as the peppers are cool enough to handle, remove them from the bag and peel off the skins. Slice the peppers in half, and scrape the seeds away with the blunt edge of a knife. Do not rinse the peppers, or flavorful juices will be lost. Slice into thin strips.

5. Finely chop the jalapeño pepper and add it, along with the roasted pepper strips, to the bowl of fromage blanc. Stir to combine, and spread the mixture in a shallow casserole or 9-inch round deep-dish pie plate. Top with the tomato and grated cheese, and place under the broiler until bubbly hot and lightly browned on top, 15 to 20 minutes. Serve hot, with corn chips for dipping.

FROMAGE BLANC

Fromage blanc is a soft fresh cheese with the texture and flavor of sour cream, but it is much lower in fat. It holds up beautifully in sauces and is a welcome substitute in recipes calling for sour cream. You can find it in the cheese section of your market.

Vidalia Onion Dip

MAKES 2 CUPS

Magnificent Georgia-grown Vidalias are so mild that just a brief cooking mellows their flavor—which means there's lots of crunch left in this superb version of the classic picnic dip. It's awesome served with really thick potato chips. Or you can spoon the dip onto small scoop-shaped slices of raw Vidalia onion. (Yes, they are *that* mild!)

◆◆◆◆◆◆◆

1 tablespoon light vegetable oil
1 clove garlic, peeled and minced
1½ cups chopped Vidalia onion (see
   About Vidalia Onions, page 115)
1½ teaspoons sugar
1 tablespoon chopped fresh thyme, or
   1 teaspoon dried
¼ cup Browned Beef Stock (page 269)
   or demi glace (see Note, page 134)
2 tablespoons medium-dry sherry
8 ounces cream cheese
¼ cup sour cream
1 tablespoon minced fresh chives, plus
   additional for garnish
Coarse (kosher) salt

◆◆◆◆◆◆

1. Heat the oil in a large skillet. Add the garlic and 1 generous cup of the onions, and sauté over medium-high heat until softened (do not brown), 3 to 5 minutes. Sprinkle with the sugar and thyme, drizzle in the stock and sherry, and simmer until the liquid is reduced to 1 tablespoon, about 2 minutes. Remove from the heat and allow to cool to room temperature (or refrigerate to speed the process).

Bright Spring Greens for Dipping

Asparagus
Sugar snap peas
Fiddleheads
Haricots verts

Complementary dips
Vidalia Onion Dip
Lemon Vinaigrette
Tapenade Yogurt
Sesame-Ginger Vinaigrette

2. Combine the cream cheese and sour cream in a mixing bowl, and whip together with an electric mixer on high speed to soften and combine. Add the cooled onion mixture and stir or blend in on low speed. Stir in the 1 tablespoon chives and the remaining raw chopped onion, and season to taste with salt as needed. Spoon into a serving bowl, top with a few additional chives, and serve. Store any remaining dip, wrapped, in the refrigerator. It will keep nicely for several days.

Bright Ideas

❦ Use as a topping for hamburgers or baked potatoes.

❦ Serve as a spread for Sunday bagels, topped with thinly sliced smoked salmon.

❦ **Vidalia Onion Tea Sandwiches:** Spread a layer of Vidalia Onion Dip on thinly sliced sandwich bread and top with thin slices of Vidalia onion and sprigs of fresh watercress.

Chunky Clam and Bacon Dip

MAKES 2 CUPS

This is catnip for people who like New England clam chowder. Brightly colored with red onions, green scallions, and red peppers, it is great with really excellent thick, sturdy potato chips and spears of celery, bell peppers, and scallions. It's perfect for a boat or beach picnic, and there's never any left to take home. You can pick up chopped fresh clams at your local seafood market.

◆◆◆◆◆◆

4 ounces thick-sliced smoked bacon,
    diced
⅓ cup chopped red onion
3 scallions, white and light green
    parts coarsely chopped
6 ounces chopped clams (meat from
    about 12 to 14 "top neck" or large
    chowder clams)
8 ounces sour cream
8 ounces cream cheese, at room
    temperature
1 red bell pepper, roasted (see How to
    Roast Peppers, page 80) and coarsely
    chopped, or 1 roasted pepper from a
    jar, coarsely chopped
Pinch of crushed red pepper flakes
2 tablespoons coarsely chopped Italian
    (flat-leaf) parsley
Ground white pepper
Coarse (kosher) salt

◆◆◆◆◆◆

1. In a large skillet, sauté the bacon over medium-high heat until crisp. Drain the fat from the pan, and add the onion, scallions, and clams. Sauté until the clams are just cooked through, about 1 minute. Remove from the heat and set aside.

2. Combine the sour cream, cream cheese, roasted bell pepper, red pepper flakes, and parsley in a large mixing bowl. Mix with an electric mixer on low speed or work with the back of a large spoon until smooth and well blended. Add the contents of the skillet along with all the pan juices, and stir well. Season to taste with pepper and salt. Serve right away, or cover and refrigerate until ready to serve (the dip will keep for several days).

Bright Ideas

❧ Toss with diced cooked potatoes for a terrific summer potato salad. Season to taste with additional salt and pepper.

❧ Serve on spears of Belgian endive.

A Warm-Weather Tea

The rejuvenating tradition of afternoon tea should be enjoyed year-round. When the weather is too sultry for a pot of hot tea, set the table on the balcony and invite a few friends for a cool afternoon tea.

❧ ❧ ❧

Iced Darjeeling Tea

Vidalia Onion Tea Sandwiches
Chunky Clam and Bacon Dip with
Herb-Toasted Pita Chips

Lemon Snap Cookies

Baby Potatoes with Chunky Clam and Bacon Dip

SERVES 8 TO 12

Tiny red or white new potatoes make wonderful doll-size "bowls" for hors d'oeuvres. Here they are lightly cooked and seasoned like a good French potato salad before filling.

◆◆◆◆◆◆

*24 bite-size (1- to 1½-inch diameter)
red or white new potatoes (select
uniform size for even cooking)
2 tablespoons tarragon vinegar
¼ teaspoon coarse (kosher) salt
½ teaspoon sweet paprika, plus
additional for garnish
1 cup Chunky Clam and Bacon Dip
(facing page)*

◆◆◆◆◆◆

1. Scrub the potatoes. Use a small melon baller to scoop out the center of each potato, creating a cavity about ½ to ¾ inch in diameter (about halfway into the potato).

2. Bring a large pot of lightly salted water to a boil, and cook the potato cups until fork-tender through the thickest portion, 5 to 7 minutes. Drain, place in a mixing bowl, and toss with the vinegar, salt, and the ¼ teaspoon paprika while still hot. Cover and chill for at least 4 hours before filling.

3. Fill each potato cup with a heaping teaspoon of the dip, mounding it up high. Finish with a dusting of paprika.

Cranberry Salsa

MAKES 2 CUPS

When they first encountered it, our customers were startled by this combination of Cape Cod and Cancún—but very soon they couldn't get enough of it. It's basically a raw salsa, delicious with sweet potato or corn chips. The garlic, vinegar, and jalapeño make it a real wake-up call for turkey at Thanksgiving, especially in post-holiday sandwiches. It's a snap to put together and is best made the day before so the flavors can develop fully.

◆◆◆◆◆◆

*½ cup coarsely chopped onion
1 fresh jalapeño pepper, seeded,
deveined, and chopped into a few
large pieces
1 clove garlic, smashed and peeled
1½ cups fresh or frozen cranberries
½ small juice orange, unpeeled,
scrubbed, quartered, and seeded
3 tablespoons white wine vinegar
1 tablespoon sugar
2 tablespoons fresh orange juice
½ teaspoon coarse (kosher) salt
Oven-Baked Sweet Potato Chips
(recipe follows)*

◆◆◆◆◆◆

47

1. Combine the onion, jalapeño, and garlic in a food processor, and pulse until finely chopped. Add the cranberries, orange quarters, vinegar, sugar, and orange juice, and pulse until uniformly coarse and chunky. Season to taste with salt. Allow to rest at room temperature for 30 minutes for the flavors to develop.

2. Refrigerate the salsa until it is thoroughly chilled, 2 hours.

3. Arrange the sweet potato chips around a platter, and place a bowl of the Cranberry Salsa in the center. Serve while the salsa is still cold. Covered and refrigerated, Cranberry Salsa will keep nicely for a couple of weeks.

Bright Ideas

❦ Serve as a condiment for smoked chicken, pheasant, or turkey.

❦ Mix with a little sour cream and serve as a zesty topping for baked sweet potatoes.

❦ In the summer, serve as a refreshing condiment for grilled turkey burgers.

Oven-Baked Sweet Potato Chips

MAKES ABOUT 70 CHIPS

Yellow- or orange-fleshed sweet potatoes make wonderful chips. A steady hand and a sharp knife will do the job, but you'll get consistent slices far more quickly with a mandoline or a food processor fitted with a thin slicing blade. Each potato yields just the right number of slices to cover a large baking sheet, so work in batches for the best results.

◆◆◆◆◆◆

*3 orange-fleshed sweet potatoes
(see Sweet Potatoes, page 202),
unpeeled, scrubbed
2 tablespoons olive oil
¾ teaspoon coarse (kosher) salt*

◆◆◆◆◆◆

1. Preheat the oven to 400°F.

2. Cut the potatoes into ⅛-inch-thick slices, using a mandoline-style slicer (resist the temptation to slice much thinner—the chips will burn too quickly). Blot the slices between paper towels.

3. Lightly wipe a large baking sheet with 2 teaspoons of the olive oil, and spread a single layer of potato slices on the sheet. Sprinkle with a bit of the salt and bake, turning once, until toasted to a dappled brown color with crisp and curly edges, 12 to 15 minutes. Remove, and set aside to cool (the chips will continue to crisp as they cool). Repeat with the remaining potato slices. If not devoured immediately, they'll keep well in an airtight plastic bag for 2 or 3 days.

Avocado and Jicama Salsa

MAKES 4 CUPS

We've always liked to serve traditional guacamole on raw jicama spears, so putting the two together for a guacamole-with-crunch was a natural next step. This salsa gets its nice texture not only from the chunks of jicama, but also from avocados that are slightly firmer than you would use for conventional guacamole. Like the classic, it's great served with good corn chips and cold beer or icy margaritas. To store it for any length of time, pack it in a small airtight container, top with a slice of lemon or lime, and place plastic wrap directly over the entire surface to prevent the avocado from browning.

◆◆◆◆◆◆

1 small jicama, peeled and diced
   (2 cups diced)
½ cup minced red onion
1 clove garlic, peeled and minced
1 or 2 green serrano chile peppers, to
   taste, minced (2 make a hot salsa)
⅓ cup fresh lime juice
2 tablespoons fresh orange juice
⅓ cup coarsely chopped fresh cilantro
2 firm ripe Hass avocados
½ teaspoon coarse (kosher) salt

◆◆◆◆◆◆

1. Combine the jicama, onion, garlic, chile pepper, lime juice, orange juice, and cilantro in a large bowl and toss together.

2. Peel, pit, and coarsely chop the avocados. Add the avocados and salt to the bowl, and toss gently and thoroughly. Serve immediately, or refrigerate (see headnote) for a few hours to allow the flavors to combine.

Bright Ideas

❧ Serve as a pretty spring condiment with poached salmon or grilled boneless chicken breasts.

❧ Spoon over small plates of grilled shrimp or sea scallops for a dazzling summer appetizer.

❧ Wrap in warm flour tortillas, along with black beans and shredded roast chicken, for a luncheon burrito.

ABOUT JICAMA

Beloved in Mexican cooking for its fresh texture, raw jicama (like apples) adds crunch to salads and salsas and makes a wonderful alternative to crackers. Because it doesn't wilt or discolor easily, it is perfect for make-ahead hors d'oeuvres. Just peel off the thin brown skin and fibrous under-layer and slice, chop, dice, or julienne.

Store whole unpeeled jicama in the vegetable bin of your refrigerator. Once cut, pieces should be well wrapped to retain moisture. Properly stored, jicama will keep for at least a week.

Skinny Dipping

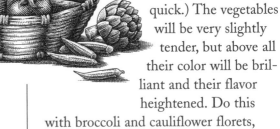

We're always glad when a customer orders a crudités platter, because assembling it is such a pleasure. If we were giving a master class on crudités, here is what we'd put in the study guide.

🍅 🍅 🍅

Crudités should be bright, crisp, and inviting. Choose the most attractive, freshest seasonal vegetables, and try to include at least one miniature. Everyone loves baby beets, mini zucchini, radishes, tiny pattypan squash, bite-size potatoes, and cherry tomatoes. Wash the vegetables well, and trim them sparingly, leaving green tops and stems intact whenever practical.

🍅 🍅 🍅

The bright color and flavor of many vegetables is vastly improved by blanching. Bring a large pot of water—preferably the kind with a basket liner—to a full rolling boil, and give the vegetables a quick dunking, uncovered, until they're brightly colored but still crisp, 1 to 3 minutes. Then drain them quickly and immerse them in cold water to stop the cooking. (Pay attention, because the whole process is very quick.) The vegetables will be very slightly tender, but above all their color will be brilliant and their flavor heightened. Do this with broccoli and cauliflower florets, Brussels sprouts (cut in half), green beans, wax beans, and haricots verts, asparagus, pattypan squash, fiddlehead ferns, zucchini (blanched *very* briefly), carrots, and sugar snap and snow peas.

🍅 🍅 🍅

A crudités platter should be abundant. Prepare plenty of vegetables so your platter looks like the produce department at harvesttime. If you do have leftovers, there will be plenty of uses for them in soups and salads, and of course they're great for snacks.

Basic crudités vegetables include carrot sticks, bell pepper strips, spears of endive, cucumber rounds or spears, celery sticks, and blanched florets of broccoli and cauliflower.

Winter vegetables include fennel spears, daikon rounds, jicama strips, turnip slices, strips of bok choy, and whole fresh tomatillas (papery skin removed).

Spring and summer vegetables include

green or purple asparagus spears, raw or blanched sugar snap or snow peas, baby pattypan and zucchini squash, baby red potatoes (boiled or steamed until tender), red and yellow cherry and teardrop tomatoes, green beans, wax beans, haricots verts, cooked artichoke leaves or baby artichoke hearts (cut in half), fiddlehead ferns, and sliced baby Vidalia onions.

❦ ❦ ❦

Many crudités stay fresh even though they're prepared in advance. Most cut fresh vegetables will keep well in the fridge, even overnight. We store raw carrots, celery, and florets of broccoli and cauliflower in water or on ice. Blanched vegetables will keep happily overnight in plastic bags or covered containers.

❦ ❦ ❦

Offer a couple of complementary sauces for dipping. Just about any savory condiment used to season salads and sandwiches can be served as a dip for vegetables. Creamy salad dressings and vinaigrettes, dips, spreads, and seasoned mayonnaise all cling to crisp vegetable chips and spears. You'll find many of the recipes for our most beloved dips for crudités right here in this chapter.

Check the Index for Roasted Garlic Mayonnaise, Tomato-Pesto Mayonnaise, Sauce Verte, Black Peppercorn Dressing, Hay Day's Roquefort Dressing, Tapenade

Yogurt, Hummus, Marvelous Mushroom Dip, Vidalia Onion Dip, Chunky Clam and Bacon Dip, Oriental Dip, Lemon Vinaigrette, Feta Vinaigrette, Sun-Dried Tomato Vinaigrette, Balsamic Vinaigrette, Cranberry Vinaigrette, Sesame-Ginger Vinaigrette, Roasted Eggplant Caviar, and Southwestern Tomato Salsa.

❦ ❦ ❦

Choose serving dishes of an appropriate size and style. Crudités are fresh garden vegetables, so we like to carry the theme through with baskets and other rustic containers rather than formal serving platters. Line the container first with plastic, then with sturdy greens for decoration. Settle the dip bowl onto the greens, and cluster the crudités around it. If your prettiest container is too big for the available quantity of vegetables, start with a bed of excelsior or straw. We like to use wide, shallow baskets; produce crates; wooden cheese boxes and lids (the kind Brie comes in, for example); and antique tinware or wooden bowls and trenchers.

Line the containers with large, sturdy leaves of kale, romaine lettuce, grape leaves, cabbage, spinach, or chard.

Put dips in large hollowed-out bell peppers, cabbages, artichokes, acorn squash, or butternut squash.

Finish the presentation with bunches of fresh seasonal herbs, edible flowers, or olives. Just remember that everything must be edible! (You need only one experience with a garnish of raw hot peppers to see the wisdom of that.)

Southwestern Tomato Salsa

MAKES 2 GENEROUS CUPS

Incredibly versatile, simple low-fat salsa has been hailed as the "ketchup of the nineties." We make it in the stores in both mild and hot versions. This is the milder one, but just add another jalapeño and an extra dash of hot sauce to the recipe if you prefer it more piquant.

◆◆◆◆◆◆

1 small Spanish onion, peeled and cut into large pieces
1 large clove garlic, smashed and peeled
½ green bell pepper, stemmed, seeded, and coarsely chopped
1 jalapeño pepper, deveined, seeded, and coarsely chopped
Juice of 1 large lime (2 tablespoons)
3 tablespoons cider vinegar
2 cups chopped fresh or good-quality canned peeled plum tomatoes, drained of excess juices
2 tablespoons coarsely chopped fresh cilantro
¼ teaspoon ground cumin
1 scant teaspoon coarse (kosher) salt
Tabasco or other hot pepper sauce (optional)

◆◆◆◆◆◆

1. Combine the onion, garlic, peppers, lime juice, and vinegar in a food processor or blender, and pulse to combine and coarsely chop. The mixture should be coarse and irregular, with bits of onion and pepper still separate and distinct but no larger than kidney beans.

2. Transfer the mixture to a large bowl and stir in the tomatoes, cilantro, cumin, and salt. Cover and allow to marinate for at least 30 minutes; then season to taste with hot sauce as desired. The salsa will keep nicely, sealed and refrigerated, for a week or two.

Bright Ideas

❦ Use the salsa as a marinade or condiment for grilled chicken, shrimp, tuna, or swordfish.

❦ Stir into a little sour cream or crème fraîche to make a dip for vegetable crudités.

❦ Spoon over whole fresh clams as they steam; then serve the clams and juices over a warm plate of linguine.

❦ Use as a light, flavorful condiment for grilled burgers.

❦ Serve with a frittata, omelet, or scrambled eggs for a Sunday morning brunch.

❦ Use as a flavoring for a savory meat loaf (see Mexican Meat Loaf, page 131).

ABOUT CURRY PASTE

Available in a range from medium to hot, prepared Indian curry pastes are a convenient way to add flavor and spice to a wide variety of foods. There are several available in the market; we're partial to one made by the Petaks company. (Don't confuse the classic Indian mixture of curry, garlic, and spices with the much hotter Thai version, which is made with crushed red chiles and is often used in Thai stir-fries.)

Curried Chutney Spread on Crisp Apple Slices

MAKES 1½ CUPS

Apple slices make wonderful substitutes for crackers with pâtés and cheeses. Choose the firmest seasonal apples in the market—we're particularly fond of Gala, Braeburn, Stayman Winesap, Macoun, and Empire—and keep the slices crisp and white in a bowl of cold water and lemon juice (acidulated water) until serving time.

We like to use homemade peach chutney for this spicy fruit spread, but it is superb with whatever good-quality fruit chutney comes to hand—try Major Grey's mango or an apricot, pear, or apple chutney.

◆◆◆◆◆◆

8 ounces cream cheese, at room
temperature
2 tablespoons milk
1 generous teaspoon Indian-style
curry paste
2 heaping tablespoons chunky fruit
chutney
⅓ cup pecan halves, toasted (see
Toasting Nuts, page 55) and coarsely
chopped
2 large crisp apples, preferably red-skin
1 tablespoon fresh lemon juice

◆◆◆◆◆◆

1. Combine the cream cheese, milk, and curry paste in a mixing bowl. Working with the back of a spoon, blend until smooth. Stir in the chutney, breaking up any excessively large pieces, and ¼ cup of the pecans (reserve the remaining pecans for garnish).

2. Cut the apples into even quarters, remove the core, and cut each quarter into four lengthwise slices. Drop the slices into a small bowl, add cold water to cover, and stir in the lemon juice. Cover and refrigerate until serving time.

3. When ready to serve, drain the apple slices and pat dry with paper towels. Smear about 1 teaspoon of Curried Chutney Spread on each apple slice, garnish with the remaining pecans, and serve immediately.

Bright Ideas

❧ Create holiday canapés with chutney spread on whole-grain bread, topped with thinly sliced pheasant, chicken, or duck.

❧ Spread on crisp sticks of celery or fennel.

❧ Use as a filling for split Medjool dates.

Lady Apples Filled with Chicken Liver Pâté

SERVES 12 TO 18

Tiny, beautiful lady apples make crisp cups for savory fall hors d'oeuvres. Their sweet, fruity flavor is a natural combination with Chicken Liver Pâté, and garnishing them with cranberries and pistachios makes a visual feast.

◆◆◆◆◆◆

36 small lady apples (no larger than
1½ inches in diameter)
Chicken Liver Pâté with Cranberries
and Pistachios (recipe follows)
1 ounce (¼ cup) dried cranberries
2 tablespoons coarsely chopped
unsalted pistachio nuts

◆◆◆◆◆◆

Using a ¾-inch apple corer, cut straight down through the center of each apple to remove the entire core. (The cored apples will keep well in the refrigerator before filling as long as they're submerged in acidulated water.) Using a small spoon,

fill the center of each apple with a generous teaspoon of the pâté. Decorate the tops with a single dried cranberry and a small dusting of pistachios, and serve. Or cover and refrigerate for up to 2 hours before serving.

Chicken Liver Pâté with Cranberries and Pistachios

MAKES 1½ CUPS

Customers come back for this rich pâté year after year—it's one of the all-time Hay Day bestsellers. Festive and elegant, creamy and fresh, it's an up-to-the-minute variation on classic chopped liver. Serve it crostini-style, spread on toasted baguette slices and topped with a few dried cranberries or chopped pistachios.

◆◆◆◆◆◆

3 strips thick-sliced bacon, diced
¾ cup chopped onion
2 cloves garlic, peeled and minced
½ tablespoon sugar
8 ounces fresh chicken livers
3 tablespoons medium-dry sherry
Coarse (kosher) salt
Freshly ground black pepper
4 ounces cream cheese
¼ cup dried cranberries
¼ cup shelled unsalted pistachio nuts,
lightly toasted (facing page)
2 tablespoons coarsely chopped fresh
Italian (flat-leaf) parsley

◆◆◆◆◆◆

TOASTING NUTS

Get in the habit of toasting all kinds of nuts; you'll be impressed with the way their rich natural flavor is intensified. To toast, scatter the nuts in a single layer on a baking sheet and bake in a preheated 350°F oven until lightly colored, crisp, and fragrant—5 to 7 minutes for pecans, pistachios, almonds, and pine nuts, 10 minutes for walnuts. (Sesame seeds, which are oily and burn quickly, should be toasted in a dry skillet; they'll take 3 minutes—stir often).

Toasting also helps in the process of removing the outer papery skins of some nuts, like walnuts, which can leave behind an unpleasant tannic flavor. Once the nuts are toasted, the skins rub off easily when the nuts are rolled inside a clean kitchen towel.

1. Sauté the bacon, onion, and garlic in a large heavy-bottomed saucepan over medium-high heat until the bacon begins to crisp and the onion is lightly colored, about 5 minutes. Sprinkle with the sugar, and stir. Then push the mixture toward the outer rim of the pan, freeing the center for the chicken livers. Add the chicken livers and cook over medium-high heat, turning occasionally, until nicely browned on all sides, 3 to 4 minutes. Sprinkle with the sherry, reduce the heat, cover, and allow to steam until the livers are just cooked through, 8 to 10 minutes. Cut one in half to check for doneness (it should be just a bit pink at the center). Remove from the heat, and sprinkle with ½ teaspoon salt and several grindings of pepper.

2. Cut the cream cheese into large chunks and place in a food processor or blender. Spoon in the warm chicken livers and the pan juices, scraping up and adding any bits clinging to the pan. Add the cranberries, pistachios, and parsley. Pulse five or six times—just enough to mix and coarsely chop. Stir, and season to taste with additional salt and pepper as needed. Transfer to a serving bowl, cover, and refrigerate for at least 4 hours before serving. The pâté will keep for up to 1 week in the refrigerator.

Belgian Endive with Smoked Trout Pâté

SERVES 12

Farm-raised hardwood-smoked trout is gorgeous as is—just skinned, broken into chunks, and served on crackers, or crumbled with a light vinaigrette in salads, or tossed in pasta with a little cream and fresh herbs—but sometimes we turn it into a savory spread. The moist, supple flesh purées easily, and the rich smoky flavor is appealing enough to need very few additions—anything more would be lily-gilding. We like to serve it very simply, with a counterpoint of crisp spears of Belgian endive and toasted walnuts.

◆◆◆◆◆◆

*1 boneless smoked trout (8 ounces),
    skin, head, and tail removed*
¼ cup sour cream
*2 ounces (¼ cup) cream cheese, at
    room temperature*
*2 tablespoons coarsely chopped red
    onion*
*1 chunk (2 inches) fresh horseradish,
    peeled and coarsely grated (about
    1 packed tablespoon; see Note)*
1 tablespoon fresh lemon juice
¼ teaspoon cayenne pepper
½ cup walnut halves
2 large heads Belgian endive
Grated fresh lemon zest, for garnish

◆◆◆◆◆◆

1. Preheat the oven to 350°F.

2. Break the trout into large chunks and place them in a food processor or blender. Add the sour cream, cream cheese, onion, horseradish, lemon juice, and cayenne. Pulse several times to form a chunky purée. Taste, and adjust the seasonings as needed. (The pâté can be prepared to this point a day or two in advance; wrap it well and refrigerate.)

3. Scatter the walnuts onto a pie plate or baking sheet, and toast in the oven until lightly browned and fragrant, 10 to 12 minutes. Remove from the oven and transfer the nuts to a clean dish towel. Fold the towel to enclose the nuts while they are still hot, allow to rest for a minute or two, then roll back and forth to loosen and remove their papery skins.

4. Cut 1 inch or so off the bottom of each head of endive to separate the leaves. Drop a rounded teaspoon of the pâté into the cup of each leaf, press a

toasted walnut on top, and garnish with lemon zest. Arrange on a decorative platter and serve immediately.

Note: You can substitute bottled horseradish in a pinch, but if you do, use only 2½ teaspoons.

Bright Ideas

❦ Serve the pâté on fresh crisp apple slices.

❦ Surround a bowl of the pâté with slices of whole-grain bread.

ABOUT HORSERADISH

Small children can be forgiven for thinking it grows in jars, but most grownups know that tall, gangly horseradish is a fall and early winter stalwart in New England vegetable gardens. It is a coarse root not unlike a parsnip, which when peeled and shredded with a box grater offers far more interesting flavor than the kind in the jar. Freshly grated raw horseradish adds punch to mixed salads; add it to a basic vinaigrette or to a marinade for fish and meat. Or marinate finely grated horseradish in white vinegar to cover for 24 hours, then mix it with sour cream for a sauce for roast beef or a dressing for potato salad.

Smithfield Ham Spread in Spears of Crimson Endive

MAKES 2 CUPS; SERVES 12

You're in luck if you have hickory-smoked Smithfield Virginia ham left over from New Year's Eve, because you can toss it in the food processor, add a few basic ingredients, and in an instant make this savory spread. But you can also buy small quantities of Westphalian ham at most good food stores, and it does just fine. Radicchio di Treviso is a lovely elongated green, which we often use instead of endive spears to cradle richly flavored dips and cheese; its crisp, bitter flavor cuts through the richness of the ham spread to make an ideal combination.

◆◆◆◆◆◆

4 ounces Smithfield or Westphalian
*   ham, coarsely chopped*
6 scallions, white and light green
*   parts coarsely chopped*
Large pinch of fresh dill
1 tablespoon coarsely chopped fresh
*   Italian (flat-leaf) parsley*
½ cup light cream
⅓ cup mayonnaise, preferably
*   homemade*
8 ounces cream cheese
Tabasco or other hot pepper sauce
4 heads radicchio di Treviso
*   (see About Radicchio, page 203) or*
*   Belgian endive*
18 cornichons, sliced in half lengthwise

◆◆◆◆◆◆

1. Combine the ham, scallions, dill, and parsley in a food processor or blender, and chop fine. Add the cream, mayonnaise, and cream cheese, and pulse several times to form a thick spread. Season to taste with hot sauce, and refrigerate until ready to serve.

2. Cut 1 inch or so off the bottom of each head of Trevisano to separate the leaves. Spoon a heaping teaspoon of the ham spread into the cup of each leaf, and top with a cornichon half. Arrange on a decorative platter and serve immediately.

Bright Ideas

❦ Serve as a spread for Sunday-brunch bagels.

❦ Spread on thin slices of whole-grain bread for canapés.

❦ Use the spread as a filling for classic country biscuits.

Tapas Skewers

SERVES 6 TO 8

Named for the colorful darts used in the bullring, *banderillas* (small hors d'oeuvres on skewers) are a staple in tapas bars all over Spain. Made with meats, peppers, olives, and cheeses, each one is usually a combination of no more than three ingredients, but the variations on the theme are almost infinite. Authentic Spanish foods—handmade cheeses, arbequina olives, marinated artichoke hearts, ham, and chorizo sausage—are now readily available in this country and are easy to assemble in a colorful array on skewers for a cocktail buffet. Here we quickly sauté shrimp and mushrooms, which go particularly well with the flavor and fragrance of Spanish sherry vinegar.

◆◆◆◆◆◆

¼ cup olive oil

3 large cloves garlic, peeled and finely minced

18 medium shrimp, cleaned and deveined, tails left on

18 small mushroom caps, wiped clean

2 tablespoons sherry vinegar

¼ teaspoon coarse (kosher) salt

1 tablespoon chopped fresh cilantro or parsley

18 small (6- to 8-inch-long) wooden skewers

18 cubes (1 inch) firm or day-old white bread, with or without crusts

◆◆◆◆◆◆

1. Heat the oil in a large skillet until nearly smoking. Add the garlic, shrimp, and mushrooms and sauté over high heat until the shrimp are bright pink and just cooked through, 2 to 3 minutes. Quickly remove the skillet from the heat. Sprinkle with the vinegar, salt, and cilantro; stir to combine.

2. Thread one shrimp, then one mushroom cap, on each skewer, and secure with a bread cube. Lightly roll the finished skewers in the pan juices and serve immediately.

Variations

◆ Cubes of manchego cheese, strips of roasted red bell pepper, and Spanish olives or caperberries (olive-size Spanish capers).

◆ Marinated artichoke hearts, Roncal or aged provolone cheese, and smoked chorizo or Italian salami.

◆ Pimiento-stuffed martini olives, chilled cooked shrimp, and aged Cheddar.

Walnut-Crusted Camembert Cheese

SERVES 4 TO 6

When several members of our cheese department returned from a week in France, where they had been learning about cheeses (talk about perks!), they brought with them the idea of marinating Camembert in Calvados, two of the great products of Normandy. We added toasted walnuts and fresh apple slices, and the result has been a fall highlight at Hay Day ever since. A fantastic hors d'oeuvre for everything from a football party to a sit-down dinner, it also works as a first course when cut into wedges and served on fresh greens flanked by the apple slices.

◆◆◆◆◆◆

*1 medium-ripe 8-ounce Camembert
cheese (see Selecting a Ripe Cheese)*
¾ cup walnut halves
*1 cup Calvados or other apple
brandy*
2 crisp tart apples
1 teaspoon fresh lemon juice
Whole-grain bread, for serving

◆◆◆◆◆◆

1. Allow the cheese to come to room
temperature by leaving it on the counter
for at least 1 hour. Preheat the oven to
350°F.

2. Spread the walnut halves out in a single layer on a small baking sheet. Toast
until lightly browned and fragrant, about
10 minutes.

3. Warm the Calvados in a small saucepan over medium-high heat. Place the
cheese in a small bowl and pour the
warm brandy over it. Set aside to mac-
erate for a minimum of 20 minutes or
as long as 2 hours, turning once.

4. Meanwhile, reserving one whole half,
finely chop the toasted walnuts. (The nuts
can be chopped in a food processor, but
take care not to overchop them; they can
quickly become soft and oily.)

5. When you are ready to serve the
cheese, core the apples and cut into thin
wedges. Combine the apples, lemon juice,
and just enough water to cover the slices
in a bowl. Toss gently (the acidulated
water will keep the apple slices from dis-
coloring). Drain the apple slices.

6. Remove the cheese from the brandy
and roll it in the nuts, pressing them

firmly onto the crust to coat it well. Place
in the middle of a cheese plate or serving
platter, surround with any remaining
nuts, and top with the reserved walnut
half. Serve at room temperature, surrounded with the apple slices and wedges
of whole-grain bread.

SELECTING A RIPE CHEESE

Soft-ripening cheeses (like Brie,
Camembert, Taleggio, and Pont
l'Eveque) ripen from the outside; so
check for ripeness by gently pressing
your fingers over the surface of the
cheese to be sure it is evenly soft
throughout (an underripe cheese
will have a hard inner core). Once
you cut into an unripe soft-ripening
cheese, it will not ripen further.
Since most cheese is kept under
refrigeration in the U.S., a few hours
at room temperature will often
speed the process and do miraculous
things for the flavor and texture.

Sun-Dried Tomato and Basil Chèvre Terrine

SERVES 8 TO 12

Serve this layered marvel on a
platter, surrounded with toasted
rounds of oil-brushed French
bread, and it pretty much makes the
party. Or slice it and serve it, drizzled
with a little olive oil, on a small bed of
fresh basil leaves for a first course, maybe

with toasted baguettes or wedges of focaccia.

◆◆◆◆◆◆

12 dry-packed sun-dried tomatoes, soaked in water until tender (about 30 minutes), coarsely chopped
1 tablespoon fresh thyme leaves
1 tablespoon extra-virgin olive oil
¼ teaspoon coarse (kosher) salt
1 pound fresh goat's-milk cheese (chèvre)
½ cup packed fresh basil leaves, coarsely chopped
⅓ cup oil-cured black olives, pitted and coarsely chopped
Sprigs of fresh thyme, for garnish
Crackers or toasted rounds of bread, for serving

◆◆◆◆◆◆

1. Lightly oil a nonreactive 2-cup (5½ × 3-inch) mini loaf pan.

2. Mix the tomatoes, thyme, oil, and salt in a small bowl. Taste for seasonings and adjust if necessary. Then press the mixture into the bottom of the prepared pan in an even layer. Crumble half of the goat cheese on top, and press firmly to form a smooth, even layer.

3. Place the basil and olives in a food processor and pulse a few times to form a coarse paste. Spread the paste over the cheese to form a third layer. Crumble the remaining goat cheese on top and again press it firmly to form a smooth, even layer. Cover and chill until ready to serve. If you're slicing the terrine for individual servings, chill overnight.

4. Run a thin sharp blade along the edges of the pan to free the terrine. Place

a serving platter, right side down, over the pan; turn, and tap the terrine out onto the platter. Garnish with thyme sprigs and surround with toast or crackers.

Note: For individual appetizer servings, cut the terrine into ½-inch-thick slices; using a very sharp serrated knife and supporting the sides of the terrine with one hand, cut in a sawing motion while applying very little pressure.

A NOTE ON CHÈVRE

Chèvre is the French word for *goat*, but the term has come to be synonymous with the pure white tangy cheese made from goat's milk. Historically the best chèvres (Crottin de Chavignol, Montrachet, and Banon) have been imported from France, but nowadays excellent cheeses are coming from farms in this country. Coach Farms, Cypress Grove, Laura Chanel, Capriole Farms, Westfield Farms, and Brier Run are a few of the American producers.

Berry Nut Brie

SERVES 18 TO 20

Your mother probably told you not to play with your food. At Hay Day we get to fiddle with different combinations and call it work! The cheese department has concocted infinite variations on the stuffed-Brie theme. This one, using wine and berries seasoned with star anise and cinnamon sticks, makes a particularly fragrant and festive centerpiece for holiday parties. Put the whole wheel on a platter, deck it with holly or cranberries and surround it with thin slices of French bread, and all you need to add is the carols.

◆◆◆◆◆◆

1 ripe Brie (8-inch round; see
  Selecting a Ripe Cheese, page 59)
1 cup dried Bing cherries
1 cup dried cranberries
1 cup light, fruity red wine
  (Beaujolais or Pinot Noir)
2 whole star anise
1 cinnamon stick (3 inches), broken
  in half
½ cup pecan pieces
½ cup sliced almonds
Thinly sliced French bread, for serving

◆◆◆◆◆◆

1. Allow the Brie to rest at room temperature for at least 4 hours. The interior of the cheese should feel buttery-soft from the outer edges to the center.

2. Preheat the oven to 325°F.

3. Combine the cherries, cranberries, wine, and star anise and cinnamon pieces in a small saucepan and place over medium heat. Heat gently until the berries are warm and have absorbed a bit of the liquid, about 5 minutes. Remove from the heat and allow to steep at room temperature.

4. Meanwhile, spread the pecans and almonds in a single layer on a large baking sheet and toast until fragrant, nicely browned, and crisp, 5 to 7 minutes. (The

berries and the nuts can be prepared to this point several hours in advance.)

5. Shortly before serving time, assemble the Brie: Using a long thin blade, slice the Brie in half horizontally, carefully lifting and separating the top from the bottom as you work. Place the top to one side, and cover the bottom layer with half of the soaked berries and juices (remove the star anise and cinnamon stick pieces as you work). Cover with half of the nut mixture. Then replace the top layer of cheese, cut side up (this will give you a sticky surface to which the nuts and berries will cling). Spoon the remaining berries over the top layer of cheese, and finish with a layer of the remaining nuts. Serve at room temperature, accompanied by thin slices of French bread. (Do not refrigerate—it will make the nuts disappointingly soggy.)

Polenta Crostini

MAKES 25 CROSTINI

Coarse-ground yellow cornmeal makes a polenta with really wonderful flavor and texture, but you can do almost as well with timesaving substitutes like the prepared version or the imported precooked instant polenta that cooks in 5 or 10 minutes. If you like, cut the polenta into star and heart shapes with cookie cutters; just be sure the shapes are simple enough to hold together. However you do it, these very pretty little hors d'oeuvres create the illusion that there's help in the kitchen—when actually there's nobody out there but the cat.

◆◆◆◆◆◆

3½ cups water

1 teaspoon coarse (kosher) salt

1¼ cups coarsely ground yellow cornmeal

1 scant tablespoon minced fresh rosemary

2 tablespoons freshly grated Parmesan cheese

Freshly ground black pepper

1 red bell pepper, roasted (see How to Roast Peppers, page 80), peeled, and minced

Splash of balsamic vinegar

2 tablespoons unsalted butter, melted

2 tablespoons shredded fresh basil leaves

◆◆◆◆◆◆

1. Lightly oil an 8-inch square baking pan.

2. Bring the water to a boil in a 4-quart stockpot. Add the salt. Then add the cornmeal in a slow thin stream, whisking continuously to prevent lumps from forming. When all the cornmeal has been whisked in, change to a large wooden spoon and reduce the heat to medium-low. If lumps have formed, press them out against the sides of the pot with the back of the spoon. Cook over medium-low heat, stirring frequently, until the corn-meal forms a smooth thick mass that easily pulls away from the sides of the pot, 15 to 20 minutes. The polenta is ready when it has the consistency of whipped potatoes. Stir in the rosemary, Parmesan, and several grindings of black pepper.

3. Spread the polenta evenly in the prepared pan; it should be about ½ inch thick. Allow it to cool until very firm, about 2 hours; or cover and refrigerate overnight.

4. Preheat the broiler. In a small bowl, combine the minced bell pepper with the vinegar; set aside.

5. Turn the polenta out onto a cutting board, and cut it into 1½-inch squares. Arrange the squares on a large baking sheet and brush with the melted butter. Broil until lightly browned with crisp edges, about 5 minutes. Remove the pan from the oven, transfer the polenta squares to a serving platter, and top each with a small mound of the minced peppers. Garnish with a few ribbons of the fresh basil, and serve while still warm.

Variation

◆ Top these Polenta Crostini with a variety of other antipasto ingredients, such as crumbled Gorgonzola and pine nuts, minced olives or sun-dried tomatoes, sautéed mushrooms, or ribbons of prosciutto and fresh basil.

Blue Cheese and Pear Bruschetta

MAKES 24 PIECES

Every fall we offer samples of sweet pears and rich, pungent blue cheese, just to remind our customers what a stunning combination it is. Here we go one step further and mix them together for an autumnal variation on the classic Tuscan chopped-tomatoes-on-toast hors d'oeuvre. Just dice the pears and toss them with blue cheese, then spoon the mixture onto toasted baguette rounds spread with creamy mascarpone. Gorgeous.

◆◆◆◆◆◆

2 red-skin Bartlett or Anjou pears
1 tablespoon fresh lemon juice
1 tablespoon minced fresh Italian
    (flat-leaf) parsley
2 ounces sharp crumbly blue cheese
    (Maytag, Roquefort, or Danish
    Blue), finely crumbled (about ⅓ cup
    crumbled)
1½ tablespoons olive oil
Freshly ground black pepper
1 baguette (12 inches), cut into
    ½-inch-thick rounds
8 ounces mascarpone cheese
¼ cup finely chopped walnuts, toasted
    (see Toasting Nuts, page 55)

◆◆◆◆◆◆

1. Rinse the pears but do not peel them. Cut them into small dice, and place in a small bowl. Sprinkle the pears with the lemon juice and toss (this prevents the pears from turning brown). Add the parsley, blue cheese, and oil, and toss gently and thoroughly. Season to taste with freshly ground black pepper, and set aside. (The topping can be prepared to this point a few hours ahead. Store, covered, in the refrigerator.)

2. Preheat the broiler.

3. Arrange the bread slices in a single layer on a baking sheet, and toast under the broiler until lightly browned and crisp, 1 to 2 minutes per side.

4. Spread each toast round with a teaspoon of the mascarpone. Top with a generous tablespoon of the diced pear mixture, mounding it up high and pressing it firmly. Finish each one with a sprinkling of walnuts, and serve.

Summer Vegetable Bruschetta

SERVES 10

Not too long ago bruschetta seemed exotic, but now they're part of everybody's summer. Hay Day's version adds bright fresh peppers and zucchini to the classic combination of tomatoes, basil, and olive oil, and intensifies the flavor with pesto and Kalamata olives to make a spectacular summer canapé or light lunch. (How to pronounce the word in Italian? Put a *k* in the middle.)

◆◆◆◆◆◆

1 small zucchini, scrubbed and cut
into small dice

2 cups diced fresh tomatoes

½ yellow bell pepper, stemmed, seeded,
and cut into small dice

12 large fresh basil leaves, shredded

10 Kalamata olives, pitted and
coarsely chopped

2 tablespoons olive oil

2 teaspoons red wine vinegar

¼ teaspoon coarse (kosher) salt, or
to taste

Coarsely ground black pepper

¼ cup Pesto (page 250)

Extra-virgin olive oil, as needed

1 round loaf country bread, cut into
¾- to 1-inch-thick slices

◆◆◆◆◆◆

1. Combine the zucchini, tomatoes, bell pepper, basil, olives, oil, vinegar, and salt in a medium-size bowl and toss to mix. Set aside to marinate at room temperature, stirring occasionally, for at least 30 minutes. Season to taste with additional salt, if needed, and coarsely ground black pepper. The mixture should taste like a good, well-seasoned salad.

2. Meanwhile, preheat the broiler. Thin the pesto with extra-virgin olive oil as needed to be spreadable with a pastry brush.

3. Cut the long center bread slices in half on an angle, to form 10 slices approximately 3½ × 3½ inches. Grill the bread under the broiler, turning the pieces once, until lightly colored and crisp on the outside, about 2 minutes per side. Brush one side of each slice with a generous amount of the pesto, and arrange the slices, pesto side up, in a single layer on a large serving platter. Top each slice with 2 heaping tablespoons of the marinated vegetable mixture, and drizzle with the remaining juices from the bottom of the bowl. Serve the bruschetta immediately.

Note: You can also grill the bread slices on your barbecue, or even the traditional way—over an open fire.

A Quintet of Drinks

Fruit-based drinks are particularly welcome and thirst quenching at a party, whether during the height of summer or at a wintry football gathering. Here are five favorites to enjoy with any small pleasure. They are a big pleasure themselves.

Spiced Cranberry-Apple Wine

SERVES ABOUT 20

Every fall Hay Day sells thousands of gallons of a cider that's pressed for us by a Hudson Valley apple grower. It's wonderful plain, or mixed with things like pears, citrus, or cranberries, or made into the Spiced Cranberry-

Apple Cider we sell in the stores. If you spike that with red wine, you get an autumnal sangría that's wonderful at all kinds of gatherings.

◆◆◆◆◆◆

1 orange, scrubbed well
½ gallon fresh apple cider
3 cups cranberry juice
2 bottles inexpensive fruity red wine
  (Beaujolais, Pinot Noir, or Merlot)
3 cinnamon sticks (each 3 inches long)
12 whole cloves
12 whole allspice berries
3 whole star anise

◆◆◆◆◆◆

1. Using a good swivel peeler or a small sharp paring knife, remove the orange zest. Slice the zest into thin slivers.

2. Combine the zest and all the other ingredients in a large saucepan. Bring to a simmer over medium-high heat and simmer gently (do not boil) until very fragrant and pleasantly spiced, about 15 minutes. Strain and serve warm, ladled into mugs.

Fresh Ginger Beer

SERVES 6

Once we had tasted true Caribbean ginger beer, made with puréed fresh ginger, we couldn't wait to try it at home. It's easy—you don't even have to peel the ginger! Our version is refreshed with lime juice for a wonderfully tropical flavor, particularly welcome in the summer. This peppery brew is a refreshingly spicy mixer for rum.

◆◆◆◆◆◆

1 chunk (2 ounces) fresh ginger,
  unpeeled, cut into several large pieces
  (see About Ginger, page 215)
Generous ½ cup fresh lime juice
  (about 5 large limes)
1 cup cold water
½ cup sugar
2 cups sparkling water
Ice
1 lime, sliced into thin rounds,
  for garnish

◆◆◆◆◆◆

1. Combine the ginger, lime juice, and water in a blender and purée to form a fragrant cloudy liquid with the ginger chopped to a very fine pulp. Line a fine-mesh sieve or colander with cheesecloth, place it over a small pitcher, and strain the mixture through it. Wring all the juices through the cheesecloth, and discard the cheesecloth and its contents. Add the sugar and stir until dissolved.

2. Stir in the sparkling water, pour into tall ice-filled glasses, garnish each one with a slice of lime, and serve immediately.

Blueberry Lemonade

MAKES 2 GENEROUS QUARTS

Okay, so everybody's had lemonade. But add fresh blueberries and you get a richly colored fragrant brew that sells out every summer in our stores. An ice-filled glass pitcher of this unusually refreshing drink makes a summer gathering a real event.

65

♦♦♦♦♦♦

1 cup sugar

6 cups water

Finely grated zest of 1 lemon
  (see About Zest, page 229)

1 pint fresh blueberries, rinsed

1 cup fresh lemon juice
  (about 6 large lemons)

Ice

Sprigs of fresh mint, for garnish

♦♦♦♦♦♦

1. Mix the sugar, water, and lemon zest in a saucepan. Warm over medium-high heat, stirring to dissolve the sugar. Once the sugar has completely dissolved, remove the pan from the heat and pour the mixture into a large glass pitcher. Refrigerate for at least 1 hour.

2. Meanwhile, make sure all the stems have been picked off the blueberries. Combine the berries with the lemon juice in a blender, and purée. Add to the pitcher and stir well to blend. Skim the excess blueberry skins off the top, or pour the lemonade through a sieve to remove all the skins if desired. (The lemonade can be fully prepared and refrigerated the day before serving.)

3. Pour Blueberry Lemonade over tall ice-filled glasses, garnish each one with a sprig of mint, and serve.

Bright Ideas

❦ Add more whole blueberries and freeze as Popsicles.

❦ Freeze in ice-cube trays to ornament tall glasses of classic lemonade.

❦ Serve as an exceptionally refreshing mixer for vodka or gin.

Cucumber-Watermelon Cooler

SERVES 2

On a boiling hot day in July, you'll feel better just reading this recipe! Two classic summer refreshers, cucumber and watermelon, are blended with lemon sorbet and accented with mint for a glorious pink concoction that brings to mind palm trees and cooling breezes.

♦♦♦♦♦♦

1 large English (hothouse) cucumber,
  peeled and halved lengthwise

2 cups cubed seedless watermelon

2 generous ice cream scoops lemon
  sorbet

1 tablespoon finely chopped fresh
  mint

Sprigs of fresh mint, for garnish

♦♦♦♦♦♦

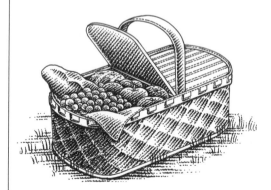

1. Place two tall glasses in the freezer to chill while you prepare the cooler.

2. Coarsely chop half the cucumber and drop the pieces into a blender along with the watermelon, sorbet, and chopped mint. Blend at high speed until smooth, and pour into the chilled glasses.

3. Slice the remaining cucumber into two long spears (trim if necessary) and drop one into each glass. Top with a sprig of mint, and serve right away.

Iced Darjeeling Tea
MAKES 2 QUARTS

On Summer Days when life is hot,
A sip of iced tea hits the spot.
"Hay Day's Iced Tea" is what
we're thinking—
"It's all the rage for summer drinking."

We don't advertise it on our label, but the best-quality Darjeeling is what makes our freshly brewed iced tea so popular. The rich, smoky flavor of this black India tea holds up well in iced preparations—it's not easily diluted with a few ice cubes. A few sprigs of fresh mint add soft flavor to the brew. In the shop we use a contraption that looks a bit like a coffee machine, with a basket on top for the tea leaves. At home we find it's simplest to wrap the leaves inside a cone-style paper coffee filter, then twist or tie the open end.

◆◆◆◆◆◆

8 cups fresh tap water
½ ounce (about 3 heaping tablespoons)
   Darjeeling tea leaves
6 or 7 fresh mint leaves
2 tablespoons fresh lemon juice
¼ cup superfine sugar, or more to taste
Ice
Fresh mint leaves, for garnish

◆◆◆◆◆◆

Backyard Summer Barbecue

Mark this page for Father's Day, Memorial Day, or the Fourth of July, and offer a quintessential backyard feast. From Bangor to Savannah, the smell of barbecue defines the summer, and the ring of ice in a pitcher of blueberry lemonade is as seductive as the cool of the shade.

❦ ❦ ❦

Blueberry Lemonade

Seasoned Baby Potatoes with
Chunky Clam and Bacon Dip

Southern Pulled Chicken Barbecue
Creamy Mustard Coleslaw
Summer Corn and Tomato Salad

Country Shortcake with
blackberries and peaches

❦ ❦ ❦

1. Bring the water to a boil in a tea kettle over high heat.

2. Meanwhile, combine the tea and mint leaves in a paper coffee filter. Twist the filter closed to fully enclose the contents (if it looks at all insecure, tie the package with a piece of kitchen string). Place the filter package in a heat-resistant 2- to 3-quart pitcher.

3. Add the boiling water to the pitcher, pouring it directly over the filter package.

Allow the tea to steep for 6 minutes. Then remove the filter package, pressing it with the back of a spoon to extract the moisture from the leaves. Stir in the lemon juice and sugar, and allow the tea to cool to room temperature.

4. Fill tall glasses with ice, and pour the tea into them. Garnish with additional mint leaves if desired.

Soups—and a Few of Our Favorite Breads

Soups and breads are the ultimate home-and-hearth foods. Sure, some of them take time to prepare, but it isn't all working time—mostly they're simmering, or rising, or baking without any attention from the cook.

At Hay Day we make all sorts of fresh soups. Warm bowls of hearty Vermont Cheddar Chowder nourish body and soul in the depths of winter. Cold Cucumber, Feta, and Sweet Red Pepper Soup is welcome when the thermometer begins to rise. Many of these classics are delicious served hot or cold, and many can be dressed up or down: Serve cups of Golden Tomato Gazpacho from a thermos at a beach picnic, or ladle it into china bowls and top it with scallop ceviche for a dinner party.

The biscuits, scones, and classic soft pan breads in this chapter are all Hay Day standbys. Making bread is one of the great simple pleasures, and it doesn't require special equipment. (A bread machine takes away all the fun, if you want our honest opinion.) All of these breads transform a bowl of soup into a full, nourishing meal.

69

Soups

Early Spring Asparagus Soup

SERVES 4 TO 6

We make this in the spring as soon as the really good asparagus comes into the market. The young spears are tender enough to purée easily, and the result is smooth and creamy (although there isn't a drop of cream in it!). The soup is wonderful in any season, actually; asparagus is available year-round in most markets, and you can always trim the spears with a vegetable peeler if the ends look at all fibrous. Complete the meal with the light, peppery counterpoint of our tender Ham and Cheddar Scones (page 96).

◆◆◆◆◆◆

1½ pounds fresh asparagus spears
¼ cup olive oil
1 large onion, peeled and coarsely chopped
2 large shallots, peeled and coarsely chopped
1 cup dry white wine
3 cups Vegetable Stock (page 271)
Coarse (kosher) salt and freshly ground black pepper
Crème Fraîche (page 255), for garnish
Large handful minced fresh chives, for garnish

◆◆◆◆◆◆

1. Rinse and dry the asparagus. Trim off and discard any tough white bottoms. Cut

ASPARAGUS

By now nobody needs to be told that thickness has nothing to do with quality. Asparagus is a perennial; more mature plantings yield thicker stalks, and any size will be tender as long as it's freshly cut. Look for bright apple-green spears and tightly closed purplish heads; the stalks should be glossy, firm, and unwrinkled, with just a little white toward the base. When you get them home, snap off the ends at the point where they break with little resistance, and store the stalks upright in water, just as if they were cut flowers—which they are, after all.

off the tips and set them aside. Coarsely chop the spears.

2. Heat the olive oil in a large heavy-bottomed soup pot over medium-high heat. Add the onion and shallots and sauté until lightly caramelized, about 10 minutes. Add the chopped asparagus spears and continue to cook, stirring occasionally, until the asparagus is bright green, 2 to 3 minutes. Pour in the wine along with 1 cup of the stock, and bring to a simmer over medium-high heat. Partially cover, and simmer gently until the asparagus is very tender, 25 to 35 minutes. Remove from the heat and allow to cool for at least 10 minutes.

3. Pour the mixture into a blender, in batches if necessary, and purée. Return the purée to the cooking pot, add the remaining 2 cups stock, and bring to a gentle simmer. Season to taste with salt and pepper. Add the reserved asparagus tips and continue to cook just until the tips are tender, about 5 minutes. Ladle the soup into bowls, float a spoonful of crème fraîche on top of each serving, sprinkle with the chives, and serve.

Bright Ideas

❧ Add a few sautéed morels and some curls of shaved Parmesan to each bowl.

❧ Serve as a sauce over poached, grilled, or oven-roasted salmon, sea bass, or halibut.

❧ Use the soup to create a dramatic setting for other foods—grilled or poached salmon, for instance, or a plate of carpaccio—by spooning a pool under each serving.

Outdoors at Last!

Winter's over and it's warm enough for brunch on the porch. Bring everyone out into the sunshine with a spring still life of fiddleheads, sugar snap peas, and baby carrots brightly flavored with Lemon Vinaigrette, followed by creamy (creamless!) asparagus soup, savory scones, and classic springtime strawberries with Lemon Sugar Snap Cookies.

❧ ❧ ❧

*Assortment of spring crudités
with Lemon Vinaigrette*

*Early Spring Asparagus Soup
Ham and Cheddar Scones*

*Fresh strawberries
Lemon Sugar Snap Cookies*
❧ ❧ ❧

Mediterranean Bean Soup

SERVES 12

Full of nourishing vegetables and spiked generously with garlic and olives, this lively, colorful soup is wonderful in any season, but it's particularly welcome in front of the fire after skiing or shoveling the driveway. Complete the meal with a basket of warm Parmesan-Sage Biscuits (page 97).

◆◆◆◆◆◆

¼ cup olive oil
*2 large cloves garlic, peeled and
    minced*
1 Spanish onion, peeled and chopped
*1 zucchini (about 12 ounces), cut into
    ½-inch dice (2½ cups diced)*
*1 small yellow bell pepper, stemmed,
    seeded, and cut into ½-inch dice*
*1 small red bell pepper, stemmed,
    seeded, and cut into ½-inch dice*
1 teaspoon dried basil
½ teaspoon dried thyme
Coarse (kosher) salt
*4 cups Vegetable Stock (page 271),
    more if needed*
*1 pound (2 cups) fresh or canned plum
    tomatoes, peeled and chopped, with
    their juice*
*⅓ cup coarsely chopped brine-cured
    black olives (Kalamata or Gaeta)*
*2½ cups cooked or canned cannellini,
    drained and rinsed (see About
    Beans, page 72)*
*4 ounces fresh spinach leaves,
    trimmed, washed, and very
    coarsely chopped*
Freshly ground black pepper

◆◆◆◆◆◆

ABOUT BEANS

Available in a dizzying (and often interchangeable) array of varieties, beans are a wonderful high-fiber, low-fat addition to everyone's diet.

There's no great magic about cooking dried beans. Just put them in a large saucepan, add 4 cups of water for every cup of beans, and simmer (gently, to keep the skins from splitting) until tender, 30 to 50 minutes. As they cook, add a bit more water if necessary to keep them covered. Then cool the beans in their cooking liquid.

If you have time, presoaking beans (*not* split peas or quick-cooking lentils) will shorten the cooking time and help leach out the indigestible sugars that sometimes cause intestinal gas. There are two methods: (1) Soak the beans for at least 4 hours, or as long as 8, in cool water to cover. (2) If you're in a hurry, put the beans in a large saucepan, add enough water to cover by 2 inches, and bring to a boil. Boil for 2 minutes, then cover the pan, remove from the heat, and set aside for 1 hour. Discard the soaking water (*never* cook the beans in their soaking water), rinse the beans, and cook as directed.

Is it okay to use canned beans? Of course it is—we do it all the time when we're in a hurry—but be sure to rinse them in a colander before using them. Cans of good-quality Great Northern and kidney beans belong right there in the pantry next to the canned plum tomatoes.

Home-cooked beans have a lovely texture, but the canned variety offers a tremendous trade-off in convenience. Do yourself a favor sometime, though, and start a soup or chili or cassoulet with dried beans; you'll see that it does make a difference. One cup of dried beans will yield 2 to 3 cups cooked, or enough for four servings.

1. Heat the oil in a large kettle or soup pot over medium heat. Add the garlic and onion and sauté until the onion is very tender and just beginning to brown, about 10 minutes. Add the zucchini, bell peppers, basil, thyme, and ½ teaspoon salt. Sauté for another 5 minutes.

2. Stir in the stock, tomatoes with their juice, and olives. Bring to a boil, reduce the heat, partially cover, and simmer gently for 25 to 30 minutes.

3. Add the beans and spinach, and cook over medium heat just until the beans have warmed and the spinach has wilted, about 5 minutes. Season to taste with salt and pepper, and add a bit more stock or water for a thinner soup if desired. Serve hot in crocks or mugs.

Bright Ideas

❧ Top bowls of the soup with Parmesan croutons: Sprinkle ½-inch-thick rounds of French bread with Parmesan cheese and black pepper, then bake at 400°F or broil briefly until the cheese is melted and crisp.

❧ Ladle a small spoonful of Pesto (page 250) into hot bowls of Mediterranean Bean Soup just before serving.

Carrot and Ginger Soup

SERVES 6

This wonderful combination of sweet carrots and peppery ginger is a Hay Day best-seller. Elegant enough for Limoges porcelain and simple enough for a thermos, it is a snap to make. If you buy carrots with their bright green tops attached, you know they'll be fresh and sweet; but since carrots' sugar content does vary, we suggest that you taste the soup and perhaps add a little sugar at the end. Serve it hot or chilled, garnished with some fresh green cilantro and a few croutons if you like. It's nice to balance the sweetness and spice of the soup with the rich whole-grain flavor of Whole-Meal Bread (page 102).

◆◆◆◆◆◆

4 tablespoons (½ stick) unsalted butter
1 piece of fresh ginger (2 ounces, about the size of a small lime), peeled and finely chopped (see About Ginger, page 215)
2 pounds carrots, scrubbed and chopped into ½-inch dice
5 cups Vegetable Stock (page 271) or Chicken Stock (page 270)
1 cup dry white wine
½ teaspoon coarse (kosher) salt, or to taste
Freshly ground black pepper, to taste
1 tablespoon sugar (optional)
Chopped fresh cilantro, for garnish

◆◆◆◆◆◆

Menu

Fireside Après Ski

This is what everyone hopes to see by the hearth after a day on the mountain: richly flavored hors d'oeuvres, a magnificent bean and vegetable soup, savory biscuits, and one of the best desserts this side of Mad River Glen.

Polenta Crostini
Tapenade and Chèvre on Spears of Fresh Fennel

Mediterranean Bean Soup
Parmesan-Sage Biscuits

Gingered Pear Crisp with Ruby Raisins
Vanilla ice cream

1. Melt the butter in a soup pot over low heat. Add the ginger and sauté until fragrant, 2 to 3 minutes. Add the carrots, stock, and wine, and bring to a boil over medium-high heat. Reduce to a simmer, partially cover, and cook until the carrots are very soft, 20 to 30 minutes. Remove from the heat and allow to cool for at least 10 minutes.

2. Purée the contents in a blender, working in batches if necessary. Return the purée to the pot, and season with the salt and pepper. Depending upon the natural sweetness of the carrots, add up to 1 tablespoon of sugar. For a finer soup, run the purée through a sieve or a food mill and return it to the pot.

3. Serve the soup hot or chilled. Ladle it into soup bowls, and garnish with a generous sprinkling of cilantro.

Bright Ideas

❦ Add a few scallops or grilled shrimp to enhance the soup.

❦ Serve a few spoonfuls of the soup as a sauce for grilled poultry or seafood.

CHOPPING TENDER HERBS

Chopping tender green herbs like cilantro can be tricky if the leaves are damp; chopping brings out additional moisture and makes the leaves clump together. If fresh herbs are thoroughly dry, they'll be easy to chop and sprinkle, so get in the habit of drying them well with a kitchen or paper towel both before and after chopping.

Vermont Cheddar Chowder

SERVES 8

Our first-choice cheese for this soup is the sweet, nutty Vermont Cheddar from rich Jersey cows' milk made by our friends at the Grafton Village Cheese Company—but the whole state of Vermont produces delicious creamy white Cheddars. If you can, select a cheese that has been aged for 12 to 18 months. People new to the idea of cheese soup are pleasantly surprised by the lightness of this one; the chunks of carrots and potatoes give it a wonderful texture.

Complete the meal with our Cheddar-Chive Biscuits (page 98) or with crisp cheese straws or slices of tangy sourdough bread.

◆◆◆◆◆◆

4 tablespoons (½ stick) unsalted butter
4 carrots, scrubbed and diced
1 Spanish onion, peeled and coarsely chopped
3 cups Chicken Stock (page 270)
1 pound red-skin potatoes, scrubbed and cut into large dice
¼ cup unbleached all-purpose flour
1½ cups whole milk
8 ounces aged Vermont Cheddar cheese, shredded
Freshly ground black pepper
2 tablespoons coarsely chopped fresh chives

◆◆◆◆◆◆

1. Melt 1 tablespoon of the butter in a large stockpot over medium-high heat. Add the carrots and onion and sauté briefly, just until the onion is transparent, 3 minutes. Add the stock and potatoes, and bring to a boil. Reduce the heat, cover, and simmer gently until the carrots are tender, 15 to 20 minutes.

2. Meanwhile, melt the remaining 3 tablespoons butter in a small saucepan over medium-high heat. Gradually whisk in the flour to make a paste. Continue to whisk over medium-high heat for 1 minute to brown and cook the flour. Whisking continuously, add the milk in a steady, even stream and whisk the mixture into a thick, smooth, creamy sauce.

Remove the pan from the heat, add the cheese, and stir until it is completely melted. Season to taste with pepper.

3. Stir the cheese sauce into the stockpot and warm the soup gently over low heat. Stir in the chives, and season to taste with additional pepper as needed. Serve hot.

Note: This and all cheese soups should be reheated very, very gently; the cheese sinks to the bottom and will burn if you don't keep a close eye on it.

Bright Idea

❦ **Creamy Cheddar Pasta Bake:** Mix some Vermont Cheddar Chowder with cooked spaghetti and chunks of country ham, add some grated Cheddar, top with fresh bread crumbs, and bake at 350°F until hot and bubbly, 30 minutes.

Amish Chicken Noodle Soup

SERVES 12

You're starving spiritually if you've only had chicken noodle soup out of a can. The homemade kind is genuine food for the soul, and nobody does it better than the Pennsylvania Dutch, who add a pinch of saffron to give the broth a rich, restorative golden color. It's worth going the extra mile for natural, free-range or organic chickens, too; they offer a lot more flavor and fewer additives than standard commercial chickens. Many of our customers swear by kosher chickens for the tastiest soup. If you do choose a kosher chicken, season the broth with half the amount of salt because these chickens arrive at the pot already salted.

Toasted slices of Hay Day's Best-Ever Potato Bread (page 103) or a basket of Cheddar-Chive Biscuits (page 98) will round out this satisfying meal.

◆◆◆◆◆

4 pounds chicken pieces
3 quarts water
2 teaspoons coarse (kosher) salt
1 large pinch saffron threads (see Cooking with Saffron, page 180)
1 large onion, peeled and quartered
2 cups thinly sliced, diced, or julienned carrots
2 cups fine egg noodles
1 cup fresh corn kernels (see Note)
Salt and freshly ground black pepper, to taste

◆◆◆◆◆

1. Rinse the chicken pieces and trim off any excess fat. Place the chicken in a large soup pot and cover with the water. Stir in the salt, saffron, and onion, and bring to a simmer over medium-high heat. Adjust the heat and continue to simmer (do not allow the broth to boil), skimming off any foam that rises to the surface, until the broth takes on a rich golden color and the chicken is cooked through, 30 to 40 minutes. Using a large slotted spoon, remove the chicken and onion pieces and set them aside until cool enough to handle. Discard the onion. Strain the broth through a fine-mesh sieve or a cheesecloth-lined colander into another large saucepan.

2. Add the carrots and noodles to the broth, bring to a simmer, and cook, uncovered, until tender, 10 to 15 minutes. Meanwhile, pull the chicken meat from the bones, discarding the skin and bones. Shred or cut the meat into large bite-size pieces, and add them to the soup along with the corn. Cook for an additional 5 minutes, season with salt and pepper, and serve.

Note: When corn is out of season, tender cooked kernels of hominy make a nice substitute. Hominy is available dried or canned. Simply simmer dried hominy in water to cover until fork-tender. If you

ABOUT COCONUT MILK

Yes, you could buy the coconut and squeeze out the milk—but what for? With the soaring popularity of Asian and Indian cooking, most stores offer excellent-quality unsweetened canned coconut milk. Look for a brand with little saturated fat and no chemical additives. Stir before using.

are using canned hominy, drain and rinse it well before adding. Hominy will add a rich smoky flavor to the soup.

Variations

◆ For a very lean soup, prepare the broth (step 1) one day in advance. Refrigerate the cooked chicken and the broth separately. When the broth has chilled, you will be able to spoon off the thin layer of fat that has risen to the surface. Then continue with step 2.

◆ All of the following make delicious substitutions or additions to the soup. Toss in with the noodles and simmer until tender: fresh garden peas, asparagus tips, sliced green beans, diced zucchini, sliced or diced celery, broccoli florets, or diced winter squash (sugar pumpkin, acorn, or butternut).

Curried Chicken and Basmati Rice Soup

SERVES 6 TO 8

On a gloomy fall or winter day, when chicken soup is balm for the soul, try this masterly variation on a familiar theme. Inspired by the great curried Senegalese Stew we've sold for years at Hay Day, this soup adds apple and fennel to echo the flavor of the curry. It is an excellent way to use leftover roast chicken, and is delicious enough to warrant picking up a roast bird at the market on the way home from work. Complete the meal with papadums (a traditional fragrant crisp Indian flatbread made from

SHOPPING FOR CURRY POWDER

Did you know that there's no single "curry powder" in Indian cooking? It is, rather, the catchall name for a blend of as many as twenty different spices, a mixture that usually includes coriander, cardamom, chiles, cumin, fennel seeds, fenugreek, ginger, anise, mustard, cinnamon, cloves, saffron, tamarind, and turmeric. Indian cooks are skilled artists at blending flavors, using a palette ranging from mild to very hot.

From brand to brand both the flavor and the heat vary considerably. Experiment with a few to select the ones you prefer. Smell the powder and test it on your tongue for flavor and heat. Buy small quantities to store in a cool, dark corner of your spice cupboard for no more than a few months (once ground, the spices lose their pungency quickly).

Beyond the familiar lamb or chicken curry, curry powder adds bold, assertive flavor to stir-fries, oven-roasted vegetables, scrambled eggs, rice, or even a plain baked potato.

---

lentil flour) or thick slices of whole-grain or our Whole-Meal Bread (page 102).

◆◆◆◆◆◆

2 tablespoons unsalted butter
1 large onion, peeled, halved
   lengthwise, and thinly sliced
1 large clove garlic, peeled and minced
1 large Granny Smith apple, peeled,
   cored, and coarsely chopped
1 small bulb fresh fennel, rinsed,
   trimmed, quartered lengthwise,
   and cut into thin slivers
2 teaspoons curry powder
5 cups Chicken Stock (page 270)
½ cup white basmati rice, well rinsed
   and drained
1 pound boneless cooked chicken,
   coarsely chopped (2½ cups chopped)
½ cup mango chutney
1 cup canned coconut milk (see About
   Coconut Milk, facing page)
Coarse (kosher) salt and freshly
   ground black pepper
⅓ cup coarsely chopped unsalted
   peanuts, for garnish
Chopped fresh cilantro, for garnish

◆◆◆◆◆◆

1. Melt the butter over medium heat in a large soup pot. Add the onion and garlic and sauté until soft, about 3 minutes.

2. Stir in the apple and fennel, sprinkle with the curry powder, and sauté briefly. Add the stock and rice, and bring to a gentle simmer. Cover, and cook until the rice is tender, 20 to 25 minutes. Then stir in the chicken, chutney, and coconut milk and warm over medium heat. Season to taste with salt and pepper. Ladle the hot soup into bowls, and garnish with a sprinkling of chopped peanuts and cilantro.

Sweet Corn and Lobster Chowder

SERVES 8

This elegant late-summer celebration is expecially good in September, when Maine lobsters are so plentiful that the cooked meat is frequently available for less than the astronomical summer price, making it sometimes even cheaper than lobsters in the shell. Garnished with fresh thyme and served with flaky Cheddar-Chive Biscuits (page 98) or Parmesan-Sage Biscuits (page 97), it's a wonderful way to make the season last just a little bit longer.

◆◆◆◆◆◆

6 ears fresh yellow corn
2 tablespoons olive oil
1 large leek, white part only, well
    washed and coarsely chopped
12 ounces cooked lobster meat, coarsely
    chopped
1 pound red-skin potatoes, scrubbed
    and diced
4 cups Fish Stock (page 271)
½ cup dry white wine
1 cup whole milk
½ cup heavy (whipping) cream
2 tablespoons fresh thyme leaves
Coarse (kosher) salt and freshly ground
    black pepper
Fresh thyme sprigs, for garnish

◆◆◆◆◆◆

1. Using a thin sharp blade, slice the corn kernels off the cobs. Set the kernels aside and reserve the cobs.

2. Heat the oil in a large soup kettle over medium-high heat. Add the leek and sauté until it is transparent and tender, about 5 minutes. Add the lobster and continue to sauté for another 5 minutes. Scoop out the leek and lobster and set aside.

3. Pile the potatoes and corncobs in the pot, and cover with the stock and wine. Bring to a simmer over medium heat, cover, and simmer until the potatoes are very tender, 25 to 30 minutes.

4. Remove the cobs from the pot and discard them. Using a slotted spoon, scoop out a generous cup of the potatoes and place in a small bowl; mash well with a fork. Return the mashed potato to the pot, and add the corn kernels, milk, cream, thyme, and reserved lobster. Stir well and return to a gentle simmer over medium heat. Cook just until the corn is crisp-tender, about 5 minutes. Season to taste with salt and pepper. Serve hot, garnished with whole sprigs of thyme.

Creamy Summer Corn Chowder

SERVES 4 TO 6

When sweet corn comes in still warm from the field, we've been known to eat it just like that, right off the truck. But for this recipe, you'll need to grate the corn. It's a messy job (you may want an apron), but there's no better way to extract all the sugars. The grater removes all the kernels and juices and actually purées them in the process. Just snap the ears in half and use a simple box grater set on a platter or in a large bowl. Fresh Tomato with Yogurt Cheese Salad (page 113) is just the thing to serve alongside.

◆◆◆◆◆◆

2 tablespoons unsalted butter

2 carrots, scrubbed and diced

3 scallions, white and light green parts finely chopped

12 ounces red-skin potatoes, scrubbed and cut into small dice (1½ cups diced)

¾ cup Chicken Stock (page 270)

2 cups whole milk

2 cups grated sweet corn (about 8 large ears)

Small pinch coarse (kosher) salt

Freshly ground black pepper

Minced fresh chives, for garnish

◆◆◆◆◆◆

1. Melt the butter in a heavy-bottomed soup pot over medium heat. Add the carrots and scallions, and sauté over medium-high heat until the scallions are meltingly tender, 3 to 5 minutes. Add the potatoes and stock, bring to a simmer, cover, and cook gently until the potatoes are fork-tender, about 10 minutes.

2. Stir in the milk and corn, return to a simmer, and cook gently for about 3 minutes. Season to taste with the salt and a generous grinding of pepper, garnish with the chives, and serve hot.

Cold Cucumber, Feta, and Sweet Red Pepper Soup

SERVES 8

Come midsummer, cooks and guests are grateful for simple, fresh, uncooked soups. They are easy to assemble in the cool of the morning and serve chilled at dinnertime. Here, feta cheese and roasted peppers make an interesting variation on a classic cucumber soup. Complete the meal with wedges of toasted Everybody's Favorite Peasant Bread (white or herbed, page 100) and a bowl of good brine-cured olives.

◆◆◆◆◆◆

1½ cups Chicken Stock (page 270)

1 quart plain yogurt

2 tablespoons olive oil

Juice of 1 large lemon

1 large clove garlic, peeled and minced

1 tablespoon honey

1 large cucumber, peeled, seeded, and coarsely grated (2 generous cups grated; see Note)

2 tablespoons chopped fresh mint

3 ounces feta cheese, crumbled (¾ cup crumbled)

1 large red bell pepper, roasted (see How to Roast Peppers, page 80), peeled, seeded, and diced (½ cup diced)

Freshly ground black pepper

◆◆◆◆◆◆

1. Combine the stock, yogurt, oil, lemon juice, garlic, and honey in a large bowl and whisk together. Stir in the cucumber

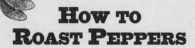

HOW TO ROAST PEPPERS

You can buy bottled roasted red bell peppers (frequently called "fire-roasted red peppers"); they're usually sold with their skins removed. Simply split them open and scrape out any seeds. Do not rinse them, or flavorful juices will be lost. Buy the peppers packed in their own juices; they also come marinated in vinegar and herbs, but these have a very different flavor.

However, you can also roast your own: Spear the pepper on a long-handled fork and roast it over a gas burner or on an outdoor grill, turning until it is charred all over, 8 to 10 minutes. Or place the pepper in a baking dish and roast in a 400°F oven, turning occasionally, until soft and charred all over, 25 to 30 minutes. Once the skin is soft and charred, place the pepper in a paper or plastic bag, seal it, and let the pepper steam for at least 15 minutes. When it is cool enough to handle, you can easily peel off the skin. Remove the core and scrape away the seeds with the blunt edge of a knife.

and mint, cover, and chill for at least 2 hours before serving.

2. Spoon the chilled soup into individual bowls, and scatter the feta and roasted bell peppers over each serving. Finish with a generous dusting of freshly ground black pepper, and serve immediately.

Note: Summer garden cucumbers are glorious, but they can be seedy and watery. If you use cucumbers from the

neighborhood patch, be sure to remove all seedy portions before grating. English (hothouse) cucumbers offer fewer seeds and involve a bit less work.

Cream of Roasted Fennel Soup

SERVES 8

Gently roasted fennel and onion combine with potato in this hearty soup. A splash of fresh grapefruit juice adds a refreshing spark of citrus, and a topping of toasted fennel seeds highlights the soup's gentle anise flavor. As with nuts, toasting whole spices enhances their flavor and fragrance.

◆◆◆◆◆◆

1 large bulb fresh fennel with
    stalks (1½ to 2 pounds)
1 large Spanish onion, peeled and
    coarsely chopped
2 teaspoons olive oil
Coarse (kosher) salt
1 large russet potato, peeled and
    cut into ½-inch cubes
4 cups Chicken Stock (page 270)
1 cup light cream
¾ teaspoon ground cumin
2 tablespoons fresh grapefruit juice
Ground white pepper
1 tablespoon fennel seeds

◆◆◆◆◆◆

1. Preheat the oven to 325°F.

2. Rinse and trim the fennel bulb; reserve the feathery fronds. Cut the bulb and stalks into ½-inch-thick rounds.

3. Scatter the sliced fennel and chopped onion in a large baking pan and arrange in a single layer. Drizzle with the oil, sprinkle with ¹/₂ teaspoon salt, and roast just until the vegetables are fork-tender but not browned, about 25 minutes.

4. Transfer the roasted fennel and onion to a large soup pot. Add the potato, cover with the stock, and bring to a simmer over medium heat. Cook until the potatoes are fork-tender, about 20 minutes. Allow to cool for at least 10 minutes. Then purée the mixture in a blender or food processor, in batches if necessary, until smooth. Return the purée to the soup pot, stir in the cream, cumin, and grapefruit juice, and warm over medium heat. Season to taste with salt and white pepper.

5. Place the fennel seeds in a small skillet over medium-high heat and toast, stirring frequently, until lightly browned and fragrant, about 3 minutes. Ladle the warm soup into individual bowls, float a small feathery tuft of fennel top on each serving, and sprinkle with the toasted fennel seeds. Serve immediately.

A NOTE ON TAMARI

Made from fermented soybeans, tamari is easy to mistake for conventional soy sauce. It's thicker than soy sauce, however, and has a richer, mellower flavor. It is commonly used as a condiment on Asian tables; we use it all the time to flavor soups, sauces, dips, and marinades.

Shiitake Mushroom Barley Soup

SERVES 6

One of the original Hay Day soups and certainly one of the best, this is the choice to take in a wide-mouth thermos on a picnic in October—it is a natural outdoors, surrounded by autumn leaves. You can make it with a combination of cremini and conventional button mushrooms, too, but shiitakes are so easy to find these days that we like to take advantage of their more intense mushroom flavor. (Always remove shiitake stems, by the way—they're too tough to use for anything but flavoring stock.) If you're serving this at home, a salad of mixed greens dressed in a fragrant sherry vinaigrette would provide a nice counterpoint.

◆◆◆◆◆◆

2 tablespoons unsalted butter
1 Spanish onion, peeled and chopped
1 large clove garlic, peeled and
    minced
8 ounces shiitake mushrooms, stems
    removed, caps wiped clean and
    thinly sliced
1 tablespoon tamari (see A Note on
    Tamari)
6 cups Chicken Stock (page 270)
¹/₂ cup pearl barley, rinsed and drained
¹/₄ cup medium-dry sherry (oloroso or
    amontillado)
Coarse (kosher) salt and freshly ground
    black pepper
Fresh thyme sprigs, for garnish

◆◆◆◆◆◆

1. Melt the butter in a large soup pot over medium-high heat. Add the onion and garlic and sauté until very lightly colored, about 5 minutes. Stir in the mushrooms and sauté, stirring frequently, until completely softened and cooked down, 8 to 10 minutes. Add the tamari and sauté for another minute.

2. Stir in the stock and barley, bring to a gentle boil, and then reduce the heat. Simmer, partially covered, over medium heat just until the barley is tender, 25 to 30 minutes. Add the sherry, stir, and warm for a couple of minutes. Season to taste with salt and pepper. Serve bowls of the hot soup topped with sprigs of fresh thyme.

Note: Like most soups, this one can easily be made ahead of time, but remember that the barley will continue to absorb the liquid. You may need to thin the soup with additional stock, and to reseason it to taste, at serving time.

ABOUT SHERRY

Sherry, like other aromatics (fresh herbs or ground pepper, for example), should be added near the end of the cooking time because heat dissipates its fragrance quickly We use a good all-purpose medium-dry sherry (oloroso or amontillado) for all our soups, stews, and sauces. Avoid "cooking sherry" like the plague—it will *definitely* ruin the soup.

Cream of Wild Mushroom Soup

SERVES 4

It's true, this is not an everyday soup, but do try it for Thanksgiving dinner or some other special occasion (this recipe doubles easily). You can, of course, substitute plain button mushrooms for any of the wild ones, but try not to skip the morels. Even Hay Day has fresh morels only briefly in the spring, but the dried ones are plentiful year-round. Their mild flavor and extraordinary texture are unique—and they're nowhere near as costly as the fresh ones. For a lovely accompaniment, serve garlic-or herb-buttered toast points sprinkled with chopped fresh parsley.

◆◆◆◆◆◆

½ ounce dried morel mushrooms, or
   6 ounces fresh (see Cooking with
   Fresh Morels, facing page)
½ cup brandy
4 tablespoons (½ stick) unsalted butter
1 clove garlic, peeled and minced
1 leek, white part only, well washed
   and finely diced
8 ounces cremini mushrooms, caps and
   stems wiped clean and sliced
4 ounces shiitake mushrooms, stems
   removed, caps wiped clean and sliced
1 tablespoon fresh thyme leaves
3 tablespoons unbleached all-purpose
   flour
4 cups Browned Beef Stock (page 269;
   see Note)
1 cup heavy (whipping) cream
Coarse (kosher) salt and freshly ground
   black pepper
Fresh thyme leaves, for garnish

◆◆◆◆◆◆

1. Place the dried mushrooms and the brandy in a small bowl. Add enough warm water to cover completely, and set aside to reconstitute for 30 minutes (or simmer over medium-high heat until softened, about 5 minutes). Drain the mushrooms, reserving 2 tablespoons of the liquid, and slice them into thin rounds. (If you are using fresh morels, clean them and slice them into thin rounds.)

2. Melt the butter in a large heavy-bottomed kettle or soup pot. Add the garlic and leek and sauté until transparent and tender, 2 to 3 minutes. Then, add all the mushrooms and sauté over medium heat until tender and wilted, about 5 minutes.

3. Add the thyme and the reserved morel soaking liquid to the pot (or add 2 tablespoons brandy if using fresh morels), and continue to cook for 2 to 3 minutes. Sprinkle the flour over the mushrooms and cook over medium heat, stirring constantly, to brown and cook the flour, about 2 minutes.

4. Stirring constantly over medium heat, add the stock in a slow, thin stream. Bring to a simmer and cook, stirring frequently, until slightly thickened, about 30 minutes. Add the cream and return to a gentle simmer. Allow the soup to simmer for several minutes. Season to taste with salt and pepper. Ladle the hot soup into bowls, and garnish each serving with fresh thyme.

Note: You'll find that when you're making a roux, as in steps 3 and 4, it is less likely to lump if the stock is cool or at room temperature.

COOKING WITH FRESH MORELS

If you prepare Cream of Wild Mushroom Soup when fresh morels are in season (roughly early spring to July), substitute 6 ounces of fresh mushrooms for ½ ounce dried. Fresh morels are perishable, so store them for only 1 or 2 days and clean them just before using (never eat them raw).

Washing mushrooms is hardly ever recommended, for they are little sponges that soak up moisture and quickly begin to rot. However, the honeycomb-shaped caps of fresh morels tend to harbor sand and grit. Trim away their heavy base tips, place in a colander, and rinse under a light spray of water, bouncing them up and down to shake and rinse away any debris.

Once the morels are cleaned, immediately blot them dry with paper towels, slice, and add them to the soup along with 2 tablespoons brandy.

Bright Idea

❧ Serve the soup as a creamy mushroom sauce: Toss it into warm cooked wild rice or ladle it over hot egg noodles.

Chilled Salmon Chowder

SERVES 6

This cool chowder is a wonderfully easy make-ahead lunch or dinner entrée for summer entertaining. Make it the night before and stash it in the refrigerator. At serving time, all you do is stir in the herbs and garnish the plates. (It's great warm, too—in fact, we have a hard time deciding which way we prefer it.) Complete the meal with a salad of mixed greens tossed in Lemon Vinaigrette (page 265).

♦♦♦♦♦♦

2 tablespoons unsalted butter
4 large red-skin new potatoes,
    scrubbed and cut into ½-inch dice
    (4 cups diced)
16 scallions, white and light green
    parts thickly sliced
3 cups Chicken Stock (page 270)
½ cup dry white wine
1 cup whole milk
1½ cups Crème Fraîche (page 255)
2 cups (1 scant pound) flaked poached
    salmon
Coarse (kosher) salt and freshly
    ground black pepper, to taste
¼ cup chopped fresh dill
⅓ cup chopped fresh chives
Minced fresh chives, for garnish
6 thin-sliced lemon rounds, for garnish

♦♦♦♦♦♦

1. Melt the butter in a large soup pot over medium heat. Stir in the potatoes and scallions and sauté over medium-high heat for 2 minutes. Add the stock and wine, and bring to a boil. Reduce the

HOT-SMOKED SALMON

The smoked salmon that we like to serve on Sunday bagels is prepared with a low-temperature cold-smoking technique that yields a tender, delicately flavored fish. The hot-smoking process, traditional in the Northwest, smokes fish at a much higher temperature for a shorter period of time and produces a flaky, heartier-flavored fish. The texture and flavor of hot-smoked salmon is best suited for cooked preparations—egg dishes, sauces, and soups—while buttery cold-smoked salmon is best enjoyed thinly sliced in salads and on canapés.

heat, partially cover, and simmer until the potatoes are tender, 10 to 15 minutes.

2. Stir in the milk and half of the crème fraîche (reserve the remainder for serving time). Warm gently over medium heat. Then stir in the salmon and season liberally with salt and pepper. Remove from the heat, cover, and refrigerate overnight.

3. Just before serving, stir in the dill and chives; taste, and adjust the seasonings if necessary. Spoon each serving into a soup bowl, top with a dollop of the remaining crème fraîche, sprinkle with minced chives, and garnish with a single lemon slice. Serve immediately.

Bright Ideas

❦ To add a rich smoky flavor to the soup, use hot-smoked salmon (facing page) in place of the poached salmon.

❦ For a formal presentation, warm the soup gently and ladle it into flaky baked puff pastry shells.

Spelt Chowder

SERVES 10 TO 12

This is a great dairy-free vegetarian chowder packed with nutrition and satisfying flavor. Whole dried chiles add a rich peppery flavor to soups and broths. To make the chowder year-round, substitute frozen or good-quality canned corn in the winter. Corn muffins are a natural accompaniment (just skip the jam filling in the recipe on page 2).

◆◆◆◆◆◆

¼ cup olive oil
1 large onion, peeled and coarsely
   chopped
1 pound ripe plum tomatoes,
   coarsely chopped (see Note)
1 large russet or Idaho potato,
   peeled and cut into ½-inch dice
2 dried medium-hot red chile peppers
   (New Mexico or pasilla), broken in
   half, seeds shaken out and discarded
6 cups Vegetable Stock (page 271)
2 teaspoons coarse (kosher) salt
1 cup spelt kernels, rinsed and drained
2 cups corn kernels (4 large ears)
⅓ cup minced fresh chives
Salt and freshly ground black pepper,
   to taste

◆◆◆◆◆◆

1. Heat the oil in a large soup pot over medium-high heat. Add the onion and sauté until nicely colored and caramelized, about 10 minutes. Stir in the tomatoes and sauté until softened and slightly thickened, 5 minutes. Add the potato, chiles, stock, and salt and allow to come to a boil.

2. Stir in the spelt and reduce the heat to a simmer. Partially cover, and cook, stirring occasionally, until the spelt is tender, 30 to 40 minutes. Remove and discard the chile pieces, and stir in the corn and chives. Continue to simmer just until the corn is crisp-tender, 2 to 3 minutes. Season with salt and pepper, and serve hot.

Note: Two cups of good-quality canned plum tomatoes can be substituted here for fresh.

ABOUT SPELT

There are so many different grains and beans on store shelves these days, and cooking with them can be a real adventure. Spelt, an ancient cereal grain with a mellow nutty flavor and a high protein content, cooks quite a bit faster than wheat berries and is highly digestible, even for people who can't eat wheat. Spelt kernels are available in most specialty and health-food stores, but if you can't find them, you can substitute wheat berries, kamut, or Italian farro.

Summer Squash Soup

SERVES 8

We sell this richly flavored, dairy-free vegetarian marvel all summer long, to serve warm or cold. It's simple and economical to make, and a natural to take in a thermos to the beach. Take along some crisp seeded breadsticks or slices of a simple focaccia in a picnic basket.

◆◆◆◆◆◆

½ cup olive oil

1 large onion, peeled and coarsely chopped

1 large clove garlic, peeled and crushed with the side of a knife

4 large ripe tomatoes, cored, seeded, and coarsely chopped

2 zucchini (total of 1 pound or less), coarsely chopped

2 yellow squash (total of 1 pound or less), coarsely chopped

1 red bell pepper, stemmed, seeded, and coarsely chopped

Coarse (kosher) salt

1 cup Vegetable Stock (page 271)

2 tablespoons red wine vinegar

½ teaspoon fennel seeds

Freshly ground black pepper, to taste

¼ cup minced or julienned zucchini and yellow squash, mixed, for garnish

◆◆◆◆◆◆

1. Heat the oil in a large kettle or stockpot over medium-high heat. Add the onion and sauté until softened and transparent, 5 minutes. Add the garlic, remaining vegetables, and 2 teaspoons salt, and sauté until the vegetables are lightly caramelized, about 15 minutes.

2. Add the stock, vinegar, fennel seeds, and black pepper to the pot, bring to a simmer, and cook, uncovered, until the vegetables are extremely tender, about 20 minutes. Remove from the heat and allow to cool for at least 10 minutes.

3. Transfer the mixture, in batches, to a blender and pulse to form a coarse purée. Return it to the pot and season to taste with additional salt and pepper. Serve hot, warm, or chilled. Ladle the soup into bowls, and garnish each one with some of the minced zucchini and yellow squash.

WHAT'S ALL THE FUSS ABOUT COARSE SALT?

We nearly always cook with coarse salt for its ease and its pure mild flavor. It's coarser in texture than standard table salt, but the crystals are actually fine flecks that cling to food and dissolve quickly. The large irregular flakes also make it easier to sprinkle evenly and discriminately, especially when seasoning food to taste with a pinch of the fingers. If you are substituting table salt for coarse salt in a recipe, begin with half the amount listed.

ABOUT CHILE PEPPERS

Besides heat, each hot pepper, in fact, offers a particular character and taste to a dish. In the market, fresh chiles should be firm and smooth-skinned; if they are wrinkled or soft, they will have lost their fresh taste. Store them wrapped in paper towels (never in airtight plastic bags) in the refrigerator.

Dried chiles should still be a bit flexible—not really brittle—but they must be dry. They keep well for several months in a cool, dry place; dampness will attract mold and cause them to spoil quickly. Soften dried chiles for cooking by toasting them lightly in a dry skillet until they are very pliable; they can then be chopped, blended into sauces and marinades, or soaked for stuffing or puréeing.

Chile peppers get their heat from an enzyme in their ribs and seeds called capsaicin, which can be extremely irritating and should be treated with the utmost respect. The ribs and seeds are usually discarded, but since they contain most of the heat, the procedure is optional; use the whole pepper (fresh or dried) if you like things extra-hot. It is wise to wear plastic gloves when handling chiles, and never, *never* rub your eyes until you've washed your hands and all cutting surfaces thoroughly with detergent (capsaicin is not soluble in plain water).

What to do for relief? If a dish is too hot, most people find that beer or wine, yogurt, milk, sour cream, bread, or tortillas will take away the fire. Water (since capsaicin is not water-soluble) doesn't do much good.

Having said all this, though, we must emphasize that chiles bring with them far more than just heat. Be careful—but do not be put off. They are magnificent flavorings and infinitely rewarding.

Remember, too, that if you're caught without chiles in mid-recipe, you can use a bottled hot sauce instead. Hot sauces offer an equally dizzying range of flavor and character, and their convenience and versatility are unbeatable.

Bright Ideas

❦ Serve Summer Squash Soup as a sauce for pasta or spaghetti squash.

❦ Toss with shredded cooked chicken and cooked egg noodles, top with bread crumbs and Parmesan cheese, and bake at 350°F until bubbly.

Winter Squash Bisque

SERVES 6 TO 8

Squash, carrots, and celery combine in a bisque that's substantial on its own—and is heavenly when enriched with a bit of crème fraîche. Its rich, aromatic quality is nicely complemented by thick slices of Herbed Peasant Bread (page 101).

◆◆◆◆◆◆

4 tablespoons (½ stick) unsalted butter

1 onion, peeled and coarsely chopped

2 carrots, scrubbed and coarsely
*   chopped*

2 large ribs celery, coarsely chopped

2 large cloves garlic, peeled and minced

1½ pounds butternut squash, peeled,
*   seeded, and cut into ½-inch dice*
*   (see Note)*

4 cups Chicken Stock (page 270)

1½ teaspoons fresh thyme leaves

½ teaspoon ground allspice

2 tablespoons Calvados or other apple
*   brandy*

Coarse (kosher) salt and freshly ground
*   black pepper*

8 ounces (1 cup) Crème Fraîche
*   (page 255)*

◆◆◆◆◆◆

1. Melt the butter in a large heavy-bottomed soup pot over medium-high heat. Add the onion, carrots, celery, and garlic and sauté just until the garlic begins to color, about 10 minutes. Stir in the squash and stock, and bring to a boil. Reduce the heat, partially cover, and simmer until the squash is very tender, 15 to 20 minutes. Remove the pot from the heat and allow to cool for at least 10 minutes.

2. Transfer the contents of the soup pot to a blender, in batches if necessary, and purée. Return the purée to the pot, place it over medium heat, and stir in the thyme, allspice, and Calvados. Bring to a gentle simmer, and season to taste with salt and pepper. Ladle into large soup bowls, and swirl a large spoonful of crème fraîche into each. Serve hot.

Note: We've specified butternut squash because it is almost universally available these days, but pumpkin, acorn, Hubbard, turban, or buttercup will do just as well here. All winter squashes are good keepers, of course, and can be peeled and diced ahead of time and kept in a plastic bag in the refrigerator for several days. They can be stubborn to peel (use a good sharp swivel peeler as you would with potatoes), but the good news is that many stores now sell the squash peeled, diced, and ready to go.

Bright Ideas

❦ Serve the soup from a tureen made from a hollowed-out sugar pumpkin.

❦ Use as a sauce for roast pheasant, quail, capon, or Cornish hen.

❦ Toss with cubed butternut squash and grated Gruyère cheese, and bake at 375°F until the squash is fork-tender, about 30 minutes, for a baked squash gratin.

PURÉE
THE EASY WAY

Hand-held immersion blenders are a soupmaker's dream appliance. Keep one conveniently mounted and you can purée the soup in a freezer container or even right in the pot, then rinse off the blender afterward without breaking stride. Sure beats washing the food processor or traditional blender.

Warm Sweet Potato Vichyssoise

SERVES 8

In this case the potatoes are sweet but the soup isn't. Balanced with leeks and onions, this warm version of the French classic is an elegant starter for fall entertaining—or even for Thanksgiving dinner. Finish each serving with a swirl of cream and a scattering of minced fresh chives or, for an unconventional touch, crushed cumin seeds. Warm cornbread or toasted slices of our Whole-Meal Bread (page 102) go perfectly with this hearty soup.

◆◆◆◆◆◆

4 tablespoons (½ stick) unsalted butter
4 large leeks, white parts only, well
   washed and thinly sliced
1 onion, peeled and thinly sliced
   (about 1 cup sliced)
1½ pounds sweet potatoes (2 large
   potatoes), peeled and thinly sliced
2 teaspoons coarse (kosher) salt
4 cups Chicken Stock (page 270)
2 cups milk
1 cup light cream, plus additional
   for garnish
Ground white pepper
¼ cup minced fresh chives, or
   2 teaspoons whole cumin seeds,
   toasted and crushed to a coarse
   powder, for garnish

◆◆◆◆◆◆

1. Melt the butter in a large heavy-bottomed soup pot over medium heat. Add the leeks and onion, and sauté over medium-high heat until tender and transparent, about 5 minutes. Stir in the potatoes, sprinkle with the salt, and continue to sauté for another minute or two. Add the stock and bring to a simmer. Reduce the heat to low, cover, and simmer until the potatoes are crumbly tender, about 30 minutes.

2. Run the contents of the soup pot through a food mill into another large saucepan (or push through a fine-mesh sieve using the back of a ladle or spoon). Stir in the milk and 1 cup cream. Warm gently over medium heat, stirring occasionally (do not let the soup boil). Season to taste with white pepper. Ladle the hot soup into individual bowls, swirl a bit of cream into each, and finish with a sprinkling of chives or cumin, if using.

Chilled Strawberry and Yogurt Soup

SERVES 4

A California classic slightly updated with peppery balsamic vinegar and mint, this simple and refreshing uncooked soup is just the thing to serve for a summertime lunch on the terrace. The soup is most refreshing when served very cold and for convenience can be prepared a few days in advance. A fresh citrus and endive salad would complement the creamy yogurt and complete the meal.

◆◆◆◆◆◆

1 generous quart ripe fresh
   strawberries, rinsed and hulled
½ cup dry white wine
3 tablespoons honey
¼ teaspoon ground allspice
1 cup plain yogurt
¼ cup sour cream or Crème Fraîche
   (page 255)
4 teaspoons balsamic vinegar
1 tablespoon chopped fresh mint

◆◆◆◆◆◆

1. Purée the berries in a food processor or blender until smooth. Pour the purée into a large pitcher or bowl, and add the wine, honey, and allspice. Whisk in the yogurt and sour cream, and chill for at least 6 hours or as long as overnight. Chill the serving bowls as well.

2. At serving time, pour the soup into the chilled bowls, and float a teaspoonful of balsamic vinegar over the surface of each. Finish with a sprinkling of mint, and serve immediately.

Bright Ideas

❧ Serve as a sauce for mixed berries or fruit salad.

❧ Use as a sauce for a simple grilled chicken breast served on a bed of baby greens.

CALIFORNIA STRAWBERRIES

At Hay Day we toot the horn for local produce all summer, but strawberries are the exception, even in July. If you can pick your own local ripe berries and take them home to eat right away, that's wonderful, but the tender sweetness that makes really ripe strawberries such a luxury also makes them too fragile to ship. If you're buying strawberries in a store, you'll probably find that the varieties grown in California seem to travel better. The ideal growing conditions of Orange, San Diego, and Ventura counties produce more than 70 percent of the strawberries sold in this country; the berries are hand-picked, then cooled and shipped to market by air.

Except for blueberries (which last much longer), *all* berries should be used within 24 to 48 hours. Remove them from their containers and arrange them in a single layer on a pan lined with paper towels (do not wash them); top with more paper towels, cover loosely with plastic wrap, and refrigerate. Berries taste better at room temperature, so remove them from the refrigerator 1 to 2 hours before using. Rinse them very gently in a colander just before serving.

Chunky Tomato and Bacon Soup

SERVES 6

This recipe belongs in the Hay Day Hall of Fame. The secret—besides really good tomatoes—is the quality of the bacon. We use thick-sliced bacon that has been smoked over apple wood or juniper, which adds a wonderful complexity to the flavor of the soup. It's a snap to make, and a great way to seize the moment when magnificent local tomatoes flood the summer markets. Like many main-dish soups, it becomes a full meal with a couple of slices of good bread, and its flavor is even richer the next day.

◆◆◆◆◆◆

6 ounces thick-sliced bacon
 (4 or 5 strips), coarsely chopped
1 large onion, peeled and coarsely
 chopped
1 tablespoon unsalted butter
3½ pounds ripe tomatoes, cored and
 coarsely chopped (8 cups chopped),
 with their juice
Coarse (kosher) salt
1 cup Chicken Stock (page 270)
Small handful fresh thyme sprigs
½ cup milk
1 cup heavy (whipping) cream
Freshly ground black pepper
Fresh thyme leaves, for garnish

◆◆◆◆◆◆

1. Combine the bacon, onion, and butter in a large heavy-bottomed soup pot, and sauté over medium-high heat until the bacon is crisp, 8 to 10 minutes.

MENU

A Farm Stand Sunday Supper

A nourishing bowl of fragrant tomato soup accompanied by some homemade bread is perfect for a Sunday supper around the kitchen table. The chunky tomato soup is easy to prepare and a great way to enjoy the abundant crop of local summer tomatoes.

Freshly harvested beets, raspberries, and tree-ripened peaches make this meal a special celebration of our summer harvest from Connecticut, Long Island, and New Jersey farms.

❧ ❧ ❧

Chunky Tomato and Bacon Soup
Everybody's Favorite Peasant Bread

Oven-Roasted Beets, Red Onions,
and Oranges

Raspberry Peach Torte

2. Stir in the tomatoes (juice and all), and scrape up the browned bits clinging to the bottom of the pot. Season with ½ teaspoon salt and bring to a simmer over medium-high heat.

3. Add the stock. Working over the soup pot, strip the leaves from the thyme sprigs, and add the leaves and the tender portions of the stems to the soup. Continue to simmer, partially covered, until the soup is fragrant and slightly thickened, about 25 minutes. Stir the soup occasionally.

4. Stir in the milk and cream, and warm over low heat for 5 minutes. Then season with additional salt, if needed, and pepper to taste. Ladle the soup into bowls, garnish with the extra thyme, and serve hot.

Bright Ideas

❦ Season with Parmesan and serve over hot pasta as a chunky Tomato Alfredo.

❦ Use as a topping for hot baked potatoes.

Variation

◆ Top ovenproof crocks of the hot soup with shredded Gruyère or aged Cheddar and run them under the broiler to melt the cheese.

Fresh Tomato and Basil Soup

SERVES 8

This is a great summertime soup, delicious served at any temperature. Finish chilled bowls of soup with a spoonful of balsamic vinegar and ribbons of fresh basil. Or on a cooler evening, serve the soup hot, topped with a dollop of crème fraîche or sour cream. Whatever the temperature of the soup, complete the meal with crisp breadsticks or slices of a simple focaccia.

We suggest plum tomatoes for this recipe, not only because of their sturdy flavor but also because they have fewer seeds; ripe beefsteak and other garden tomatoes are glorious, but you may want to seed them first.

◆◆◆◆◆◆

3 tablespoons olive oil
3 carrots, scrubbed and coarsely chopped
1 large onion, peeled and coarsely chopped
4 cups Vegetable Stock (page 271)
1 teaspoon fresh thyme leaves
¼ teaspoon paprika
1 cup tomato juice
3 pounds fresh plum tomatoes, peeled and coarsely chopped
1 cup loosely packed fresh basil leaves
Coarse (kosher) salt and freshly ground black pepper
Balsamic vinegar or Crème Fraîche (page 255), for garnish

◆◆◆◆◆◆

1. Heat the oil in a large stockpot over medium-high heat. Add the carrots and onion, and sauté until the onion is limp and translucent, about 5 minutes. Stir in the stock, thyme, and paprika, bring to a simmer, and cook, stirring occasionally, for another 10 minutes. Add the tomato juice, tomatoes, and half of the basil. Return to a simmer and cook, uncovered, until slightly thickened and fragrant, about 40 minutes. Remove from the heat and add the remaining basil, reserving 4 leaves for the final garnish.

2. In small batches, pulse the soup two or three times in a blender to form a slightly chunky purée.

3. *To serve the soup cold,* season it to taste with salt and pepper and refrigerate it overnight. Just before serving, slice the reserved basil leaves into fine ribbons. Ladle the chilled soup into individual bowls, drizzle a spoonful of balsamic vinegar over each, and finish with a few ribbons of basil.

To serve the soup hot, return the purée to the pot and reheat it gently, seasoning it to taste with salt and pepper. Slice the reserved basil into fine ribbons. Ladle the hot soup into individual bowls, top each one with a dollop of crème fraîche and a few basil ribbons, and serve immediately.

Bright Ideas

❦ Serve as a light sauce for pasta, topped with some toasted pine nuts.

❦ Serve warm or at room temperature as a sauce for crab cakes or grilled shrimp, tuna, or swordfish.

HOW TO PEEL A TOMATO

Score the blossom end of the tomato (opposite the stem) and drop it into a pot of boiling water. Blanch for 30 seconds (a bit less if the tomato is very ripe), and then transfer it to a bowl or sink filled with cold water. The skin will wrinkle immediately and slip off or peel away easily.

Golden Tomato Gazpacho

SERVES 6

Very elegant and pretty, this soup is a light meal in itself. You can use red tomatoes, but yellows are increasingly available, and their low acidity makes them very easy to digest. For hearty appetites, serve some thick slices of country bread that have been grilled or toasted and rubbed with split garlic cloves. You could simply use ground cumin to season the soup, but you'll get the most flavor if you start with the whole seed and toast it.

◆◆◆◆◆◆

3 pounds ripe golden tomatoes, cored, seeded, and coarsely chopped

1 small Spanish onion, peeled and coarsely chopped

2 large cloves garlic, peeled

1 yellow bell pepper, stemmed, seeded, and coarsely chopped

½ cup extra-virgin olive oil

3 tablespoons white wine vinegar

¼ teaspoon whole cumin seeds, toasted (see Toasting Spices, page 94)

1 teaspoon coarse (kosher) salt, or more as needed

1 cucumber, peeled, seeded, and diced

¼ cup diced red bell pepper

⅓ cup finely chopped fresh cilantro, chervil, or Italian (flat-leaf) parsley

◆◆◆◆◆◆

TOASTING SPICES

As with nuts, a quick toasting of whole spices accents and enlivens their flavor. A skillet is the most convenient tool for toasting small batches at home. Simply scatter the seeds into a small skillet placed over medium heat, and stirring occasionally, cook the seeds until they are fragrant and toasty brown, 2 to 3 minutes. Use the seeds whole, or crush into a coarse powder using a rolling pin or a mortar and pestle.

1. Working in batches, place the tomatoes, onion, garlic, yellow bell pepper, oil, vinegar, cumin, and salt in a food processor or blender, and pulse to coarsely chop. Transfer to a large bowl.

2. Season to taste with additional salt as needed. Stir in the cucumber and refrigerate, covered, for at least 4 hours.

3. Pour or ladle the soup into chilled bowls, sprinkle with the red bell pepper and cilantro, and serve immediately.

Bright Ideas

❦ Add tender cooked white beans for a more substantial vegetarian entrée.

❦ Serve as a refreshing relish for tuna steaks or grilled shrimp.

❦ Make quick fajitas by rolling slices of charred flank steak or London broil in warm flour tortillas and spreading them with a little Golden Gazpacho topping.

Variation

◆ **Gazpacho with Scallop Ceviche:** Turn Golden Gazpacho into a real event by adding a ceviche of either 1 pound of bay scallops or sea scallops: Leave bay scallops whole; if using sea scallops, cut them crosswise into thin medallions. In a mixing bowl, combine the scallops with 3 finely chopped scallions and enough freshly squeezed lime juice (5 or 6 limes) to cover completely. Refrigerate, covered, for 4 hours. As soon as the flesh of the scallops has become completely opaque, remove them from the juice, pat them dry, and roll them in finely chopped fresh Italian (flat-leaf) parsley or cilantro. Float a few scallops on top of each bowl of gazpacho, and serve.

Oven-Charred Vegetable Soup

SERVES 6 TO 8

This is a relatively new invention at Hay Day, great year-round but best at the end of summer when you can bring the vegetables straight in from the garden, give them a quick wash, and toss them with a little olive oil and coarse salt. We use sweet little cipollini onions, which are a good size for roasting, but quartered Spanish onions will do just fine. Turn the soup into a meal by serving some toasted bread rounds spread with a creamy fresh goat cheese.

◆◆◆◆◆◆

1 small eggplant (just under 1 pound), unpeeled, cut into 1-inch chunks

1 red bell pepper, stemmed, seeded, and coarsely chopped

8 ounces cipollini onions (see About Cipollini Onions), peeled

1 pound ripe plum tomatoes (about 6 large tomatoes), quartered

1 large zucchini (just under 1 pound), cut into 1-inch chunks

3 large cloves garlic, peeled

⅓ cup olive oil

Coarse (kosher) salt and freshly ground black pepper

1 tablespoon chopped fresh rosemary

3 cups Chicken Stock (page 270) or Vegetable Stock (page 271)

◆◆◆◆◆◆

1. Preheat the oven to 400°F.

2. Combine the vegetables and garlic in a large bowl. Toss with the oil, 1 teaspoon salt, and several grindings of black pepper.

3. Spread the seasoned vegetables in a single layer on a large baking sheet or jelly roll pan, and roast for 20 minutes. Sprinkle the rosemary over the vegetables and continue roasting until they are nicely charred around the edges, another 15 to 25 minutes.

4. Remove the vegetables from the oven and set aside a few charred morsels for garnish. Using a large spatula, transfer half the vegetables to a blender, scraping up and adding any caramelized bits clinging to the pan. Add ½ cup of the

stock and purée the mixture. Transfer the purée to a soup pot and repeat with the remaining vegetables and another ½ cup stock.

5. Add enough of the remaining 2 cups stock to thin the soup to the desired consistency, and heat thoroughly over low heat. Season to taste with salt and pepper. Ladle the hot soup into individual bowls, and garnish each serving with a few of the reserved roasted vegetable morsels.

Bright Ideas

❧ Use as a sauce for grilled fish, lamb, or even a grilled fillet of beef.

❧ Spoon over warm pasta and top with a bit of crumbled aged goat cheese.

ABOUT CIPOLLINI ONIONS

They look a bit like baby onions, but cipollini are actually the bulbs of a flowering plant native to the Italian Mediterranean. You'll often see them, already prepared, in specialty markets, but the fresh ones are turning up more often on produce stands, since cipollini seeds are now being planted in American soil. Their distinctive disk-shaped bulbs are harvested throughout the autumn months. Fresh cipollini are sweet and tender, and delicious simply peeled, drizzled with a bit of good olive oil, and braised or oven-roasted. Cipollini can be either yellow or red; the red are even a bit sweeter.

Breads

Ham and Cheddar Scones

MAKES 8 LARGE SCONES

The visual impact of these scones will be heightened if you use a bright orange Wisconsin or New York Cheddar, but their flavor will be fine with whatever good-quality sharp Cheddar comes to hand. They are moist and tender and will keep well for a couple of days; toast them lightly on the second day to perk up their flavor and texture.

◆◆◆◆◆◆

2 cups unbleached all-purpose flour
2 teaspoons sugar
½ teaspoon salt
1 tablespoon baking powder
¼ teaspoon cayenne pepper
6 tablespoons (¾ stick) unsalted butter, chilled
3 ounces sharp Cheddar cheese, shredded (1 lightly packed cup shredded)
4 ounces baked Virginia or Black Forest ham, diced
1 egg
Scant ⅔ cup milk, plus 2 tablespoons for glaze (see Note)

◆◆◆◆◆◆

1. Preheat the oven to 400°F.

2. Toss the flour, sugar, salt, baking powder, and cayenne together in a large bowl or in a food processor. Cut the butter into several pieces and add them to the dry ingredients. Using a hand-held pastry blender, two knives, or the food processor, work in the butter until the bits are no larger than small grains of rice. Transfer the mixture to a large bowl, add the cheese and ham, and toss, separating any clumps of cheese that form.

3. Whisk the egg and ⅔ cup milk together in a small bowl, and add to the dry ingredients. Stir until the dry ingredients are moistened and a soft dough forms (the dough should be slightly tacky and crumbly). With lightly floured hands, gather the dough together. Using the palm of your hand, press it out on an ungreased or parchment-lined baking sheet to form an 8-inch round.

BAKING WITH PARCHMENT

We recommend baking on parchment paper for ease and for simple cleanup. It's particularly convenient when you are glazing baked goods, since the unavoidable spillage around the edges is apt to caramelize and fuse the pastries to the pan, making both removal and cleanup more difficult.

If you are using a plain ungreased baking sheet, take care to brush the milk or glaze neatly on top in order to avoid excess runoff.

4. If you like your scones to have crisp edges, use a long sharp knife or a dough cutter to divide the round into eight equal wedges. Pull the wedges apart. If you prefer tender edges, leave the round intact and simply score the divisions with the knife. Brush with the 2 tablespoons milk, and bake until lightly browned and nearly doubled in size, 18 to 20 minutes. Serve warm or at room temperature.

Note: In our bakeries we always use whole milk for the tenderest pastry, but at home 1 percent or 2 percent makes a fine stand-in. Do avoid using skim milk in baking, however.

ABOUT SAGE

Look for bottles labeled "rubbed sage" when buying the herb. Any type should be fine, but crumbled or "rubbed" leaves have more volatile aromatic oils than the powdered kind.

Parmesan-Sage Biscuits

MAKES 8 TO 10 BISCUITS

Thyme, sage, and Parmesan flavor these tall, flaky biscuits—exceptional with soup for brunch or with a classic omelet or frittata. In an ideal world, biscuits are always served piping hot right from the oven, but these will be fine on the second day if you perk them up with a light oven toasting.

◆◆◆◆◆◆

2 cups unbleached all-purpose flour
1 tablespoon baking powder
¾ teaspoon salt
5 tablespoons unsalted butter, chilled, cut into chunks
2 tablespoons solid vegetable shortening, chilled, cut into chunks
½ cup freshly grated Parmesan cheese
1 teaspoon dried thyme
1 teaspoon dried sage (see About Sage)
¾ teaspoon freshly ground black pepper
¾ cup milk (see Note, left)
¼ cup fine cornmeal, for dusting
1 tablespoon unsalted butter, melted

◆◆◆◆◆◆

1. Preheat the oven to 400°F.

2. Combine the flour, baking powder, and salt in a food processor. Add the butter and shortening, and pulse until the bits are no larger than small grains of rice. Transfer to a large mixing bowl and add the cheese, thyme, sage, and pepper; toss to mix.

3. Add the milk and stir it in gently, using a large spoon or spatula, just until all the dry ingredients are moistened and a soft, slightly crumbly dough forms.

4. Dust a work surface with the cornmeal. Turn the dough out onto the work surface and gather it up into a ball. Roll the dough out to form a ½-inch-thick rectangle. Fold the short ends of the rectangle to meet in the middle; then fold it in half at the seam to create four layers.

A NOTE ON BISCUITS

Biscuits transform soup or a salad into lunch. The method described in the two biscuit recipes in this chapter may appear more labor-intensive than conventional directions, but it is not difficult. Rolling and folding biscuit dough to suspend the shortening in layers is a technique we've followed over the years, and there is absolutely no question that it produces taller, flakier biscuits.

Biscuits are only as light as the flour that goes into them, so avoid heavy, high-protein bread flour. Use an all-purpose flour with a maximum of 12 grams of protein per cup—any more than that and the biscuits won't be tender and flaky.

In an ideal world, biscuits and scones are always served piping hot from the oven, but they last beautifully for another day or two. Just before serving preheat the oven to 350°F and place the biscuits directly on the oven rack. Heat until they are warm and lightly crisp around the edges, 5 to 8 minutes.

Like scones, biscuits should be baked on ungreased pans, which allow them to get a grip on the bottom surface and rise more efficiently. To split these flaky biscuits, just pull the layers apart with your fingers or split them with a fork as you would an English muffin. Splitting them with a knife will crush the tender layers.

Roll the dough out again to form a ½-inch-thick rectangle.

5. Grease and flour a 2½-inch biscuit cutter and neatly cut the dough into rounds. Reflour the cutter after each cut, and do not twist as you cut, or you will compress the biscuit layers. Pinch together the remaining scraps of dough, fold in half, reroll, and cut out additional biscuits. Place the cut biscuits on an ungreased baking sheet, and brush the tops with the melted butter. Bake until roughly doubled in height and nicely browned on top, 12 to 15 minutes.

Bright Idea

❦ Split the biscuits and fill them with sliced tomato and ham for little teatime sandwiches, or what the Italians call *panini*.

Cheddar-Chive Biscuits

MAKES 8 TO 10 BISCUITS

At Hay Day we make these tall, flaky biscuits with an extra-sharp, bright orange aged Cheddar for color and flavor. They are divine served hot with soup, chili, or chowder, or with ham and scrambled eggs for brunch (they make great mini sandwiches, too).

◆◆◆◆◆◆

2 cups unbleached all-purpose flour

1 tablespoon baking powder

¾ teaspoon salt

3 tablespoons unsalted butter, chilled, cut into small pieces

2 tablespoons solid vegetable shortening, chilled

2 tablespoons finely chopped fresh chives

3 ounces aged New York Cheddar cheese, shredded (1 lightly packed cup, shredded)

¾ cup milk

1 tablespoon unsalted butter, melted

◆◆◆◆◆◆

1. Preheat the oven to 400°F.

2. Combine the flour, baking powder, and salt in a food processor. Add the butter and shortening and pulse until the bits are no larger than small grains of rice. Transfer to a large mixing bowl and add the chives and cheese; toss to mix.

3. Add the milk and stir it in gently using a large spoon or spatula, just until all the dry ingredients are moistened and a soft, slightly crumbly dough forms.

4. Dust a work surface lightly with flour. Turn the dough out onto the work surface and gather it up into a ball. Roll the dough out to form a ½-inch-thick rectangle. Fold the short ends of the rectangle in to meet in the middle; then fold the dough in half at the seam to create four layers. Roll the dough out to form a ½-inch-thick rectangle.

5. Grease and flour a 2½-inch biscuit cutter, and neatly cut the dough into rounds. Reflour the cutter after each cut, and do not twist as you cut or you will compress the biscuit layers. Pinch together the remaining scraps of dough, fold in half, reroll, and cut additional biscuits. Place the biscuits on an ungreased baking sheet, and brush the tops with the melted butter. Bake until roughly doubled in height and nicely browned on top, 12 to 15 minutes.

A NOTE ON ORANGE CHEDDAR

For centuries, Cheddar-makers in many regions have colored their cheeses with annato seeds, a natural vegetable coloring. The custom originated in England (as did Cheddar, of course), when cheesemakers sought to give their winter cheeses the rich glow that occurred naturally in the milk from cows grazing in summer pastures. In later years the bright orange color became a hallmark of English cheeses like Double Gloucester, and of American Cheddars from Wisconsin and parts of upstate New York, but the color is just a sort of trademark—it has nothing whatever to do with quality, age, taste, or texture.

Everybody's Favorite Peasant Bread

MAKES 2 LOAVES

Peasant Bread was Hay Day's very first bread twenty years ago, and it was an immediate hit—people love it for both toast and sandwiches. After all these years, this is the first time we've printed the recipe. It's a soft pan bread that, unlike crusty hearth breads, keeps well when wrapped in plastic. The unusual combination of yeast and baking soda gives it a chewy, moist English-muffin texture. Peasant Bread is unconventional—it is too sticky to be kneaded by hand. Slow stirring replaces the kneading process to develop the gluten (and therefore the structural strength) in the dough. In the Hay Day bakeries we bake Peasant Bread as a round loaf, but the size of pan we use isn't readily available to home cooks. So, we suggest you use a standard loaf pan instead.

◆◆◆◆◆◆

1½ cups hot water (105° to 115°F)
2 tablespoons sugar
1 package (2¼ teaspoons) active dry
  yeast
¼ teaspoon baking soda
¾ cup cool water
5½ to 6½ cups unbleached all-purpose
  flour
2 teaspoons coarse (kosher) salt
1 tablespoon unsalted butter, melted

◆◆◆◆◆◆

1. Combine the hot water, sugar, and yeast in a large mixing bowl. Stir quickly

MEASURING FLOUR

When measuring flour for baking, always use the scoop-and-sweep method (empty the flour into a large bowl, scoop with a large spoon, sprinkle into the measuring cup, and level or sweep off with the flat side of a knife). Even then, variations in the exact quantity may occur with changes in the weather (specifically the humidity) and in the brand of flour. For the most consistent results, stick to one brand and pay careful attention to the look and feel of your dough.

to dissolve the yeast and sugar; let stand until the mixture is nice and bubbly on top, 5 minutes.

2. In a small bowl, dissolve the baking soda in the cool water. Combine with the yeast mixture.

3. In a large bowl, stir 5 cups of the flour with the salt. Over a period of 10 to 15 minutes, gradually stir the flour into the liquid, using a large wooden spoon or the paddle attachment on a heavy-duty mixer set on low speed. The mixture should form an elastic dough that just begins to ball up and pull away from the sides of the bowl in ribbons. Work in enough of the remaining flour with your hands to form a firm yet sticky dough that comes together in a ball. It should not be as firm as traditional bread dough and will be too sticky to knead in the traditional manner. Cover the bowl loosely with a clean kitchen towel, and set it aside to rest at room temperature until the dough has doubled in size, 1 to 1½ hours.

4. Butter two 5- to 6-cup loaf pans.

5. Using buttered hands, turn the dough from the bowl onto a lightly floured surface, and divide it in half. Shape the halves and tuck them inside the prepared pans. Set the loaves aside, uncovered, in a warm, draft-free corner of the kitchen until they have doubled in size and risen about 1 inch above the sides of the pans, about 2 hours.

6. Preheat the oven to 400°F.

7. Brush the tops of the loaves with the melted butter, arrange the pans on a baking sheet, and bake until crisp and nicely browned on top, 30 minutes. (The loaves will not have risen further.) To test for doneness, tap the bottom of a loaf. If it

ABOUT YEAST

In Hay Day's production bakery, we use compressed cake yeast for its reliable fast action and mild flavor. But for occasional home baking, active dry yeast is the most readily available version. Fleischmann's and Red Star are two trustworthy brands. Be sure to check the expiration date on the back of the package, and store the yeast, well sealed, in a cool, dark section of the refrigerator. If the yeast does not foam and bubble once combined with liquid and sugar, discard it and start over with a fresh batch.

sounds hollow, the bread is done. Turn them out of the pans to cool on a wire rack. The lightly crisp crust will soften as the loaves cool. Slice thickly and use for toast and sandwiches. Everybody's Favorite Peasant Bread will keep well for 2 or 3 days, stored in an airtight plastic bag or in plastic wrap.

Variations

◆ **Whole-Wheat Cinnamon Raisin Peasant Bread.** A favorite Sunday-morning variation, this is delicious toasted and served with blueberry, peach, or apricot preserves. Or slice it thickly and use it for very special peanut butter and honey or cream cheese and jam sandwiches.

Substitute the following:

1 cup stone-ground whole-wheat flour for 1 cup of the all-purpose.

Add 1 tablespoon ground cinnamon to the dry ingredients.

Decrease the salt to 1 teaspoon.

Increase the sugar to 3 tablespoons.

Mix 2 cups raisins into the dough just before the first rising.

◆ **Herbed Peasant Bread.** A flavorful, chewy loaf speckled and seasoned with fresh herbs, this variation is possibly even more popular than the original. Its flavor adds style to just about any meal. It's a great way to dress up a bowl of homemade soup, and it's delicious for turkey, roast beef, or cheese sandwiches. It's our favorite choice for summer tomato and cucumber sandwiches. You can cube and toast any leftovers to make delicious salad croutons.

Before the first rising, stir 3 tablespoons each of chopped fresh dill, parsley, and scallions into the dough. (Rinse and dry the herbs thoroughly before chopping.)

Whole-Meal Bread

MAKES 2 LOAVES

This is one of Hay Day's signature breads. It was printed in our first cookbook, and it got so much fan mail that we're including it here. The rich flavors of whole wheat and molasses go well with winter soups, and the bread makes fantastic grilled cheese sandwiches.

◆◆◆◆◆◆

1 cup milk
1 cup cold water
1/4 cup safflower oil or unsalted butter
1/4 cup blackstrap molasses (see Note)
1/4 cup unsulfured molasses
1 tablespoon coarse (kosher) salt
1 tablespoon (1 package plus
   3/4 teaspoon) active dry yeast
1/4 cup hot water
2 cups whole-wheat flour
3 1/2 to 4 cups unbleached all-purpose
   flour

◆◆◆◆◆◆

1. Combine the milk, cold water, oil, blackstrap and unsulfured molasses, and salt in a saucepan. Place over medium heat and stir until melted and combined; then remove from the heat.

2. In a large mixing bowl, stir the yeast into the hot water; let stand until nice and bubbly on top, about 5 minutes. Then add the contents of the saucepan.

3. Using a large wooden spoon or the paddle attachment of a heavy-duty mixer set on low speed, gradually stir in all the whole-wheat flour and 3 1/2 cups of the all-purpose flour to make a stiff dough that easily pulls away from the sides of the bowl. Add more all-purpose flour, if necessary.

4. Turn the dough out on a lightly floured surface and knead until it is smooth and elastic, about 10 minutes. Place the dough in an oiled bowl and turn it to coat all surfaces. Cover with a kitchen towel and set aside in a warm draft-free spot until the dough has doubled in volume, 1 1/2 to 2 hours.

5. Lightly oil two 8-cup loaf pans.

6. Turn the dough out of the bowl, divide it in half, and shape the halves into loaves. Tuck them into the prepared loaf pans, cover loosely with a clean kitchen towel, and allow to rise again until doubled, 2 to 2 1/2 hours.

7. Preheat the oven to 350°F.

8. Bake the loaves until risen and nicely browned, about 45 minutes. To test for doneness, tap the bottom of a loaf. If it sounds hollow, the bread is done. Immediately turn the loaves out of the pans and set them to cool on a wire rack.

Note: Available at any health-food store, blackstrap molasses is a rich source of iron. You can skip it and use 1/2 cup unsulfured molasses, but the bread won't have the dark color and rich flavor it gets from the combination of the two. On the other hand, don't be overzealous and use only the blackstrap—it will inhibit the action of the yeast.

Hay Day's Best-Ever Potato Bread

MAKES 3 LOAVES

Made with chunks of high-starch russet potatoes, this cousin of brioche is easy to prepare and keeps beautifully. Try making it with sweet potatoes in the fall and winter for a richly colored bread that makes incredible toast. Potato bread recipes are not uncommon, but this one is amazing. It's so good that our friend Lydie Marshall included it in her book *A Passion for Potatoes*.

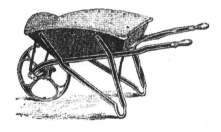

◆◆◆◆◆◆

1 pound russet potatoes or orange-
  fleshed sweet potatoes (about 2 large)
1 cup milk
8 tablespoons (1 stick) unsalted butter
4 teaspoons coarse (kosher) salt
8 tablespoons sugar
1 package (2¹⁄₄ teaspoons) active
  dry yeast
2 large eggs, lightly beaten
6 to 7 cups unbleached all-purpose flour

◆◆◆◆◆◆

1. Scrub and quarter the potatoes, leaving the skins on. Place them in a saucepan and add water to cover. Bring to a boil, partially cover, and cook until just fork-tender (not mushy!), 12 to 15 minutes. Drain the potatoes into a colander or sieve placed over a large bowl to catch the cooking water. Measure out ¹⁄₂ cup of the cooking water and discard the rest. When the potatoes are cool enough to handle, crumble them into small pieces.

2. Return the potatoes to the saucepan and set aside.

3. Combine the milk and butter in a small saucepan over low heat. When the butter has melted, add the salt and stir to dissolve. Set aside and allow to cool to room temperature.

4. Meanwhile, pour the reserved potato water into a large mixing bowl. The potato water should be warm, not hot; if you need to cool it more quickly, put it in the refrigerator for a few minutes. Stir 1 tablespoon of the sugar and the yeast into the potato water. Let it stand until nice and bubbly on top, about 5 minutes. Then add the milk mixture, eggs, potatoes, and the remaining 7 tablespoons sugar. Using a large wooden spoon or mixer set on low speed, stir to roughly combine. Gradually stir 6 cups of the flour into the mixture. Then work in enough of the remaining 1 cup flour with your hands until the dough is firm and pulls away from the sides of the bowl. Form the dough into a ball, return it to the bowl, cover the bowl loosely with plastic wrap, and set aside to rest at room temperature until the dough is doubled in size, 1 to 1¹⁄₂ hours.

5. Generously butter three 6-cup loaf pans.

6. Remove the dough from the bowl and place it on a lightly floured surface. Divide it into three portions, shape them into loaves, and gently tuck the loaves into the prepared loaf pans. Once again, cover and set aside until the dough has doubled in size and reaches up to the rims of the pans, 1½ to 2 hours.

7. Preheat the oven to 350°F.

8. Bake the loaves until nicely risen and golden brown on top, 40 to 45 minutes. To test for doneness, tap the bottom of a loaf. If it sounds hollow, the bread is done. Let the loaves rest in the pans for 15 minutes; then turn them out on a wire rack to cool.

Salads for All Seasons

What's a salad? Certainly not just the traditional lettuce tossed in a vinaigrette. Hay Day Salads are really compositions—some artfully arranged, some tossed casually together—all inspired by the cornucopia of fresh seasonal vegetables and grains we find in the markets every day.

These salads are wonderfully versatile. They're great on picnics, or served as side dishes with simple entrées, and many—like Spinach and Citrus Salad, for example, or Peppered Peach and Vidalia Onion Salad—are easy to assemble and serve on individual plates as an appetizer.

Unlike green salads, which wilt in a vinaigrette, most of these salads are even better with a little mellowing—even for a day or so. They're all designed to be made ahead of time and served chilled or at room temperature. Above all, like everything else at Hay Day, they celebrate the pleasure of cooking with fresh produce and other superb ingredients. We know from experience that after a long day in the office or the carpool, it can be truly therapeutic to spend quality time with beautiful vegetables!

New Potatoes and Fiddlehead Ferns

SERVES 4

Serving fiddleheads will win you points for creativity. Their flavor is somewhere between asparagus and string beans, and they bring a springtime accent to this warm salad—which would go beautifully with poached salmon. You can also serve the salad over a bed of tender young greens for a delightful springtime starter.

◆◆◆◆◆◆

1 pound tiny new potatoes, scrubbed, trimmed, and sliced in half if larger than a marble (see About "New" Potatoes, page 109)
5 ounces fiddlehead ferns, cleaned, rinsed well, and trimmed (2 generous cups; see About Fiddleheads)
1 tablespoon red wine vinegar
3 tablespoons extra-virgin olive oil
1 teaspoon fresh lemon juice
1 teaspoon Dijon mustard
12 large cornichon pickles
Coarse (kosher) salt and freshly ground black pepper
½ cup coarsely chopped fresh Italian (flat-leaf) parsley
1 hard-cooked egg, chopped

◆◆◆◆◆◆

1. Pour water to a depth of 1 inch in a large pot. Set a large steamer basket inside the pot and fill with the potatoes and fiddlehead ferns. Bring the water to a boil, reduce the heat, cover, and steam until the potatoes are fork-tender and the ferns are bright green and crisp-tender, 8 to 10 minutes. Remove the vegetables from the steamer and place them in a large serving bowl.

2. Meanwhile, combine the vinegar, oil, lemon juice, and mustard in a food processor or blender. Add 6 cornichon pickles and blend to form a chunky purée. Season to taste with salt and pepper, then pour over the potatoes and fiddleheads. Add the parsley and toss.

3. Thinly slice the remaining cornichons. Serve the salad either warm or at room temperature, topped with the chopped egg and sliced cornichons.

ABOUT FIDDLEHEADS

Fiddleheads, the first tender shoots of the ostrich fern, come into the market during April and May. Because the ferns must be picked while their tops are still tightly furled, their season is short. Fiddleheads often have a papery brown skin protecting their green coils; rub it away before rinsing them well. Choose bright green, firm fiddleheads that are not much larger than a quarter in diameter, and trim the stems to within half an inch of the coil. Then steam or boil them until tender throughout, 8 to 10 minutes. Drain and serve warm, tossed with melted butter and lemon, or at room temperature or chilled, dressed in a light vinaigrette.

Purple Potato and Snap Pea Salad

SERVES 6 TO 8

Potato salads made with vinaigrettes are wonderfully light. This one is spectacular when made with Peruvian Purple potatoes, but any variety of new potato will be fine. The effect will be most vivid if you toss in the snap peas just before serving—otherwise the acid in the dressing will fade their brilliant color.

◆◆◆◆◆◆

2 pounds purple-skin new potatoes, scrubbed, trimmed, and cut into large bite-size chunks
2 tablespoons white wine vinegar
1 generous tablespoon finely minced shallots
Juice and grated zest of 1 large lemon (see About Zest, page 229)
⅓ cup extra-virgin olive oil
½ teaspoon sugar
Coarse (kosher) salt and freshly ground black pepper
12 ounces sugar snap peas, trimmed, blanched, and refreshed in cold water (see Note)
¼ cup finely minced fresh chives

◆◆◆◆◆◆

1. Place the potatoes in a large pot and cover with cold water. Lightly salt the water and bring to a boil. Reduce the heat, and simmer, partially covered, until fork-tender, about 7 minutes. Drain and transfer to a large bowl. While the potatoes are still warm, sprinkle the vinegar over them. Toss, and set aside to cool to room temperature.

2. Whisk the shallots, lemon juice, lemon zest, oil, and sugar together in a small bowl. Season to taste with salt and pepper.

3. Add the snap peas and chives to the bowl of potatoes. Sprinkle with the dressing and toss. Season to taste with additional salt and pepper, and serve at room temperature. (If you prefer to serve the salad chilled, add the snap peas just before serving.)

Note: The fully edible pods of sugar snap peas require hardly any cooking. In fact, raw sugar snaps make a delightful and nutritious springtime snack. However, a brief blanching (no more than 30 seconds) in a large pot of lightly salted boiling water brings up their brightest shade of green and heightens the sweetness. As with asparagus and other green vegetables, the blanched vegetables should be quickly cooled in a pot of cold water to set the color and stop the cooking.

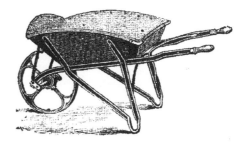

Buttermilk Ranch Potato Salad

SERVES 6 TO 8

Creamy, tangy Buttermilk Ranch is one of our most popular and versatile dressings. It's great drizzled over sliced tomatoes or tossed into a chicken, pasta, potato, or green salad. The rich flavor and creamy texture of Yukon Gold potatoes makes them ideal for this slightly crumbly American-style potato salad; their butter-yellow color makes them decorative as well. Yukon Golds are usually available in good produce stores beginning in the spring, but any other medium-starch potato will work just as well.

◆◆◆◆◆◆

*3 pounds Yukon Gold potatoes,
  peeled and cut into 1-inch dice*
¾ cup buttermilk
¾ cup mayonnaise
1 tablespoon cider vinegar
1 large clove garlic, peeled and minced
1 teaspoon fresh lemon juice
*2 tablespoons chopped fresh Italian
  (flat-leaf) parsley*
*2 scallions, white and light green
  parts finely chopped*
1 teaspoon olive oil
*1 fresh poblano chile, stemmed, seeded,
  and coarsely chopped (see About
  Poblano Chiles, page 148)*
*1 small red onion, peeled, halved
  lengthwise, and sliced into thin
  crescents*
Freshly ground black pepper
*4 thick-cut slices smoked bacon, cooked
  until very crisp, crumbled*

◆◆◆◆◆◆

1. Place the potatoes in a large pot and cover with cold water. Lightly salt the water and bring to a boil. Reduce the heat, and simmer, partially covered, until fork-tender, 12 to 15 minutes.

2. Meanwhile, whisk together the buttermilk, mayonnaise, vinegar, garlic, lemon juice, parsley, and scallions in a small bowl.

3. Drain the potatoes, transfer them to a large bowl, and pour the dressing over them while they are still warm. Toss and set aside. (It may seem that there is too much dressing at first, but the hot potatoes will absorb quite a bit of the liquid.)

4. Heat the oil in a large skillet and sauté the poblano chile until slightly softened but still crisp, about 2 minutes. Add it to the potatoes along with the red onion, and toss to combine well. Season to taste with black pepper. Cover and refrigerate to chill for at least 2 hours. Just before serving, top with the crumbled bacon.

Sweet Potato Salad

SERVES 8

If you think nothing can take the place of a favorite traditional potato salad, wait until you try this one. The festive combination of sweet potatoes, dried fruits, and nuts in a mustard vinaigrette

ABOUT "NEW" POTATOES

What exactly are "new" potatoes? First of all, they aren't always red-skinned. They're simply "new crop" potatoes—of any variety and size, though they're usually small. They are thin skinned, tender, low in starch, and unbelievably fresh-tasting because they have been harvested from a growing potato plant. These qualities make them ideal for steaming, boiling, braising, oven-roasting—and for use in salads because they don't soak up all the dressing the way a high-starch potato would.

Fully grown mature potatoes are dug at the end of the season, when the dying plants have turned yellow and brown. Potatoes like the all-purpose Yukon Golds and Idaho Russets are harvested at this point and have a higher starch content, making them ideal for baking, mashing, and frying.

Although all potatoes are relatively good keepers (if stored in a cool, dry environment), spring is the primary harvest season for new crop potatoes and therefore the time to enjoy them at their peak. These days we have a wonderful selection of potato varieties in a rainbow of colors, with names like Peruvian Purple, Cherry Red, Yellow Finn, Russian Banana, All Blue, and the already noted Yukon Gold. Because new potatoes are freshly dug and delicate, they're often still colored with some of the earth they grew in. Scrub the skin well with a vegetable brush under running water, and enjoy the potatoes, skin and all. Be sure to select very firm smooth-skinned "new" potatoes with few eyes.

---

has become a staple on the Hay Day fall menu. It is a natural for a Thanksgiving buffet, but make it a day ahead so the flavors can develop.

◆◆◆◆◆◆

4 orange-fleshed sweet potatoes,
*   peeled and cut into ½-inch dice*
*   (see Sweet Potatoes, page 202)*
1 tablespoon Dijon mustard
¼ cup cider vinegar
¼ cup honey
⅓ cup vegetable oil
⅔ cup diced red onion
½ cup dried cranberries
⅓ cup dried currants
⅔ cup coarsely chopped pecans,
*   preferably lightly toasted*
*   (see Toasting Nuts, page 55)*

◆◆◆◆◆◆

1. Bring water to a boil in a vegetable steamer. Put the sweet potatoes in the steamer basket, cover, and steam until just fork-tender, about 20 minutes.

2. Meanwhile, whisk the mustard, vinegar, honey, and oil together in a small bowl until smooth.

3. In a large bowl, combine the red onion, cranberries, and currants. Add the steamed sweet potatoes along with the honey mustard dressing, and toss to coat evenly. Chill for at least 1 hour before serving. Just before serving, toss in the pecans.

Mediterranean Crouton Salad

SERVES 6 TO 8

A bright summer variation on Italian *panzanella* or Middle Eastern *fatoush*, this is simply an assemblage of chopped fresh vegetables, good olive oil, green herbs, and chunks of crisp bread (day-old hearth bread, toasted pita wedges, or baked unseasoned croutons) to add texture and soak up all the divine juices. Add olives and some crumbled aged chèvre (Bûcheron, for example) or feta, and it's a full-dress salad for a luncheon or light supper.

The flavor of the oil really stands out in straightforward salads like this, so now's the time to use that cold-pressed extra-virgin olive oil you've been saving since Christmas.

❖❖❖❖❖❖

1 English (hothouse) cucumber, peeled and coarsely chopped

1 red bell pepper, stemmed, seeded, and coarsely chopped

1 yellow bell pepper, stemmed, seeded, and coarsely chopped

2 large ripe tomatoes, cored, seeded, and coarsely chopped

6 scallions, white and light green parts chopped

1 large bunch fresh Italian (flat-leaf) parsley, coarsely chopped

¼ cup chopped fresh mint leaves

Juice of 1 large lemon

⅓ cup extra-virgin olive oil

1 tablespoon crushed sumac berries (optional; see About Sumac)

Coarse (kosher) salt and freshly ground black pepper

2 cups Oven-Baked Croutons (unseasoned; page 253) or crumbled shards of toasted pita bread

❖❖❖❖❖❖

ABOUT SUMAC

Sumac (*not* our roadside version!) is the dark reddish-purple berry of a shrub that grows throughout the Middle East, where it is ground and kept on the table, like salt. It has a pleasantly tart lemony flavor that goes well with salads or on roast chicken or vegetables. Ground sumac will stay fresh and flavorful for a good long time in an airtight jar in a cool, dark spice cupboard. You can find it in specialty markets and through mail-order catalogs.

1. Toss the cucumber, bell peppers, tomatoes, scallions, parsley, and mint in a large serving bowl. Sprinkle with the lemon juice and oil, and toss to coat evenly. Toss in the sumac if you are using it, and season to taste with salt and pepper. Chill, covered, until ready to serve. (The salad can be prepared to this point up to 6 hours in advance.)

SOME SERIOUS THOUGHTS ABOUT TOMATOES

First rule: Don't store tomatoes in the refrigerator. The aroma of a vine-picked tomato can be maintained at room temperature while the fruit is ripening, but it evaporates quickly in the refrigerator and is not replaced. So keep whole fresh tomatoes at room temperature. Refrigerate them only in an effort to maintain very ripe or sliced or chopped fruit.

Now. According to a recent Harvard study, reported in *The New York Times,* significant health benefits accrue from eating tomatoes (raw or cooked) about seven times a week, but only if they are consumed with a little fat at the same time. Tomatoes contain a carotenoid called lycopene, which makes them red (that's right—yellow and green tomatoes,

therefore, don't count), and since it is fat-soluble, its absorption into the body is enhanced when a little fat is consumed as well. We all know that nutrition theories come and go, but isn't it interesting how the Mediterranean diet seems to survive? It wasn't so long ago that we learned that pasta and beans are better eaten together (proving the worth of *pasta e fagioli*); now we have the reason for pizza with Parmesan, and for tomato slices with olive oil and mozzarella.

For the ultimate in tomato enjoyment, slice a ripe fresh-from-the-garden tomato just before serving. The aroma will be its peak—and your nose is every bit as important as your tastebuds in delivering the real tomato experience.

2. Shortly before serving, toss in the croutons. Allow just enough time for the croutons to absorb some of the juices yet still remain fairly crisp. Serve immediately.

Summer Corn and Tomato Salad

SERVES 8 TO 10

Some of the dishes we sell at Hay Day are really simple to make. Customers buy them from us to save time, but it really takes little effort to chop four tomatoes and cut the kernels off ten ears of corn. The reward is a wonderful (and highly portable) summer salad to make ahead for picnics and cookouts.

5 cups fresh corn kernels
   (from about 10 large ears)
¼ cup safflower or canola oil
3 tablespoons raspberry vinegar
Juice of 1 lime
Coarse (kosher) salt and freshly
   ground black pepper
4 ripe tomatoes, cored, seeded, and
   coarsely chopped
10 scallions, white and light green
   parts chopped
⅓ cup chopped fresh cilantro

◆◆◆◆◆◆

1. Bring salted water to a boil in a vegetable steamer. Put the corn kernels in the steamer basket, cover, and steam until just crisp-tender, 3 to 5 minutes.

FRESH MOZZARELLA

Technically speaking, mozzarella is a spun-curd cows'-milk cheese. The aged version is familiar melted on pizza, but the fresh version, which comes packed in its own whey or brine, is very different. Often packaged and labeled as *fiore de latte*, fresh mozzarella is lightly salted, with a delicate flavor and creamy texture. It is not dense enough to melt really well. Instead, it comes into its own when combined in salads with fresh vegetables and vinaigrettes; marinated, it makes a wonderful addition to an antipasto platter.

Mozzarella di bufala is fresh cheese made from the milk of water buffalo; it is flown in from Italy. For this reason you'll pay a premium price for it, but it does have a rich flavor unequaled by cow's-milk mozzarella. However, be aware that mozzarella di bufala is quite perishable and should be purchased as fresh as possible. Buy it only from a reputable cheese shop. Fresh mozzarella, whether made from cow's or buffalo's milk, should be moist, sweet, and tender, yet firm enough to be sliced and enjoyed in salads. For the best texture and flavor, store the fresh cheese, packed in its liquid, in the refrigerator and use it within 2 days.

Bocconcini, little balls of fresh mozzarella packed in seasoned olive oil, are great served as is on skewers.

---

2. Meanwhile, whisk the oil, vinegar, and lime juice together in a small bowl. Season to taste with salt and pepper.

3. Combine the corn, tomatoes, scallions, and cilantro in a large bowl. Toss with the dressing, and serve at room temperature or chilled. (The salad will keep, covered and refrigerated, for up to 3 days.)

Mozzarella, Tomato, and Grilled Fennel Salad

SERVES 4

The combination of ripe tomatoes and fresh mozzarella is a summer classic; grilled fresh fennel makes it new and different. Our good friend Sallie Williams (author of the first *Hay Day Cookbook*) showed us the virtues of fennel in this combination: It is sturdy enough to survive grilling and develops a rich smoky flavor. Serve this as a summer first course, perhaps followed by a simple entrée of grilled fish. For easy entertaining, grill the fennel ahead of time, then assemble the salad just before serving.

❖❖❖❖❖❖

1 large or 2 small fennel bulbs,
scrubbed, feathery ends trimmed
Olive oil for grilling
⅓ cup extra-virgin olive oil
2 tablespoons sherry vinegar
Coarse (kosher) salt and freshly
ground black pepper
2 ripe tomatoes, cored, seeded, and
coarsely chopped
8 ounces fresh mozzarella cheese,
sliced into thin rounds (see Fresh
Mozzarella, facing page)

❖❖❖❖❖❖

1. Preheat the grill to high.

2. Cut the fennel lengthwise, from root to stalk, into ¼-inch-thick slices, leaving the inner core in place. Brush lightly all over with olive oil and grill until the fennel is translucent, tender, and lightly charred on both sides, about 5 minutes per side. Remove from the heat and set aside.

3. Whisk the extra-virgin olive oil and vinegar together in a small bowl. Season to taste with salt and pepper, and drizzle over the chopped tomatoes.

4. Divide the mozzarella slices among four salad plates. Top with the grilled fennel, then spoon the tomatoes and their dressing on top. Serve at room temperature.

Fresh Tomato and Yogurt Cheese Salad

SERVES 6 TO 8

Freshly made yogurt cheese is wonderful with sweet ripe summertime tomatoes. Olives, fresh basil, and a bright scattering of sweet peppers add rich color and flavor to the dish. Use top-quality extra-virgin olive oil to finish the salad—or showcase a fresh Basil-Infused Oil (page 261). You can prepare the yogurt cheese a day or two in advance, then arrange the platter shortly before serving time.

❖❖❖❖❖❖

1 head red-leaf or Boston lettuce,
rinsed and dried
2 large or 4 medium-size ripe summer
tomatoes
1 generous cup Yogurt Cheese (page
254)
¼ cup minced Kalamata olives
2 to 3 tablespoons shredded fresh basil
leaves
⅓ cup minced yellow or orange bell
pepper
2 tablespoons extra-virgin olive oil
Freshly ground black pepper

❖❖❖❖❖❖

Arrange the lettuce leaves on a large round serving platter. Slice the tomatoes thickly, and arrange them on the lettuce in an overlapping circular pattern. Mound the yogurt cheese in the center of the platter, letting it overlap the tomatoes a bit. Scatter the olives, basil, and bell pepper over the cheese and tomatoes. Drizzle the oil on top, and grind some black pepper to taste over it all. Serve the salad immediately.

Creamy Mustard Coleslaw

SERVES 8 TO 10

This excellent all-purpose creamy coleslaw takes advantage of the light crisp texture and mild flavor of Napa cabbage. Mustard gives it a bright, refreshing flavor, and substituting yogurt for mayonnaise makes it entirely virtuous.

◆◆◆◆◆◆

1 cup Yogurt Cheese (page 254; see Note)
¼ cup coarse-grain mustard
¼ cup honey
Juice of 1 lime
1 tablespoon white wine vinegar
½ teaspoon coarse (kosher) salt
Freshly ground black pepper
3 large carrots, scrubbed and coarsely grated
1 small head red or green cabbage (12 ounces), cored and shredded
½ small head Napa cabbage (1 pound), cored and shredded
1 small sweet onion (Vidalia, Walla Walla, or Oso Sweet), peeled and thinly sliced

◆◆◆◆◆◆

1. In a mixing bowl, whisk together the yogurt cheese, mustard, honey, lime juice, vinegar, and salt. Season to taste with pepper.

2. Combine the carrots, cabbage, and onion in a large bowl. Pour the dressing over the vegetables, and toss to combine well. Cover and chill for at least 1 hour before serving.

Note: Using yogurt instead of mayonnaise or sour cream gives creamy dressings a wonderful flavor and makes them lower in fat. Yogurt straight from the container, however, makes a watery dressing. The solution is to use Yogurt Cheese, which is perfectly simple to make.

Peppered Peach and Vidalia Onion Salad

SERVES 6 TO 8

With Vidalia onion for crunch and cayenne pepper for spice, this celebration of summer peaches is magnificent alongside any spicy barbecued meat, fish, or seafood, and it's obviously right at home with Southern-style barbecued ribs or chicken. And it's not exactly difficult. If you can't find Vidalias (see About Vidalia Onions, facing page), substitute another sweet onion variety.

ABOUT VIDALIA ONIONS

Vidalias are uniquely juicy and sweet, but that makes them unsuitable to store for any length of time, and their season (May and June) is short.

Even though you can't keep Vidalias all the way through the summer, you can still extend their season a bit by storing them properly. The key is to keep them in a cool, dry place, stored individually (without touching). We've stored them successfully wrapped in dry cotton napkins, but we have friends who swear by the old-style nylon-stocking method: Drop the onions into a stocking, tie knots between them to keep separated, and hang the whole thing in the pantry. Just cut them off from the bottom as needed.

So what do we do the rest of the year? Encouraged by Vidalias' runaway success, growers have produced several new sweet onion varieties: California Imperials (Smoothies) and Texas 1015s begin the season with a jump start on Vidalias (both harvests begin in April and run into early summer); succulent Hawaiian Mauis are generally available during the early summer; Walla Wallas, from Washington State, follow in mid-summer and continue into fall; and Chilean Oso Sweets are in the market from November through February. They're not the real thing, but they are perfectly acceptable substitutes.

◆◆◆◆◆◆

6 ripe peaches, peeled and thinly sliced
  (see Note)
1 large Vidalia onion, peeled, halved
  lengthwise, and sliced into thin
  crescents
Juice of 1 large lemon
$\frac{1}{8}$ teaspoon cayenne pepper
$\frac{1}{2}$ teaspoon coarse (kosher) salt
Freshly ground black pepper
1 large bunch fresh arugula,
  rinsed well and dried

◆◆◆◆◆◆

1. Combine the peach and onion slices in a large bowl. Sprinkle with the lemon juice, cayenne, salt, and several grindings of black pepper. Toss thoroughly, and refrigerate to chill for at least 1 hour before serving. (The salad can be prepared to this point up to a day in advance.)

2. Arrange a small bed of crisp green arugula on each salad plate, and top with the chilled peaches and onions. Drizzle the juices from the bowl over all, and serve immediately.

Note: A peach skin will slip off easily if you first dunk the whole peach into a large pot of rapidly boiling water for 15 seconds, then refresh it under cold running water. However, if thin-skinned fuzz-free peaches are available, it's fine to leave those skins on.

Pineapple, Papaya, and Berries in Fresh Lime-Chile Dressing

SERVES 4

This truly excellent summer fruit salad, which gets a tiny unexpected flavor explosion from the spice of fresh chile peppers, is a good example of how things have changed. Five years ago, this combination of fruits would have been served as a tropical dessert! The simple addition of lime juice and fresh chiles transforms it into a refreshing appetizer or luncheon salad. If you're a cilantro fan, by all means substitute it for the mint.

◆◆◆◆◆◆

¼ cup fresh lime juice (1½ to 2 large limes)

1 to 2 fresh serrano chiles, deveined, seeded, and minced

1 tablespoon chopped fresh mint or cilantro

1 large ripe papaya (about 1 pound), peeled, seeded, and cut into ½-inch cubes (see About Papayas)

1 cup raspberries

1 cup blueberries

1 head butterhead lettuce, rinsed and patted dry

½ ripe pineapple, peeled and cored

◆◆◆◆◆◆

1. Whisk together the lime juice, chile, and mint in a small bowl.

2. Combine the papaya, raspberries, and blueberries in a large bowl. Pour the dressing over the fruit and toss gently, taking care not to crush the berries.

3. Line four plates with the lettuce leaves. Slice the pineapple in half lengthwise, then cut each half into 2-inch spears. Scatter the spears at random (like Lincoln Logs) over the lettuce, and spoon the papaya, berries, and juices on top. Serve immediately.

ABOUT PAPAYAS

Papayas should be delicately sweet; unripe ones will be musky and sour. Choose ripe papayas the way you do pears: They should be firm but should yield to gentle pressure, and should be turning from green to yellow. Try to find strawberry papayas for special occasions; their rich, rosy flesh and sweet flavor are really spectacular.

Orange and Jicama Slaw

SERVES 4

If you've never purchased jicama because you're not sure what to do with it, this crisp, cool salad with sliced oranges and a peppery chili vinaigrette should change all that. You'll find that after just a quick shredding on a box grater (or a processor's largest shredding disk), jicama will reward you with a superbly textured slaw that goes just beautifully with grilled fish or any casual summer barbecue.

◆◆◆◆◆◆

4 juicy seedless oranges, peeled and thinly sliced

1 small jicama, peeled, quartered, and shredded (see About Jicama, page 49)

3 tablespoons fresh orange juice

Juice of 1 lime

1 tablespoon red wine vinegar

½ teaspoon chili powder

¼ teaspoon coarse (kosher) salt

⅓ cup olive oil

Pinch of cayenne pepper, or to taste

2 tablespoons chopped fresh cilantro

◆◆◆◆◆◆

1. Divide the orange slices among four chilled salad plates. Top the oranges with a generous mound of shredded jicama, and set aside or cover and refrigerate up to 3 hours before serving.

2. In a small bowl, whisk together the orange and lime juices, vinegar, chili powder, and salt. Add the oil in a slow thin stream, whisking continuously. Season with the cayenne pepper. Drizzle the dressing over each salad, sprinkle with the cilantro, and serve.

Menu

Cool Summer Spice

On a warm evening, after the heat of a bright yellow sun has given way, serve a rich island menu that balances spicy peppers and ginger with fresh sweet summer fruits.

🌿 🌿 🌿

Fresh Ginger Beer

Pineapple, Papaya, and Berries in Fresh Lime-Chile Dressing

Jamaican Spiced Snapper with Rum-Glazed Plantains

Gingerbread-Peach Upside-Down Cake

🌿 🌿 🌿

Sunchokes and Pears in Walnut Vinaigrette

SERVES 4 TO 6

Pears, walnuts, and sunchokes (often called Jerusalem artichokes) are all at their best in the fall and winter, which makes this salad richly autumnal. The crisp texture of the sunchokes contrasts nicely with the sweetness and buttery texture of the pears. Great with French bread and a good country pâté for lunch or tailgating.

◆◆◆◆◆◆

1 pound sunchokes, peeled and sliced
   into thin rounds (see About
   Sunchokes)
¼ cup walnut oil
1½ tablespoons fresh lemon juice
1 tablespoon finely minced scallions
1 tablespoon coarse-grain mustard
Coarse (kosher) salt and freshly ground
   black pepper
3 large red-skin pears, rinsed, cored,
   and coarsely chopped
1 large bunch fresh watercress, rinsed
   well and dried
⅓ cup coarsely chopped walnuts,
   toasted (see Toasting Nuts, page 55)

◆◆◆◆◆◆

1. Bring a small saucepan of water to a boil. Add the sunchoke slices, return to a simmer, and cook for 1 minute. Drain immediately.

2. Meanwhile, whisk the oil, lemon juice, scallions, and mustard together in a small bowl. Season to taste with salt and pepper.

3. Combine the blanched sunchokes and the chopped pears in a large bowl. Add the dressing, toss, and adjust the seasoning as needed. Arrange a small bed of watercress on each plate, and spoon the sunchokes and pears on top. Scatter the toasted walnuts generously over each plate, and serve immediately.

ABOUT SUNCHOKES

Entirely native to North America (Native Americans called them sunroots), Jerusalem artichokes are unrelated to either Jerusalem or the artichoke family; they are tubers with a crisp, clean flavor. They make great crudités, and since they don't get soggy in a vinaigrette, they're ideal in salads (blanch them for just a minute to bring out their flavor). They can also be lightly steamed, boiled, stir-fried, or roasted (peeled or un-peeled). They look a little like ginger root. Fresh, firm sunchokes with the fewest knobs and protrusions will be the least wasteful and easiest to peel. Store them in the refrigerator for up to 1 week, and scrub or peel them thoroughly before cooking.

Spinach and Citrus Salad in Cranberry Vinaigrette

SERVES 4 TO 6

We've always loved the combination of oranges and spinach for a winter salad. It's ideal with pretty little seedless clementines, but when that season's over, you can make this bright salad just as well with California navel oranges, crimson blood oranges, or sweet ruby grapefruits. Fragrant fresh fennel is wonderful with citrus, but if you're not a fennel fan, feel free to substitute thinly sliced red onion.

◆◆◆◆◆◆

1 small bulb fresh fennel, rinsed
    and trimmed of feathery tops
6 ounces fresh spinach leaves,
    trimmed, rinsed well, and dried
1/3 cup pine nuts
6 clementines, 3 oranges, or 2 red
    grapefruits
Cranberry Vinaigrette (recipe
    follows)

◆◆◆◆◆◆

1. Preheat the oven to 325°F.

2. Slice the fennel in half lengthwise from root to stalk. Using a small paring knife, cut out and discard the hard V-shaped inner core at the base of each half. Slice the halves crosswise into thin rounds, and toss with the spinach in a large salad bowl.

3. Scatter the pine nuts in a small cake pan or baking dish, and toast in the oven until lightly browned and fragrant, 5 to 7 minutes. Remove from the oven and set aside to cool.

4. Meanwhile, peel the clementines, removing as much of the white pith as possible. Separate the sections, and toss them in the salad bowl along with a generous amount of the Cranberry Vinaigrette. Arrange the salad on serving plates, and top each one with a small handful of toasted pine nuts. Serve immediately.

A NOTE ON SALAD GREENS

Make it a rule to rinse and dry fresh greens—lettuces, spinach, tatsoi, arugula, broccoli rabe—not later, not tomorrow, but as soon as you get them home. Clean and fresh, they'll keep nicely for several days when stored in aerated plastic bags in the fridge, and they'll be ready not only to serve on their own with a vinaigrette, but also to embellish other salads, or wilt into soup, or add to pasta or risotto.

Cranberry Vinaigrette
MAKES 1 GENEROUS CUP

This outstanding holiday vinaigrette keeps well for several weeks in the refrigerator. Keep it on hand from Thanksgiving to New Year's to add color and flavor to a wide variety of mixed greens. Or use it as a marinade before grilling turkey cutlets, boneless chicken breasts, or pork tenderloin. The appeal of these tart berries transcends seasons.

◆◆◆◆◆◆

1/2 cup whole fresh or frozen cranberries
3 tablespoons raspberry vinegar
1 small clove garlic, peeled
1 teaspoon minced shallots
1/2 teaspoon Dijon mustard
1/4 cup cranberry juice
3 tablespoons walnut oil
1 tablespoon honey
3 leaves fresh mint, or 1 small pinch
    dried
1/3 cup vegetable oil
Coarse (kosher) salt to taste

◆◆◆◆◆◆

1. Place the cranberries, vinegar, garlic, shallots, and mustard in a food processor or blender, and pulse several times to coarsely chop. Add the cranberry juice, walnut oil, honey, and mint, and blend until thin and smooth.

2. With the machine running, add the vegetable oil in a steady thin stream, and blend to form a slightly thickened and emulsified dressing. Season with salt as needed.

MAKE-IT-YOURSELF MESCLUN

R ight beside the beautiful mesclun mixes of tender baby salad greens, produce stands often set out fresh arugula, radicchio, frisée, mâche, tatsoi, and baby spinach. This makes it easy to create your own combination; you can always toss in a handful of whole fresh basil leaves, cilantro, parsley, chives, sorrel, or mint for an additional spark of flavor.

Tender baby salad greens are highly perishable; when shopping, look for leaves that are light, fluffy, brightly colored, and fresh-scented. Rinse and spin them dry as soon as you get home; they will keep well for only a couple of days in an aerated bag in the fridge.

"Wild" Greens and Chèvre in a Blackberry Cider Vinaigrette

SERVES 6 TO 8

T hese days, nearly every decent supermarket in the U.S. offers mesclun, a potpourri of mixed baby greens that includes pungent peppery varieties like arugula, frisée, mizuna, and radicchio. Not too long ago, flavorful mixed salad greens like these were a rarity. Legend has it that mesclun originally was simply a mélange of wild spring shoots eagerly clipped from French gardens after a long winter. Today mesclun is enormously popular in both France and the U.S., and although no longer clipped from the wild, it's a delicious and elegant cultivated mixture of "wildly" flavorful greens whose assertive quality is set off nicely by this tart, fruity late-summer vinaigrette.

◆◆◆◆◆◆

8 ounces (1 pint) fresh blackberries
¼ cup apple cider
1 tablespoon cider vinegar
½ teaspoon Dijon mustard
¼ cup vegetable oil
¼ teaspoon sugar (optional, depending on the tartness of the berries)
8 ounces mesclun (mixed baby salad greens), rinsed well and dried
½ cup walnut pieces, toasted (see Toasting Nuts, page 55) and coarsely chopped
4 ounces aged chèvre (Bûcheron or Crottin)

◆◆◆◆◆◆

A Salad Sampler

A colorful trio of salads makes a great warm-weather meal—particularly during the dog days of summer, when it's too hot to turn on the grill. Prepare as much as possible the night before or in the cool of the morning, and spend the heat of the day by the pool.

🍂 🍂 🍂

Iced Darjeeling Tea

"Wild" Greens and Chèvre in a
Blackberry Cider Vinaigrette
Three-Grain Salad
Purple Potato and Snap Pea Salad

Berries in Passion Fruit Cream
Lemon Sugar Snap Cookies

🍂 🍂 🍂

---

1. Place half the blackberries in a food processor or blender. Add the apple cider, vinegar, and mustard, and blend to form a thin smooth purée. With the machine running, add the oil in a thin even stream and blend to form a creamy, slightly thickened dressing. If desired, add sugar to taste.

2. In a large bowl, toss the greens with a generous amount of the dressing to evenly coat. Taste, and add more dressing as needed. Divide the greens among serving plates, sprinkle with the toasted nuts, and crumble a small portion of the chèvre over each. Garnish each plate with the remaining blackberries, and serve immediately.

B.L.T. Pasta Salad

SERVES 4 TO 6

At Hay Day we make this year-round with bow-tie pasta; at the height of summer we switch to green spinach noodles and bright yellow cherry tomatoes. This very American combination of flavors makes a superb picnic salad, with peppery green arugula standing in assertively for the usual "L."

◆◆◆◆◆◆

8 ounces bow-tie pasta, cooked,
   rinsed, and drained
1 pint cherry tomatoes, rinsed and
   sliced in half
6 scallions, white and light green
   parts thinly sliced
1 cup packed arugula leaves, rinsed
   well and torn into bite-size pieces
⅓ cup extra-virgin olive oil
1 teaspoon Dijon mustard
2 teaspoons fresh lemon juice
3 tablespoons red wine vinegar
Coarse (kosher) salt and freshly
   ground black pepper
8 thick-cut slices smoked bacon,
   cooked until very crisp

◆◆◆◆◆◆

1. In a chilled bowl, combine the pasta, tomatoes, scallions, and arugula.

2. Whisk the oil, mustard, lemon juice, and vinegar together in a small bowl. Season to taste with salt and pepper, and toss into the pasta and vegetables. Crumble in the bacon, toss, and serve.

121

Three-Grain Salad

SERVES 8 TO 10

We sell tons of this in the summer; if you like the lemon and mint flavors of a good tabbouleh, you'll like this, too. Light and refreshing, it's a great introduction to some of the new and nourishing grains we're all supposed to be eating.

◆◆◆◆◆◆

1 quart water
Coarse (kosher) salt
1 cup wheat berries, rinsed well
1 cup pearl barley, rinsed well
1 cup millet seeds (see It's Not Just
    Birdseed, facing page)
Grated zest of 2 large lemons
    (see Note)
Grated zest of 1 orange (see Note)
6 scallions, white and light green
    parts chopped
½ cup coarsely chopped fresh Italian
    (flat-leaf) parsley
⅓ cup coarsely chopped fresh mint
    leaves
⅓ cup dried currants
Juice of 1 large lemon
½ cup extra-virgin olive oil
Freshly ground black pepper

◆◆◆◆◆◆

1. Bring the water to a boil in a large saucepan. Add 1 teaspoon salt and the wheat berries. Reduce the heat, cover, and simmer for 30 minutes. Add the barley, and cook for another 20 minutes.

2. Meanwhile, toast the millet in a large dry skillet over medium-high heat, stir-

ABOUT RINSING GRAINS

Unless the package specifically forbids it, all grains (including rice) should always be rinsed well before cooking. Grown in fields like any other vegetable, they may contain earth or even tiny pebbles. An exception to this rule is arborio rice and other rices used for risotto. Natural starches are essential to these small round grains and should never be washed away.

ring and shaking the skillet until you hear the grains "pop" and see them turn a shade darker, about 5 minutes.

3. After the barley has cooked for 20 minutes, add the millet to the barley and wheat berries, and cook until all the grains are tender and the water has been completely absorbed, about 15 minutes. (If any water remains when the grains are done, simply drain if off.) Transfer the grains to a large bowl.

4. Add the lemon zest, orange zest, scallions, parsley, mint, and currants to the grains. Toss well.

5. Whisk the lemon juice and oil together in a small bowl. Season to taste with salt and pepper, and pour over the salad. Toss, and chill for at least 1 hour before serving.

Note: For the best appearance, peel the lemon and orange zest with a hand-held zester. If you don't have a zester, use a vegetable peeler and then cut the strips of zest into thin slivers.

Bright Ideas

❦ Pack into hollowed ripe summer tomatoes for a lovely light luncheon salad.

❦ Serve as a bed for grilled shrimp or pork tenderloin.

Wild Rice and Cranberries

SERVES 6 TO 8

This is both a natural with post-Thanksgiving turkey sandwiches and elegant enough for any kind of holiday buffet. Hearty and refreshing, it's best served warm or at room temperature (not cold) for the most delicious flavor. By all means substitute dried sour cherries or coarsely chopped dried apricots if you can't find dried cranberries.

◆◆◆◆◆◆

3 cups water
1½ cups wild rice, rinsed well
½ cup dried cranberries
¼ cup fruity red wine (such as Merlot, Pinot Noir, or Beaujolais)
⅓ cup olive oil
2 tablespoons red wine vinegar
1 teaspoon Dijon mustard
Coarse (kosher) salt
6 scallions, white and light green parts coarsely chopped
2 large firm-ripe pears, preferably Comice, cored, peeled, and diced
½ cup coarsely chopped pecans, preferably toasted (see Toasting Nuts, page 55)

◆◆◆◆◆◆

1. Bring the water to a boil in a saucepan. Lightly salt the water, and add the wild rice as soon as it comes back to a boil. Reduce the heat to low, cover, and simmer until tender but still firm to the bite, 25 to

IT'S NOT JUST BIRDSEED

Millet is an ancient grain that has nourished a major portion of the world's population for centuries. A source of protein, iron, calcium, and riboflavin, it is healthful and delicious, with a delicate flavor. It readily absorbs seasonings and adds texture to soup, salads, and pilafs. The late Bert Greene, our most trusted authority on the subject of grains, taught us the technique of toasting the grain in a dry skillet before cooking it, to bring out the best flavor.

Look for millet in specialty and health-food markets. A small, perfectly round bead, millet should be bright gold and have very little aroma. It has a relatively long shelf life, so when you find it, don't hesitate to purchase a little extra; you can store it in an airtight jar in a cool dry place for several months.

And as for its other use: The millet in birdseed is unhulled and unfit for human consumption. Don't even think of using it.

30 minutes. Drain the rice well of any excess water.

2. Meanwhile, place the cranberries in a small bowl, cover with the wine, and set aside to plump.

3. Whisk the oil, vinegar, mustard, and ¼ teaspoon salt together in a small bowl.

4. Toss the warm cooked rice in a large bowl with the scallions, dressing, pears, and cranberries and their soaking wine. Season to taste with additional salt as needed. The salad can be prepared a day ahead to this point. Cover and refrigerate; allow the salad to come to room temperature, and toss the pecans in just before serving.

About Quinoa

Hard to believe, since many people have never heard of it, but quinoa is one of the oldest grains on the planet. A nutritional wonder too, it's 17 percent protein and very high in calcium. Most quinoa comes from South America, where it was the primary grain for the Incas, but a couple of excellent varieties are now being grown on small farms in Colorado. The little round grains cook quickly, and their springy crunch gives a welcome texture and variety to salads, soups, stuffings, pilafs, and baked goods. Quinoa should be right up there beside the rice on your pantry shelf.

Quinoa-Tabbouleh Salad

SERVES 4 TO 6

Nutritious quinoa (keen-wah) stands in nicely for bulgur wheat in this bright summer salad. We prefer our tabbouleh packed with more greenery and vegetables than grain, so the quality of this salad depends almost completely on the freshness of the parsley, mint, and tomatoes—prepare it only when these crops are at their peak. The refreshing lemony flavor of the salad is excellent with grilled or poached fish or with grilled kebabs of chicken or lamb.

◆◆◆◆◆◆

¾ cup water
½ cup quinoa (see About Quinoa),
    rinsed well in a fine-mesh sieve
2 lightly packed cups chopped fresh
    Italian (flat-leaf) parsley
⅓ cup finely chopped fresh mint
6 scallions, white and light green
    parts, finely chopped
1 large ripe tomato, cored, seeded,
    and cut into ¼-inch dice
¼ cup fresh lemon juice (about
    2 lemons)
⅓ cup extra-virgin olive oil
Coarse (kosher) salt
3 ounces feta cheese, finely crumbled
    (generous ½ cup crumbled)
Freshly ground black pepper

◆◆◆◆◆◆

1. Bring the water to a boil in a small saucepan. Lightly salt the water, and add the quinoa as soon as it comes back to a boil. Reduce the heat to low, cover, and simmer until most of the water has been absorbed and the quinoa is just tender, about 5 minutes. (Properly cooked grains of quinoa should be translucent with the exception of a small white opaque center.) Drain well of any excess water, and toss the quinoa in a large bowl with the parsley, mint, scallions, and tomato.

2. In a small bowl, whisk the lemon juice, oil, and ½ teaspoon salt together. Drizzle over the quinoa mixture. Add the feta and toss with a fork to combine and dress everything thoroughly. Season to taste with freshly ground black pepper and additional salt as needed.

Bright Ideas

❧ Spoon portions of Quinoa-Tabbouleh Salad over thick slices of ripe summer tomatoes.

❧ Serve the salad inside hollowed cherry tomatoes for a lively summer appetizer.

❧ Pack inside pita pockets for a light, nutritious sandwich (add morsels of grilled tuna or chicken if you like).

A Picnic for All Seasons

We know people who are so hooked on portable meals, they keep a picnic basket right under the kitchen table. Sandwiches and salads are easy to wrap and pack for a meal on the go. Transport the soup in a thermos for pouring into tall cups—warm or cold, depending on the time of year. The crumb bars can be prepared a day in advance and wrapped individually— a delicious chewy treat for munching on the road.

❧ ❧ ❧

Carrot and Ginger Soup

Quinoa-Tabbouleh Salad
in Pita Pockets
Buttermilk Ranch Potato Salad

Cherry-Apricot Crumb Bars
Assorted fresh fruit
❧ ❧ ❧

Wheat-Berry Waldorf

SERVES 6 TO 8

What's a Waldorf? Traditionally it's a salad of apples, celery, walnuts, and mayonnaise, named for the hotel that created it. Ours is an even healthier Waldorf. It's still an apple salad, but it's made with wheat berries, currants, fennel, and a lovely walnut oil vinaigrette.

◆◆◆◆◆◆

1 cup wheat berries or kamut (see
  About Kamut), rinsed well
1¼ cups water
⅓ cup olive oil
¼ cup walnut oil (see About Walnut
  Oil, facing page)
⅓ cup red wine vinegar
Juice of 1 lemon
Coarse (kosher) salt and freshly ground
  black pepper
3 large scallions, white and light green
  parts finely chopped
¼ cup chopped fresh Italian (flat-leaf)
  parsley
2 crisp red-skin apples (such as
  Stayman Winesap, Empire, or
  Braeburn), unpeeled, cut into
  small dice
⅔ cup diced fresh fennel
½ cup dried currants
½ cup coarsely chopped walnuts,
  preferably toasted (see Toasting Nuts,
  page 55)

◆◆◆◆◆◆

1. Place the wheat berries in a medium-size saucepan, add the water, and bring to a boil over medium-high heat. Reduce the heat, cover, and simmer until most of the water has been absorbed and the kernels are tender and pleasantly chewy, 30 to 35 minutes. Drain any excess water and transfer the wheat berries to a large bowl.

2. Meanwhile, whisk the oils, vinegar, and lemon juice together in a small bowl. Season to taste with the salt and pepper. Add the dressing to the bowl of warm wheat berries.

3. Add all the remaining ingredients to the bowl, toss, and refrigerate, covered, until ready to serve. (Well wrapped, this salad will keep in the refrigerator for up to 2 days.)

ABOUT KAMUT

By now many of us are familiar with the toothsome charm of standard wheat berries, so wonderful in salads, soups, and pilafs. Our latest discovery in the world of grains is kamut (pronounced ka-moot). It's a large-kerneled type of wheat sold in whole "wheat berry" form. The fragrant cooked kernels are bigger and fatter than conventional wheat berries, with a decidedly nutty flavor. Actually an ancient strain—originally from Egypt, where it nourished pharaohs for centuries—kamut is now being cultivated in this country.

Texas Caviar

SERVES 6

Black-eyed peas are supposed to bring good luck at New Year's. Whether you believe that or not, they make a lively salad to serve at parties all year long. This combination is a great way to experience the fabulous texture and flavor of whole-grain hominy.

◆◆◆◆◆◆

½ cup dried whole hominy, or
   1 generous cup (14-ounce can)
   cooked whole-grain hominy
   (see About Hominy, page 128)
1 cup dried black-eyed peas, rinsed
   and sorted
1½ cups diced ripe tomato
1 large clove garlic, peeled and
   minced
1 yellow or orange bell pepper,
   stemmed, seeded, and diced
1 or 2 fresh jalapeño peppers, seeds
   and ribs removed, finely minced
   (see About Chile Peppers, page 87)
½ cup finely chopped onion
½ cup chopped fresh cilantro
½ teaspoon coarse (kosher) salt
1 cup Red Wine Vinaigrette
   (page 263)
Sliced ripe tomatoes or lettuce leaves,
   for serving

◆◆◆◆◆◆

1. Place the dried hominy in a saucepan, add water to cover by 1 inch, and bring to a rapid simmer over medium-high heat. Simmer for 1 minute, then cover, remove from the heat, and allow to rest for 1 hour. Drain, and add 3 cups fresh water to the pot. Once again bring to a simmer over medium-high heat. Reduce the heat slightly and simmer, uncovered, until the hominy is just tender, about 30 minutes. Drain, and set aside. (If you're using the precooked hominy, skip this step; just drain and rinse.)

2. While the hominy is cooking, place the black-eyed peas in a stockpot, and add water to cover (about 4 cups). Bring to a simmer over medium-high heat. Reduce the heat slightly and simmer gently until just tender, 20 to 25 minutes. Remove from the heat and drain well.

3. In a large bowl, combine the black-eyed peas, hominy, and all the remaining ingredients except the sliced tomatoes or lettuce leaves. Stir well, and allow to marinate for at least 2 hours, stirring occasionally to distribute the flavors.

ABOUT WALNUT OIL

Walnut oil adds a delicious nutty flavor and fragrance to salad dressings and sauces. It's both richly flavored and expensive, so you'll want to use it sparingly. Combine it with another milder oil for the best balance of flavor. Like the nuts, the oil is susceptible to spoilage, and therefore once opened is best stored in the refrigerator.

4. Line a large platter with the sliced tomatoes or lettuce leaves, mound the Texas Caviar high in the middle, and serve.

Bright Ideas

❦ Serve as a refreshing, lively accompaniment to grilled or blackened chicken or fish fillets.

❦ Offer as a dip at a New Year's celebration, surrounded with corn chips for scooping.

ABOUT HOMINY

A form of whole-grain dried corn traditionally used in Native American cooking, hominy adds rich smoky flavor and texture to all kinds of soups, stews, and salads. We sell it dried, and it is also frequently available precooked in jars and cans. People who think they've never heard of hominy may know it in its roasted and salted form: corn nuts.

The Main Attraction

Contrary to popular myth, food people are just as tired as everybody else when they get home from work, and just as anxious to make something easy for dinner. We keep long hours at Hay Day, and we, too, stand hopefully in front of the fridge, praying that just this once our fairy godmother's left supper all ready to pop into the oven. And she doesn't any more often at our house than she does at yours.

We've learned from experience that good food needn't take long to make. There's nothing time-consuming in this chapter—no wrapping in pastry, no long sauce reductions—and almost everything can be prepared ahead of time.

Along with the ease of preparation, these recipes highlight how far we've come in terms of inventiveness and sophistication. Our customers love masterpieces like Mediterranean Turkey Loaf and Maryland Crab Cakes, but like us, they're eager for new things too. Their adventurousness inspires combinations like the smoky chiles and sweet apples in Pecan-Crusted Chicken, the fragrant coffee-and-peppercorn coating in Kona-Crusted Beef, and the lightness of couscous in a vegetable lasagne.

So here's what's for dinner. We hope you'll like it.

Meat

Kona-Crusted Beef with Sweet Onion Jam

SERVES 4

This is a variation on classic steak au poivre in which the tang of Sechuan pepper is mellowed by the rich, smoky coffee flavor. We introduced this recipe during a Hawaii-inspired food festival in our shops. The rich mellow flavor of Kona coffee is particularly delicious when seared on the steak, but whatever type of coffee you use, make sure the beans are aromatic and freshly roasted. As soon as you open the bag, the fragrance of good rich coffee should be unmistakable. A serving of Buttermilk-Chive Mashed Potatoes (page 201) or Oven-Roasted Winter Vegetables (page 208) would round this out beautifully.

◆◆◆◆◆◆

¼ cup roasted coffee beans, preferably Kona
⅓ cup Sechuan peppercorns
1 tablespoon coarse (kosher) salt
4 shell steaks (8 ounces each), about 1 inch thick
Caramelized Onion Jam (recipe follows)

◆◆◆◆◆◆

1. Preheat the oven to 400°F.

2. Coarsely crush the coffee beans and peppercorns together, using a mortar and pestle, a spice mill, or a mini food processor. The bits should be no larger than small grains of rice. Add the salt and stir together to combine. Coat both sides of the steaks with a thin uniform layer of the coffee mixture.

3. Heat a large ovenproof skillet, preferably cast iron, over high heat. As soon as the pan is smoking hot, sear the steaks until nicely browned, 2 to 3 minutes per side. Then transfer the pan to the oven and cook for 10 to 12 minutes for medium-rare. Serve hot from the oven, accompanied by a generous portion of the onion jam.

STORING COFFEE BEANS

For optimum flavor, we recommend that you purchase and store coffee beans much as you would spices: buy only what you'll use in the near future (for coffee, one to two weeks), and store the beans in a cool, dark, dry location. Send the beans to the freezer for long-term storage only, and then be sure to let them come to room temperature before using them.

Caramelized Onion Jam

MAKES 2 CUPS

We sell this intensely rich, sweet onion jam as a condiment with the beef, but keep it in mind as a mellow contrast for other spicy dishes, like blackened fish, spiced grilled chicken, or spicy roast pork.

◆◆◆◆◆◆

2 to 3 large Spanish onions,
 peeled, quartered, and sliced
 into thin crescents (8 cups sliced)
¼ cup (firmly packed) light brown sugar
1 tablespoon red wine vinegar
4 tablespoons (½ stick) unsalted
 butter, cut into chunks
1 tablespoon honey

◆◆◆◆◆◆

1. Place the onions in a large saucepan. Sprinkle with the sugar and vinegar, dot with the butter, and drizzle with the honey. Cover and cook over medium-high heat until the onions are tender, 15 minutes.

2. Uncover, raise the heat to high, and cook, stirring occasionally, until the onions are browned and caramelized, about 10 minutes. They should have a very sweet smoky flavor. Serve warm or at room temperature. Store covered, in the refrigerator for up to 1 week.

Mexican Meat Loaf

SERVES 8

Where is it written that meat loaf has to be rectangular? It's a country pâté, after all, and if you slice a round loaf in pie-shaped wedges there aren't any end-pieces to argue about. Tomato salsa and a topping of crisp corn tortillas make a wonderful south-of-the-border variation on the traditional theme.

◆◆◆◆◆◆

2 pounds ground beef, preferably
 sirloin
2 large eggs
16 large brine-cured black olives,
 pitted and sliced
¾ teaspoon ground cumin
1 teaspoon chili powder
1 teaspoon coarse (kosher) salt
5 ounces Monterey Jack cheese,
 shredded (generous 1½ cups
 shredded)
2 cups Southwestern Tomato Salsa
 (page 253) or another fresh salsa
1 cup freshly dried bread crumbs
 (see Note)
3 corn tortillas (8-inch size)
1 small head red or green leaf lettuce,
 rinsed, dried, and shredded
½ cup sour cream

◆◆◆◆◆◆

1. Preheat the oven to 350°F.

2. Combine the beef, eggs, olives, cumin, chili powder, salt, and a heaping cup of the shredded cheese in a large mixing bowl. Measure 1 even cup of the salsa, and add

to the mixing bowl along with the bread crumbs. Blend together thoroughly.

3. Press the meat mixture into a 9-inch round deep-dish pie plate, cake pan, or casserole. Spread ½ cup of the remaining salsa evenly over the top of the meat.

4. Slice the tortillas into thin ribbons. Cut the ribbons in half, and scatter them evenly over the meat. Sprinkle the remaining ½ cup shredded cheese on top. Bake until the meat has pulled away from the edges of the pie plate and the tortilla shreds are nicely browned and crisp on top, 50 to 60 minutes. Remove from the oven and let cool for 10 minutes before serving.

5. Place a small pile of shredded lettuce on eight plates. Slice the meat loaf into pie-shaped wedges. Arrange the servings on the lettuce, and top each one with a spoonful of the reserved tomato salsa and a small spoonful of sour cream. Serve immediately.

Note: To make fresh bread crumbs, place thinly sliced white bread on a baking sheet, and place in a preheated 350°F oven until completely dried and slightly browned around the edges, about 15 minutes. Crumble the bread into pieces, dropping them right into the food processor. Pulse until the bread is coarsely ground. If you don't have a processor, place the bread on a cutting board and use a rolling pin to crush it into crumbs. Store the crumbs in an airtight container for up to 1 week.

Veal Chops on a Bed of Leeks

SERVES 4

Augment the spicy sweetness of Dan's Mustard with shallots, white wine, and a little cream, and the result is a sauce that is gorgeous over sautéed veal and tender oven-roasted leeks. Lamb chops make a wonderful substitute, but the cooking time should be shortened if you like your lamb on the rare side. Complete the meal with a side dish of Green Beans, Tomatoes, and Pine Nuts (page 196) or Honey and Ginger Glazed Carrots (page 194).

◆◆◆◆◆◆

6 large leeks, white portions well washed (see Note), patted dry, and thinly sliced (4 cups sliced)
4 loin veal chops, 1 inch thick
Coarse (kosher) salt and freshly ground black pepper
1 tablespoon clarified butter (see About Clarified Butter, facing page)
1 tablespoon unsalted butter
¼ cup minced fresh shallots
½ cup dry white wine
⅓ cup Dan's Mustard (page 252) or another sweet mustard
¼ cup light cream
1 tablespoon minced fresh rosemary

◆◆◆◆◆◆

ABOUT CLARIFIED BUTTER

Clarified butter has a much higher smoke, or burning, point (350°F) than pure butter, making it useful for sautéing and browning foods at a high temperature (just a bit lower than the smoke point of olive oil). Clarifying butter is quite easy: Slowly melt the butter over very low heat. The nonfat ingredients will separate and rise or sink to the bottom, leaving the liquid clarified butter underneath the top layer of white foam. Skim off and discard the foam; then ladle out or pour off the clear butter just until the bottom particles emerge. (Or simply transfer it all to a clean container and refrigerate for at least 1 hour; then scrape the thin white layers of residue from the top and bottom.) The remaining clarified butter will store beautifully in the refrigerator for several months. Ghee, a form of superclarified butter used in Indian and Middle Eastern cooking, is frequently available in specialty food shops.

1. Preheat the oven to 400°F. Butter a gratin or baking dish that is large enough to accommodate the chops in a single layer.

2. Arrange the leeks in the prepared dish and place in the oven. Roast, stirring once or twice, until they are tender and just beginning to color, 15 to 20 minutes. Remove from the oven, but keep the oven on.

3. Season the chops on both sides with a sprinkling of salt and pepper. Melt the clarified butter in a heavy skillet over high heat and sauté the chops until they are nicely browned, 2 to 3 minutes per side. Remove the chops from the skillet, arrange them in a single layer over the leeks, and return the gratin dish to the oven.

4. Add the unsalted butter and shallots to the skillet, and sauté over medium heat until the shallots are tender, about 2 minutes. Add the wine, increase the heat, and stir up any browned bits clinging to the pan. Add the mustard, cream, and rosemary, and whisk until smooth. Bring to a gentle simmer, and then pour the sauce evenly over the chops. Continue to cook in the oven, occasionally spooning the sauce over the chops, just until the chops are cooked through and the sauce is thickened, 10 to 12 minutes (tender veal chops are best cooked until just slightly pink around the bone). Transfer the chops to serving plates, and ladle the tender leeks and mustard sauce on top. Serve hot.

Note: Even if they appear pristine, leeks are notoriously sandy and must always be washed thoroughly. Before cooking leeks, always trim away their root ends and dark green tops; then split the remaining white portions in half lengthwise and soak them in a sink filled with lukewarm water.

133

Pan-Seared Venison in Dried Cherry Demi-Glace

SERVES 2

This is not your everyday dinner— we bring out the venison and demi-glace when it's Valentine's Day or another special occasion. Venison is so lean that quick cooking is crucial; nothing takes the glamour out of any dinner more surely than tough, overcooked meat. Leave the venison rounds in the refrigerator until cooking time, or even put them in the freezer for 20 to 30 minutes before cooking, and then give them a quick pan-searing to keep the interior moist.

The velvety rich fruit sauce balances the spectacular game flavor of the venison. All you need alongside is a few Lacy Two-Potato Pancakes (page 201) or some Wild Rice and Couscous (page 210).

◆◆◆◆◆◆

2 tablespoons unsalted butter

1 tablespoon minced shallot

1 tablespoon light brown sugar

½ cup fruity red wine (such as Pinot Noir, Merlot, or Cabernet)

6 ounces veal demi-glace (see Note)

⅓ cup dried tart cherries (see About Dried Cherries, page 224)

Coarse (kosher) salt

8 ounces boneless venison loin, cut into four ½-inch-thick rounds, chilled

2 teaspoons dried green peppercorns, crushed

1 tablespoon chopped fresh parsley

◆◆◆◆◆◆

1. Melt the butter in a small saucepan over medium heat. Add the shallot and sauté until transparent and tender, about 2 minutes. Sprinkle with the brown sugar, stir in quickly, and then add the red wine, demi-glace, and cherries. Stir to combine, and simmer gently until thick enough to coat the back of a spoon, about 15 minutes. Season to taste with a pinch of salt, and reserve over very low heat while you prepare the venison.

2. Place a large skillet (preferably cast iron and/or ridged) over high heat. Rub both sides of the venison rounds with the crushed green peppercorns to coat lightly. When the skillet is smoking hot, sear the meat just until nicely browned outside and, at most, medium-rare inside, 2 to 3 minutes per side. Serve at once, topped with a large spoonful of the warm cherry sauce and a sprinkling of the chopped parsley.

Note: Demi-glace is the basis for many of the classic sauces that characterize great French cooking. Making this rich brown essence yourself from a reduction of meat bones, stock, and vegetables takes forever, but nowadays good-quality demi-glace can be bought either concentrated or frozen—and given the time and effort it saves, you can forgive the price. Keep it on hand to add quick flavor to an array of sauces for meat, fish, and vegetables.

Pork and Apple Chili

SERVES 6 TO 8

At one time Venison-Apple Chili was a popular Hay Day recipe, but the venison was horribly expensive and easily overcooked. So at home we make this chili with pork loin, and save the venison (when we're lucky enough to have it) to cook as medallions. This is spectacular fall and winter comfort food, especially with some steamed white rice and a basket of warm cornbread or corn muffins.

◆◆◆◆◆◆

3 tablespoons corn oil

2 pounds pork loin, cut into ½-inch chunks

1 tablespoon Cajun seasoning (see Note)

1 small red onion, peeled and coarsely chopped

1 large clove garlic, peeled and minced

1 red bell pepper, stemmed, seeded, and coarsely chopped

1 Scotch bonnet chile, finely minced (see Scotch Bonnet Peppers, page 161)

1 large can (35 ounces) peeled tomatoes, drained and coarsely chopped

1½ cups Browned Beef Stock (page 269)

2 Granny Smith apples, peeled, cored, and coarsely chopped

2 bay leaves

1 teaspoon chili powder

1 tablespoon light brown sugar

1½ cups cooked or canned kidney beans, drained and rinsed

Coarse (kosher) salt

◆◆◆◆◆◆

1. Heat the oil in a large heavy-bottomed kettle or stockpot over high heat. In a large bowl, toss the meat with the Cajun seasoning to coat. Working in small batches, add the meat to the pot and brown on all sides, 2 to 3 minutes. Transfer the browned meat to a small bowl and set aside.

2. Add the onion, garlic, bell pepper, and chile to the pot and sauté until fragrant and tender, about 2 minutes. Stir in the tomatoes and stock. Bring to a boil, scraping up any browned bits clinging to the bottom of the pan, and simmer gently for 5 minutes.

3. Add the apples, bay leaves, chili powder, and brown sugar, and continue to simmer until the apples are tender, about 30 minutes. Stir in the beans and reserved browned meat, along with any accumulated juices, and continue to simmer just until the meat is warmed and cooked through, 10 to 15 minutes. Season with salt to taste and serve hot.

Note: Spicy, bold Cajun seasonings—sometimes called "blackened" seasonings—can be found on almost any grocery store's spice shelf. Use the mixture that's formulated for pork if there is a choice. Or refer to page 172 for blending your own mixture.

Maple-Glazed Pork Chops with Roasted Corn Relish

SERVES 4

This savory sweet glaze gives a rich flavor to succulent smoked pork chops, which are already fully cooked and are quickly finished off on the grill. They make a great late-summer meal paired with the crunchy bright corn relish.

◆◆◆◆◆◆

6 tablespoons maple syrup
2 tablespoons balsamic vinegar
Freshly ground black pepper
4 thick-sliced smoked pork chops
Roasted Corn Relish (recipe follows)

◆◆◆◆◆◆

1. Combine the maple syrup and vinegar in a small saucepan and bring to a gentle simmer over medium-high heat. Simmer until reduced by half and just thick enough to coat the back of a spoon, about 5 minutes. Season with several grindings of pepper and set aside.

2. Preheat the grill to medium-high. When ready to cook, oil the grill rack.

3. Brush the glaze generously over both sides of the pork chops, and grill until lightly charred and warmed through, 3 to 4 minutes per side. Arrange the chops over a bed of the warm corn relish, and serve immediately.

Roasted Corn Relish

MAKES 3 CUPS

A colorful cooked pan relish to serve with country ribs, barbecued chicken, or salmon steaks—or grilled anything, really. Pancetta and balsamic vinegar give it a nice peppery accent.

◆◆◆◆◆◆

4 ounces pancetta or thick-cut peppered bacon, diced
½ cup finely chopped red onion
3 scallions, white and light green parts coarsely chopped
2 cups fresh corn kernels (from about 4 large ears)
1 red or orange bell pepper, stemmed, seeded, and diced
2 tablespoons balsamic vinegar
Coarse (kosher) salt and freshly ground black pepper

◆◆◆◆◆◆

1. Cook the pancetta in a large skillet over medium-high heat until crisp, 10 minutes. Drain all but 1 teaspoon of fat from the pan, add the onion, and sauté until lightly colored, 3 to 5 minutes.

2. Stir in the scallions, corn, and bell pepper. Raise the heat and add the balsamic vinegar. Bring to a boil, scraping up any browned bits. Sauté over high heat, stirring constantly, until the vegetables are warmed yet barely cooked through, 1 to 2 minutes.

3. Remove from the heat, and season to taste with salt and pepper. Serve warm or at room temperature. The relish will keep, covered, in the refrigerator for 2 to 3 days; gently reheat it in the microwave.

Grilled Pork and Apricots

SERVES 4

This is so easy it practically makes itself. You just grill pork and apricots together, glazing them with the savory apricot sauce. Add a side dish of orzo, steamed rice, or our Three-Grain Salad (page 122), and dinner's ready!

◆◆◆◆◆◆

*2 whole boneless pork tenderloins
    (1¼ to 1½ pounds total)
Coarse (kosher) salt and freshly ground
    black pepper to taste
½ cup Apricot-Mustard Glaze (recipe
    follows)
6 firm ripe apricots, split in half, pits
    removed*

◆◆◆◆◆◆

1. Preheat the grill to high. When ready to cook, oil the grill rack.

2. Season the pork on all sides with salt and pepper. Place on the grill and cook for 10 minutes, turning once. Then brush the meat generously with the Apricot-Mustard Glaze. Brush a generous amount of the remaining glaze over the apricots, and add them, cut side down, to the grill alongside the meat. Continue to cook, turning the meat occasionally and reapplying the glaze once or twice, until the tenderloins are lightly browned and just cooked through, 8 to 10 minutes. The apricots should be softened (not mushy) and lightly charred.

3. Using a large spatula, remove the pork and apricots from the grill. Slice the pork into thin medallions and arrange them on plates, accompanied by the grilled apricots, cut side up.

Apricot-Mustard Glaze

MAKES 1¼ CUPS

This popular Hay Day concoction is great on grilled pork, chicken, ham, duck, or sea scallops, and it keeps well in the refrigerator for 6 to 8 weeks.

◆◆◆◆◆◆

*⅓ cup apricot preserves
½ cup honey
2 tablespoons dry sherry
1 tablespoon maple syrup
⅓ cup Dijon mustard
6 sprigs fresh Italian (flat-leaf)
    parsley, stems removed
½ teaspoon coarse (kosher) salt
Freshly ground black pepper*

◆◆◆◆◆◆

Blend all the ingredients except the pepper in a food processor or blender until smooth. Season to taste with black pepper. Transfer to a clean jar and store in the refrigerator.

Honey-Mustard Baked Ham

SERVES 6

People sometimes forget how spectacular good ham can be. Next time you're celebrating almost anything, buy one of the premium smoked hams from a New England smokehouse, roast it with this sweet and spicy (and almost effortless) glaze, and watch it disappear. You could use Dan's Mustard all by itself, but mixing it with honey, cloves, and rum turns the merely delicious into the extraordinary.

◆◆◆◆◆◆

1 New England–style smoked ham
(6 to 8 pounds), rump or shank half
⅓ cup honey
½ cup Dan's Mustard (page 252)
¼ teaspoon ground cloves
2 tablespoons dark rum or whiskey

◆◆◆◆◆◆

1. Preheat the oven to 325°F.

2. Place the ham, fat side up, in a roasting pan. Pour water into the pan to the depth of 1 inch, slide the pan into the oven, and roast for 1½ hours.

3. Meanwhile, stir the honey, mustard, cloves, and rum together in a small bowl until smooth. Set aside.

4. Remove the roasting pan from the oven and brush a generous amount of the glaze all over the ham. Roast, brushing a bit more glaze over the ham every 10 minutes or so, until the crust is golden brown and bubbly, another 30 minutes.

5. Slice, and serve hot or warm.

Lamb and Red Onion Kebabs

SERVES 4

This aromatic blend of Middle Eastern spices is a classic combination with lamb, as is the quick, refreshing cucumber-and-yogurt sauce. For a change of pace, substitute a spoonful of creamy hummus for the sauce. Roasted Vegetable Couscous (page 209) makes an excellent accompaniment.

◆◆◆◆◆◆

2 red onions, peeled and cut in half,
leaving the root and stem ends intact
1½ pounds boneless leg of lamb, cut
into 1½-inch cubes
¼ teaspoon cayenne pepper
¼ teaspoon ground cinnamon
2 teaspoons ground cumin
½ teaspoon coarse (kosher) salt
3 tablespoons olive oil
Cucumber Sauce (recipe follows)

◆◆◆◆◆◆

1. Cut each onion half into six large wedges, and place them in a large dish along with the lamb. Combine the cayenne, cinnamon, cumin, and salt in a small bowl. Sprinkle the spice mixture over the lamb and onions. Drizzle with the oil and toss to coat evenly. Cover and refrigerate for at least 30 minutes or as long as overnight.

2. Preheat the grill to medium-high, or preheat the broiler.

3. Thread the meat and onions alternately onto skewers, and brush with the spices and oil remaining in the dish. When ready to cook, oil the grill rack, if using. Place the skewers on the rack and grill or broil, turning once, until the meat is lightly charred on the outside and pink to medium-rare inside, 8 to 10 minutes. The onions should soften, becoming translucent, and char lightly around the edges.

4. Slide the meat and onions off the skewers onto serving plates, and pass the chilled Cucumber Sauce to spoon on top.

Cucumber Sauce
MAKES 1½ CUPS

This is great not only with lamb, but also with grilled swordfish or salmon, or with any smoked fish.

◆◆◆◆◆◆

1 small cucumber, peeled and coarsely
    chopped
1 cup plain yogurt
2 tablespoons finely chopped fresh mint
1 large clove garlic, peeled, minced
    with a pinch of coarse (or kosher) salt

◆◆◆◆◆◆

In a small bowl, stir together all the ingredients for the cucumber sauce, cover, and set aside in the refrigerator while you prepare the kebabs.

Poultry

Cornish Hens with Cornbread Stuffing
SERVES 4

A simple dry rub of spices adds new flavor to these roasted hens, and the flavor is delightfully complemented by the rustic Cajun-style cornbread stuffing.

◆◆◆◆◆◆

Stuffing and Hens
2 tablespoons unsalted butter
6 ounces andouille sausage, cut into
    medium dice
3 large carrots, scrubbed and cut into
    medium dice
½ cup coarsely chopped onion
3 ribs celery, cut into medium dice
2 cloves garlic, peeled and minced
1 bay leaf
2 tablespoons chopped fresh sage leaves
Southern–Style Cornbread, crumbled
    (recipe follows)
¼ cup Chicken Stock (page 270)
4 Cornish hens (1½ pounds each)

Spice Rub
¾ teaspoon coarse (kosher) salt
1 tablespoon chili powder
1 teaspoon ground cumin
½ teaspoon cayenne pepper

1 tablespoon unsalted butter, melted

A Cozy Holiday Supper

Set the winter table by the fire, serve individual roast birds with wild rice, and after dinner gather around to read *A Christmas Carol* out loud.

❦ ❦ ❦

Cream of Wild Mushroom Soup

Spinach and Citrus Salad in Hay Day's Cranberry Vinaigrette

Cornish Hens with Cornbread Stuffing

Wild Rice and Cranberries

Pumpkin Cheesecake with Gingersnap Crust

❦ ❦ ❦

1. Prepare the stuffing: Melt the butter in a large skillet over medium-high heat and add the andouille, carrots, onion, celery, garlic, and bay leaf. Sauté until fragrant, about 5 minutes. Add the sage and cornbread and continue to cook for a few minutes, stirring continuously to blend the flavors. Add the chicken stock, stir, and continue to cook until just heated through, about 2 minutes. The stuffing should be just slightly moist, not wet. Taste for seasonings, and set aside for at least 30 minutes before stuffing the birds. (The stuffing can be prepared and refrigerated, covered, up to a day in advance.) Remove the bay leaf before stuffing.

2. Preheat the oven to 375°F.

3. Thoroughly rinse and dry the hens.

4. Prepare the spice rub: Stir the salt, chili powder, cumin, and cayenne together in a small bowl. Rub the hens inside and out with the spice mixture, and fill the cavity of each hen with approximately ¾ cup stuffing. Spoon the remaining stuffing into a well-buttered baking dish, and cover with a tight-fitting lid or aluminum foil.

5. Arrange the hens in a roasting pan, and brush with the melted butter. Place the pan and baking dish in the oven, and roast until the hens are nicely browned and crisp and the juices run clear when a thigh is pricked with a fork, 40 to 45 minutes. The dish of stuffing should be piping hot.

6. Serve each hen on a small bed of additional stuffing.

Southern-Style Cornbread

SERVES 8;
MAKES 2 QUARTS CRUMBLED

A classic unsweetened Southern cornbread, perfect for a round or rectangular loaf, a savory stuffing, and corn sticks.

◆◆◆◆◆◆

1½ cups coarse-ground yellow cornmeal
¾ cup unbleached all-purpose flour
¾ teaspoon salt
2 teaspoons baking powder
2 eggs, well beaten
½ cup buttermilk
1 cup milk
3 tablespoons unsalted butter, melted

◆◆◆◆◆◆

1. Preheat the oven to 375°F. Butter a 2-quart (10 × 7-inch) glass baking dish.

2. In a mixing bowl, stir together the cornmeal, flour, salt, and baking powder. In a separate bowl, beat the eggs with the buttermilk and milk. Add the egg mixture to the cornmeal mixture, and stir together until just moistened. (The batter will be slightly lumpy, like pancake batter.) Stir in the melted butter.

3. Pour the batter into the prepared baking dish, and bake until the top is golden brown and a toothpick inserted in the center comes out clean, about 25 minutes.

4. Allow the cornbread to cool in the pan for about 10 minutes before cutting it into squares and serving. If you are using it for stuffing, let the cornbread cool in the pan for 10 minutes, then turn it out onto a large baking sheet. Using your fingers, crumble the cornbread into coarse bits. Spread the crumbles out on the baking sheet and allow them to air-dry for about 2 hours. Then prepare the stuffing or store the cornbread in a plastic bag for up to 2 days.

Variation

◆ For savory cornbread, stir into the batter a generous handful of crumbled crisp bacon or cut corn kernels, some minced fresh jalapeños or chopped scallions, or a cup of shredded Monterey Jack cheese.

Pecan-Crusted Chicken with Spicy Apple Butter

SERVES 4

The simple combination of pecans, cornmeal, and oats forms a crisp golden crust for boneless chicken, with egg whites as a light binder. We like the contrast with the sweetness and spice of the apple butter, but a bit of good old-fashioned applesauce fills the bill too. Complete the meal with Maple-Roasted Sweet Potato Spears (page 203) or Cider-Glazed Autumn Medley (page 207).

◆◆◆◆◆◆

2 whole boneless, skinless chicken breasts, about 1½ pounds, tenderloins removed (see Note)
⅓ cup old-fashioned rolled oats
⅔ cup pecan pieces
3 tablespoons stone-ground cornmeal
¼ teaspoon coarse (kosher) salt
Freshly ground black pepper
2 egg whites
2 tablespoons vegetable oil
1 tablespoon unsalted butter
Spicy Apple Butter (recipe follows), or Aunt Maud's Apple Cider Applesauce (page 255)

◆◆◆◆◆◆

1. Rinse and dry the chicken breasts. Slice each in half down the center to make four serving portions.

2. Place the oats in a food processor or blender, and process to form a coarse meal. Add the pecans and pulse until the nuts are uniformly chopped, with the bits no larger than small grains of rice. Add the cornmeal, salt, and a couple of grindings of black pepper, and pulse to combine. Spread the mixture out on a flat plate or cutting board.

3. Beat the egg whites until foamy, and pour them onto a plate. Dip each chicken breast in the egg whites, then in the oat mixture, pressing it lightly to coat evenly on all sides. Shake lightly to remove any excess crumbs. (The chicken can be prepared to this point up to a day in advance; wrap in plastic wrap and refrigerate.)

4. Heat the oil and butter in a large skillet over medium-high heat until hot. Add the chicken breasts and sauté until nicely browned on both sides (taking care not to scorch the nuts) and just cooked through, 2 to 3 minutes per side. Serve warm, accompanied by a large spoonful of the apple butter.

Note: Because pecans can scorch easily, choose chicken breasts that are not too plump, so they'll cook quickly and evenly.

Spicy Apple Butter

MAKES 1 GENEROUS CUP

This savory fruit preserve is traditionally made with fresh apples that are cooked very slowly, but with their concentrated flavor, dried apple rings are a great shortcut. Chipotle peppers give it a smoky spiciness, but you can omit them and still have a rich, aromatic sweet apple butter. Try this as a holiday condiment with roast chicken, pork, turkey, or smoked pheasant. It's also great on a cracker with a bit of sharp Cheddar.

◆◆◆◆◆◆

1 packed cup (3 ounces) dried apple rings
1 small dried chipotle pepper, broken into large pieces, seeds removed (see Note)
1⅓ cups apple cider or juice
½ teaspoon ground cinnamon
¼ teaspoon ground allspice
1 tablespoon Calvados or other apple brandy

◆◆◆◆◆◆

Combine all the ingredients in a small saucepan and bring to a boil. Reduce the heat to low, cover, and simmer until the apples are very tender, about 20 minutes. Pour the contents of the saucepan into a blender or food processor, and purée until smooth. Serve at room temperature. Keeps well for several weeks in the refrigerator.

Note: Chipotles are dried smoked jalapeño peppers with an intense smoky flavor. Make sure you use the dried variety for this recipe (they are also sold reconstituted in a rich adobo sauce). See About Chile Peppers, on page 87, for instructions on handling chiles.

If you are wary about the amount of heat the chipotle will add to the apple butter, don't add any to the blender until after you have puréed the mixture. Then you can add the pieces bit by bit, puréeing and tasting as you go.

Lemon-Chèvre Chicken

SERVES 4

This almost takes more time to describe than it does to prepare: chicken breasts stuffed with herbs and goat cheese, sautéed, and napped with a simple Greek-style lemon sauce. You could skip the sauce and serve the stuffed breasts, warm or cold, with red pepper jelly or a tangy fruit chutney. A side dish of Spring Pea Medley (page 198) or Roasted Vidalias and Red Peppers (page 197) would complete the meal perfectly.

◆◆◆◆◆◆

2 whole boneless, skinless chicken breasts (about 1½ pounds total), halved, tenderloins removed
4 ounces creamy fresh chèvre (see A Note on Chèvre, page 60)
4 tablespoons minced fresh chives, basil, and parsley, mixed
½ teaspoon plus scant 2 tablespoons olive oil, more if needed
Coarse (kosher) salt and ground white pepper
½ cup Chicken Stock (page 270)
1 teaspoon light brown sugar
1 egg
1½ tablespoons fresh lemon juice

◆◆◆◆◆◆

1. Preheat the oven to 200°F.

2. Using a thin boning knife, cut a lengthwise pocket in the thickest side of each breast half, without cutting through to either surface.

3. In a small bowl, mash together the goat cheese, 3 tablespoons of the mixed herbs, and the ½ teaspoon oil with the back of a fork; add a dash more oil if needed to work into a creamy consistency. Season to taste with salt and pepper. Spoon the mixture into a pastry bag fitted with a ½-inch round tip, and pipe a generous tablespoon into each breast pocket (or use a teaspoon to fill the pocket). Secure the openings with a single wooden toothpick, and season the outside of each breast with a sprinkling of salt and pepper. Refrigerate, covered, until ready to cook (the chicken can be prepared to this point up to 1 day in advance).

4. Heat the remaining 2 tablespoons oil in a large heavy skillet over medium-high heat. Add the chicken and sauté until nicely browned, about 5 minutes. Turn, carefully loosening the chicken from the bottom of the skillet, and continue to sauté until it is cooked through and nicely browned on both sides, another 3 to 5 minutes. Transfer to an ovenproof dish and place in the oven.

5. Drain the fat from the pan, add the stock, and warm gently over medium heat, scraping up any browned bits. Stir in the brown sugar and bring to a gentle simmer.

6. Meanwhile, whisk the egg vigorously in a small bowl until it is fluffy and light

143

in color. Then whisk in the lemon juice. Add this to the simmering liquid, whisking continuously. Add the cooked chicken, along with any accumulated juices, and cook over low heat, frequently spooning the sauce over the chicken, until the sauce is lightly thickened, 1 to 2 minutes. Season the sauce to taste with salt and pepper.

7. Remove the toothpicks and serve, topping each chicken breast with a spoonful of the sauce and a sprinkling of the remaining herbs.

Chicken and Olive Stew

SERVES 4 TO 6

This quickly cooked, aromatic stew gets its distinctive Spanish flavor from chorizo sausage, briny green olives, generous amounts of garlic and bell peppers—and sherry. Use a medium-dry Spanish sherry like oloroso or amontillado for the best flavor and fragrance. All you need to complete this meal is a platter of steamed rice.

◆◆◆◆◆◆

3 tablespoons unbleached all-purpose flour
Coarse (kosher) salt and freshly ground black pepper
2 tablespoons olive oil, more if needed
1½ pounds boneless, skinless chicken breasts, cut into 1-inch-thick strips
1 clove garlic, peeled and minced
1 Spanish onion, peeled and coarsely chopped
2 chorizo sausages, coarsely chopped
1 red bell pepper, stemmed, seeded, and cut into strips
1 green bell pepper, stemmed, seeded, and cut into strips
⅓ cup Chicken Stock (page 270)
⅓ cup medium-dry sherry (see About Sherry, page 82)
1 can (14 ounces) peeled plum tomatoes, drained and coarsely chopped
½ cup pitted brine-cured green olives (Spanish manzanilla or other good-quality olives)
1 teaspoon fresh thyme leaves

◆◆◆◆◆◆

1. In a small bowl, combine the flour with 1 teaspoon each salt and black pepper.

2. Heat the oil in a large Dutch oven or skillet over high heat.

3. Toss the chicken strips in the seasoned flour, add to the pan, and brown on all sides, 2 to 3 minutes. Transfer the chicken to a small bowl and set aside.

4. Add the garlic and onion to the pan, along with a dash more oil if needed, reduce the heat, and sauté over medium-high heat until just transparent, about 2

CANNED PLUM TOMATOES

We revel in the abundance of fresh local tomatoes in July and August, but what do we do the rest of the year? Although the quality of imported fresh tomatoes gets better all the time, supplies are not always reliable. So it is a relief to be able to fall back on canned plum tomatoes, which are packed at the peak of their season and can be substituted for fresh tomatoes in all of our recipes for cooked soups, stews, and sauces (unless otherwise specified).

When you buy canned tomatoes, always buy them whole—they'll be the best quality—and chop or crush them as needed for the recipe. The best of the lot are the imported Italian San Marzano tomatoes, but they are packed by a number of companies. The quality can vary widely, so be selective. Buy one can of a brand at a time, and look for firm, whole, bright red tomatoes packed with very little juice and no fragments. They should taste fresh and sweet and be firm enough to slice. Once you have found a brand you like, keep a supply in the pantry. If you're like us, you'll use them all the time—just as we do in this book.

---

minutes. Add the chorizo and bell pepper strips, and continue to sauté until fragrant and tender, 5 minutes.

5. Add the stock and stir up any browned bits clinging to the pan. Then add the sherry, tomatoes, olives, and sautéed chicken along with any accumulated juices in the bowl. Stir together and simmer gently until the tomatoes have thickened, the peppers are extremely tender, and the stew is hot and aromatic, 10 to 15 minutes. Add the thyme and simmer for another minute. Season to taste with salt and pepper, and serve hot.

Chicken Pies with a Puff Pastry Lid

SERVES 6

Hay Day's bestselling chicken potpie has been an essential comfort food in Fairfield County for as long as we can remember. Chicken, mushrooms, carrots, and celery are cloaked in a silky tarragon white sauce and baked under a crisp "comforter" of puff pastry for the kind of suppertime classic that mothers used to make (theoretically) at least once a week. Even if you make it only once a year, it's nice to have this definitive recipe. Individual potpies really are the best, especially if family schedules don't mesh. Have the filling ready in one container, the egg glaze in another, and the thawed puff pastry circles in the fridge, and then the

145

pies can be baked to order. That way the last person home still gets a fair share of supper—and of comfort, too.

◆◆◆◆◆◆

3 large bone-in chicken breast halves
(about 2 pounds total)
3 cups Chicken Stock (page 270)
2 bay leaves
18 to 20 bite-size pearl onions,
trimmed and peeled
3 carrots, scrubbed and cut into
¼-inch-thick rounds
⅓ pound button mushrooms, wiped
clean and thickly sliced
2 ribs celery, cut into ¼-inch-thick
slices
4 tablespoons (½ stick) unsalted butter
⅓ cup unbleached all-purpose flour
1½ cups plus 1 tablespoon milk
1½ tablespoons chopped fresh tarragon
leaves or sage leaves
3 tablespoons medium-dry sherry
(see About Sherry, page 82)
Coarse (kosher) salt and freshly
ground black pepper to taste
1 package frozen puff-pastry sheets
(17¼ ounces, 2 sheets), thawed
1 egg

◆◆◆◆◆◆

1. Place the chicken in a medium-size saucepan, add the stock, and bring to a simmer over medium-high heat. Add the bay leaves and simmer very gently until the chicken is cooked to the bone, about

20 minutes. Remove with a slotted spoon and set aside to cool.

2. Add the pearl onions to the simmering stock and poach for 5 minutes. Then add the carrots, mushrooms, and celery, and continue to simmer gently until the carrots and celery are bright and tender, about 5 minutes more. Strain the contents of the saucepan into a bowl through a fine-mesh sieve. Set the vegetables aside.

3. Remove and discard the skin and bones from the chicken breasts, and shred the meat into bite-size pieces (see Pulled Meat, facing page)

4. Melt the butter in a small saucepan over medium heat. Whisk in the flour and cook until the flour is very lightly browned, 2 to 3 minutes. Add 2 cups of the strained stock and the 1½ cups milk in a steady, even stream, whisking constantly until smooth. Bring to a gentle simmer, add the tarragon, and continue to simmer until the sauce is slightly thickened, about 1 minute. Then add the sherry, and stir in the chicken and vegetables. Season to taste with salt and pepper. (The filling can be prepared to this point a day or two in advance and refrigerated, covered, until serving time.)

5. Preheat the oven to 400°F.

6. Set out eight individual ovenproof crocks or ramekins. Roll the puff pastry out on a lightly floured work surface, and trace around the outside rim of a crock to cut lids for the potpies. Mix the egg with the remaining 1 tablespoon milk to use as a wash for the pastry.

7. Spoon the chicken and vegetables into the crocks, and place on a large baking sheet. Arrange the pastry rounds alongside the crocks. Prick each in several places with the tines of a fork and brush with the egg wash. Bake until the pastry is nicely browned and puffed and the filling is bubbling hot, 15 to 20 minutes. Remove from the oven, place a pastry round on each crock, and serve.

PULLED MEAT

The rough irregular texture of shredded, or pulled, meat grabs and cradles sauces better than smooth, evenly chopped chunks of meat. Two small table forks are the only tools needed to shred the chicken. Spear one upright into the meat to hold it in place while raking the other fork back and forth, pulling the meat from the bone in shreds.

Rosemary Chicken Kebabs

SERVES 4

Serving skewered chicken on pitas, Middle-Eastern style, is great for casual summer entertaining. The pitas keep the chicken warm and soak up the juices (to be authentic they should be torn into small pieces and used as utensils to hold individual bites of meat).

The fresh sweet and hot peppers add succulent flavor. We sell sturdy rosemary branches for use as skewers in our produce department; the stems give a nice flavor to lamb, chicken, fish, and vegetables. You can make your own if the rosemary in your garden is mature enough: Just rinse, and whittle the woody ends a bit to make a point. If you can't obtain rosemary skewers, use traditional metal or bamboo skewers. And if you run out of charcoal, the kebabs can easily be cooked under the kitchen broiler.

Complete the meal with a traditional tabbouleh or with Quinoa-Tabbouleh Salad (page 124).

◆◆◆◆◆◆

8 rosemary skewers (at least 8 inches long)
1 red bell pepper
1 yellow or orange bell pepper
1 large dark-green poblano chile (see About Poblano Chiles, page 148)
2 whole boneless, skinless chicken breasts (about 1½ pounds), cut into bite-size chunks
¾ cup fresh lemon juice (3 to 4 large lemons)
⅓ cup olive oil
6 scallions, white and light green parts finely minced
1 teaspoon coarse (kosher) salt
Freshly ground black pepper
4 round pita breads (8-inch size), split horizontally into 8 rounds (see Note)

◆◆◆◆◆◆

1. Place the rosemary skewers (or bamboo, if using) in a flat dish of water to cover, and set aside to soak for at least 15 minutes.

2. Cut the bell and poblano peppers into 1-inch chunks, removing the stems and seeds. Place in a large nonreactive bowl along with the chicken, lemon juice, oil, scallions, salt, and several grindings of pepper. Toss to coat, cover, and set aside to marinate in the refrigerator for at least 1 hour or as long as overnight.

3. Preheat the grill to medium-high.

4. Thread the chunks of chicken and peppers onto the skewers in an alternating pattern, dividing the pepper varieties evenly among the eight skewers. Reserve the marinade for basting at the grill.

5. When ready to cook, oil the grill rack. Place the skewers on the grill and cook, turning and basting occasionally with the marinade, until the chicken is nicely browned and cooked through and the peppers are tender and a bit charred around the edges, about 15 minutes. Discard any remaining marinade.

6. Meanwhile, place half of the split pita rounds on a serving platter, rough sides up.

7. Place the kebabs on top of the pita rounds, and quickly cover with the remaining rounds to keep warm and collect the juices. Serve immediately.

Note: Vastly different from the leathery supermarket version, good-quality fresh pitas are in a class by themselves. You will find the best quality sold fresh and unrefrigerated. Large Middle Eastern flatbreads called lavash, or mountain shepherd bread, make a fine substitute.

ABOUT POBLANO CHILES

Beautiful dark-green fresh poblano chile peppers (the kind most commonly used in the preparation of chiles rellenos) look like small, thin green bell peppers. Readily available in most markets, they're richly flavored but not fiercely hot and are therefore a good place to start if you're a newcomer to the whole idea of cooking with chiles.

Southern Pulled Chicken Barbecue

SERVES 6

Pulled pork barbecue is a way of life in the South; we make a wonderful version at Hay Day with slowly smoked Boston butts. At home, however, we use the same technique with chicken thighs, which cuts down on fat and saves hours of time and labor. We season the thighs with a simple dry rub, leave the skin on to protect them in cooking, then discard the skin and shred the meat (you can't do this with chicken breasts), and mix it with a traditional Georgia-style mustard-based barbecue sauce. This method of long slow cooking over a low fire is what classic barbecue is all about. Anything else is grilling.

The chicken is great with soft potato rolls and Hay Day's Creamy Mustard Coleslaw (page 114) or Buttermilk Ranch Potato Salad (page 108), and it also makes a terrific sandwich. The spice rub is great stuff to keep on hand; it'll give an instant flavor infusion to chicken, beef, ribs, or fish steaks.

◆◆◆◆◆◆

Spicy Dry Rub

3 tablespoons light brown sugar
1 tablespoon coarse (kosher) salt
1 tablespoon ground cumin
2 tablespoons sweet paprika
1 tablespoon chili powder
1 tablespoon cracked black pepper
½ teaspoon cayenne pepper

4 pounds bone-in chicken thighs,
 skin on
About 1 cup Savannah Barbecue
 Sauce (page 268) or other mustard-
 based barbecue sauce
6 soft rolls, split

◆◆◆◆◆◆

1. Preheat the grill to very low.

2. Combine the dry rub ingredients in a small bowl. Stir together well, and rub a thin layer all over the chicken.

3. When ready to cook, oil the grill rack and grill the chicken, skin side down, covered, until the skin has begun to blacken and the meat easily separates from the bone, about 1 hour. During the last 15 minutes, repeatedly turn and baste with a bit of the barbecue sauce.

4. Remove the chicken from the grill and allow to rest until cool enough to handle.

Remove and discard the skin. Pull the meat off the bones and shred it, discarding any fat, and placing the shreds in a bowl (see Pulled Meat, page 147). Add the remaining barbecue sauce to taste and serve warm, tucked inside the soft rolls. (The barbecued meat can be prepared a day or two in advance. To reheat, simply pile it into an ovenproof dish, cover tightly with aluminum foil, and place in a 350°F oven until warm throughout.)

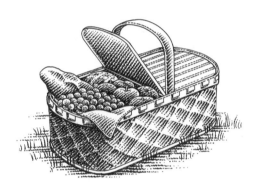

Grilled Chicken Fajita Salad

SERVES 4 TO 6

This was one of the first things we made when the big charbroilers were installed in the Hay Day commissary; it's a great way to enjoy all the color and flavor of fajitas without the last-minute work. You just rub the chicken with classic south-of-the border spices and grill it with the bell peppers, then slice and toss in lime juice with onion and tomatoes. This salad is even better when it's made a day or two ahead so the flavors can mingle.

To round out the Southwestern meal, serve wedges of warm flour tortillas alongside.

◆◆◆◆◆◆

1½ teaspoons ground cumin
1 teaspoon dried thyme leaves
2 teaspoons freshly ground black pepper
2 teaspoons hot paprika
2 teaspoons chili powder
Coarse (kosher) salt to taste
2 whole boneless, skinless chicken
  breasts (about 1½ pounds)
4 tablespoons vegetable oil
1 red bell pepper, halved, stemmed,
  and seeded
1 yellow bell pepper, halved, stemmed,
  and seeded
1 green bell pepper, halved, stemmed,
  and seeded
1 to 2 large Spanish onion, peeled,
  halved, and sliced into thin crescents
  (2 cups sliced)
3 large ripe plum tomatoes, cut
  lengthwise into thin slices
¼ cup coarsely chopped fresh Italian
  (flat-leaf) parsley or cilantro
Juice of 1 large lime
2 tablespoons red wine vinegar

◆◆◆◆◆◆

1. Preheat the grill to medium-high.

2. Toss the cumin, thyme, pepper, paprika, chili powder, and ¼ teaspoon salt together in a small jar or bowl.

3. Rinse the chicken, pat dry, and trim off any excess fat. Place the chicken in a baking dish and sprinkle with 2 tablespoons of the spice mixture. Drizzle with 2 tablespoons of the oil and toss to coat evenly. Brush the bell peppers with a bit of the remaining oil.

Menu

A Well-Orchestrated Summer Picnic

From Tanglewood to Wolf Trap, Spoleto to Santa Fe, America's summer festivals are the inspiration for simple, imaginative picnic menus that can be prepared ahead, packed in a cooler, and then spread on the grass as the shadows lengthen across the lawn and the setting sun gilds a glass of Chardonnay.

❦ ❦ ❦

*Avocado and Jicama Salsa
with corn chips*

Chilled Fresh Tomato and Basil Soup

*Grilled Chicken Fajita Salad
with flour tortillas*

Summer Plum Torte

❦ ❦ ❦

4. When ready to cook, oil the grill rack. Grill the chicken until it is a bit charred around the edges and just cooked through, 3 to 5 minutes per side; grill the bell peppers until they have softened and the skins are nicely charred, 3 to 5 minutes per side.

5. Cut the chicken and bell peppers into ¼-inch-wide diagonal strips and toss in a large bowl. Add the remaining spice mixture, the remaining 2 tablespoons oil, and the onion, tomatoes, parsley, lime juice, and vinegar. Toss, and season with additional salt as needed. Serve warm, or prepare a day or two in advance and store, covered, in the refrigerator.

Mango Chicken Salad

SERVES 4

Curried chicken salad has been a standby at Hay Day for years. This is a seductive hot-weather version, made with fresh summer mangoes and green grapes, and lightened with yogurt. Beautiful, assertive dark-green tatsoi balances the flavor and color of the spicy golden chicken.

◆◆◆◆◆◆

3 large bone-in chicken breast halves
(about 2½ pounds)
1 cup Chicken Stock (see page 270)
2 bay leaves
6 black peppercorns
2 tablespoons mayonnaise
¼ cup plain yogurt
3 tablespoons mango chutney
1 teaspoon curry powder
1 tablespoon finely chopped fresh
cilantro or parsley
¼ teaspoon coarse (kosher) salt, or
to taste
2 large ripe mangoes (see About
Mangoes, page 218)
1 large rib celery, diced
1 cup green grapes, sliced in half
4 ounces tatsoi greens (see About
Tatsoi) or fresh spinach
½ cup unsalted roasted peanuts

◆◆◆◆◆◆

1. Place the chicken in a saucepan and add the stock, bay leaves, and peppercorns. Pour in enough water to just cover the chicken. Bring to a simmer, cover, and poach until just cooked through, 15 to 20 minutes.

2. Meanwhile, combine the mayonnaise, yogurt, chutney, curry powder, and cilantro in a small bowl. Stir together to blend, season with the salt, cover, and refrigerate.

3. Drain the poached chicken breasts and set aside until cool enough to handle.

4. Cut the flesh of 1 mango into bite-size chunks, and slice the flesh of the remaining mango into thin wedges.

5. Remove and discard the skin and bones from the chicken breasts; then chop or shred the meat into bite-size chunks. Combine in a large bowl with the celery, grapes, and the mango chunks. Add the reserved dressing and toss to coat evenly. Cover and refrigerate until ready to serve.

ABOUT TATSOI

So many people are buying fresh salad mixtures nowadays that once-exotic greens like tatsoi and mizuna have become almost commonplace. Tatsoi is the cute little succulent one with the round dark-green leaves and pronounced white rib and stem. A member of the mustard family, it has a very faint but pleasant cabbage-like taste. We get it locally in the summer, but it is grown year-round in greenhouses and on small specialty farms in California.

6. At serving time, divide the tatsoi evenly among four plates, and top with the mango slices and the chicken salad. Sprinkle a small handful of the peanuts over each plate, and serve.

Smoked Chicken and Arugula Salad

SERVES 4

I nspired by Hay Day's Cranberry Vinaigrette and the succulent smoked chicken breasts now available from any number of small smokehouses, this is about as easy as a recipe can get. Just toss arugula and blue cheese with vinaigrette, arrange the salad to make a crisp base for thin slices of smoked chicken, and top with a few dried cranberries and toasted walnuts. Piece of cake.

◆◆◆◆◆◆

4 ounces arugula (2 large bunches), trimmed, soaked in cold water, and dried

4 ounces sharp blue cheese (Roquefort, Maytag, or Bleu d'Auvergne), crumbled

½ cup coarsely chopped walnuts

½ cup Cranberry Vinaigrette (page 119)

8 ounces smoked chicken breast, thinly sliced

¼ cup dried cranberries

◆◆◆◆◆◆

1. Preheat the oven to 350°F.

2. In a large bowl, toss the arugula with the blue cheese.

3. Spread the walnuts on a small baking sheet and toast in the oven until fragrant and lightly colored, 5 to 7 minutes. Remove from the oven and set aside to cool.

4. Sprinkle ¼ cup of the Cranberry Vinaigrette over the arugula, and toss to dress evenly. Divide the salad among four plates, and top each portion with some of the sliced chicken breast. Drizzle the remaining ¼ cup vinaigrette over the chicken, sprinkle each serving with the walnuts and dried cranberries, and serve.

The Comforts of Home

W hen it gets dark earlier, we gather once again around the hearth. This is the moment for comfort foods we put aside for the summer: nurturing fall classics that go naturally with quiet suppertime conversation.

Cream of Roasted Fennel Soup

*Mixed Greens with
Olive Oil Vinaigrette*

*Mediterranean Turkey Loaf
Buttermilk-Chive Mashed Potatoes*

Pear and Apple Potpies

Mediterranean Turkey Loaf

SERVES 6 TO 8

Combining the comfort level of meat loaf with the virtues of low-fat turkey, this is another gem from the Hay Day Hall of Fame. Dark turkey meat makes the juiciest meat loaf—the white breast meat is just too lean and dry. You'll get the best texture if you handle the meat gently and don't work it too hard.

If you like, heat up some additional Classic Ratatouille to serve as a sauce over the meat loaf. Complete the meal with a scoop of Buttermilk-Chive Mashed Potatoes (page 201) topped with a little more ratatouille.

◆◆◆◆◆◆

1 teaspoon olive oil
1½ cups old-fashioned rolled oats
2 pounds fresh ground turkey
   (dark meat)
⅓ cup shredded fresh basil leaves
½ cup plus 3 tablespoons freshly grated
   Parmesan cheese (see Grating
   Cheeses, page 251)
1 generous cup Classic Ratatouille
   (page 258)
2 eggs, lightly beaten
2 teaspoons coarse (kosher) salt
Freshly ground black pepper
Tabasco or other hot pepper sauce
½ cup fresh or good-quality canned
   peeled plum tomatoes, crushed,
   with their juices

◆◆◆◆◆◆

1. Preheat the oven to 350°F. Grease a 1½-quart loaf pan with the oil.

2. Place the oats in a food processor or blender and process to form a coarse meal.

3. Place the turkey, basil, oats, ½ cup cheese, ratatouille, eggs, and salt in a large mixing bowl. Add several grindings of pepper and a dash or two of hot pepper sauce. Mix together gently and thoroughly.

4. Pack the turkey mixture into the prepared pan and top with the crushed tomatoes. Cover with aluminum foil and bake for 1 hour.

5. Raise the oven temperature to 375°F, remove the foil, sprinkle on the remaining 3 tablespoons cheese, and continue to bake until the tomatoes are lightly caramelized on top, 10 to 15 minutes. Remove the meat loaf from the oven and let it rest for 10 minutes before slicing.

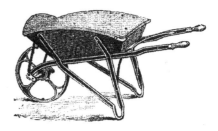

All-American Turkey Salad

SERVES 6

This guilt-free autumn salad is one of the prettiest things we make and one of the lightest. There's no oil in the dressing, which works beautifully with the healthful mix of wild and brown rice, lean smoked turkey, and golden butternut squash. And the bright fall accent of tart-sweet dried cranberries is wonderful all year round.

◆◆◆◆◆◆

Dressing

½ cup Chicken Stock (page 270)
½ cup fresh orange juice
3 tablespoons sherry vinegar
1 tablespoon raspberry vinegar
Pinch of ground allspice
½ teaspoon sugar
*Coarse (kosher) salt and freshly
    ground black pepper to taste*

Salad

2 tablespoons olive oil
½ cup wild rice, well rinsed
1 cup brown rice
3⅓ cups plus ¼ cup water
½ teaspoon coarse (kosher) salt
*12 ounces butternut squash or sugar
    pumpkin, peeled and cut into
    ½-inch dice*
*10 ounces smoked turkey breast, cut
    into ½-inch dice*
*2 ounces (approximately ½ cup)
    dried cranberries*
*Finely chopped fresh mint,
    for garnish*

◆◆◆◆◆◆

1. Whisk together all the dressing ingredients in a small bowl and set aside.

2. Heat the oil in a small saucepan, and sauté the wild and brown rice over medium-high heat to seal and separate the grains, 1 to 2 minutes. Add the 3⅓ cups water and ½ teaspoon salt and bring to a boil. Reduce the heat, cover, and simmer gently until the grains are just tender, about 45 minutes. Remove the pan from the heat, and separate and fluff the grains with a fork.

3. Meanwhile, place the squash in a small saucepan and add the ¼ cup water. Bring to a simmer, reduce the heat to low, cover, and steam until just barely fork-tender (not mushy!), 5 to 7 minutes. Drain.

4. Combine the hot rice, squash, turkey, and cranberries in a large salad bowl. Whisk the dressing again and drizzle it on top. Stir together gently and thoroughly. Season to taste with salt and pepper, and refrigerate, covered, for at least 1 hour. Serve cold, topping each serving with a pinch of chopped fresh mint.

DUCKS: PEKIN OR PEKING?

This is important: Pekin (rhymes with *reckon*) is a breed of duck; Peking (named for the city now called Beijing) is a preparation. Pekin ducks are specially bred to be tender, mild in flavor, and low in fat; recent USDA studies show that their skinless white meat contains less fat and fewer calories than skinless chicken breasts! Since Muscovy and Moulard ducks are bred as sources of foie gras, they are naturally higher in fat (the duck meat labeled *magret* is the meaty breast of a Muscovy duck). We find the smaller, leaner Pekin breasts ideal for grilling.

Grilled Duck Breast with Fresh Citrus-Cherry Relish

SERVES 4

Boneless Pekin duck breasts (they're smaller and less fatty than other varieties of duck) are readily available these days, and they're extraordinary when grilled. Here the duck is cooked skin side down to protect the lean meat from the fire and to allow the skin to brown while its fat cooks off. Cut the meat, with its sublimely succulent browned skin (unlike that of a roast bird, it will not crisp completely), into thin slices, and serve the fruity relish as a refreshing complement.

◆◆◆◆◆◆

2 whole boneless Pekin duck breasts
Coarse (kosher) salt and freshly ground
* black pepper to taste*
4 handfuls mâche (lamb's lettuce)
Citrus-Cherry Relish (recipe follows)

◆◆◆◆◆◆

1. Preheat the grill to low. When ready to cook, oil the grill rack.

2. Jab the tines of a fork randomly into the skin side of the duck breast, piercing through to the flesh, to allow some of the fat to cook off during grilling. Season liberally on both sides with salt and pepper, and place skin side down on the grill. Cook over low heat until the skin is nicely browned and crisped around the edges and the meat is tender and pink, 25 to 30 minutes. For medium-done meat, flip the breasts and cook for another 5 minutes. Remove from the grill and cut into thin lengthwise slices, along the grain of the meat.

3. Arrange a small bed of mâche on each plate, spoon a portion of the fruit relish on top, and fan a portion of the duck slices alongside. Spoon relish juices over the meat, and serve warm or at room temperature.

Citrus-Cherry Relish

MAKES 2 CUPS

This also makes a delicious and attractive summer accompaniment to grilled pork chops, chicken, or tenderloin. In the off-season make the relish with dried cherries that have been plumped in the vinegar.

◆◆◆◆◆◆

3 seedless oranges, peel and pith removed
8 ounces fresh sweet cherries (Bing
* or Rainier), pitted and quartered*
6 scallions, white and light green parts
* coarsely chopped*
6 large fresh basil leaves, cut into
* fine shreds*
Juice of 1 large lime
1½ tablespoons red wine vinegar
3 tablespoons light vegetable oil
Coarse (kosher) salt and freshly ground
* black pepper*

◆◆◆◆◆◆

Working over a medium-size glass bowl to collect the juices, free the orange sections and drop them into the bowl. Add the cherries, scallions, basil, lime juice, vinegar, and oil. Stir to combine well, and season to taste with salt and pepper. Set aside at room temperature for at least 15 minutes to allow the flavors to mingle. Covered tightly and refrigerated, the relish will keep nicely for a day or two.

Seafood

East Coast Fisherman's Stew

SERVES 6

This fragrant, quick-cooking fish stew is a hearty, healthful classic for fall and winter. It was brought to our shores by the Portuguese fishermen who settled along the New England coast in the earliest days of the colonies. You can substitute any other sturdy white-fleshed fish—haddock, monkfish, pollock—for the traditional cod. Be sure

to cook the stew just until the shellfish have opened (don't let one or two stubborn mussels fool you—if they don't open, discard them).

Serve some warm Portuguese rolls or toasted slices of Hay Day's Best-Ever Potato Bread (page 103) with the stew— and don't be a snob about using the bread to sop up the delicious juices!

◆◆◆◆◆◆

½ cup extra-virgin olive oil
1 small onion, peeled and chopped
1 bulb fresh fennel, rinsed, trimmed, and coarsely chopped
5 cups coarsely chopped fresh or good-quality canned peeled tomatoes
4 large cloves garlic, peeled and minced
1 large pinch saffron threads, preferably toasted (see Cooking with Saffron, page 180)
1 cup dry white wine
Coarse (kosher) salt
¼ cup shredded fresh basil leaves
⅓ cup coarsely chopped fresh Italian (flat-leaf) parsley
1½ pounds fresh cod, cut into bite-size chunks
1 pound medium shrimp, deveined, shells left on (see Note)
24 fresh mussels or clams, shells well-scrubbed (if using mussels, remove beards)

◆◆◆◆◆◆

1. Heat the oil in a large heavy-bottomed kettle or soup pot over medium-high heat. Add the onion and fennel, and sauté until lightly caramelized, 8 to 10 minutes. Stir in the tomatoes, garlic, saffron, and wine, and simmer gently until slightly thickened, 15 to 20 minutes. Season to taste with salt.

2. Add the basil and parsley to the pot. Season the cod with 1 teaspoon salt, and add the fish to the pot in an even layer. Then add the shrimp in a layer, and finally the mussels. Cover and simmer, stirring gently once, just until the mussels have opened and the shrimp are completely pink and the fish opaque, 10 to 12 minutes. Discard any mussels that do not open. Spoon the seafood into large warm shallow bowls, and ladle the juices on top. Serve hot.

Note: Shrimp cooked in its shell retains the most juice and seasonings for the best flavor and texture. To clean the shrimp, just split it along the back ridge, using a pair of kitchen shears or a sharp knife, cutting just deep enough to expose the dark vein. Rinse the vein away under cold running water. Once cooked, the shells are easy to peel away with your fingers.

Curried Sea Bass and Butternut Stew

SERVES 4 TO 6

We originally made this recipe with sugar pumpkin, but sweet butternut squash is so universally available nowadays (you can even get it peeled and cubed) that we use it a lot—it goes beautifully with the curry and tomatoes. The firm white flesh of sea bass holds up well in a stew, and here it absorbs all the rich autumnal flavor. Toasted slices of Whole-Meal Bread (page 102) or a basket of warm garlic bread would be a nice addition to the meal.

◆◆◆◆◆◆

¼ cup light vegetable oil
1 large onion, peeled, halved
  lengthwise, and sliced into thin
  crescents
1 large clove garlic, peeled and minced
2 tablespoons curry powder
1 pound butternut squash, peeled
  and cut into 1-inch cubes (4 cups
  chopped)
½ cup Chicken Stock (page 270) or
  Fish Stock (page 271)
16 ounces fresh or good-quality
  canned plum tomatoes, coarsely
  chopped, with their juices (2 cups)
1½ pounds sea bass fillet
Coarse (kosher) salt and freshly
  ground black pepper, to taste
Chopped fresh Italian (flat-leaf)
  parsley, for garnish

◆◆◆◆◆◆

1. Heat the oil in a large heavy-bottomed saucepan over medium heat. Add the onion and garlic, and sauté until the onion is transparent and limp, 3 to 5 minutes. Stir in the curry powder, and sauté until hot and fragrant, another minute. Add the squash, stock, and tomatoes along with their juices, and bring to a simmer over medium-high heat. Cover and cook until the squash is fork-tender, 15 to 20 minutes.

2. Meanwhile, season the fish on both sides with salt and pepper, and then cut it into 1-inch chunks. As soon as the squash is tender, scatter the seasoned fish into the saucepan and ladle some of the pan juices over it. Cover and simmer just until the fish is cooked through (the flesh should be opaque throughout and should flake easily with the tines of a fork), 5 to 10 minutes. Ladle into large serving bowls and top with chopped parsley. Serve hot.

Pan-Fried Rainbow Trout with Black Bean Salsa

SERVES 4

Like everybody else, we've cut back severely on fried foods—but for small rainbow trout, a quick pan-fry in a coating of golden cornmeal is just about the best preparation there is. The cleaned butterflied fish are completely edible (except for their heads, of course, and any tiny bones along the spine), and their skin becomes crisp and delicious. Serve them with refreshing, crunchy Black Bean Salsa for a spectacularly impressive lunch entrée.

◆◆◆◆◆◆

1 generous cup medium-grain stone-ground cornmeal (see Stone-Ground Cornmeal, page 4)
1 cup whole milk
4 small (8 ounces each) butterflied rainbow trout (or golden trout, char, or baby salmon)
3 tablespoons chopped mixed fresh herbs (such as chives, parsley, and/or cilantro)
Coarse (kosher) salt and freshly ground black pepper
½ cup vegetable oil
Black Bean Salsa (recipe follows)

◆◆◆◆◆◆

1. Preheat the oven to 200°F.

2. Spread the cornmeal over a large plate or work surface. Pour the milk into a wide shallow bowl.

3. Wash and dry the fish fillets thoroughly. Dip each one into the milk to moisten both sides, then rub a portion of the herbs over the inside surface of each fish. Season each fillet on both sides with salt and pepper. Then dredge in the cornmeal, coating them evenly and thoroughly, and shake off any excess. (The fillets can be prepared to this point up to 6 hours in advance; cover and refrigerate until ready to serve.)

4. Heat the oil in a skillet that is large enough to hold one whole butterflied fish. When the oil is very hot (close to the smoke point), cook one trout, skin side up, until crisp and golden brown, 2 to 3 minutes. Flip it over and cook until crisp and just cooked through, another 2 to 3 minutes. Remove from the pan, drain on paper towels or a clean, split-open brown paper bag, and reserve in the oven while you cook the remaining fish. Top each trout with a generous spoonful of the salsa, and serve.

Black Bean Salsa

MAKES 3 GENEROUS CUPS

This great Hay Day salsa keeps well in the refrigerator and is a godsend for brightening up a variety of summer foods. If you're really in a hurry, mix the black beans and corn with a cup of your favorite store-bought tomato salsa; the result will be surprisingly satisfying.

1 cup tender cooked black beans, drained and rinsed
1 cup fresh corn kernels (from about 2 large ears)
2 large ripe garden tomatoes, cored, seeded, and coarsely chopped
1 small green bell pepper, stemmed, seeded, and chopped
4 scallions, white and light green parts finely chopped
1 tablespoon chopped fresh cilantro
1 tablespoon white wine vinegar
½ cup tomato juice
Juice of 1 large lime
½ teaspoon ground cumin
1 teaspoon coarse (kosher) salt, or to taste
Several dashes of Tabasco or other hot sauce, to taste

◆◆◆◆◆◆

Combine all the ingredients except the salt and Tabasco sauce in a large nonreactive bowl, and stir to combine. Then add salt to taste, and season with Tabasco. Set aside for at least 30 minutes to allow the flavors to develop. Covered and refrigerated, this will keep well for several days.

Bright Ideas

❧ Serve as a dip for tortilla chips.

❧ Use as a condiment for grilled salmon, chicken, or shrimp.

❧ Mix with chunks of shredded roast chicken or flaked grilled tuna for a crunchy summer salad (you can also use canned chunk white albacore tuna).

Jamaican Spiced Snapper with Rum-Glazed Plantains

SERVES 4

Commonly referred to as jerk seasoning, this fragrant, fiery Jamaican spice rub—a blend of peppers and spices—is made throughout the Caribbean. Our version creates a wet rub that gives the fish a protective coating of moisture—and is equally good on chicken, pork chops, or pork tenderloin. It's hot as blazes but fragrant and flavorful as well. The rub can be made in advance and refrigerated for at least 2 weeks.

Grouper, mahi-mahi, halibut, or any other firm-fleshed fish will work well here, but for the best flavor we do prefer fillets to thick steaks. It's always a good idea to combine "jerk" fish or meat with something sweet and mellow, like these grilled plantains, to smooth the spice.

◆◆◆◆◆◆

Jamaican Spice Rub

1 fresh Scotch bonnet chile pepper,
split in half, seeds removed, cut into
large chunks (see Scotch Bonnet
Peppers, facing page)
6 scallions, white and light green
parts coarsely chopped
2 tablespoons coarsely chopped
fresh ginger (see About Ginger,
page 215)
Juice of 1 lime
3 tablespoons fresh orange juice
½ teaspoon ground cinnamon
1 teaspoon whole allspice berries
1 tablespoon light brown sugar
1 teaspoon coarse (kosher) salt
1 tablespoon coarsely chopped fresh
thyme

4 red snapper fillets (8 ounces each),
skin on
Rum-Glazed Plantains (recipe
follows)

◆◆◆◆◆◆

1. Prepare the rub: Combine the chile pepper, scallions, ginger, lime juice, orange juice, cinnamon, allspice, brown sugar, and salt in a food processor or blender, and purée to form a thin coarse paste. Stir in the thyme, and allow to rest for at least 30 minutes for the flavors to blend.

2. Brush a thin coating of the spice rub evenly over the flesh side of each fillet, and set aside to marinate for at least 30 minutes.

3. Preheat the grill to medium-high. When ready to cook, oil the grill rack.

4. Place the fish, skin side up, on the grill and cook without turning until the flesh is just cooked through (the fish should flake easily at its thickest point), 8 to 10 minutes. Using a large flat spatula, remove the fillets from the grill. Serve immediately with the plantains.

Rum-Glazed Plantains

SERVES 4

Plantains are fully ripe when their skins are truly black—far beyond anything you'd tolerate in a banana. Very ripe plantains store well for a couple of weeks in a cold drawer in the refrigerator, and they are so good prepared this way that you'll want to grab them whenever ripe ones turn up in the market. Serve them as a nice counterpoint to any spicy grilled fish or meat.

◆◆◆◆◆◆

¼ cup light rum
3 tablespoons honey
Juice of 1 large lime
2 black-ripe plantains

◆◆◆◆◆◆

1. Preheat the grill to medium-high.

2. Whisk together the rum, honey, and lime juice in a small bowl.

SCOTCH BONNET PEPPERS

Tiny, lantern-shaped Scotch bonnets come in a range of colors from yellow to orange to red. They are fiercely hot and can be used interchangeably with the equally fiery Jamaican hot or habanero chile (both considered to be the hottest chiles grown and cultivated). As with all fresh chiles, use care in handling (see page 87).

If fresh chile peppers are not available, look for a good Caribbean hot sauce to season the dish. Caribbean hot sauces are based on these fiery chile peppers and have more flavor and body than Tabasco or other Southern-type hot sauces. There are as many versions as there are Caribbean countries, but do try Inner Beauty Caribbean Hot Sauce if you come across it. Grilling guru Chris Schlesinger makes it, and we use it all the time.

3. Trim off the stem ends of the plantains, and cut them in half lengthwise, straight through the skin.

4. When ready to cook, oil the grill rack. Place the plantains, cut side down, on the grill and cook until lightly browned and softened, 5 to 7 minutes. Turn them over and brush the cut sides with the reserved glaze. Serve the plantains hot, in their jackets just as you would a baked potato (but don't eat the skin).

Amaranth-Crusted Fillet of Sole

SERVES 4

Toasted amaranth (which is a bit like very tiny popcorn) creates a very crispy coating on classic sautéed fillet of sole. Complete the meal with a side of our Spring Pea Medley (page 198) or Oven-Roasted Beets, Red Onions, and Oranges (page 193).

◆◆◆◆◆◆

¼ cup amaranth (see About Amaranth, page 162)
4 sole fillets (6 ounces each)
Pinch of coarse (kosher) salt
½ tablespoon unsalted butter
1 tablespoon olive oil
2 tablespoons minced fresh parsley or cilantro
1 large lemon, cut into wedges

◆◆◆◆◆◆

1. Heat a large heavy-bottomed, tall-sided pot over high heat for 5 minutes. Sprinkle in a few of the amaranth grains; if the pot is hot enough, they will begin to pop almost immediately. When the pot is ready, add the remaining grains in a slow, even stream. Cover partially, to keep the grains from jumping all over your kitchen, and shake to prevent them from scorching. Remove from the heat as soon as the popping subsides, 1 to 2 minutes, and transfer the popped grains to a cool plate.

2. Rinse the fish and thoroughly pat it dry. Season the fillets on both sides with a small pinch of salt. Then press the fish into the amaranth to coat the fillets evenly on both sides.

3. Combine the butter and oil in a large skillet and heat over medium-high heat until sizzling hot. Add the fillets and sauté until lightly browned and just cooked through, 2 to 3 minutes per side. Sprinkle with the parsley and serve warm, with the lemon wedges on the side.

ABOUT AMARANTH

Amaranth, an ancient grain that's coming back into modern markets, looks a little like couscous. When it is poured into a very hot dry pot, it explodes into tiny popcorn. Popped amaranth is great sprinkled over salads, soups, and stews or used as a light, crisp breading. The trick to popping the grain is to add it to the pot sparingly, in a thin stream, so it won't be overcrowded, and then to shake the pot to prevent scorching—just as you would with popcorn. (Don't be discouraged if all the grains don't pop.) The popped grains will keep well for several days in an airtight container.

Amaranth is also available as a flour, which is used for baking.

Swordfish Kebabs

SERVES 4

You could serve swordfish steaks in this preparation, but we think cutting them into individual kebabs makes a more graceful presentation. The fresh relish of ripe summer tomatoes, capers, and olive oil suits the kebabs nicely, and serves as both marinade and finishing sauce. Complete the meal with servings of orzo or rice pilaf, and pass rounds of grilled bread for scooping up the juices.

◆◆◆◆◆◆

⅓ cup large capers packed in vinegar (balsamic, if available), drained and coarsely chopped
2 anchovy fillets, rinsed and minced
2 cloves garlic, peeled and minced
2 large ripe tomatoes, cored and coarsely chopped
⅓ cup coarsely chopped fresh Italian (flat-leaf) parsley
⅓ cup extra-virgin olive oil
Coarse (kosher) salt and freshly ground black pepper
2 swordfish steaks, 1 inch thick (about 2 pounds total)

◆◆◆◆◆◆

1. Combine the capers, anchovies, garlic, tomatoes, parsley, and oil in a large bowl. Stir well to combine, and season to taste with salt and pepper.

2. Cut the fish into 1-inch cubes, place them in a mixing bowl, and stir in half of the tomato relish. Set aside to marinate for a minimum of 30 minutes; or cover, refrigerate, and allow to marinate for several hours or overnight. Cover the remaining tomato relish and set it aside at room temperature.

3. Preheat the grill to medium-high. If you will be using wooden skewers, soak them in water for at least 15 minutes.

4. Thread the fish onto long metal or wooden skewers, and discard the marinade.

5. When ready to cook, oil the grill rack. Place the kebabs on the grill and cook, turning once, until the fish is lightly colored on the outside and evenly cooked throughout, 10 to 12 minutes. Transfer the kebabs to a clean serving platter, spoon the reserved tomato relish on top, and serve immediately.

Variation

◆ You can substitute any other firm-fleshed fish that holds up well on the grill—such as tuna, salmon, monkfish, mako, or halibut.

Tuna and Flageolets Niçoise

SERVES 4 TO 6

Fresh flageolets (tiny French kidney beans) are rarely available in the U.S., but the dried kind is wonderful in European-style summer salads. Here we incorporate them in a traditional Salade Niçoise, which profits from

being made ahead of time and needs only a baguette and a bottle of chilled Bandol to make a complete picnic. (Many restaurants in this country use seared fresh tuna in their Niçoise salads, but the next time you're in Nice, you'll see that the French use the canned variety. Seared tuna is wonderful, but since good-quality canned tuna is authentic in this case, there's no need to bother.)

◆◆◆◆◆◆

Dressing
½ cup extra-virgin olive oil
1½ tablespoons tarragon vinegar
2 tablespoons fresh lemon juice
1½ tablespoons coarse-grain mustard
1 shallot, peeled and minced
Salt and freshly ground black pepper

Salad
1 cup dried flageolet beans, rinsed and sorted to remove pebbles and broken pieces
4 cups water
8 ounces fresh haricots verts or thin green beans, trimmed
12 ounces water-packed solid white or light tuna, drained
3 tablespoons large capers, rinsed and drained
4 scallions, white and light green parts coarsely chopped
1 tablespoon fresh thyme leaves
2 small heads Bibb lettuce, leaves separated, rinsed, and thoroughly dried
6 hard-cooked eggs, halved
2 large ripe tomatoes, cut into wedges
½ cup Niçoise olives

◆◆◆◆◆◆

1. Whisk together all the dressing ingredients except the salt and pepper, and set aside at room temperature for the flavors to develop. Before serving, season to taste with salt and pepper.

2. Place the flageolet beans in a medium-size saucepan, and cover with the water. Bring to a boil, reduce the heat, and simmer gently until tender, 40 to 60 minutes. Drain.

3. While the flageolets are cooking, cook the haricots verts in boiling water until crisp-tender, 2 to 3 minutes. Drain, refresh under cold water, and pat dry. Set them aside.

4. Combine the flageolets, tuna, capers, scallions, thyme, and haricots verts in a large bowl. Whisk the dressing, and add to the salad, tossing gently and thoroughly.

5. Divide the lettuce leaves among individual plates, or arrange on one large serving platter. Top with the tuna and vegetables, garnish with the eggs, tomato wedges, and olives, and serve.

Peppered Tuna with Port and Pears

SERVES 4

Fresh tuna is substantial enough to stand in successfully for beef in this classic steak *au poivre* preparation. The sweet pears and port make a nice counterpoint for the heat of the peppercorns. The mixture of peppers suits the tuna and is both more colorful and a little mellower than the traditional black pepper coating.

◆◆◆◆◆◆

1 large bunch watercress, rinsed, tough stems trimmed
2 ripe Bartlett or Anjou pears, cored and very thinly sliced
1 tablespoon fresh lemon juice
1½ tablespoons poivre irisé or mixed rainbow peppercorns (see About Peppercorns)
4 tuna steaks (each 1 inch thick, 5 to 8 ounces), rinsed and patted dry
1½ tablespoons olive oil
⅔ cup port

◆◆◆◆◆◆

ABOUT PEPPERCORNS

We take peppercorns for granted today, but in the Middle Ages they were such a rarity that they were used as a measure of wealth. Green, black, and white peppercorns come from the same *Piper nigrum* plant but are picked at different stages of ripeness; pink peppercorns come from a totally different plant that is actually a member of the rose family.

Poivre irisé is a lively medley of mixed dried peppercorns: black, white, pink, and green.

Pink and green peppercorns are also often cured and packed in a brine solution.

1. Combine the watercress and pears in a large bowl. Sprinkle the lemon juice on top, toss together gently, and set aside.

2. Coarsely crush the peppercorns using a mortar and pestle; or wrap them in wax paper and smash them with a rolling pin. Press the crushed pepper evenly onto both sides of the tuna steaks.

3. Heat the oil in a heavy-bottomed skillet, large enough to hold the tuna steaks in a single layer, over high heat. Add the steaks and sear just until the tuna is nicely browned on the outside and still pink in the center, about 3 minutes per side. Transfer to a warm platter and cover with aluminum foil.

4. Add the port to the skillet, and stir up any bits clinging to the bottom of the pan. Simmer over high heat until the liquid is reduced by half, 4 to 5 minutes. Pour the pan liquid over the watercress and pear mixture, toss, and divide evenly among four dinner plates. Arrange the tuna steaks on top, drizzle with the juices from the salad bowl, and serve immediately.

Sesame-Ginger Grilled Tuna Steaks

SERVES 4

This recipe started with the Sesame-Ginger Vinaigrette we sell in the stores and emerged as one of our favorite summer entrées. The dressing works well with tuna steaks not only because the flavors go well together, but because it is lower in acid than traditional vinegar-based marinades and therefore the fish is less likely to "cook" as it marinates. It's equally delicious on sea bass, halibut, scallops, and shrimp. Make the dressing ahead of time—it keeps well in the refrigerator.

◆◆◆◆◆◆

4 tuna steaks, 1 inch thick
1 cup Sesame-Ginger Vinaigrette
   (recipe follows)
6 ounces mesclun (mixed baby salad
   greens)
4 teaspoons sesame seeds, lightly
   toasted (see Toasting Nuts,
   page 55)

◆◆◆◆◆◆

1. Rinse and dry the tuna steaks. Place them in a single layer in a shallow nonreactive baking dish, and pour ¾ cup of the vinaigrette over them. Cover and set aside to marinate for at least 30 minutes. (If you plan to marinate the fish longer, put it in the refrigerator.)

2. Meanwhile, preheat the grill to high.

3. When ready to cook, oil the grill rack. Remove the tuna from the dressing and discard the vinaigrette. Grill the tuna steaks until nicely browned on the outside but still translucent in the center—

2 to 3 minutes per side for rare, 3 to 5 minutes for medium-rare.

4. While the fish is cooking, toss the salad greens with the remaining ¼ cup vinaigrette (or to taste) and divide the salad among four dinner plates. Arrange the grilled fish over the greens, sprinkle each steak with a teaspoon of the toasted sesame seeds, and serve immediately.

Sesame-Ginger Vinaigrette

MAKES ABOUT 1 CUP

One of the most versatile Hay Day vinaigrettes, this keeps well for several weeks in the refrigerator. It is splendid on grain salads, in stir-fries, and as a marinade for seafood, chicken, or beef.

◆◆◆◆◆◆

¾ cup vegetable oil
¼ cup rice wine vinegar
1 tablespoon finely minced fresh ginger
1 small clove garlic, peeled and finely minced
Finely grated zest of 1 orange (see About Zest, page 229)
¼ cup fresh orange juice
1 teaspoon toasted sesame oil
1 teaspoon soy sauce or tamari (see A Note on Tamari, page 81)
Coarse (kosher) salt and freshly ground black pepper

◆◆◆◆◆◆

Combine all the ingredients except the salt and pepper in a small bowl. Whisk together, and season with salt and pepper to taste. Set aside or refrigerate until ready to use.

Potato-Crusted Salmon in Fresh Avocado "Mayonnaise"

SERVES 4

Running the Hay Day Cooking School means cooking side by side with some of the best chefs in the nation. The great Emeril Lagasse introduced our staffers to this technique for crusting fish fillets with crisp potatoes. Served on a creamy avocado sauce, these succulent salmon fillets are very impressive—and very easy. We've chosen Yukon Gold potatoes for their buttery yellow color, but if you can't find them, any fairly high-starch baking potato will do as well. If calories are an issue or the avocados aren't ripe, a fresh tomato salsa makes a fine substitute for the avocado sauce.

◆◆◆◆◆◆

½ teaspoon coarse (kosher) salt
1½ pounds salmon fillet, skin removed, cut into 4 portions of equal size and thickness
1 teaspoon fresh lemon juice
1⅓ cups peeled and coarsely grated Yukon Gold potatoes (about 3 potatoes)
¼ cup vegetable oil
Fresh Avocado "Mayonnaise" (recipe follows)
1 lemon, cut into 4 wedges

◆◆◆◆◆◆

1. Press the salt onto both sides of the fish fillets, and sprinkle with the lemon juice.

2. Squeeze out the excess moisture from the grated potatoes, and press a thin layer onto one side of each fillet, covering the entire surface.

3. Heat the oil in a heavy-bottomed skillet, large enough to hold all four pieces of fish without touching, over medium-high heat. When the oil is very hot, slide the fillets in, potato side up. Cover and cook for 2 to 3 minutes. Then, using a large spatula, carefully turn each fillet over onto the potato side. Cover and continue to cook until the potato crust is brown and crisp and the fish is just cooked through, 3 to 4 minutes.

4. Meanwhile, spread a portion of the Fresh Avocado "Mayonnaise" on each dinner plate, using the back of a spoon to make a pool of sauce for the fillet. Position the fish, potato side up, on the sauce. Garnish with the lemon wedges, and serve immediately.

Fresh Avocado "Mayonnaise"

MAKES A GENEROUS ½ CUP

Although it's totally egg-free and contains only a single tablespoon of oil, this beautiful sauce has the thick, creamy texture of a good homemade mayonnaise.

1 large ripe avocado, skin and pit
 removed
2 tablespoons fresh lemon juice
6 large cilantro leaves, or to taste
1 tablespoon olive oil
Coarse (kosher) salt and freshly ground
 black pepper

Combine the avocado, lemon juice, and cilantro in a food processor or blender and process to form a chunky purée. With the machine running, add the oil in a slow thin stream, and continue to blend until the sauce is smooth and thickened. Season to taste with salt and pepper, and set aside. Covered tightly and refrigerated, this will keep well for 2 to 3 days.

Bright Ideas

❦ Use as a spread for a roast turkey sandwich.

❦ Serve as a condiment with grilled shrimp or boneless chicken breasts.

❦ Use as a topping for very grown-up hamburgers.

Martini-Glazed Salmon

SERVES 4

When we sell this in the stores, it's made with salmon that has been cold-smoked over apple wood. Here we simplify the preparation and add a bit of apple jelly, whose caramelized sweetness makes a nice accent for the rich salmon fillets. The juniper gives them a wonderfully earthy flavor. Complete the meal with a warm wild rice pilaf, Hay Day's Three-Grain Salad (page 122), or Wild Rice and Couscous (page 210).

◆◆◆◆◆◆

2 teaspoons fresh thyme, finely
    minced
1 teaspoon fresh rosemary, finely
    minced
2 teaspoons dried juniper berries,
    crushed (see About Juniper Berries)
1/4 cup dry vermouth
1/3 cup apple jelly
1 1/2 to 2 pounds salmon fillet
    (1 inch thick, skin on), cut into
    4 equal portions
Coarse (kosher) salt and freshly
    ground black pepper

◆◆◆◆◆◆

1. Preheat the oven to 400°F.

2. Set aside a large pinch each of the thyme and rosemary to use as a garnish.

3. Place the juniper berries in a small saucepan over medium-high heat and toast until fragrant, about 1 minute. Add the vermouth and the remaining thyme and rosemary and bring to a simmer. Whisk in the apple jelly, and simmer just until dissolved, about 1 minute. Remove from the heat and set aside.

4. Heat an ovenproof nonstick skillet, large enough to hold the fish in a single layer, over high heat. Sear the salmon, skin side up, until lightly browned, about 2 minutes. Turn the pieces with a large spatula, and season each one with a small pinch of salt and a grinding of pepper. Spoon the reserved glaze generously over each fillet, and transfer the skillet to the

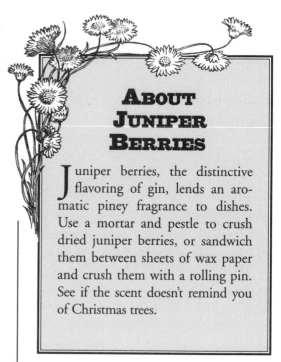

ABOUT JUNIPER BERRIES

Juniper berries, the distinctive flavoring of gin, lends an aromatic piney fragrance to dishes. Use a mortar and pestle to crush dried juniper berries, or sandwich them between sheets of wax paper and crush them with a rolling pin. See if the scent doesn't remind you of Christmas trees.

oven. Bake until the salmon is just cooked through and the glaze is nicely browned and caramelized, 8 to 10 minutes. Remove the skillet from the oven, sprinkle the reserved herbs over the fillets, and serve immediately.

Smoked Salmon and Spinach Rotollo

SERVES 4 TO 6

This simple make-ahead entrée is designed to be sliced and arranged on a salad of fresh baby spinach greens for an impressive addition to a spring buffet. Fresh pasta rotollos were one of the first things we made in the early days at the Westport store, and people seem never to tire of them.

◆◆◆◆◆◆
Rotollo

1 pound fresh spinach

6 scallions, white and light green
  parts chopped

½ cup ricotta

2 ounces feta cheese, crumbled (½ cup
  crumbled)

2 teaspoons capers, drained, rinsed,
  and coarsely chopped

Freshly ground black pepper

2 sheets (each 10 × 6 inches) fresh
  pasta

Generous ⅓ pound thinly sliced
  smoked salmon

1 egg lightly beaten with 2 teaspoons
  water

Salad

6 large handfuls fresh baby spinach
  leaves or other tender spring greens

½ cup Lemon Vinaigrette (page 265)
  or another light vinaigrette
◆◆◆◆◆◆

1. Rinse the spinach thoroughly and place it in a large pot with the water still clinging to the leaves. Cover and steam over medium-high heat until the leaves are tender and wilted, about 5 minutes. Remove from the pot, squeeze out as much excess moisture as possible, and coarsely chop.

2. In a large bowl, combine the spinach, scallions, ricotta, feta, and capers. Stir together to combine thoroughly, and season to taste with pepper.

3. Spread ½ cup of the filling evenly over one of the pasta sheets, leaving a ½-inch border on all sides. Top with one half of the salmon slices in a single layer, and fold the long edges in over the filling.

Begin rolling from the short end, jelly-roll fashion, keeping the long edges tucked in. Roll loosely, applying as little pressure as possible and taking care not to squeeze the filling out. Using a pastry brush, brush the egg wash along the remaining ½-inch border, and lightly press in place to seal and complete the roll. Wrap the entire roll in a single layer of cheesecloth, twisting the ends to seal them. Repeat with the remaining pasta sheet. (The rolls can be prepared to this point up to 1 day in advance; cover with plastic wrap and refrigerate.)

4. Bring a large pot of lightly salted water to a boil. Reduce the heat to a low simmer and add the pasta rolls in their cheesecloth wrapping. Poach in the simmering water for 15 minutes. Remove, drain, and allow to cool for at least 30 minutes.

5. Rinse the baby spinach leaves and pat them dry. Toss in a bowl with the vinaigrette, and arrange a bed of spinach salad on each serving plate.

6. Remove the cheesecloth from the rolls and slice them into ¾-inch-thick rounds. Serve warm or at room temperature, on top of the spinach salad.

Shrimp and Jasmine Rice Stir-Fry

SERVES 4

This recipe for a lovely, light, ginger-spiced fried rice describes one of those techniques that can be used in a variety of combinations. We make it here with shrimp and snow peas, but it is great for scallops or strips of chicken or beef. We suggest fragrant, aromatic jasmine rice from Thailand because its slightly sticky texture helps the grains hold together—but leftover rice from Japanese or Thai take-out will work just as well. If you have some chopsticks, set them out on the table.

A NOTE ON SESAME OILS

Small golden sesame seeds produce two different kinds of oil. Sesame oil is very light in both color and flavor and can be used for sautés and salad dressings just as olive oil is. *Toasted* sesame oil, on the other hand, is a far more richly colored and intensely flavored Asian condiment, used very sparingly to add flavor to sauces, marinades, and stir-fries.

Note to Santa: Consider an electric rice steamer. It's one of those great inventions that seems like a frill only until you get it home. Quietly and loyally, it makes a perfect pot of rice every single time.

◆◆◆◆◆◆

3 tablespoons peanut oil
½ cup whole unsalted cashew nuts
1 large onion, peeled and thinly sliced
2 large eggs, lightly beaten
2 teaspoons chopped fresh cilantro
1 teaspoon coarse (kosher) salt
1 teaspoon toasted sesame oil
  (see A Note on Sesame Oils)
1 tablespoon minced fresh ginger
  (see About Ginger, page 215)
12 ounces small fresh shrimp, shelled
  and deveined
4 ounces snow peas, trimmed and
  sliced lengthwise into narrow strips
4 cups cooked jasmine rice
2 tablespoons soy sauce or nam pla,
  or to taste (see About Fish Sauce,
  facing page)

◆◆◆◆◆◆

1. Heat 1 tablespoon of the peanut oil in a large skillet over medium-high heat. Add the cashews and stir-fry until nicely browned and crisp, 1 to 2 minutes. Using a slotted spoon, transfer the cashews to paper towels to drain.

2. Add another tablespoon of the peanut oil to the skillet and sauté the onion over medium-high heat until golden brown, about 5 minutes.

3. Meanwhile, whisk the eggs, cilantro, and salt together in a small bowl. When the onions are nicely colored, add the egg mixture to the skillet all at once, and cook without stirring over medium-high heat

170

until very lightly colored and set underneath, 1 to 2 minutes. Using a large wooden spoon, stir the eggs with a few wide strokes so they cook throughout. Then scoop the egg mixture from the pan in medium-size chunks and set it aside.

4. Add the remaining 1 tablespoon peanut oil and the sesame oil to the skillet and place over medium-high heat. Add the ginger and sauté quickly until fragrant, about 30 seconds. Add the shrimp and snow peas and continue to sauté just until the shrimp are bright pink and cooked through and the snow peas are bright green and crisp, 2 to 3 minutes. Stir in the rice, egg mixture, and reserved cashews, and toss over medium heat until warmed throughout. Season to taste with the soy sauce and serve hot in shallow bowls.

Low-Country Shrimp

SERVES 4

This simple one-pan, super-fast entrée is a great way to bring barbecue flavors indoors; the cream finish is the Creole way of rounding out the sharpness of the Cajun seasonings. We suggest Hay Day's Low-Country Barbecue Sauce, which is made in the western North Carolina tradition with a

tomato base spiked with vinegar—but you can use another favorite just as well.

Complete the meal with a warm basket of Hay Day's Cheddar-Chive Biscuits (page 98) or a bowl of fluffy steamed rice; fragrant popcorn rice from Louisiana would be ideal.

◆◆◆◆◆◆

1 pound medium to large shrimp, shelled and deveined but tails intact
2 teaspoons Cajun Seasonings (recipe follows)
2 tablespoons olive oil
8 scallions, white and light green parts coarsely chopped
2 cups fresh corn kernels (from about 4 large ears)
⅔ cup Low-Country Barbecue Sauce (page 267) or any good liquidy tomato and vinegar–based sauce
⅓ cup heavy (whipping) cream

◆◆◆◆◆◆

1. In a mixing bowl, sprinkle the shrimp with the Cajun seasonings and toss to coat evenly.

2. Heat the oil in a large skillet over medium-high heat and sauté the scallions until they are bright green and tender, about 2 minutes. Add the shrimp and sauté until pink and just cooked through, 3 to 5 minutes. Add the corn and sauté for another minute. Reduce the heat to medium-low and stir in the barbecue sauce. Drizzle in the cream, stir well to heat and combine, and serve immediately.

Cajun Seasonings

MAKES ABOUT ¼ CUP

Like curries, these spicy seasonings come in every conceivable formula. If you don't have a favorite blend in your cupboard already, here's a quick version to make on your own.

◆◆◆◆◆◆

1 tablespoon chili powder
1 tablespoon sweet paprika
1 teaspoon coarse (kosher) salt
1 teaspoon onion powder
1 teaspoon granulated garlic
½ teaspoon freshly ground black pepper
½ teaspoon cayenne pepper
½ teaspoon dried oregano
½ teaspoon dried thyme

◆◆◆◆◆◆

Combine all the ingredients thoroughly in a small bowl. Transfer to an airtight container and store in a cool, dry spot.

Grilled Shrimp with Tropical Fruit Salsa

SERVES 4

There are few things better than simple grilled shrimp with cumin and garlic, but serving the shrimp with a collage of bright tropical fruits does make the stars come out. When a large contract or a year-end bonus is on the line, this is what you serve for dinner. Complete the meal with mixed greens dressed in our velvety Lemon Vinaigrette (page 265) or with Three-Grain Salad (page 122).

◆◆◆◆◆◆

4 large cloves garlic, peeled and minced
¾ teaspoon ground cumin
½ teaspoon coarse (kosher) salt
2 tablespoons olive oil
2 tablespoons chopped fresh Italian (flat-leaf) parsley
24 medium-size shrimp (about 1½ pounds), shelled and deveined
Tropical Fruit Salsa (recipe follows)

◆◆◆◆◆◆

1. Preheat the grill to medium-high. If you are using wooden skewers, soak them in water for at least 15 minutes.

2. Combine the garlic, cumin, salt, oil, and parsley in a mixing bowl. Add the shrimp and toss to coat thoroughly.

3. Thread the shrimp onto metal or wooden skewers, and brush any remaining marinade over the shrimp. When ready to cook, oil the grill rack. Grill the

ABOUT TOMATILLOS

The tomatillo bears an obvious relationship to members of both the tomato and the Cape gooseberry families. A parchment-like papery outer skin easily peels away to reveal the fruit, which resembles a small unripe tomato. While tomatillos will ripen to a soft yellow fruit, the firm green unripe fruit adds crunch and a delicious fruity, acidic flavor to salsas, salads, and sauces. Select hard fruit with dry, closely fitting outer skins and store them in a cold dry corner of the refrigerator (they will keep well for several weeks like this). When ready to use, peel away the outer skins, rinse to remove any sticky residue, then chop, slice, or serve whole, like cherry tomatoes.

shrimp until they are just cooked through and a bit charred around the edges, 3 to 5 minutes per side.

4. Slide the shrimp off the skewers and serve hot, topped with a generous portion of the fruit salsa.

Tropical Fruit Salsa

MAKES 2 GENEROUS CUPS

Don't worry if you can't find a mango and a pineapple in good condition; you can substitute papaya, citrus, kiwi, melon, or split grapes, as long as the combination creates a contrast in color and texture. If you do use papaya, remember that the seeds are fully edible—a tablespoon or more will add crunch and a nice peppery accent.

◆◆◆◆◆◆

1 cup diced ripe pineapple

1 large ripe mango, peeled, seeded, and diced (see *About Mangoes*, page 218)

3 fresh tomatillos, papery husks discarded, rinsed and diced (½ cup diced; see *About Tomatillos*)

1 fresh jalapeño pepper, deveined, seeded, and minced (see *About Chile Peppers*, page 87)

Juice of 1 lime

⅓ cup diced red onion

2 tablespoons coarsely chopped fresh cilantro

1 tablespoon olive oil

Coarse (kosher) salt, to taste

◆◆◆◆◆◆

Combine all the ingredients in a large nonreactive bowl. Toss thoroughly and allow to rest at room temperature while you prepare the shrimp. Or prepare the salsa up to 1 day in advance, cover, and refrigerate.

Gingered Shrimp Fettuccine

SERVES 6 TO 8

One of our more elegant pasta salads, this Hay Day classic is a natural for summer picnics—at Tanglewood, for example, or on a boat at sunset. All you need to add is a tossed green salad or a platter of sliced ripe garden tomatoes.

◆◆◆◆◆◆

2 egg yolks (see Using Raw Eggs)

¼ cup rice wine vinegar

2 tablespoons fresh lemon juice

1 chunk fresh ginger (1 ounce),
peeled and coarsely chopped
(2½ tablespoons chopped; see
About Ginger, page 215)

1 teaspoon coarse (kosher) salt

½ cup extra-virgin olive oil

1 tablespoon toasted sesame oil (see
A Note on Sesame Oils, page 170)

¼ cup heavy (whipping) cream

1 pound fettuccine noodles

1 pound medium-size shrimp,
shelled and deveined, cut in half
lengthwise

8 ounces snow peas, trimmed
(see Note)

6 scallions, white and light green
parts chopped

Freshly ground black pepper

2 tablespoons sesame seeds, lightly
toasted (see Toasting Nuts, page 55),
for garnish

◆◆◆◆◆◆

1. Place a large pot of water on to boil for the fettuccine.

2. In a food processor or blender, combine the egg yolks, vinegar, lemon juice, ginger, and salt. Blend until smooth. With the machine running, add the olive and sesame oils in a slow thin stream. Blend until slightly thickened. Add the cream, blend it in, and set the dressing aside, covered, in the refrigerator.

3. Lightly salt the boiling water, and add the fettuccine. Stir and cook until al dente (just tender to the bite), 4 to 6 minutes. Then add the shrimp and snow peas, and boil just until the shrimp are

opaque throughout and the snow peas are bright green and crisp, about 30 seconds. Drain immediately into a large colander and rinse under cold water to stop the cooking. Transfer to a large bowl, add the dressing and scallions, and toss well to mix and coat evenly. Season to taste with pepper, and refrigerate, covered, to chill for at least 30 minutes. Garnish with toasted sesame seeds if desired.

Note: If you're making the salad several hours ahead of serving time, the acid in the dressing may rob the snow peas of some of their green color. To avoid this, drop the snow peas into boiling water, cook for 30 seconds, drain, and refresh under cold water; then add the peas to the salad just before serving.

USING RAW EGGS

To avoid the very real hazards of salmonella, eggs must be fresh, uncracked, and constantly refrigerated. Buy them from a reputable supplier, always check for cracks, and be sure they've been stored in the refrigerator case—which means never, *never* buying eggs from a cute farm-style stack of cartons kept out at room temperature.

Maryland Crab Cakes

SERVES 4

One of the most popular items at Hay Day, these crab cakes are luxuriously meaty. Toss some mixed salad greens with Lemon Vinaigrette (page 265), arrange the crab cakes on top, and you have a complete meal. Even though it's expensive, it is important to go the whole nine yards and use only fresh jumbo lump crabmeat; backfin crabmeat and fresh Maine claw meat just won't be the same. An added bonus: These can be prepared a day ahead, then sautéed just before serving.

◆◆◆◆◆◆

2 tablespoons Sauce Verte (page 250)
*   or fresh-herb mayonnaise*
1 tablespoon Dijon mustard
6 scallions, white and light green
*   parts finely chopped*
¼ cup minced fresh herbs (such as
*   parsley, basil, and/or chives)*
Juice of 1 lemon
1 pound jumbo lump crabmeat,
*   drained and picked through to*
*   remove any cartilage or shell*
Coarse (kosher) salt and freshly
*   ground black pepper*
2 large egg whites, lightly beaten
½ cup unseasoned bread crumbs,
*   preferably fresh*
2 tablespoons unsalted butter
1 tablespoon light vegetable oil

◆◆◆◆◆◆

1. Combine the Sauce Verte, mustard, scallions, minced herbs, and lemon juice in a medium-size mixing bowl, and stir together well with a fork.

2. Add the crabmeat and fold in gently, taking care not to overmix (retain as many large clumps of crabmeat as possible). Season to taste with salt and pepper. Stir in the egg whites and about ¼ cup of the bread crumbs—enough to form a loose mixture that is just firm enough to shape. Form into eight 3-inch patties (flatten them slightly), cover, and refrigerate for at least 30 minutes. (The crab cakes can be held at this point for up to 24 hours.)

3. Heat the butter and oil in a large skillet over medium-high heat. Press the crab cakes into the remaining bread crumbs to coat, and sauté until nicely browned and crisp, about 5 minutes per side. Serve immediately.

Bright Ideas

❦ Serve warm crab cakes in a bright pool of tomato coulis, using our Fresh Tomato and Basil Soup (page 92).

❦ Make a great sandwich: crab cakes on toasted Everybody's Favorite Peasant Bread (page 100) with sliced tomato and fresh basil or arugula.

❦ Use this recipe to make about two dozen bite-size mini crab cakes for an appetizer. Form them ahead of time and sauté them just before serving. Tuck each one into a small cup of tender lettuce along with a bit of Sauce Verte. Allow 2 to 3 per person.

Crab and Citrus Salad

SERVES 4

The crisp astringent flavors of fresh citrus and cilantro make a deliciously refreshing crabmeat salad. Citrus is at its peak throughout the winter season, but the bright light flavor of this salad can certainly be enjoyed year-round. Use seedless varieties, if possible, of the juiciest, most flavorful citrus available.

◆◆◆◆◆◆

1 tablespoon Dijon mustard
2 teaspoons white wine vinegar
2 cups coarsely chopped mixed citrus
   sections (from approximately
   4 oranges, 2 grapefruits, 2 limes,
   1 lemon), juices reserved
¼ cup olive oil
Coarse (kosher) salt and freshly
   ground black pepper
1 pound fresh jumbo lump crabmeat,
   drained and picked through to
   remove any cartilage or shell
2 tablespoons chopped fresh cilantro
¼ cup minced fresh chives
6 ounces mesclun (baby salad greens)
1 cup diced fresh tomatoes

◆◆◆◆◆◆

1. Whisk together the mustard, vinegar, and 4 teaspoons of the reserved citrus juice in a small bowl. Whisk in the oil until the dressing is emulsified, and season with salt and pepper to taste. Refrigerate while you prepare the salad.

2. In a large bowl, gently toss the citrus, crabmeat, cilantro, and chives together. Arrange the mesclun on individual plates, and then top with a generous amount of the crab and citrus mixture. Scatter a small handful of the tomatoes over each plate, drizzle the dressing on top, and serve immediately.

Confetti Lobster Salad

SERVES 2

A rainbow of diced bell peppers and fresh green herbs makes this pretty lobster salad a natural for a summer celebration on the beach or the terrace. Good lobster salad needn't be loaded with mayonnaise to be spectacular. Here the sweet lobster meat is enhanced with the crisp sweet bite of bell peppers, sparked with fresh lemon juice, and accented with fresh basil and chives. It's a great way to serve leftover lobster meat— if you're lucky enough to have any—from the Fourth of July clambake. And it is equally divine made with any combination of lobster, shrimp, and/or crabmeat.

Hollowed-out red or yellow bell peppers make a pretty dish for the lobster salad, or you can return it to the empty shells for a dramatic presentation. Complete the meal with Summer Corn and Tomato Salad (page 111) or Creamy Mustard Coleslaw (page 114).

♦♦♦♦♦♦
*2 live Maine lobsters (1¼ pounds
    each), preferably female (see Note)*
1 cup dry white wine or water
1 tablespoon fresh lemon juice
¼ cup diced red bell pepper
¼ cup diced yellow bell pepper
6 fresh basil leaves, shredded
*2 tablespoons coarsely chopped fresh
    chives*
*2 tablespoons Sauce Verte (page 250)
    or fresh-herb mayonnaise*
Freshly ground black pepper
♦♦♦♦♦♦

1. Rinse the lobsters under cool running water.

2. Place the wine in a pot that is large enough to hold the lobsters. Bring to a boil. Place the lobsters in the pot and cover tightly. Steam the lobsters until their shells are completely bright red, about 12 to 15 minutes (twist off one of the small legs to check the meat for doneness). Remove the lobsters from the pot and set aside until cool enough to handle. Crack the claws with a small mallet and remove the meat. Turn the lobsters belly side up and using a long sharp knife, split the tail end open lengthwise, straight down between the rows of little legs. Pull out the tail meat. Coarsely chop all the extracted meat, reserving only a few whole claw tips for garnish. If your lobsters are female, there will be chunks of bright red roe located along the top portion of the tail. Remove and reserve the roe, covered, in the refrigerator.

3. Place the chopped meat in a large bowl, and drizzle the lemon juice on top. Add the bell peppers, basil, chives, and

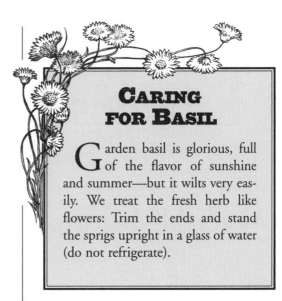

CARING FOR BASIL

Garden basil is glorious, full of the flavor of sunshine and summer—but it wilts very easily. We treat the fresh herb like flowers: Trim the ends and stand the sprigs upright in a glass of water (do not refrigerate).

Sauce Verte. Toss to combine and dress evenly, and season with black pepper to taste. Garnish with the reserved claw tips. Refrigerate, covered, to chill for at least 2 hours before serving.

4. Using your fingertips, crumble the roe, if any, over the salad and serve.

Note: Female lobsters are easily identified by checking the smallest pair of inner legs, located where the tail joins the chest. On a female these legs will be fringed with hair; on a male they'll be smooth and pointed.

Bright Ideas

❦ For a delicious variation on the traditional Maine lobster roll, serve this pretty salad inside split grilled frankfurter rolls, brushed with a bit of our Basil-Infused Olive Oil (page 261).

❦ Chop this celestial mixture a bit more finely and use it for canapés: Fill ripe cherry tomato or cucumber cups, celery sticks, or fennel boats with the salad, or serve it as a luxurious dip for crisp corn tortilla chips.

Vegetable Entrées

Summer Vegetable Risotto

SERVES 6

A bowl of warm, creamy risotto is profoundly satisfying. If you make it with chopped vegetables, you have a complete, nourishing meal. And if it is high summer and you have access to tender yellow squash blossoms, stir them in at the end of the cooking time for a colorful addition.

◆◆◆◆◆◆

4½ cups Vegetable Stock (page271) or
   Chicken Stock (page 270)
1 yellow bell pepper, stemmed, seeded,
   and diced
2 cups diced zucchini (1 large zucchini)
1½ cups diced peeled fresh tomatoes
   (2 medium-size tomatoes, or
   4 large plum tomatoes)
Coarse (kosher) salt
¼ cup olive oil
½ small red onion, peeled and finely
   chopped
1½ cups arborio or Vialone Nano rice
   (see Note)
⅓ cup freshly grated Parmesan cheese
   (see Grating Cheeses, page 251)
1 cup packed fresh basil leaves, shredded
¼ cup pine nuts, lightly toasted
   (see Toasting Pine Nuts, page 250)

◆◆◆◆◆◆

1. Place the stock in a small saucepan over medium heat, and bring to a very gentle simmer.

2. Meanwhile, combine the bell pepper, zucchini, and tomatoes in a bowl. Sprinkle with ½ teaspoon salt, toss, and set aside.

3. Heat the oil in a large heavy-bottomed stockpot or flameproof casserole over medium-high heat. Add the onion, and sauté until lightly colored, about 5 minutes.

4. Add the rice and stir to coat the grains thoroughly. Add 1 cup of the warm stock, and cook, stirring frequently, until the liquid has been completely absorbed, 5 to 7 minutes. Add one third of the diced vegetables along with another 1 cup of stock, stirring continuously. Repeat, adding stock and vegetables each time the liquid in the pot has been absorbed, every 7 minutes or so. The risotto is ready when both the rice and the vegetables are tender and cooked through, yet firm to the bite. (You may not need to use all of the stock.) This should take a total of 25 to 30 minutes.

5. Remove the pan from the heat, stir in the Parmesan and almost all the basil, and season to taste with additional salt as needed. Serve immediately in warm bowls, topped with the remaining basil and the toasted pine nuts.

Note: In Italy classic risotto is made not just with arborio rice, but with Carnaroli and Vialone Nano as well. Vialone produces the creamiest results, arborio the most texture, and Carnaroli (the traditional rice of the Veneto region) something between the two. Any of the three will work well in this version

Unlike most other grains, these beautiful rices should never be washed before cooking; many of their vitamins and starches will disappear with the rinse water.

Bright Idea

❦ **Risotto Fritters or Puffs:** Cold risotto holds together well enough to make wonderful fritters or even bite-size crisp hot hors d'oeuvres—which can be formed and refrigerated in advance, then sautéed at serving time. Just shape the risotto into flattened cakes for an entrée or into small balls for an hors d'oeuvre, coat lightly in plain fresh bread crumbs, and brown in a bit of hot vegetable oil. Serve warm or at room temperature.

Pasta and Snap Peas in Saffron Lemon Cream

SERVES 4 TO 6

This richly flavored, luxurious sauce transforms simple pasta and spring vegetables into an elegant appetizer or a light main course. The sauce gets its rich color and deep flavor from the saffron and goes beautifully with the sweet spring sugar snaps, baby spinach, and fresh chives. Freshly shelled

peas, asparagus tips, and tender greens like arugula are effective substitutes.

◆◆◆◆◆

½ cup Chicken Stock (page 270)
1 large pinch saffron threads (about 24 threads), preferably toasted (see Cooking with Saffron, page 180)
6 ounces (scant ¾ cup) Crème Fraîche (page 255)
Finely grated zest of 1 lemon (see About Zest, page 229)
1 tablespoon fresh lemon juice
Coarse (kosher) salt and freshly ground black pepper
10 ounces penne rigate (or other short tubular pasta; see Note)
1 pound fresh sugar snap peas, trimmed
2 large handfuls fresh baby spinach leaves (about 4 ounces)
½ cup freshly grated Parmesan cheese
3 tablespoons finely chopped fresh chives

◆◆◆◆◆

1. Place a large pot of water on to boil for the pasta.

2. Pour the stock into a large saucepan and place over medium-high heat. Crumble the saffron into the stock, bring to a gentle simmer, and cook for 5 minutes, allowing the saffron to infuse the stock. Whisk in the crème fraîche, return to a gentle simmer, and cook until slightly thickened, about 5 minutes. Stir in the lemon zest and juice, and season to taste with salt and pepper. Cover and keep warm over low heat while you cook the pasta and vegetables.

3. Cook the pasta in the boiling water until al dente (just tender to the bite), adding the snap peas to the pot for the last minute of cooking time (they should be just tender and crisp). Drain immediately in a large colander, shake to remove the excess water, and return to the cooking pot. Add the warm sauce and the spinach, and stir until the spinach has wilted and the pasta and vegetables are evenly coated with sauce. Add the Parmesan and 2 tablespoons of the chives, and toss gently. Spoon into individual bowls, top with a sprinkling of the 1 tablespoon remaining chives, and serve immediately.

Note: Different pasta shapes are not just whimsical: Pastas formed with nooks and ridges (*rigate*) provide more surface area for sauces to cling to.

Vegetable-Pasta Frittata

SERVES 4 TO 6

A classic pasta frittata is just pasta and eggs (a favorite way to use up leftover pasta) seasoned with herbs and cheese; the whole thing is cooked until it forms a golden-brown

COOKING WITH SAFFRON

Saffron, the orangish stigmas of a particular kind of crocus, is a richly flavored and fragrant spice that adds its distinctive flavor to Mediterranean classics like bouillabaisse, paella, risotto Milanese, and couscous.

Saffron is much too costly to use in an extravagant manner. Happily, though, a little goes a long way; just a pinch gives flavor and golden color to most dishes. What's a pinch? It's the easiest way to measure saffron (a lot easier than piling the wispy tendrils in a spoon). For us, a small pinch is ten or twelve threads, a big one twice as many.

Although you can purchase saffron as either threads or powder, the powdered kind is often diluted with less costly natural colorings like turmeric, so threads are a more reliable source of pure flavor. Choose deeply colored threads with the fewest pale yellow strands, and store them in a tight, moisture-proof container away from heat and light.

The flavor of saffron threads is intensified with a quick toasting. Toss threads (never the powder) in a heavy-bottomed saucepan over medium heat just until they turn from red to dark brown and give off a distinctive saffron aroma, 1 to 2 minutes. Immediately remove the pan from the heat and turn the threads out onto a cool surface to keep them from scorching.

crust, then sliced and served with fresh tomato sauce to make an easy supper dish that many of us fondly call spaghetti pie. If you add a few vegetables you get a real one-dish meal, which is great warm or at room temperature, with a simple green salad alongside.

◆◆◆◆◆◆

2 ounces fresh morel mushrooms, or
½ ounce dried (see Cooking with
Fresh Morels, page 83)
2 tablespoons unsalted butter
1 large leek, washed well, white and
light green parts chopped
1 small bunch asparagus (about
1 pound), tips and tender green
stalks cut into 1-inch lengths
4 large eggs
3 tablespoons chopped fresh chives
1 tablespoon chopped fresh Italian
(flat-leaf) parsley
⅓ cup freshly grated Pecorino
Romano cheese
½ teaspoon coarse (kosher) salt
Freshly ground black pepper
8 ounces linguine, cooked until tender,
or 3 cups leftover cooked linguine
Fresh Tomato Marinara Sauce
(page 257), heated

◆◆◆◆◆◆

1. Preheat the broiler.

2. If using fresh mushrooms, clean them well and slice lengthwise. If you are using dried mushrooms, soak them in hot water to cover until tender, about 5 minutes. Then drain and slice thinly lengthwise.

3. Melt 1 tablespoon of the butter in a 10-inch ovenproof heavy-bottomed skillet or omelet pan over medium-high heat. Add the leek and asparagus, and

sauté until the asparagus is bright green and just barely fork-tender, 3 to 5 minutes. Remove the vegetables from the pan, and set them aside. Wipe the skillet clean.

4. In a large mixing bowl, beat the eggs with 2 tablespoons of the chives, the parsley, cheese, salt, and several grindings of black pepper. Add the pasta, mushrooms, and leek and asparagus. Toss thoroughly.

5. Melt the remaining 1 tablespoon butter in the skillet over medium-high heat. Swirl to coat the sides evenly, and as soon as the foam subsides, pour in the contents of the bowl. Quickly spread in an even layer. Cook, rotating the skillet to distribute and cook the egg evenly, and shaking it frequently to prevent the frittata from sticking, about 5 minutes. Use a spatula to check the underside and when a golden crust has formed, transfer the skillet to the broiler. Cook until the top is set and lightly colored, about 2 minutes. Invert the frittata onto a large serving platter. Garnish with the remaining 1 tablespoon chives, and serve warm or room temperature, cut into wedges. Spoon some of the marinara sauce onto each serving.

Variations

◆ Long pastas like spaghetti and linguine work particularly well in frittatas because they hold everything together, but the sky's the limit on the vegetables. Lightly steam or sauté vegetables before adding them. Consider:

◆ Fresh peas and slivers of sun-dried tomatoes

◆ Ribbons of prosciutto and asparagus tips

◆ A rainbow of julienned bell pepper and fresh basil

Couscous-Vegetable Lasagne

SERVES 8

This has all the virtues of classic lasagne, but using quick-cooking couscous instead of the traditional lasagne noodles makes it incredibly light. It's easy too—just toss the couscous (here seasoned with sun-dried tomatoes) with grated cheeses, then layer with a simple sautéed vegetable ragout. The whole thing holds together well—you can cut it in neat squares—

and like the traditional lasagne, it's wonderful reheated the next day.

All you need to complete the meal is some fresh bread and a simple green salad. Or, for a more elaborate dinner, serve the lasagne as an accompaniment to butterflied leg of lamb, marinated in Balsamic Vinaigrette (page 264) and grilled.

◆◆◆◆◆◆

1½ cups water
1¼ cups couscous
1 ounce oil-packed sun-dried tomatoes, finely chopped (2 generous tablespoons chopped)
1 tablespoon olive oil
1 onion, peeled and coarsely chopped
2 cloves garlic, peeled and minced
6 ounces cremini mushrooms, wiped clean and thinly sliced
1 zucchini (8 ounces), cut into ¼-inch dice
1 red bell pepper, stemmed, seeded, and diced
1 yellow bell pepper, stemmed, seeded, and diced
½ teaspoon coarse (kosher) salt
2 generous cups chopped fresh or good-quality canned peeled plum tomatoes, with their juices
½ cup dry white wine
2 tablespoons chopped fresh basil
Coarsely ground black pepper
8 ounces fontina cheese, shredded (2 firmly packed cups shredded; see About Fontina, facing page)
⅓ cup freshly grated Parmesan cheese, plus additional for topping (see Grating Cheeses, page 251)

◆◆◆◆◆◆

1. Bring the water to a simmer in a small saucepan.

DOUBLE THE PLEASURE

By all means, double the Couscous-Vegetable Lasagne recipe for a party, but remember that doubling can make some ingredients hard to handle. In this case, soak the couscous in a wide pan or shallow bowl to avoid large clumps, and be sure it is at room temperature when you mix it with the grated cheese—otherwise the cheese will melt prematurely. The doubled quantity will require a larger baking pan, obviously, and the cooking time should be extended until all the cheese is thoroughly melted and the lasagne has browned nicely around the edges.

2. Combine the couscous and sun-dried tomatoes in a shallow bowl. Add the hot water, cover with plastic wrap, and set aside to cool to room temperature while you prepare the sauce.

3. Preheat the oven to 350°F. Lightly oil an 11 × 7-inch lasagne or baking pan.

4. Heat 1 tablespoon of the oil in a large skillet over medium-high heat. Add the onion and sauté until lightly colored, 5 minutes. Stir in the garlic, mushrooms, zucchini, and bell peppers. Sprinkle with the salt, and continue to sauté until the volume is reduced by half and the vegetables are fork-tender, about 5 minutes. Add the tomatoes, wine, and basil. Bring to a simmer, cover, and cook for another 10 minutes. Season to taste with pepper and remove from the heat.

5. Fluff the couscous with a fork to separate the grains, breaking apart any clumps. Transfer it to a large bowl, add the grated cheeses, and toss, breaking apart any large lumps of cheese. Spread half of the couscous mixture in the prepared pan. Top with half of the vegetable sauce, then repeat the layers. Finish with a light sprinkling of additional Parmesan, cover tightly with aluminum foil, and bake until heated through, 30 to 35 minutes. Remove from the oven and allow to rest for 5 minutes before cutting into rectangular pieces. Serve hot.

ABOUT FONTINA

For cheese with the absolute best flavor, look for Fontina Val d'Aosta. Made from whole unpasteurized cows' milk from the alpine meadows of the northern Piedmont, this is true Italian fontina—softer than most Swiss cheese, and brine-washed during aging to give it a dark golden crust with a distinctive hearty aroma. Val d'Aosta melts like a dream and really transforms casseroles and potatoes au gratin into world-class dishes; look for the official D.O.C. (Denominazione di Origine Controllata) stamp on the rind.

Eggplant, Tomato, and Caper Lasagne

SERVES 10

Our wonderfully chunky vegetable sauce makes a spectacular lasagne, especially because its robust flavor is highlighted with aged provolone. The sauce in this recipe is great year-round, made either with fresh garden tomatoes during the summer or good-quality canned plum tomatoes the rest of the year. Since the whole thing freezes beautifully—and for a long period of time—you can make a pan when the farm stands are bursting with produce, and stash it away for a hearty midwinter meal.

◆◆◆◆◆◆

16 ounces ricotta cheese

2 cups (6 ounces) shredded aged provolone cheese

¾ cup freshly grated Parmesan cheese (see Grating Cheeses, page 251)

2 eggs

3 tablespoons coarsely chopped fresh Italian (flat-leaf) parsley

½ teaspoon coarse (kosher) salt

¼ teaspoon freshly ground black pepper

5 cups Eggplant, Tomato, and Caper Sauce (page 259)

1 pound dried lasagne noodles, cooked and drained (or uncooked fresh pasta sheets)

◆◆◆◆◆◆

1. Preheat the oven to 350°F.

2. In a large bowl, combine the ricotta, provolone, ½ cup of the Parmesan, the eggs, parsley, salt, and pepper.

3. Spread 1 cup of the eggplant sauce over the bottom of a 13 × 9-inch baking pan. Top with an overlapping layer of the pasta, then a layer of one-third of the cheese mixture. Spread another cup of sauce over the cheese. Repeat the layers of pasta, cheese, and sauce two more times. Finish with a layer of pasta, then spread the remaining cup of sauce on top. Sprinkle with the remaining ¼ cup of Parmesan cheese and cover the pan tightly with aluminum foil. (At this point the lasagne can be refrigerated overnight— or frozen as long as 6 months.)

4. Bake the lasagne until hot and bubbly, about 30 minutes. Remove the foil and bake until very lightly crisped around the edges, 10 minutes more. Allow to rest for 10 minutes before cutting into serving pieces. Serve hot.

The Glories of Grains

No doubt you know people who are willing to venture beyond the ordinary. Gather a few of your more adventurous friends and prove that a whole menu can be created from versatile, fragrant, nourishing grains. The Couscous Vegetable Lasagne (page 182) alone will send them out into the world as converts.

Shiitake Mushroom Barley Soup
Herbed Peasant Bread

Couscous-Vegetable Lasagne
Mixed Greens with Balsamic Vinaigrette

Arborio Rice Pudding with
Fresh Mango

Wild Mushroom, Spinach, and Goat Cheese Lasagne

SERVES 10

It isn't always easy to say why some things go well together—they just *do*. In this case, the tang of the goat cheese complements the fragrant earthiness of the mushrooms and spinach; they make a real crowd-pleaser in the tradition of our Vegetarian Lasagne, one of the big successes of our first book. Packaged dry lasagne noodles work fine, but you can save yourself some labor by using fresh pasta, which is available in most good stores in wide strips or sheets.

1 pound fresh spinach, trimmed of
roots and any tough stems
⅓ cup olive oil
3 tablespoons finely minced shallots
2 large cloves garlic, peeled and
finely minced
1 pound large white or cremini
mushrooms, wiped clean and sliced
8 ounces shiitake mushrooms, stems
removed, caps wiped clean and sliced
⅓ cup dry white wine
2 tablespoons shredded fresh basil
1 tablespoon chopped fresh thyme
1 cup ricotta cheese
Coarse (kosher) salt and freshly
ground black pepper
8 ounces mozzarella cheese, grated
(2 cups grated)
10 ounces soft fresh chèvre, crumbled
(see A Note on Chèvre, page 60)
½ teaspoon freshly grated nutmeg
1 pound dried lasagne noodles, cooked
and drained (or uncooked fresh
pasta sheets)

◆◆◆◆◆◆

1. Preheat the oven to 350°F. Lightly butter an 11 × 7-inch baking pan.

2. Place the spinach in a large bowl or sink filled with cold water, and allow it to soak while you cook the mushrooms.

3. Heat the oil in a large saucepan over medium-high heat. Add the shallots and garlic, and sauté until just tender and transparent, not browned, 2 minutes. Add the mushrooms, toss quickly to coat evenly with the oil, and sauté, stirring frequently, until they are tender and reduced by half, 4 to 5 minutes. Add the wine and simmer, scraping up any browned bits clinging to the bottom of the pan, until most of the liquid has evaporated. Remove from the heat, stir in the basil, thyme, and ricotta, and season to taste with salt and pepper. Stir in half of the grated mozzarella and set aside.

4. Shake the spinach free of excess water and place it in a large saucepan along with the water that is left clinging to the leaves. Cover and cook over medium heat until wilted and tender, about 5 minutes. Drain the spinach in a fine-mesh sieve or colander, and press it lightly with the back of a spoon to extract excess moisture. Coarsely chop the spinach.

5. In a large bowl, combine the spinach with the remaining mozzarella and just over half of the chèvre. Add the nutmeg and salt to taste, and using a fork, stir together gently until creamy.

6. Spread one third of the mushroom mixture over the bottom of the prepared pan. Top with a layer of the pasta, then spread on half of the spinach mixture. Top with another layer of pasta, and repeat the layers of mushrooms, pasta, and spinach. Finish with a layer of the mushrooms, and scatter the remaining crumbled chèvre on top. Cover the pan tightly with aluminum foil. (At this point the lasagne can be refrigerated overnight.)

7. Bake, covered with foil, until hot throughout, 35 to 40 minutes. Remove the foil and run the pan under the broiler until the cheese is nicely browned on top and bubbling hot. Allow to rest for a couple of minutes before cutting into serving pieces. Serve hot.

Great Northern Bean and Roasted Vegetable Stew

SERVES 6 TO 8

Here's a dish for winter Sundays: a hearty vegetarian stew that can sustain an army. Oven-roasting brings out the sweetness of root vegetables and intensifies their flavor, transforming even the humble rutabaga. We have been known to use a lot more garlic than is suggested here—but we leave that to you. Don't be put off by the long list of ingredients; once you've diced the vegetables, they roast and simmer serenely by themselves. You can prepare them in advance, too; just drop the dice in a bowl of cold water to prevent discoloration.

This is a meal-in-one. But do serve some county bread alongside for sopping up the juices.

♦♦♦♦♦♦

1 small celery root, scrubbed, peeled, and cut into 1-inch dice (about 8 ounces trimmed)

1 small rutabaga (about 1 pound), peeled and cut into 1-inch dice

2 parsnips, peeled and sliced into thick rounds

1 russet potato, peeled and cut into 1-inch dice

3 carrots, peeled and sliced into thick rounds

1 onion, peeled, halved, and sliced into thick crescents

Several large cloves garlic, peeled and crushed

Coarse (kosher) salt

Freshly ground black pepper

3 tablespoons olive oil

3 large fresh tomatoes, cut in half

4 ounces shiitake mushrooms, stems discarded, caps wiped clean and thickly sliced

2 cups Vegetable Stock (page 271)

2 bay leaves

3 cups cooked Great Northern beans, drained and rinsed (see Note)

♦♦♦♦♦♦

1. Position two oven racks evenly apart and preheat the oven to 350°F.

2. Combine the celery root, rutabaga, parsnips, potato, carrots, onion, and garlic in a large bowl. Sprinkle with 1 teaspoon of the salt, several grindings of black pepper, and 2 tablespoons of the oil. Toss the vegetables to coat evenly and spread them in a single layer in a large baking dish or jelly roll pan. Roast, uncovered, on the upper rack of the oven until the vegetables are fork-tender and lightly charred around the edges, about 1 hour.

3. Meanwhile, place the tomatoes, cut side up, on a baking sheet and sprinkle with ½ teaspoon salt. Toss the mushrooms with the remaining 1 tablespoon oil, and scatter them around the tomatoes. Place on the bottom rack of the oven to roast until extremely tender and lightly charred, about 30 minutes.

4. Transfer the vegetables to a large soup pot. Stir in the stock, bay leaves, and beans, and bring to a gentle simmer over medium-high heat, stirring occasionally. Season to taste with additional salt and pepper as needed. Remove the bay leaves, spoon the stew into large bowls, and serve.

Note: Particularly popular in baked bean dishes, small, classic white Great Northern beans have a distinctive delicate flavor and a firm texture that holds up well in soups and stews. Other white beans such as navy beans, cannellini, or baby limas can be substituted.

Bright Idea

❧ Transform this into a warming hunter's stew or a variation on cassoulet by adding game sausage, venison, or duck confit.

Rosy Root Vegetable Chili

SERVES 8 TO 10

Except that oven-roasted vegetables replace the meat, this is a fairly traditional chili. The beets give it a wonderful wine-rich color (even the white beans turn rosy pink!). Our customers buy it by the ton for ski weekends. For a great color and flavor accompaniment, serve some cornbread or muffins (try the ones on page 2, skipping the filling). Or go one step further and serve the chili in a cornbread crust (recipe follows).

CHOOSING AND USING ROOT VEGETABLES

Like carrots, parsnips should be unwrinkled, firm to the touch, and not too enormous. If they are larger than 1½ inches in diameter, cut away the inside core before dicing or slicing.

Some homelier vegetables, like celery root and rutabaga, are often a little daunting and don't reveal their true worth until you've scrubbed off the mud and peeled them with a sharp swivel peeler. Don't worry about the dirt, but be sure to choose vegetables that are firm and heavy for their size.

Turnips and rutabagas (sometimes sold as Swedish turnips or Swedes) are closely related; turnips tend to be smaller, with white flesh and a distinctive radishy bite, while the flesh of the bigger rutabagas is light yellow, mild, and sweet. Cutting rutabagas in halves or quarters before peeling makes them easier to handle.

◆◆◆◆◆◆

1 pound russet potatoes, peeled and cut into ½-inch dice

2 leeks, white parts only, well washed and coarsely chopped

1 parsnip (approximately 8 ounces), scrubbed and cut into ½-inch dice

4 carrots, scrubbed and cut into ½-inch dice

1 large beet (⅓ pound), scrubbed and cut into ½-inch dice

3 tablespoons olive oil

Coarse (kosher) salt

2 cups dark beer

2 bay leaves

2 cloves garlic, peeled and smashed with the side of a knife

5 cups chopped fresh plum tomatoes or canned plum tomatoes

2½ cups cooked white beans (navy, Great Northern, or cannellini), drained and rinsed

4 teaspoons chili powder

1 teaspoon ground cumin

1 teaspoon hot paprika

Freshly ground black pepper

Grated Monterey Jack or sharp white Cheddar cheese, for garnish

◆◆◆◆◆◆

1. Preheat the oven to 375°F.

2. Combine the potatoes, leeks, parsnip, carrots, beet, oil, and 1 teaspoon salt in a large bowl and toss to mix well. Spread in a single layer in a large baking pan and roast until tender and lightly charred, 20 to 25 minutes.

3. Transfer the roasted vegetables to a large soup pot. Add the beer, bay leaves, and garlic (the beer will just barely cover the vegetables). Bring to a boil over high heat, reduce the heat, and simmer

gently until fragrant, 10 minutes. Then add the tomatoes, beans, chili powder, cumin, and paprika. Season to taste with salt and pepper. Return to a boil, reduce the heat, cover, and simmer, stirring occasionally, until slightly thickened, about 15 minutes. Season as needed with additional salt and pepper. Remove the garlic and bay leaves. Serve hot, topping each serving with a handful of the grated cheese.

Bright Idea

❦ Create a chili potpie by prebaking circles of puff pastry until they are browned and flaky, then fitting them on top of bowls of the hot chili.

Cornbread-Crusted Chili

SERVES 4 TO 6

Cornbread is classic with chili, of course, and here the time-honored pairing makes a casserole that is a substantial one-dish meal. Make this with our Rosy Root Vegetable Chili or any other favorite chili recipe.

✦✦✦✦✦✦
2 tablespoons unsalted butter, at
room temperature
1 cup stone-ground yellow cornmeal
(see Stone-Ground Cornmeal,
page 4)
1 cup unbleached all-purpose flour
1 tablespoon baking powder
¼ teaspoon salt
¼ teaspoon baking soda
1¼ cups buttermilk
1 egg
¼ cup sugar
¼ cup corn oil
1 generous quart chili, warmed
✦✦✦✦✦✦

1. Preheat the oven to 375°F. Generously grease the inside of an 8-inch round ovenproof casserole with the butter.

2. Whisk the cornmeal, flour, baking powder, and salt together in a large bowl.

3. In a separate bowl, dissolve the baking soda in the buttermilk; then whisk in the egg, sugar, and oil. Stir the wet ingredients into the dry ingredients until thoroughly moistened and combined.

4. Spoon half of the batter into the prepared casserole. Ladle the warm chili on top, mounding it high in the center, then spoon the remaining cornbread batter around the edges, leaving the center uncovered. Bake until the cornbread on top is nicely browned and cooked through, 35 to 40 minutes.

5. Serve hot, spooned into serving bowls.

Grilled Portobello Mushrooms in Mustard Sauce

SERVES 4

Portobello mushrooms are substantial enough to serve as an entrée on their own. You can grill, roast, or sauté the caps and serve them like steak (save the stems for stock). Here their rich, meaty flavor is nicely complemented by a robust, grainy mustard sauce. These are incredibly popular when we serve them in the stores during grilling season—which seems to lengthen every year.

✦✦✦✦✦✦
1 teaspoon olive oil
2 large shallots, peeled and minced
¼ cup coarse-grain mustard
12 ounces (1½ cups) Crème Fraîche
(page 255)
⅔ cup Olive Oil Vinaigrette
(page 262)
8 large portobello mushrooms (about
5 inches in diameter), stems
removed, tops wiped clean
8 ounces mesclun (mixed baby salad
greens)
✦✦✦✦✦✦

1. Preheat the grill or broiler to medium-high.

2. Heat the oil in a large saucepan over medium-high heat. Add the shallots, and sauté for 1 minute. Whisk in the mustard and crème fraîche and simmer very gently until slightly thickened, 3 to 5 minutes. Cover and keep warm over very low heat while you cook the mushrooms.

3. When ready to cook, oil the grill rack, if using the grill. Brush some of the vinaigrette lightly and evenly over both sides of the mushroom caps. Grill until lightly charred and softened throughout, 4 to 5 minutes per side. (Or broil for the same time until browned and softened.)

4. Dress the salad greens to taste with the remaining vinaigrette, and spread a large handful on each plate. Place the warm mushrooms on the greens, and spoon a generous portion of the warm mustard sauce over each. Serve immediately.

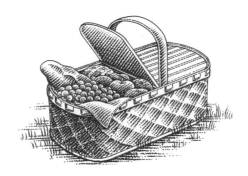

A Harvest of Vegetables and Grains

When Hay Day started in 1978, the word "harvest" conjured up images of apples, pears, squashes, onions, pumpkins, and all the other life supports our forefathers put away for the winter.

But now our produce department is as global as the Internet, and the harvest follows the sun around the earth. No longer just the tawny orange and red and brown of New England in November, the image of "harvest" is as green as California artichokes in April, as red as local strawberries in June.

And the quality is excellent, too. Now we await magnificent Haitian mangoes, Italian blood oranges, Peruvian pepino melons, Chilean nectarines, and Spanish clementines as eagerly as we do our own summer corn and tomatoes.

When we published our first cookbook in 1986, there wasn't a roasted vegetable to be seen. Fruits were relegated to breakfast or dessert; grains were limited to rices and whole-grain flours; and we didn't mention salsa anywhere! Now that our horizons embrace India, the Pacific Rim, and the Middle East, we know the pleasures of cooking with yogurt, chiles, dried fruits, and a myriad of grains, and of flavoring dishes with saffron, curry, sumac, cumin, and lemon grass.

It's a wonderful world out there!

Steamed Baby Artichokes in Feta Vinaigrette

SERVES 4

Baby artichokes (not really babies at all, but rather fully mature dwarf buds) are plentiful from March through May. Small enough to fit in the palm of your hand, they're fully edible. The fresh tang of feta cheese in the herb vinaigrette gives these artichokes a bright springtime character.

◆◆◆◆◆◆

1/2 cup dry white wine
3 tablespoons fresh lemon juice
1 tablespoon minced shallot
6 baby artichokes, each about the size
  of a large plum
1/4 cup Feta Vinaigrette (recipe follows)

◆◆◆◆◆◆

1. Combine the wine, lemon juice, and shallot in a medium-size saucepan.

2. Snap off and discard three or four outer rows of leaves from each artichoke, until the remaining leaves are pale green and tightly closed. Using a small paring knife, trim the base of the artichoke and peel the stem, removing only a thin layer of tough outer skin and any discoloration. Cut the artichokes in half lengthwise, and trim 1/2 inch off their tops. As you prepare them, place the artichokes, cut side down, in the saucepan.

3. Bring the liquid to a simmer over medium-high heat. Cover, and steam the artichokes until the flesh around the

stem of each artichoke is easily pierced with the tip of a sharp knife, 10 to 12 minutes. Drain the artichokes, arrange them cut side up on a serving platter, and spoon a generous teaspoon of the vinaigrette over each artichoke half. Serve warm or at room temperature.

Feta Vinaigrette

MAKES 1 GENEROUS CUP

The slight sharpness of feta cheese combined with fresh green herbs makes a versatile vinaigrette that goes beautifully with lightly steamed asparagus or sliced summer tomatoes as well as artichokes. It is a lovely dressing in potato, pasta, or shrimp salad, too.

◆◆◆◆◆◆

1/4 cup white wine vinegar
1 teaspoon minced fresh basil
1 teaspoon minced fresh dill
1 teaspoon minced fresh mint
2 ounces feta cheese, finely crumbled
  (1/2 cup crumbled)
1/2 cup olive oil
1/4 cup safflower oil
Coarse (kosher) salt and freshly ground
  black pepper

◆◆◆◆◆◆

In a small bowl, whisk together the vinegar, herbs, and cheese. Add the olive and safflower oils in a slow thin stream, whisking constantly until combined and emulsified. Season to taste with salt and pepper, and set aside until ready to use. Covered and refrigerated, it will keep up to 1 week. Stir or shake well before using.

Oven-Roasted Beets, Red Onions, and Oranges

SERVES 4

This popular Hay Day dish proves that beets taste even better roasted than they do steamed or boiled; the oven-roasting heightens and enhances their sweet earthy flavor. This recipe gives the right amount for one baking pan, but it can be easily doubled. In the stores we offer the beets simply tossed with the red onions and sherry vinegar, but this version goes one step further—adding oranges for a rich color combination that will light up the dinner table. It is superb with a very simple sautéed or broiled fillet of sole. Or arrange servings over a bed of tender lettuce for a light first course.

◆◆◆◆◆◆

1 pound red beets, trimmed and
   scrubbed but skin left on
1 small red onion, peeled
2 tablespoons olive oil
¼ teaspoon coarse (kosher) salt
1 tablespoon plus 1 teaspoon
   sherry vinegar
2 large navel or other juicy seedless
   oranges
4 small blood oranges, or 2 navel
   oranges

◆◆◆◆◆◆

1. Preheat the oven to 375°F.

2. Using the slicing disk of a food processor, a vegetable slicer, or a mandoline, cut the beets into rounds approximately ⅛ inch thick. Scatter the slices in a single layer on a large baking sheet. Slice the onion in the same manner, break the slices into rings, and scatter them over the beets. Drizzle with the oil and sprinkle with the salt.

3. Roast until the beets are tender and have begun to char around the edges, 30 to 35 minutes. Remove from the oven, transfer to a large bowl, and sprinkle with the 1 tablespoon sherry vinegar while still warm. Cover the beets and set them aside while you prepare the oranges.

4. Using a small serrated knife, cut away the peel and white pith from all the oranges. Slice the oranges into thin rounds and arrange them, alternating varieties, on four serving plates. Sprinkle with the remaining 1 teaspoon sherry vinegar. Then arrange a mound of the beets and onions alongside the oranges, overlapping them slightly. Serve at room temperature or chilled.

Honey and Ginger Glazed Carrots

SERVES 4

In this classic dish, sweet glazed carrots get an infusion of bright flavor from the addition of fresh ginger.

◆◆◆◆◆◆

1 pound carrots, trimmed and
* peeled*
¼ cup water
2 tablespoons unsalted butter,
* cut into small bits*
1 tablespoon finely minced fresh
* ginger (see About Ginger, page 215)*
2 tablespoons honey
Coarse (kosher) salt

◆◆◆◆◆◆

1. Cut the carrots diagonally into ¼-inch-thick slices. Scatter the slices in a large skillet that is wide enough to accommodate them in a single overlapping layer. Add the water and dot with 1 tablespoon of the butter bits. Bring to a simmer over medium-high heat. Reduce the heat, cover, and simmer until just fork-tender, 5 to 8 minutes.

2. Remove the lid and scatter the minced ginger over the carrots. Add the honey and the remaining 1 tablespoon butter. Raise the heat to medium-high and cook, stirring constantly, until all the liquid has been absorbed and the carrots are coated with a shiny glaze and are just beginning to caramelize. Season with salt to taste, transfer to a warm serving dish, and serve immediately.

Corn on the Cob with Lime Basil Butter

SERVES 3 TO 6

In the middle of July, it seems downright un-American to serve corn on the cob any way but rolled in just a bit of sweet cream butter. But, by August, even diehard corn fanatics will accept a little variety. Don't ever allow corn to become a same-old, same-old summer vegetable. Once you've exhausted your time-honored preparation, try a different cooking method or add a new spice or seasoning. Freshly minced summer herbs, such as chives, cilantro, basil, and thyme, or bold spices like chili powder and cumin, add lively flavor. We enjoy the kick fresh lime juice and basil offer in this simple seasoned butter.

◆◆◆◆◆◆

3 tablespoons unsalted butter
Juice of 1 large lime
1 tablespoon minced fresh red serrano
* or other small hot red chile pepper*
* (see About Chile Peppers, page 87)*
½ teaspoon coarse (kosher) salt
Freshly ground black pepper, to taste
6 ears fresh corn
1 tablespoon minced fresh basil

◆◆◆◆◆◆

1. Melt the butter in a small saucepan over low heat. Add the lime juice, minced chile, salt, and pepper, and whisk until light and creamy. Keep warm while you cook the corn.

2. Cook the corn by one of the following methods:

The 3-minute plunge: Three minutes is really all it takes to tenderize the kernels and heighten their natural sweet flavor. Bring a large pot of water to a boil. Shuck the corn and plunge the ears into the boiling water. Cook for 3 minutes after the water returns to a boil. (Do not add anything to the water—no sugar, no salt.) Drain, and enclose in a clean kitchen towel to hold the heat.

On the grill: Pull back the husks (don't pull them off entirely), remove the silks, and draw the husks back to once again enclose the ears of corn. Soak them in a sink or tub of cold water for 30 minutes. Meanwhile, preheat the grill to medium-hot. Drain the corn, and toss the ears, in their husks, on the grill. Cook, turning occasionally, until tender and steaming hot, about 15 minutes. Pull back the husks and return the ears to the grill for just long enough to acquire a few strategic grill marks. Wrap in a clean kitchen towel to hold the heat.

In the microwave: This is one of the simplest methods for preparing corn. Toss the whole unshucked ears, silks and all, into the microwave and cook on high for 3 minutes per ear (for example, if cooking 2 ears, total cooking time is 6 minutes). To retain the heat until serving time, allow the cooked cobs to rest in their husks until you're ready to sit down. The silks will peel right off with the husks.

3. Pile the hot corn onto a large serving platter. Stir the basil into the warm butter and pour it over the corn, turning each ear to coat it thoroughly. Deliver to the table and serve immediately.

FRESH SWEET CORN

Every year during corn season, we put up a sign in the produce department: WE SELL NO DAY-OLD CORN. The reason is straightforward: The sugars in sweet corn turn to starch very rapidly, so it should be cooked within hours of picking. Nowadays, though, new varieties have made it possible to ship corn for longer distances and still bring an acceptable product (not the absolute best, but amazingly good) to the market. There are three types of sweet corn, distinguished by the amount of sugar they contain: Normal Sugary (the old-fashioned native corn with 5 to 10 percent sugar, which is mostly lost after 24 hours), Sugary Enhanced (still local, with an equally short shelf-life but a 15 to 18 percent sugar content), and Supersweet, grown in Florida and Texas, which has 20 to 30 percent sugar and keeps for several days under refrigeration. Supersweets may not be as crisp as local corn, but in the months before the local varieties kick in, we're awfully glad to have them.

Green Beans, Tomatoes, and Pine Nuts

SERVES 6

This summer beauty is a favorite at Hay Day and a snap to make. The fresh green beans set off the bright tomatoes and the lightly browned shallots like jewels, and the golden pine nuts add crisp texture and rich flavor. To maintain the crisp freshness of this dish, be sure to rescue the beans from the boiling water the minute their bright color peaks.

◆◆◆◆◆◆

Coarse (kosher) salt
1¼ pounds fresh green beans,
    trimmed and rinsed
2 tablespoons extra-virgin olive oil
2 large shallots, peeled, cut in half, and
    thinly sliced (generous ½ cup sliced)
3 tablespoons pine nuts
1½ cups diced fresh tomatoes or
    halved cherry tomatoes

◆◆◆◆◆◆

1. Fill a large bowl with very cold water and set aside.

2. Bring a large saucepan of water to a boil. Add a dash of salt, then add the beans. Cook, uncovered, until bright green and crisp-tender, about 5 minutes. Drain, and immediately immerse in the cold water to stop the cooking and set the bright green color. Drain and pat dry. (The beans can be prepared to this point a couple of hours in advance; let them rest at room temperature.)

3. Heat the oil in a large skillet over medium heat. Add the shallots and pine nuts, and sauté until the shallots are lightly browned and begin to crisp and the pine nuts are lightly colored, 3 to 4 minutes.

4. Add the tomatoes and green beans. Toss together to warm. Season to taste with salt, and serve immediately.

Quinoa-Stuffed Mushrooms

SERVES 4

We use fragrant, nutty, healthful quinoa here instead of bread crumbs in what are otherwise traditional stuffed mushroom caps. They make a pretty fall accompaniment for anything from roast chicken and steak to grilled, baked, or poached fish.

◆◆◆◆◆◆

8 white or cremini mushrooms
    (2-inch diameter), caps and stems
    wiped clean
2 tablespoons walnut or olive oil
1 tablespoon unsalted butter
1 scant tablespoon minced garlic
1 small leek, white part only,
    well washed and chopped
    (⅓ cup chopped)
¼ cup quinoa (see About Quinoa,
    page 125), well rinsed
¼ cup Chicken Stock (page 270)
1 to 2 teaspoons fresh lemon juice
2 tablespoons chopped walnuts
2 tablespoons chopped fresh Italian
    (flat-leaf) parsley
Small pinch of coarse (kosher) salt

◆◆◆◆◆◆

1. Preheat the oven to 425°F.

2. Separate the mushroom stems from the caps. Finely chop the stems, measure out a generous ⅓ cup, and set aside.

3. Brush the mushroom caps inside and out with 1 tablespoon of the oil. Arrange them, open side up, on a baking sheet or in a baking dish.

4. Melt the butter in a skillet over medium-high heat. Add the garlic, leek, and reserved mushroom stems and sauté until fragrant and tender, 3 to 4 minutes. Stir in the quinoa and chicken stock, and bring to a boil. Reduce the heat, cover, and simmer until all the liquid is absorbed and the quinoa is tender, 8 to 10 minutes. Stir in the lemon juice to taste, then the walnuts and parsley, and season with the salt.

5. Using a teaspoon, pack the stuffing inside the mushroom caps, mounding it up high. Drizzle the remaining 1 tablespoon oil over the mushrooms and roast until they are hot and fork-tender, about 10 minutes. Serve hot.

Roasted Vidalias and Red Peppers

SERVES 4 TO 6

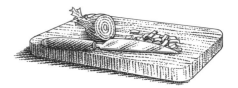

It's hard to believe that some of us grew to adulthood without knowing about Vidalia onions—now summer is unimaginable without them. A roasted Vidalia is one of Nature's noblest foods; here it is quartered and tossed with roasted peppers in a balsamic vinaigrette for a simple but glorious accompaniment to grilled lamb or beef fillet.

◆◆◆◆◆◆

3 Vidalia onions (see About Vidalia Onions, page 115)
4 assorted bell peppers (red, yellow, and orange in any combination)
1 tablespoon large capers, rinsed and drained
4 large fresh basil leaves, shredded
¼ teaspoon coarse (kosher) salt
1 tablespoon balsamic vinegar
¼ cup extra-virgin olive oil

◆◆◆◆◆◆

1. Preheat the oven to 350°F.

2. Place the whole unpeeled onions and the whole bell peppers on a large baking sheet or in a baking dish. Roast, turning the vegetables once or twice, until the onions are very soft and lightly caramelized and the peppers are soft and lightly charred, about 1 hour. Remove from the oven and place the peppers inside a paper or plastic bag to cool for at least 10 minutes. Set the onions aside to cool.

3. When the onions are cool enough to handle, trim and peel them. Cut the onions into quarters, separate the layers, and drop them into a salad bowl.

4. Remove the peppers from the bag. Pull out the stems and peel off the charred skin. Split the peppers open and scrape out the seeds with a blunt knife. Slice the peppers into thick strips and add them to the salad bowl.

5. Add the capers and basil, sprinkle with the salt, and drizzle with the vinegar and oil. Toss, and serve warm or at room temperature.

Celebrating Spring

This is what you serve when the daffodils are up and the forsythia's blooming. Have a glass of white wine on the terrace and serve tender pod peas, fiddlehead ferns, and chicken transformed for spring by creamy young chèvre, lemon, and fresh green herbs.

New Potatoes and Fiddlehead Ferns

Lemon Chèvre Chicken

Spring Pea Medley

Strawberry-Mango Fruit Torte

Spring Pea Medley

SERVES 8

Sweet spring peas hardly need embellishment, but if you toss them with sugar snaps, mint, and shredded lettuce, you get something that transcends mere vegetables.

◆◆◆◆◆◆

2 tablespoons unsalted butter
1 large leek, white portion only,
*   well washed and coarsely chopped*
1½ cups shelled English shell peas
*   (see About Peas, facing page)*
½ cup Vegetable Stock (page 271) or
*   Chicken Stock (pages 270)*
12 ounces sugar snap peas, rinsed
*   and trimmed*
1 tablespoon minced fresh mint
½ head Bibb or other tender green
*   leaf lettuce, well rinsed and sliced*
*   into thin shreds (1 generous packed*
*   cup shredded)*
Coarse (kosher) salt and freshly
*   ground black pepper*

◆◆◆◆◆◆

1. Melt the butter in a large saucepan over medium heat. Add the leek and sauté until transparent and tender, about 2 minutes. Stir in the shell peas and stock, cover, and simmer gently until the peas are nearly tender, 3 to 5 minutes.

ABOUT PEAS

There are several types of fresh peas, all of which are available nearly year-round these days, but they are at their peak during the spring and early summer months. Like corn, the natural sugar in peas converts quickly to starch; so buy the peas fresh, store them in the refrigerator, and use them within a day or two.

The *English shell pea* is the familiar round green pea. Frozen tiny tender green peas, while enjoyable and convenient throughout the winter months, bear little resemblance to the texture and bright flavor of fresh peas. The springtime ritual of shelling peas is just as satisfying as shucking summer corn, and their flavor and texture are worth every minute. When shopping for English peas, look for bright green smooth, succulent pods filled with evenly plump, round seeds. The freshness of the pods is an indication of the freshness of the peas. For the most reliable test, pop open a pod and taste a pea. Fresh peas should taste sweet and grassy. A pound of English shell peas in their pods yields about 2 cups of shelled peas—2 to 3 servings.

Both *sugar snaps* and *snow peas* are edible-pod peas—no shelling required. And as their name implies, sugar snaps are delightfully sweet. Sugar snaps are delicious raw, but their flavor is heightened with a brief cooking. As with all other peas, look for bright, smooth, succulent, tender green pods with fresh-looking stems.

---

2. Stir in the sugar snap peas and mint, replace the cover, and cook until the snap peas are bright green and crisp-tender, about 3 minutes. Then add the lettuce, stir to evenly cloak in the juices, and season with a generous pinch of salt and with pepper to taste. Serve immediately.

Provençal Stuffed Peppers

SERVES 6

Served warm or at room temperature, these fragrant roasted bell peppers make a splendid centerpiece for a platter of antipasti. They're easy to make; bake them in the cool of the morning, then surround them with a mélange of good olives, grilled marinated vegetables, and sliced aged cheeses at serving time. Best in summer when bell peppers and tomatoes are really spectacular, this can nonetheless be made year-round with good-quality canned plum tomatoes. And it makes a deliciously simple accompaniment to grilled chicken or fish.

◆◆◆◆◆◆

1 red bell pepper
1 yellow bell pepper
1 orange bell pepper
*4 large cloves garlic, peeled and
    coarsely chopped*
8 anchovy fillets, rinsed
*6 large fresh basil leaves, shredded,
    plus more for garnish*
6 large ripe plum tomatoes, peeled
*2 tablespoons extra-virgin
    olive oil*

◆◆◆◆◆◆

1. Preheat the oven to 375°F.

2. Cut the bell peppers in half, slicing straight through the stem. Scrape out the seeds and veins with a blunt knife, leaving the stems in place. Arrange, cut side up, in a gratin or baking dish that is just large enough to accommodate the peppers in a single layer.

3. Mince the garlic, anchovies, and 6 shredded basil leaves together to make a coarse paste, and spread a teaspoon of the paste inside each pepper. Place a plum tomato inside each pepper, and press it in gently to fill the cavity. Spread the remaining anchovy paste over the tomatoes, and drizzle a teaspoon of oil over each. Bake until the peppers are very tender and lightly charred around the edges, 35 to 40 minutes. Remove from the oven, spoon the pan juices over the peppers, and serve warm or at room temperature, garnished with additional fresh basil.

Chèvre-Topped Spring Potatoes

SERVES 6 TO 8

Small tender thin-skinned potatoes roast quickly and easily all by themselves. When they're cooked, we pinch them open and top them with a mixture of chèvre and fresh seasonings for a superb accompaniment to steak or grilled fish.

◆◆◆◆◆◆

18 small (2-inch-diameter) thin-skinned new potatoes, such as baby Yukon Gold, Red Bliss, or Peruvian Purple (see About "New" Potatoes, page 109)
2 teaspoons plus 1 tablespoon olive oil, more if needed
4 ounces fresh chèvre (see A Note on Chèvre, page 60)
1 small clove garlic, peeled and minced
2 tablespoons fresh lime juice
1 tablespoon chopped fresh cilantro
Coarse (kosher) salt and freshly ground black pepper

◆◆◆◆◆◆

1. Preheat the oven to 375°F.

2. Scrub the potatoes, pat them dry, and spread them out in a single layer in a roasting pan. Sprinkle with the 2 teaspoons oil and toss to coat evenly. Roast, shaking the pan occasionally so they brown evenly, until extremely tender, 30 to 40 minutes. Remove from the oven and set aside just until they are cool enough to handle, about 5 minutes.

3. Meanwhile, combine the chèvre, garlic, lime juice, cilantro, and remaining 1 tablespoon oil in a small bowl and blend with the back of a spoon until smooth. (The mixture should be soft and smooth, the consistency of sour cream; if it is too thick, add a bit more oil.) Season to taste with salt and pepper.

4. Slice an X across the top of each potato with a small paring knife and firmly pinch the sides, crushing the cooked potato a bit and popping the top open. Top each potato with a generous teaspoon of the cheese mixture, and finish with a sprinkling of black pepper. (The potatoes can be prepared to this point up to an hour before guests arrive.)

5. Preheat the broiler.

6. Cook the potatoes under the hot broiler until the topping is piping hot and very lightly browned, 3 to 5 minutes. Serve hot.

Buttermilk-Chive Mashed Potatoes

SERVES 4 TO 6

High-starch russet ("Idaho") potatoes are the classic choice for fluffy mashed potatoes, but medium-starch Yukon Golds will do just as well and have a rich buttery color. Plenty of people just mash potatoes with an old-fashioned hand-held masher or the back of a fork, but we are convinced that a ricer or a food mill really does the job best.

◆◆◆◆◆◆

Generous 2 pounds russet or
*   Yukon Gold potatoes, unpeeled,*
*   cut into 2-inch pieces*
1 cup buttermilk
2 tablespoons unsalted butter
1 teaspoon coarse (kosher) salt
Freshly ground black pepper, to taste
3 tablespoons minced fresh chives

◆◆◆◆◆◆

1. Place the potatoes in a large pot and cover with cold water. Lightly salt the water and bring to a boil. Reduce the heat and simmer, partially covered, until fork-tender, about 20 minutes.

2. Meanwhile, warm the buttermilk in a saucepan over low heat.

3. Drain the potatoes and run them through a food mill or ricer into the pan of warm buttermilk. Add the butter and whisk until fluffy and smooth. Stir in the salt, pepper to taste, and chives, and serve immediately.

Lacy Two-Potato Pancakes

MAKES 12 PANCAKES; SERVES 6

Classic potato pancakes are divine, but add the rich color and flavor of sweet potatoes and you have something really spectacular. Grating the potatoes in a food processor is not only quick and efficient—it also yields the crispest, laciest pancakes. Serve the pancakes in the fall with roast chicken or pork, or top them with a little crème fraîche or sour cream and

SWEET POTATOES

The sweet potatoes we know best, whether deep orange, pale yellow, or almost white fleshed, are all variants of the North American sweet potato, a member of the morning glory family, which came originally from Central America and now grows in warm climates around the world. The deep orange ones that flourish in sandy southern soils are often referred to as yams, but don't be confused—a yam (actually *nyami* or *name*), grown in Africa, is a totally different botanical species. The word has been adopted in this country as a marketing term to distinguish moister, orange-fleshed sweet potatoes from their drier, yellow-fleshed cousins (varieties like white sweets or Jersey sweets) or the white-fleshed Cuban sweet potato (boniato), which is now being harvested in southern Florida. All of these are in the same family, and they are not true yams.

Sweet potatoes are readily available all year round, but they're freshest and at their best from August through October, when they tend to come straight from the fields. They will keep well in a cool, dry place and should not be refrigerated.

minced chives to serve as a main course with a tossed green salad.

◆◆◆◆◆◆

1 orange-fleshed sweet potato
  (about 12 ounces, see Sweet Potatoes)
2 russet potatoes (about 1 pound total)
6 scallions, white and light green
  parts finely chopped
1 teaspoon minced fresh thyme
2 eggs, lightly beaten
2 tablespoons unbleached all-purpose
  flour
1 teaspoon coarse (kosher) salt
Freshly ground black pepper,
  to taste
1/3 cup peanut oil

◆◆◆◆◆◆

1. Preheat the oven to 200°F.

2. Peel and coarsely grate the potatoes, using a food processor fitted with the shredding blade that has the largest holes, or on the largest holes on a box grater. Toss in a large bowl with the scallions and thyme. Add the eggs, flour, salt, and pepper, and stir with a fork until moistened and thoroughly combined. The mixture will be wet but not runny.

3. Heat the oil in a large nonstick skillet or countertop griddle over high heat. When the oil is hot (a drop of the potato mixture should sizzle immediately), add 1/4-cup amounts of the mixture, flattening them out to form 4-inch disks. Cook, a few at a time, over high heat until golden brown and crisp, 1 to 2 minutes per side.

4. Remove the pancakes with a slotted spatula or a skimmer, and place them on paper towels to drain. Transfer them to an ovenproof platter and keep warm in the oven while you cook the rest. Serve warm.

Maple-Roasted Sweet Potato Spears

SERVES 6 TO 8

We sell tons of these in the fall and winter, especially around Thanksgiving, and they could not be easier. Even finicky children munch on them happily at mealtime.

◆◆◆◆◆◆

3 large orange-fleshed sweet potatoes (about 12 ounces each), scrubbed and patted dry (see Sweet Potatoes, facing page)
2 teaspoons olive oil
½ teaspoon coarse (kosher) salt
¼ cup pure maple syrup
1 tablespoon cider vinegar
1 teaspoon fresh thyme leaves, or ½ teaspoon dried

◆◆◆◆◆◆

1. Preheat the oven to 425°F.

2. Cut the potatoes in half lengthwise, and then slice each half into four spears ¾ to 1 inch wide.

3. Line a large jelly-roll pan or baking sheet with parchment paper or lightly oil. Toss the potato spears with 1 teaspoon of the olive oil and the salt in a large bowl. Scatter the sweet potatoes on the prepared pan in a single layer and place in the oven. Roast, turning once, until fork-tender and lightly browned, about 25 minutes.

4. Meanwhile, whisk together the maple syrup, vinegar, and remaining 1 teaspoon

oil. Brush this glaze lightly over the roasted potato spears (you may not need it all). Return them to the oven and continue roasting until they are caramelized, about 10 minutes. Remove from the oven, sprinkle with the thyme, and serve.

Wilted Radicchio with Gorgonzola and Walnuts

SERVES 4 TO 6

This recipe comes from friends of ours who served it one autumn evening at their home on the Connecticut River. It's a wonderfully simple side dish full of intense flavor. The

ABOUT RADICCHIO

Radicchio, a dark red-leaf Italian chicory with tender firm leaves and a slightly bitter flavor, is commonly used as a salad green, but it is also great grilled, sautéed, or baked. It grows in two forms: radicchio di Verona, a small rounded head of compact leaves, and radicchio di Treviso, also referred to as Trevisano, a narrow pointed cluster of leaves rather like Belgian endive. Use either one, but where the round Verona variety is quartered in this recipe, skinny Trevisano should just be cut in half and broiled cut-side up.

light bitterness of the radicchio matches the richness of the Gorgonzola, and the whole thing is deeply satisfying. The radicchio loses a little of its intense burgundy color in cooking but gains a lot of flavor.

◆◆◆◆◆◆

1 large head radicchio di Verona, or
  2 heads radicchio di Treviso
  (see About Radicchio, page 203)
¼ cup Balsamic Vinaigrette
  (page 264)
Scant 4 ounces mountain Gorgonzola
  cheese, crumbled (see About
  Gorgonzola)
¼ cup finely chopped walnuts

◆◆◆◆◆◆

1. Preheat the broiler.

2. Slice the radicchio in half lengthwise, cutting through the root end. If using radicchio di Verona, slice each half into quarters, leaving a small portion of the root end attached to each wedge. Pour the vinaigrette onto a small plate and dip the radicchio wedges in it, turning to coat them lightly on all sides (nearly all of the vinaigrette should be absorbed). Arrange the radicchio in a small flameproof baking dish that is just large enough to accommodate the wedges in a single layer. Scatter the cheese evenly on top, gently tucking it in between the layers of leaves, and cook under the broiler just until the cheese has melted and the radicchio is very lightly charred around the edges, 2 to 3 minutes.

3. Turn off the broiler and remove the dish. Sprinkle the chopped nuts over the radicchio, and return the dish to the warm broiler. Let sit just until the radicchio has wilted, 2 to 3 minutes. Serve warm or at room temperature.

ABOUT GORGONZOLA

One of Italy's most celebrated cheeses, this intensely flavored cow's-milk blue is imported from the Lombardy region. Highly aromatic and richly flavored, Gorgonzola is prepared and marketed in two different forms: Gorgonzola dolce (sweet) and mountain or aged Gorgonzola. The aged variety is firmer, drier, and more intensely flavored—good for crumbling—while Gorgonzola dolce is generally milder and creamier. The creamy texture of Gorgonzola dolce is best enjoyed thinly sliced over a salad or spread on slices of pear or on crackers. Either form is delicious served alongside fresh sweet figs and grapes.

Warm Spinach with Balsamic Basil Butter

SERVES 4

Balsamic vinegar and red wine combine with fresh basil to create a syrup with an intense fruity flavor—a wonderful (and almost effortless) combination with wilted fresh spinach.

◆◆◆◆◆◆

¹/₄ cup balsamic vinegar

3 tablespoons dry red wine

3 tablespoons unsalted butter,
cut into bits

6 large fresh basil leaves,
finely chopped

16 ounces fresh spinach, well rinsed,
thick stems removed

Coarse (kosher) salt and freshly
ground black pepper

◆◆◆◆◆◆

1. Combine the vinegar and wine in a small saucepan. Bring to a simmer over medium heat and cook until reduced by half, 8 to 10 minutes. Whisk in the butter and basil, and simmer gently for another minute. Remove from the heat, cover, and set aside.

2. Place the spinach, with the water from rinsing still clinging to the leaves, in a large saucepan. Cover, and cook over medium heat, turning once with kitchen tongs, until wilted, about 4 minutes. Drain well, then season with a pinch of salt and pepper to taste. Transfer to a warm serving dish. Drizzle the sauce on top and serve immediately.

GRILLING VEGETABLES

◆ Be sure the grill rack is clean; brush it lightly with oil right before grilling the vegetables.

◆ Keeping onion slices together for grilling can be tricky; the sweet onion varieties work best, not only for their mellow flavor but because of their premium size. Slice them thickly and turn only once.

◆ Eggplant has a tendency to dry out during grilling, so make sure that your slices are at least ¹/₄ inch thick, and grill them just until golden and soft and very lightly charred around the edges.

Grilled Ratatouille Vegetables

SERVES 6

It's hard to imagine improving on classic ratatouille, but this version will come into its own on hot summer days when you don't want to go within a mile of the stove. Serve it either hot or cold with roasted or grilled meats or fish. It can also serve as an appetizer on rounds of French bread or as a vegetable topping for pizza; and it makes an outstanding salad when topped with crumbled feta cheese and toasted pine nuts. The quantity given here will probably fill the grill rack twice over, unless you have a huge one, but the vegetables cook quickly and can even be grilled a day ahead.

◆◆◆◆◆◆

2 tablespoons fresh lemon juice
¼ cup plus 2 tablespoons extra-virgin olive oil
1 large sweet onion (Vidalia, Walla Walla, Maui, or Oso Sweet), peeled and sliced into 1-inch-thick rounds
1 large zucchini, scrubbed and sliced lengthwise into ¼-inch-thick slices
1 large yellow summer squash, scrubbed and sliced lengthwise into ¼-inch-thick slices
1 large red bell pepper, stemmed, seeded, and quartered
1 small eggplant, unpeeled, sliced into ¼-inch-thick rounds
⅓ cup shredded fresh basil
1 pint ripe cherry tomatoes, rinsed and sliced in half
1 tablespoon balsamic vinegar
Coarse (kosher) salt and freshly ground black pepper

◆◆◆◆◆◆

1. Preheat the grill to medium-high.

2. In a small bowl, whisk the lemon juice with the ¼ cup oil. Lightly brush this over the slices of onion, zucchini, yellow squash, bell pepper, and eggplant. When ready to cook, oil the grill rack.

3. Grill the vegetables, turning them once or twice, until tender and just cooked through. (You want the vegetables to soften, color, and char lightly around the edges yet remain moist.) Remove them from the grill as they are done: 5 to 7 minutes for the zucchini and

yellow squash, 8 to 10 minutes for the bell pepper and eggplant, and 10 to 12 minutes for the onion.

4. Chop the vegetables into large bite-size pieces and toss together in a large bowl. Add the basil, tomatoes, vinegar, and remaining 2 tablespoons oil. Season to taste with salt and pepper, and serve immediately or at room temperature. The flavors of this dish develop nicely as it sits.

Hot Off the Grill

A great menu for beach house holidays when outdoor grilling is the preferred way to cook. Grill the ratatouille vegetables in the morning when the air's still cool; their flavor will only get richer by suppertime. Set the table on the porch and serve the fennel and swordfish kebabs straight from the grill. The cake can be prepared a couple of days in advance, then lightly toasted on a clean grill rack for a very impressive finale.

🍅 🍅 🍅

Mozzarella, Tomato, and Grilled Fennel Salad

Swordfish Kebabs

Grilled Ratatouille Vegetables

Grilled Sour Lemon Cake with Poached Summer Berries

Cider-Glazed Autumn Medley

SERVES 4 TO 6

This easy, pretty mélange of autumn fruits and vegetables is wonderful with roast pork, poultry, or braised game sausages. The vegetables can be prepared several hours in advance; then just before serving time, all you have to do is to chop the apple and quickly finish off the dish.

◆◆◆◆◆◆

2 tablespoons unsalted butter
6 ounces buttercup squash, cut
    into ½-inch dice
4 ounces cremini mushrooms,
    wiped clean and quartered
4 ounces Brussels sprouts, trimmed
    and quartered
1 large tart cooking apple (Granny
    Smith or Greening), peeled, cored,
    and cut into ½-inch dice
8 ounces roasted whole peeled chestnuts
    (see Note)
1 tablespoon minced fresh sage
½ cup Chicken Stock (page 270)
¼ cup apple cider
½ teaspoon coarse (kosher) salt
Freshly ground black pepper, to taste

◆◆◆◆◆◆

1. Melt the butter in a large skillet over high heat. Add the squash, mushrooms, and Brussels sprouts and sauté until the vegetables are lightly browned, 5 to 7 minutes.

2. Stir in the apple, chestnuts, and sage. Then slowly pour in the stock and cider. Bring to a simmer, scraping up any browned bits in the pan, and cook over medium-high heat, shaking the pan occasionally, until the Brussels sprouts are fork-tender and the sauce has thickened slightly, about 5 minutes. Immediately remove from the heat, and season with the salt and pepper. Transfer to a covered serving dish and serve.

Note: Lighting the fire and roasting chestnuts is all very romantic—but a little impractical for the preparation of this dish. Instead, as soon as the cool weather comes, pick up a few jars of roasted whole peeled chestnuts. Their sweet flavor and rich texture add a nice earthy quality to a wide variety of winter preparations.

Hay Day's Vegetable Pancakes

MAKES ABOUT 10 PANCAKES;
SERVES 4 TO 6

Okay, they're fried. But it's not deep fat (there's only a quarter of a cup), and they are worth it. The recipe looks labor-intensive, but it's not a difficult process, and again, they are worth it. Customers go bonkers when we offer these in the stores. They make a great fall or winter side dish with roast pork, poultry, or game, and they're hearty enough to serve as a main course.

♦♦♦♦♦♦

1 large orange-fleshed sweet potato,
    baked (see Sweet Potatoes, page 202)
2 carrots, scrubbed and grated
1 red bell pepper, stemmed, seeded,
    and finely chopped
1 small onion, peeled and chopped
1 zucchini, scrubbed and grated
    (1 packed cup grated)
2 cloves garlic, peeled and minced
6 ounces (1 generous cup) tender cooked
    white kidney or cannellini beans,
    drained and rinsed
1/3 cup dry bread crumbs (see Note,
    page 133)
1/2 cup old-fashioned rolled oats,
    shredded in a food processor
1/2 cup freshly grated Parmesan cheese
    (see Grating Cheeses, page 251)
1 teaspoon coarse (kosher) salt
Coarsely ground black pepper, to taste
1/4 cup vegetable oil
Unbleached all-purpose flour, for dusting

♦♦♦♦♦♦

1. Scrape the flesh out of the baked
sweet potato (discard the skin), and mash
it. You should have about 1 cup cooked
mashed sweet potato.

2. Place the carrots, bell pepper, onion,
zucchini, and garlic in a large saucepan.
Cover and cook over medium-low heat,
stirring occasionally and adjusting the
heat as needed to prevent the vegetables

from scorching, until they are very tender
and reduced by half, 15 to 20 minutes.
(Without any fat, the vegetables will
steam-cook in their own juices.) Remove
the pan from the heat and set it aside.

3. Meanwhile preheat the oven to 200°F.

4. Place the beans in a large mixing bowl
and mash them coarsely with the tines of
a fork or with a potato masher. Add the
sweet potato, steamed vegetables, bread
crumbs, oats, and cheese; mix together
thoroughly. Season with the salt and
pepper, and form into 3-inch flattened
patties. For the best results, cover and
refrigerate for at least 30 minutes before
pan-frying.

5. Heat the oil in a large skillet over
medium-high heat. Lightly dust both
sides of the patties with a small amount
of flour and sauté them, in batches, until
nicely browned on both sides and heated
through, 3 to 5 minutes per side. Pat the
patties dry with a paper towel, and keep
them warm in the oven while you sauté
the remainder. Serve immediately.

Oven-Roasted
Winter Vegetables

SERVES 4 TO 6

I t's amazing to think that ten years ago
only a handful of people were roasting vegetables! Oven-roasting caramelizes the natural sugars, which makes
the vegetables taste wonderful. Here they
are nicely accented by rich, nutty walnut
oil and peppery-sweet balsamic vinegar.
We offer them on the Hay Day store

menu pretty much every day all winter, and there are *never* any leftovers. The mixture can vary, but try to match cooking times so individual vegetables are neither undercooked nor mushy. It's no problem substituting button mushrooms for the shiitakes, for example; but if you use carrots or parsnips instead of sweet potatoes, they should be parboiled first.

◆◆◆◆◆◆

1 orange-fleshed sweet potato, peeled and cut into 1-inch cubes (see Sweet Potatoes, page 202)
1 small bulb fennel, scrubbed, trimmed, and cut into thick wedges
8 ounces new potatoes, scrubbed and cut into 1-inch cubes (see About "New" Potatoes, page 109)
6 ounces shiitake mushrooms, stems discarded, caps wiped and cut in half
4 large shallots (the size of walnuts), peeled and cut into quarters
3 tablespoons walnut oil
2 tablespoons balsamic vinegar
1½ teaspoons coarse (kosher) salt

◆◆◆◆◆◆

1. Preheat the oven to 400°F.

2. In a large bowl, toss all the vegetables with the oil, 1 tablespoon of the vinegar, and the salt. Arrange on a large baking sheet and roast, stirring and tossing once or twice, until the vegetables are nicely browned and caramelized, 30 to 35 minutes.

3. Remove the baking sheet from the oven, and using a large spatula, scrape the roasted vegetables into a large serving bowl along with all the bits clinging to the pan. Sprinkle with the remaining 1 tablespoon vinegar, and serve warm or at room temperature.

Roasted Vegetable Couscous

SERVES 4 TO 6

Sweet oven-roasted root vegetables make a lovely combination with the hearty flavor of whole-wheat couscous (you can use regular, too), especially when you add fragrantly spiced stock and sweet currants. A superb side dish with roast chicken or game.

◆◆◆◆◆◆

¾ cup diced parsnips
¾ cup diced carrots
2 tablespoons unsalted butter
2 cups Chicken Stock (page 270)
1 large pinch saffron threads (see Cooking with Saffron, page 180)
½ teaspoon ground cinnamon
1¼ teaspoons coarse (kosher) salt
½ cup dried currants
2 cups whole-wheat or regular couscous

◆◆◆◆◆◆

1. Preheat the oven to 375°F.

2. Scatter the diced vegetables in a large roasting pan. Cut 1 tablespoon of the butter into small bits and scatter them among the vegetables. Roast, stirring once, until the vegetables are lightly browned and tender, 15 to 20 minutes. Remove from the oven and reduce the oven temperature to 300°F.

3. Combine the stock, saffron, cinnamon, salt, currants, and remaining 1 tablespoon butter in a saucepan and bring to a simmer over medium-high heat.

4. Meanwhile, toss the couscous and roasted vegetables together in an oven-proof casserole. Pour the simmering stock mixture on top, cover, and bake until the liquid has been absorbed and the couscous is tender, about 10 minutes. Remove the casserole from the oven, and when you are ready to serve it, lift the lid and fluff the couscous with the tines of a fork. Serve hot.

Wild Rice and Couscous

SERVES 6 TO 8

Wild rice is the classic partner for vividly flavored foods like pheasant, quail, salmon, and venison, but many people like to lighten its dense texture by adding conventional white rice. We offer here an airy pilaf that is a lot easier to prepare than cooking two kinds of rice. Just add some quick-cooking couscous to the wild rice toward the end of its cooking time, let it rest off the heat for 10 minutes, and then toss with scallions and toasted nuts. Couldn't be simpler.

◆◆◆◆◆◆

1 cup wild rice, well rinsed
2 cups water
Coarse (kosher) salt
1 tablespoon olive oil
⅓ cup regular or whole-wheat couscous
6 scallions, white and light green parts minced
⅓ cup pine nuts, lightly toasted (see Toasting Pine Nuts, page 250)

◆◆◆◆◆◆

1. Combine the wild rice, water, ½ teaspoon salt, and the oil in a saucepan and bring to a boil. Reduce the heat to medium-low, cover, and simmer until the rice is al dente (just tender to the bite) and beginning to split, 35 to 40 minutes.

2. Place a fine-mesh sieve over a bowl and drain the rice into it. Return the rice to the saucepan, and add ⅓ cup of the strained cooking liquid. Stir in the couscous, cover, and allow to rest off the heat until most of the liquid has been absorbed, about 10 minutes.

3. Remove the cover, add the scallions and pine nuts, and fluff with a fork. Season to taste with additional salt as desired, and serve hot.

Sweet Endings

"What's for dessert?" During the day, dessert (except for a peach, maybe, or a handful of cherries) is probably the thing you skip. But when you're entertaining, or looking for a simple project on a rainy afternoon, or making supper on one of the rare nights when everybody's home at the same time—dessert is the good part, the treat, the smile of relief in the seriousness of life.

The first Hay Day bakery started in 1979 in the back of the Westport store, and the results weren't all that different from the things we made at home. The pies and muffins were just as cheerfully irregular and lumpy as the ones from our own kitchen. People who love good food are suspicious of perfection. They know that only a machine can turn out a perfectly regular crust or a symmetrical muffin, and who needs that? Good pastries look as handmade as they are.

Many of the desserts included here are Hay Day classics—like the Sour Lemon Cake and Bourbon-Apple-Walnut Pie, which we have been selling forever. But here as well are wonderful fruit-filled cobblers, crisps, and summer puddings that are too fragile to sell at the stores but will make a special occasion out of an ordinary supper or a picnic at the beach. Whether they come out of the oven picture perfect or a little lopsided, their taste will be spectacular.

Strawberry-Apple Pie

SERVES 8

Spring strawberries can be almost too juicy to hold up in a pie, but snappy Granny Smith apples (splendid in pies, and reliable in the marketplace year-round) give them some substance. If you like, make a lattice top with this cornmeal pastry; it holds up well and its rich yellow color shows off the filling. (The recipe also works fine with an all-purpose pie crust.)

◆◆◆◆◆◆

4 cups thinly sliced, peeled Granny
  Smith apples (about 4 apples)
1 quart fresh ripe strawberries,
  rinsed, hulled, and thickly sliced
  (3 cups sliced)
2 teaspoons fresh lemon juice
2 teaspoons pure vanilla extract
5 tablespoons granulated sugar
5 tablespoons dark brown sugar
3 tablespoons unbleached
  all-purpose flour
2 tablespoons arrowroot (see About
  Arrowroot)
$1/2$ teaspoon salt
$1/2$ teaspoon ground cinnamon
$1/4$ teaspoon freshly grated nutmeg
Sweet Butter Cornmeal Crust, rolled
  out for a 2-crust pie (page 274)
1 egg, separated
1 tablespoon milk

◆◆◆◆◆◆

1. Preheat the oven to 350°F.

2. Toss the apples, strawberries, lemon juice, and vanilla together in a large bowl.

ABOUT ARROWROOT

Arrowroot, a white powder ground from a tropical tuber, is a great help in thickening fruit pies, tarts, puddings, and sauces. As a thickener it is twice as effective as flour, and it is also absolutely tasteless, becoming clear when cooked. We use a combination of flour and arrowroot to thicken the juices in pies made with very soft, juicy fruits like strawberries.

If you unearth a jar of arrowroot that has been in the back of the cupboard long enough to count as a genuine antique, fear not. Unlike spices, which should be replaced periodically, arrowroot seems to keep its effectiveness indefinitely.

3. In another bowl, stir and toss the sugars, flour, arrowroot, salt, cinnamon, and nutmeg. Sprinkle the mixture over the fruit, toss to coat evenly, and set aside.

4. Lay the bottom crust in a 9-inch deep-dish pie plate (preferably glass), and crimp the edges. Lightly beat the egg white and brush it over the bottom crust. Spoon in the fruit mixture and any accumulated juices, cover with the top crust, and crimp the edges to seal. Whisk the egg yolk with the milk, and brush this wash over all exposed surfaces of the crust. Then, using the tines of a fork, prick the crust in several places to create vent holes.

5. Bake in the middle of the oven until the juice is bubbling through the vents and the crust is nicely browned, 45 to 50 minutes. Place the pie on a wire rack and allow it to cool for at least 30 minutes before serving it either warm or at room temperature.

Variation

◆ **Blackberry-Apple Pie:** Use 2 heaping cups of blackberries instead of the strawberries. Raspberries make a delicious pie, too.

Bourbon-Apple-Walnut Pie

SERVES 8

This was one of the original Hay Day fall recipes, invented in the tiny Westport bakery when the first apple crop tumbled in. The raisins are steeped in bourbon for extra flavor, and the easy crumb topping adds a lovely crunch. When our bakeries go into twenty-four-hour holiday overdrive, especially at Thanksgiving, pie boxes are stacked to the ceiling, and we even recruit the office staff to help with labeling and deliveries!

◆◆◆◆◆◆

Pie

½ cup raisins

3 tablespoons bourbon

6 cups thickly sliced, peeled, tart, crisp apples (Greening, Cortland, Northern Spy, Winesap, or Granny Smith; about 6 apples)

½ cup granulated sugar

3 tablespoons unbleached all-purpose flour

¼ teaspoon freshly grated nutmeg

1 teaspoon ground cinnamon

½ cup walnuts, preferably toasted (see Toasting Nuts, page 55), coarsely chopped

All-Purpose Pie Pastry rolled out for a 1-crust pie (page 272)

1 egg white, lightly beaten

Walnut Crumb Topping

1 cup walnuts, coarsely chopped

3 tablespoons light brown sugar

3 tablespoons granulated sugar

1 teaspoon ground cinnamon

◆◆◆◆◆◆

1. Preheat the oven to 350°F.

2. Combine the raisins and bourbon in a small saucepan and warm gently over low heat until the raisins begin to swell, about 10 minutes. Remove from the heat and set aside to steep.

3. Toss the apples with the sugar, flour, nutmeg, and cinnamon in a large bowl. Add the walnuts and the raisins, along with their soaking liquid, and toss to mix.

4. Place the pie crust in a 9-inch deep-dish pie plate and crimp the edges. Brush the egg white generously over the crust, and then spoon in the apple mixture.

5. In another mixing bowl, combine all the ingredients for the crumb topping. Stir thoroughly, and sprinkle evenly over the fruit. Bake until the apples are fork-tender and the crumb topping is nicely browned, 45 to 55 minutes. Remove the pie from the oven and let it cool on a wire rack for at least 30 minutes before serving it either warm or at room temperature.

Pear and Apple Potpies

SERVES 6

At Hay Day this is made as a traditional double-crust pear-apple pie, but at home we had such fun cutting out pastry leaves and stars that we changed the recipe to make individual "potpies." Filling the ramekins with fruit and topping them with a collage of pastry cutouts is a lot easier than fussing with top and bottom pie crusts; do it with young friends home from school on a rainy afternoon and let everybody create his or her own masterpiece. Fresh ginger gives the pears a clear, crisp flavor that goes particularly well with a whole-wheat crust, but classic all-purpose pie pastry is fine, too.

◆◆◆◆◆◆

4 cups coarsely chopped, peeled tart, crisp apples (Greening, Cortland, Northern Spy, Winesap, or Granny Smith; about 4 apples)
3 cups thickly sliced, peeled medium-ripe Bosc or Bartlett pears (about 3 pears)
1 tablespoon minced fresh ginger (see About Ginger, facing page)
2 teaspoons fresh lemon juice
2 teaspoons pure vanilla extract
5 tablespoons dark brown sugar
2 tablespoons unbleached all-purpose flour
1/2 teaspoon salt
1/2 teaspoon freshly grated nutmeg
Whole-Wheat Pie Pastry for a 2-crust pie (page 273)
1 egg
1 tablespoon milk
Granulated sugar, for dusting

◆◆◆◆◆◆

1. Preheat the oven to 350°F.

2. In a large bowl, toss the apples and pears with the ginger, lemon juice, and vanilla.

3. In another bowl, combine the sugar, flour, salt, and nutmeg. Add this to the fruit and toss to coat evenly.

4. Place six 4-inch ramekins or individual pie plates on a large baking sheet and spoon in the fruit mixture, piling it up high and dividing it evenly among the six dishes.

5. Roll the pastry out thin on a lightly floured cutting board. Using cookie cutters, cut out your shapes of choice (you'll need 3 to 4 cutouts per ramekin). Arrange them over the fruit in an overlapping pattern, leaving a few small open spaces to vent the pies as they bake. Allow the pastry to reach down over the rims of the ramekins, and gently crimp the pastry edges where they meet.

6. Whisk the egg and milk together in a small bowl, and brush this wash over the pastries to form a glaze. Sprinkle with a pinch of granulated sugar, and bake until the juice is bubbling through the vents and the pastry is nicely browned, 30 to 35 minutes. Remove the pies from the oven and allow them to cool on a wire rack for at least 15 minutes. Serve warm or at room temperature.

Variation

◆ Roll out the pastry for a two-crust pie, and spread the bottom crust in an 8-inch square baking dish. Fill it with the fruit mixture, then cover with the top crust, crimp the edges, and pierce the top to make vent holes. Bake, then cut into squares to serve with brown-sugar-glazed ham for a holiday brunch.

ABOUT GINGER

There was a time when you could only get ground ginger, but those days are long gone. We sell fresh gingerroot by the bushel nowadays. Finely minced fresh ginger makes something special out of all kinds of fruit desserts and adds new life to gingerbread, cookies, and pies.

We get fresh ginger from Hawaii (a disease decimated the crop early in this decade, but it's coming back), Fiji, Brazil, Costa Rica, and Honduras—and a wonderful ginger from Jamaica that has a pinkish color and a floral scent.

Ginger should be fat, firm, and substantial when you buy it; avoid lightweight, dull, shriveled tubers (actually they're rhizomes—the term ginger "root" is just plain wrong). Depending on how fresh it was to begin with, ginger

will keep well for at least 3 weeks in the refrigerator. If you're going to use it right away, keep it in the vegetable crisper; for longer storage, it's best wrapped in a paper towel in a plastic bag. Or you can wrap it tightly in plastic wrap and store it in the freezer.

To cut up a large piece of ginger, first slice off the little knobs, then peel it with a vegetable peeler or a small paring knife. The thin skin of young, tender springtime ginger usually needs no peeling at all. Cut the ginger into very thin slices; then stack the slices and cut them into very thin strips. To mince ginger, gather the strips and cut them crosswise into tiny dice. Friends of ours swear by their old garlic press for ginger, but we're pretty much wedded to the knife method.

Blueberry-Peach Crumb Pie

SERVES 8

This crumb topping is great with soft summer fruits, which sometimes cook way down under a conventional top crust, leaving an airy dome of empty pastry. The oats and cornmeal in the topping give it extra crunch, too. We make the pie here with blueberries and peaches, one of our most popular summer fruit pie combinations, but it's just as good when you pair blackberries or raspberries with peaches.

Three-Grain Crumb Topping

¼ cup unbleached all-purpose flour
½ cup medium-grain stone-ground cornmeal (see Stone-Ground Cornmeal, page 4)
¼ cup (firmly packed) light brown sugar
5 tablespoons unsalted butter, chilled, cut into large chunks
⅓ cup old-fashioned rolled oats

Pie

5 cups sliced, peeled ripe peaches (about 4 large peaches)
1 pint blueberries, stemmed and rinsed
1 tablespoon pure vanilla extract
1 tablespoon fresh lemon juice
½ cup granulated sugar
3 tablespoons unbleached all-purpose flour
2 tablespoons arrowroot (see About Arrowroot, page 212)
¼ teaspoon freshly grated nutmeg
¼ teaspoon salt
All-Purpose Pie Pastry, rolled out for a 1-crust pie (page 272)
1 egg white, lightly beaten with a fork

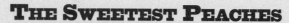

THE SWEETEST PEACHES

It's simple: To develop its sugars, a peach has to spend as much time as possible on the tree. So if it's picked green to withstand shipping, it will never reach the sweetness we all dream of in summer peaches. Which is why local peaches, like local strawberries, will always be worth waiting for. But having said all that, we have to admit that growers in the Central Valley of California are getting pretty good at sending them farther afield. The peach-growing conditions are ideal to begin with—lovely soil, hot summers, and fog that keeps the winter temperature just a hair above freezing. Encouraged by consumer demand, growers are leaving the fruit on the trees longer, packing it more carefully, and flying it to market more frequently. Still, you'll want to watch for the really special and fragile peaches—white ones, for example—from closer-to-home orchards in July and August.

1. Preheat the oven to 350°F

2. Prepare the topping: Combine the flour, cornmeal, and brown sugar in a food processor. Add the butter and oats and pulse to form a uniform coarse meal, with the bits of butter no larger than small grains of rice. Refrigerate until ready to use.

3. In a large mixing bowl, toss the peaches and blueberries with the vanilla and lemon juice. In a small bowl, stir the sugar, flour, arrowroot, nutmeg, and salt together. Add this to the fruit and toss to coat evenly and thoroughly.

4. Place the pie crust in a 9-inch deep-dish pie plate (preferably glass), crimp the edges, and brush generously with the egg white. Spoon in the fruit mixture along with any accumulated juices, and sprinkle with an even layer of the crumb topping.

5. Bake until the fruit juices come bubbling up through the crumb topping and the crust is nicely browned, about 1 hour. Remove from the oven and place on a wire rack to cool for at least 25 minutes before cutting. Serve warm or at room temperature.

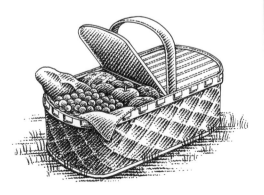

Blackberry-Mango Tart

MAKES 1 TART

This striking combination of exotic summer fruits is seasoned with fresh lime juice and set off by a crisp cornmeal crust to make a lovely free-form open-faced pie, ideal for a picnic in the shade. These days mangoes are readily available just about any time of year, but they are at their peak during the summer months. This recipe works well with blueberries, too, so you can enjoy the tart before the blackberries hit the stands in August.

◆◆◆◆◆

½ cup plus 1 teaspoon sugar
1 teaspoon freshly grated nutmeg
2 tablespoons arrowroot (see About Arrowroot, page 212)
2 ripe mangoes, peeled, halved, and thickly sliced (see About Mangoes, page 218)
2 cups fresh blackberries, gently rinsed and drained
Juice of 1 lime
¾ recipe Sweet Butter Cornmeal Crust (page 274), chilled (reserve the remainder for another use)
1 egg, separated
1 tablespoon milk

◆◆◆◆◆

1. Preheat the oven to 375°F.

2. Combine the ½ cup sugar, the nutmeg, and the arrowroot in a large bowl. Stir and toss together. Add the mangoes and blackberries, sprinkle with the lime juice, and toss to coat evenly.

ABOUT MANGOES

Most mangoes come from Mexico and Central America, with good ones also arriving from Haiti, Hawaii, Florida, and Jamaica. They're in season from January through September, with the peak in May, June, and July. Like ripe peaches, mangoes should be tender to the touch but not mushy; look for ones that yield to very gentle pressure and have a nice orange-red color.

Mangoes have big flat pits in the middle (shaped sort of like a skipping stone), which are no particular problem once you're used to them. Just remember that you'll never be able to slice a mango exactly in half. Start your cut at the stem and slice downward, following the curve of the pit as closely as possible, to produce two halves; then trim the remainder of the flesh off the sides of the pit. If you're going to slice the mango, peel the fruit before cutting into it. For cubes, cut the unpeeled mango in half, then score the flesh vertically and horizontally into squares without piercing the skin. Press each half inward from the skin side to turn it inside out and make the squares pop into a sort of rough hedgehog shape. Then slice them off, forming cubes.

3. Roll out the pie crust between two sheets of lightly floured wax paper, forming a round 12 inches in diameter. Remove the top sheet of wax paper and invert the pastry into a 9-inch deep-dish pie plate, allowing the edges to drape over the sides. Using your fingertips, lightly press the crust into the dish.

4. Beat the egg white with a fork, and generously brush it over the crust. Pile the fruit mixture inside, and fold the draped edges in over the fruit, forming large pinwheel pleats.

5. Whisk the egg yolk with the milk and brush this over the exposed edges of the pastry. Sprinkle the pastry with the remaining 1 teaspoon sugar, and bake until the juices are bubbling and the crust is nicely browned, 45 to 50 minutes. Remove from the oven and set aside to cool on a wire rack for at least 20 minutes before serving it warm or at room temperature.

Fresh Apricot Coulis

SERVES 4

In this simple, summery dessert bisque, honey and cardamom add an exotic touch to a creamy apricot purée—an elegant finish for a special meal. This recipe doubles beautifully.

◆◆◆◆◆◆

1 generous pound fresh apricots (9 to 10 apricots), rinsed, split, and pits removed
2 tablespoons honey
⅓ cup lightly fruity sweet white wine (Alsatian Riesling, Sémillon, or Chenin Blanc)
¼ teaspoon ground cardamom
1 tablespoon sugar
4 teaspoons heavy (whipping) cream, chilled

◆◆◆◆◆◆

1. In a food processor or blender, purée (in batches, if necessary) all but 1 of the apricots with the honey and wine until smooth. Transfer to a clean container, cover, and refrigerate to chill for at least 2 hours or until ready to serve.

2. Meanwhile, combine the cardamom and sugar in a small dish. Slice the reserved apricot into twelve thin crescents.

3. At serving time, divide the chilled purée among four small dessert bowls or goblets, and swirl a teaspoon of heavy cream into each. Top with the reserved apricot slices, and finish with a sprinkling of the cardamom sugar. Serve immediately.

ABOUT PASSION FRUIT

There is no more vivid contrast than that between the homely outside of a passion fruit and its intensely fragrant, luxurious interior. Ripe passion fruits look like wrinkly little rubber balls; buying the first one takes a real leap of faith. But their gorgeous juice has the intensity of an extract and can be used almost as you would vanilla; it makes an instant sauce for ice cream and transforms creams, mousses, custards, sorbets, puddings, and blended drinks. Stir it into plain yogurt or into unsalted butter to make a spread for scones and muffins.

Ripe passion fruits will be dusty brown, wrinkled, sweetly fragrant, and heavy for their size; the insides will be perceptibly juicy. They're available in early spring through early summer.

Berries in Passion Fruit Cream

SERVES 6

Golden passion fruit juice makes a fragrant sauce that transfigures a simple bowl of berries and cream. Make this when you can get museum-quality ripe berries.

◆◆◆◆◆◆

1 quart fresh ripe strawberries, blueberries, raspberries, or blackberries
2 ripe passion fruits (see About Passion Fruit)
1 tablespoon honey
6 ounces (⅔ cup) Crème Fraîche (page 255)
2 teaspoons light brown sugar

◆◆◆◆◆◆

1. Gently rinse and drain the berries. Hull the strawberries or stem the blueberries, if using.

2. Set a small sieve over a bowl. Slice the tops off the passion fruit as you would a soft-boiled egg. Scrape the pulp and juices out into the sieve. Using the back of a spoon, firmly push the pulp and juices through the sieve to extract the juice; then discard the remaining seeds and pulp.

3. Using the tines of a fork, mash 2 large strawberries or ¼ cup blueberries, raspberries, or blackberries with the honey in a mixing bowl. Work into a thick purée. Add the strained passion fruit, and stir in the crème fraîche.

4. Cut the remaining strawberries in half if they are larger than a mouthful, and divide them evenly among six chilled dessert bowls. Spoon the sauce on top. Finish each with a light sprinkling of the brown sugar, and serve immediately.

Rhubarb and Raspberry Compote

SERVES 6

A real summer classic, designed to be served warm or at room temperature. (We find people seldom have the patience to wait until it's cooled!)

◆◆◆◆◆◆

6 ounces (²/₃ cup) Crème Fraîche
  (page 255)
2 teaspoons honey
1½ pounds fresh rhubarb stalks,
  rinsed, trimmed, and chopped into
  ½-inch chunks (4 cups chopped)
2 cups water
½ cup sugar
1 tablespoon minced fresh ginger
½ pint fresh raspberries, gently rinsed
  and drained
1 tablespoon chopped fresh mint

◆◆◆◆◆◆

1. Combine the crème fraîche and honey in a small bowl, stir well, cover, and refrigerate until serving time.

2. Place the rhubarb in a large saucepan and cover with the water. Bring to a simmer over medium-high heat, and cook just until the rhubarb begins to release its color and juices, 3 to 5 minutes. The fruit should be fork-tender but still holding its shape. Using a slotted spoon, transfer the rhubarb to a clean bowl.

3. Pour off and reserve ½ cup of the cooking juices (discard the rest). Return the reserved juice to the saucepan along with the sugar and ginger. Place over medium-high heat and simmer just until the sugar dissolves. Remove from the heat, add the rhubarb and the raspberries, and stir together gently. Divide the fruit among six dessert dishes. Serve warm or at room temperature, topped with a generous spoonful of the crème fraîche mixture and a sprinkling of mint.

CHOOSING POMEGRANATES

B ecause ripe pomegranates keep well in the refrigerator, you can seize the moment during their short season and buy them even several weeks before they'll be used. The fruit should be firm and relatively heavy for its size, with thick, supple, ruby-red skin. Pomegranate seeds make a superb garnish for a whole spectrum of savories and desserts, from mixed greens with crumbled Roquefort to lemon pound cake, chocolate cake, and ice cream. A few seeds and a splash of pomegranate juice in Champagne make an elegant variation of kir royale.

Festive Winter Fruit Salad

SERVES 6 TO 8

In the depths of winter the combination of golden fresh pineapple, bright oranges, and emerald kiwis is just as dazzling as the jeweled fruit tarts of midsummer. Assemble the salad in a crystal bowl or on individual plates, and finish it with tangerine sauce and pomegranate seeds. If you've missed the brief season for fresh pomegranates, dried tart cherries or cranberries are a splendid substitute.

◆◆◆◆◆◆

1 cup fresh tangerine juice (5 or 6 tangerines)
3 tablespoons sugar
1 tablespoon pomegranate or grenadine syrup
1 ripe pomegranate (see Choosing Pomegranates, facing page)
4 large navel oranges
1 ripe pineapple, peeled, cored, and sliced into thin rounds (see Note)
6 firm-ripe kiwi, peeled and sliced into thin rounds

◆◆◆◆◆◆

1. Combine the tangerine juice, sugar, and pomegranate syrup in a small nonreactive saucepan. Place over medium heat and simmer until reduced by half, 10 to 15 minutes. Remove from the heat and strain through a fine-mesh sieve or a cheesecloth-lined colander into a bowl. Cover and refrigerate to chill for several hours or overnight.

2. Put on an apron (crimson pomegranate juice stains hands and clothing) and using a sharp paring knife, cut the blossom end off the pomegranate. Then score the thick outer skin in quarters from top to bottom. Pull the skin back to reveal the bright seeds. Working over a large bowl, break off sections in clumps and gently separate the seeds from the thin layers of membrane. (This sounds trickier than it is. If you have a good ripe fruit, the seeds will practically jump out at you. The seeds will keep for several days, well covered and refrigerated.) Set the seeds aside.

3. Peel the oranges and remove all the white pith. Cut the oranges into thin rounds. Arrange the orange rounds in a single overlapping layer in a serving bowl or on individual plates. Follow with layers of pineapple and kiwi. Drizzle the tangerine sauce on top, and sprinkle with a handful of pomegranate seeds. Serve right away, or cover and refrigerate to chill until serving time.

Note: If already peeled, cored pineapple isn't available at the market, and if you don't own a hand-held pineapple peeler/corer (yes, there is such a thing), then forget about rounds. Simply slice the pineapple lengthwise through the middle, cut away the outer rind with a thin sharp knife, and remove the core. Then slice the pineapple into half moons.

Buttermilk Wild-Berry Cobbler

SERVES 6

This is a very easy and relatively virtuous cobbler—buttermilk being very low in fat. It's easy because the dough is just dropped on top to form tender biscuits. You can serve it right out of the oven, but it holds up well enough to be baked shortly before guests arrive and kept in a cool place until dessert time.

◆◆◆◆◆◆

Fruit
Scant 4 cups mixed fresh berries:
  strawberries, blueberries, raspberries,
  and blackberries, gently rinsed and
  drained
⅔ cup sugar
Finely grated zest of 1 lemon (see
  About Zest, page 229)
1 tablespoon fresh lemon juice
¼ teaspoon ground
  cinnamon

Biscuit Topping
1¾ cups unbleached all-
  purpose flour
1 tablespoon baking
  powder
1 teaspoon baking soda
4 tablespoons sugar
5 tablespoons unsalted
  butter, at room
  temperature
1 cup buttermilk (see About
  Buttermilk)

◆◆◆◆◆◆

1. Preheat the oven to 375°F.

2. Prepare the fruit: Gently rinse and drain the berries. Hull and slice the strawberries; stem the blueberries. In a mixing bowl, toss the berries with the sugar, lemon zest, lemon juice, and cinnamon. Spoon into a 9-inch deep-dish pie plate or baking dish, and bake in the middle of the oven until the juices begin to bubble around the edges, about 10 minutes.

3. Meanwhile, prepare the topping: Stir and toss the flour, baking powder, baking soda, and 3½ tablespoons of the sugar in a mixing bowl. Work the butter in with your fingertips or the tines of a fork to form a coarse meal. Then stir in the buttermilk to form a slightly soft, lumpy batter.

ABOUT BUTTERMILK

In the old days, buttermilk was what was left in the butter churn. Now, it's manufactured with healthful bacteria, like yogurt.

Buttermilk is made with very little fat or none at all; either way, it adds a nice fresh tang and texture to baked goods. At home in the summer we purée peaches with a little sugar, add buttermilk, and freeze the whole business in the hand-cranked Donvier ice-cream maker to create a healthful, lowfat home-made version of frozen yogurt.

Buttermilk will keep for several weeks in the coldest part of your refrigerator.

4. Remove the berries from the oven, and drop large spoonfuls of the batter over the fruit, approximately ½ inch apart (they will spread and bake together). Sprinkle with the remaining ½ tablespoon sugar, and bake until the topping is nicely browned and puffed and just cooked through between the biscuits (pry two biscuits apart near the center to check for doneness), 20 to 25 minutes. To serve, scoop a portion of the biscuit topping into six serving bowls, then spoon the warm berries and juice on top.

Raspberry-Nectarine Crumble

SERVES 6 TO 8

Tender-skinned, colorful nectarines are nice and firm, but you could make this with peaches and blueberries (instead of raspberries), too. Crisps and crumbles are so simple to put together (just slice and season the fruit and pile on the crumb topping) that they are wonderful projects for young cooks. This one can be assembled and refrigerated several hours before you plan to bake it.

◆◆◆◆◆◆

Crumb Topping

½ cup unbleached all-purpose flour
½ cup medium-grain stone-ground cornmeal (see Stone-Ground Cornmeal, page 4)
⅓ cup (firmly packed) light brown sugar
Finely grated zest of 1 lime (see About Zest, page 229)
Pinch of salt
½ cup old-fashioned rolled oats
8 tablespoons (1 stick) unsalted butter, chilled, cut into bits

Fruit

5 cups sliced ripe nectarines (about 6 nectarines)
2 pints fresh ripe raspberries, gently rinsed and drained
Juice of 1 lime
½ cup granulated sugar
¼ teaspoon freshly grated nutmeg

Vanilla ice cream, for serving (optional)
◆◆◆◆◆◆

1. Preheat the oven to 375°F.

2. Prepare the topping: Combine the flour, cornmeal, brown sugar, lime zest, salt, and oats in a mixing bowl. Add the butter and blend with an electric mixer on medium speed until the topping pulls together into coarse crumbs, 3 to 5 minutes. Refrigerate, covered, until ready to use.

3. Prepare the filling: In a large bowl, toss the nectarines and raspberries with the lime juice, sugar, and nutmeg, taking care not to break up the berries. Spoon the fruit into an 11 × 8-inch baking dish, and sprinkle the crumb topping evenly over it.

4. Bake until the topping is nicely browned and the fruit juices have begun to bubble up and caramelize around the edges, about 30 minutes. Allow to cool for at least 10 minutes before serving. Serve warm or at room temperature, with a scoop of vanilla ice cream if you like.

Cherry-Apple-Pecan Crisp

SERVES 8 TO 10

We make this with a combination of crisp, tart Granny Smiths and softer, mellower Rome Beauty apples, but you can use any fresh fall apple that comes to hand. This is a great make-ahead dessert for casual fall entertaining.

◆◆◆◆◆◆

Fruit
8 cups thinly sliced, peeled apples, half
  Granny Smith and half Rome Beauty
¾ cup dried tart cherries (see About
  Dried Cherries)
⅓ cup fresh orange juice
¼ cup (firmly packed) light brown sugar

Crumb Topping
¾ cup old-fashioned rolled oats
½ cup unbleached all-purpose flour
½ cup (firmly packed) light brown sugar
1½ teaspoons ground cinnamon
¼ teaspoon freshly grated nutmeg
8 tablespoons (1 stick) unsalted butter,
  chilled, cut into large chunks
1 cup pecans, preferably toasted
  (see Toasting Nuts, page 55),
  coarsely chopped

◆◆◆◆◆◆

ABOUT DRIED CHERRIES

Primarily made from Montmorency cherries grown in Michigan, dried tart cherries are no longer exotic—they're now readily available in better supermarkets, on the same shelf as the dried cranberries and blueberries. Look for plump, shiny red berries. It's worth searching them out for the rich flavor they give to muffins and other baked goods.

There are also dried sweet cherry varieties, such as Bing and Rainier, which make delicious additions to baked goods, salads, and snack mixes.

1. Preheat the oven to 350°F.

2. Prepare the fruit: Toss the apples and cherries in an 11 × 8-inch baking dish. Add the orange juice and brown sugar, toss, and spread evenly in the dish.

3. Prepare the topping: Combine the oats, flour, brown sugar, cinnamon, and nutmeg in a food processor and pulse once or twice to mix. Add the butter and pulse to form a crumbly meal, with the bits of butter no larger than small grains of rice. Transfer to a large bowl and stir in the pecans.

4. Sprinkle the crumb topping evenly over the fruit, and bake until the topping is nicely browned and the fruit juices have begun to bubble up and caramelize around the edges, 40 to 45 minutes. Allow to cool for at least 10 minutes before serving. Serve warm or at room temperature.

Gingered Pear Crisp with Ruby Raisins

SERVES 6 TO 8

This aromatic, juicy compote, hidden under a crisp crust, is simple to make and festive enough for Thanksgiving. It's a terrific holiday combination of pears, ginger, and cranberries ("ruby raisins" is the trade term for dried cranberries), wonderful with vanilla ice cream or frozen yogurt or even over a thin slice of chiffon or angel food cake. As with our apple crisp, we use a combination of firm (Bosc) and juicy (Comice) fruit for the best flavor and texture.

◆◆◆◆◆◆

Fruit

3 ripe Bosc pears, peeled, cored, and thinly sliced (about 3 cups)

2 ripe Comice pears, peeled, cored, and thinly sliced (about 2 cups)

¼ cup fresh lemon juice

½ cup dried cranberries

2 teaspoons minced fresh ginger

¼ cup granulated sugar

1 teaspoon pure vanilla extract

2 tablespoons unbleached all-purpose flour

¼ teaspoon ground cinnamon

Crumb Topping

⅔ cup old-fashioned rolled oats

⅔ cup unbleached all-purpose flour

½ cup (packed) dark brown sugar

¼ teaspoon ground cloves

8 tablespoons (1 stick) unsalted butter, chilled, cut into small pieces

◆◆◆◆◆◆

1. Preheat the oven to 375°F. Lightly butter a 2-quart baking dish.

2. Prepare the fruit: In a large bowl, toss the pears with the lemon juice, cranberries, ginger, sugar, vanilla, flour, and cinnamon. Then spoon the mixture into the prepared baking dish.

3. Prepare the topping: Combine the oats, flour, brown sugar, and cloves in a food processor and pulse once or twice to mix. Add the butter and pulse to form a crumbly meal with the bits of butter no larger than small grains of rice. Sprinkle the topping evenly over the fruit.

4. Bake until the topping is nicely browned and the fruit juices have begun to bubble up and caramelize around the edges, 30 to 35 minutes. Allow to cool for at least 10 minutes before serving. When you are ready to serve the crisp, break through the crust with a large serving spoon and scoop the warm fruit, juices, and topping into individual bowls.

Mixed-Fruit Summer Pudding

SERVES 8 TO 10

In England, "pudding" often just means dessert; here it means something delightfully light, summery, and spectacular. Easily assembled, this pudding is designed to be made ahead of time, allowing the juices of the berries to permeate the layers of bread and give the whole thing an intensely fresh, clean flavor. It's especially good topped with crème fraîche and fresh mint. And it works just fine substituting summer strawberries, blackberries, or currants.

◆◆◆◆◆◆

1 pint fresh blueberries, stemmed, rinsed, and drained

1 pint fresh raspberries, gently rinsed and drained

3 cups coarsely chopped, peeled ripe peaches (about 3 large peaches)

¾ cup sugar

1 cup water

3 tablespoons fresh lemon juice

17 slices firm white sandwich bread, crusts removed

2 tablespoons chopped fresh mint

6 ounces (⅔ cup) Crème Fraîche (page 255; optional)

Fresh mint sprigs, for garnish

◆◆◆◆◆◆

1. Combine the berries and peaches with the sugar, water, and lemon juice in a large saucepan. Stir together gently, taking care not to break up the berries, and bring to a simmer over medium heat. Simmer, uncovered, until the fruit releases its juices and the liquid has just about doubled in volume, 5 to 10 minutes. Remove the saucepan from the heat and pour the contents into a large bowl to cool.

2. Meanwhile, cut each piece of bread into two triangles.

3. Add the chopped mint to the cooled fruit mixture, and ladle ½ cup of the fruit into a 2-quart dome-shaped mixing bowl or mold. Dip the triangles of bread one at a time into the remaining fruit mixture, quickly saturating the bread with the juices. Place a single solid layer of bread slices over the fruit in the bowl, forming a neat pinwheel with the points meeting at the center (absolute geometric perfection is not required). Ladle 1 cup of fruit and juices over the bread. Repeat the layering, increasing the quantity of fruit by ½ cup each time and finishing with a layer of bread. You should have four layers each of fruit and bread. Cover with plastic wrap, laying it directly on the bread, and set a light weight on top of the plastic wrap to compress the layers (a plate topped with a soup can will do). Refrigerate overnight.

4. To unmold the pudding, gently loosen the sides with a knife and invert it onto a large serving platter. Slice, and top each serving with a large spoonful of crème fraîche if desired. Garnish with sprigs of fresh mint.

Key Lime Pudding Cakes

SERVES 8

This simple, old-fashioned dessert is really a light summer soufflé, but here the egg whites float to the top, leaving a silky pudding beneath. It is traditionally made with lemon juice, but it's truly exceptional when made with tiny yellow Key limes from Florida— which are generally sold in bags throughout the summer months. Make it well ahead of time and serve it chilled or at room temperature, topping each ramekin with a beautiful fresh summer berry. And yes, you can use the preservative-free Key lime juice that is bottled and shipped by growers in Florida. No household should be without it, not only for this beautiful dessert but for daiquiris and ceviches as well. But, if only conventional limes are available, by all means use them instead.

◆◆◆◆◆◆

3 tablespoons unsalted butter,
  at room temperature
1½ cups sugar
4 eggs, separated
6 tablespoons unbleached all-purpose
  flour
Pinch of salt
2 cups whole milk
⅔ cup fresh Key lime juice (10 to
  12 Key limes)
Fresh berries or thin lime slices,
  for garnish

◆◆◆◆◆◆

1. Preheat the oven to 325°F. Lightly butter eight 3-inch (¾-cup) ramekins or custard cups.

2. In a mixing bowl, cream the butter and sugar together to form a crumbly meal. Add the egg yolks one at a time, beating well after each addition.

3. Whisk together the flour and salt in a small bowl, and add to the creamed mixture in batches, alternating with the milk. Blend until the mixture is smooth. Add the lime juice, mix in well, and set aside.

4. Bring a large tea kettle of water to a boil.

5. In a mixing bowl, beat the egg whites until they form firm moist peaks. Fold them into the reserved batter, incorporating them thoroughly. Spoon the mixture into the prepared ramekins and place the ramekins in a shallow baking dish. Pour the boiling water into the baking dish to reach halfway up the sides of the ramekins. Place the whole thing in the oven and bake until the tops are very lightly browned and springy to the touch, 25 to 30 minutes.

6. Remove the ramekins from the water bath and allow to cool. Serve warm, at room temperature, or chilled, topped with a single berry or a thin slice of lime. Or, if you prefer, chill them thoroughly and then use a knife to gently unmold the cakes onto serving plates.

Arborio Rice Pudding

SERVES 4

Just wait until you try this fresh, creamy short-grain rice pudding. The vanilla bean gives it the intense flavor of really good vanilla ice cream, and serving it with fresh fruit is a revelation—the result is more like peaches-and-cream than traditional rice pudding. We're using the juicy, plush texture of ripe mango here, but a soft, ripe Hachiya persimmon would be excellent, too. So would fresh peaches, for that matter.

◆◆◆◆◆◆

1 quart whole milk
6 tablespoons sugar
1 whole vanilla bean
¾ cup cold water
½ cup arborio rice
Diced flesh of 1 large ripe mango
  (see About Mangoes, page 218)

◆◆◆◆◆◆

1. Combine the milk and sugar in a large saucepan. Using a small paring knife, split the vanilla bean open lengthwise. Scrape the seeds from the bean into the milk, then add the bean to the milk. Bring to a boil over medium-high heat, stirring continuously to prevent scorching.

2. Stir in the water and rice, and return to a boil. Reduce the heat to medium and simmer gently, stirring frequently, until the mixture is creamy and has thickened to the consistency of a hearty porridge, 35 to 40 minutes.

3. Remove and discard the vanilla bean. Serve the warm pudding in small bowls, topped with the diced mango. To serve it cold, spoon the pudding into four lightly buttered ramekins, cover, and refrigerate until firm, at least 2 hours. When ready to serve, dip the bottoms of the ramekins into warm water, run a hot knife along the inside edge, and turn the puddings out onto serving plates. Top each serving with a scattering of the diced mango.

Sour Lemon Cake with Poached Berries

MAKES 2 LOAVES; SERVES 16

This popular, versatile cake was one of the first things we produced in the Westport bakery. We make it in bundts, muffins, and tiny loaves at Christmastime, and our customers can't seem to get enough of it. Here we serve it for dessert with a simple warm berry sauce; if you're entertaining outdoors, toast the cake slices lightly on the grill (make sure the rack is clean) before topping them with cooled sauce. (The berry sauce is glorious over vanilla ice cream, too, and the cake is excellent in a berry trifle.)

♦♦♦♦♦♦

14 tablespoons (1¾ sticks) unsalted
   butter, at room temperature
2 cups granulated sugar
4 eggs
Grated zest of 2 lemons (see About
   Zest)
3 cups sifted unbleached all-purpose
   flour
1 tablespoon baking powder
1 teaspoon salt
1 cup milk
⅓ cup confectioners' sugar
Juice of 2 lemons
Poached Berries (recipe follows)

♦♦♦♦♦♦

1. Preheat the oven to 325°F. Lightly butter and flour two 6-cup loaf pans.

2. In a large bowl, cream the butter and sugar together with an electric mixer on high speed until light and fluffy. Add the eggs one at a time, blending until each one is fully incorporated. Stir in the lemon zest.

3. In another bowl, whisk together the flour, baking powder, and salt. Add the dry ingredients to the creamed mixture in batches, alternating with the milk, and blend until smooth. Spoon the batter into the prepared pans, spreading it out evenly. Bake until the cakes are lightly browned on top and spring back to a light touch, about 1 hour. Remove from the oven and allow the cakes to cool in the pans for at least 15 minutes before turning them out onto wire racks.

4. Combine the confectioners' sugar with the lemon juice in a small saucepan and simmer gently until slightly thickened, 2 to 3 minutes. Brush the glaze generously over

ABOUT ZEST

The intense aroma and flavor of citrus zest adds amazing flavor to so many foods, from soup to cookies. The only real trick in using lemon, orange, or lime zest is to remove only the outer, colored layer of the peel, avoiding the bitter white pith underneath. First, scrub the citrus well with a vegetable brush or coarse sponge to clean off any dirt or markings. Then simply grate the zest, using a zester or the smallest holes on a conventional box grater; or slice the zest off with a sharp paring knife or vegetable peeler and then mince it finely.

the warm cakes. (Thoroughly cooled and then well wrapped in plastic, the cakes will keep for several days in the refrigerator.)

5. Using a slotted spoon, ladle the warm poached berries over slices of the cake; then drizzle with a bit of the poaching liquid. Or refrigerate the berries until serving time and ladle them over warm toasted slices of the cake.

Variation

♦ **Almond-Crusted Lemon Bundt Cakes:** Scatter 2 tablespoons slivered almonds into two buttered and floured 6-cup bundt pans; then spoon in the batter and bake as described.

Poached Berries

MAKES 2 CUPS

Succulent summer berries require little embellishment. Here we delicately poach them to hold their form and heighten their natural sweet flavor. Using a slotted spoon, scoop the warm berries over cake, ice cream, or frozen yogurt; then drizzle a bit of the juices on top.

4 cups mixed berries: raspberries,
blueberries, blackberries, and/or
sliced hulled strawberries, gently
rinsed and drained
1 cup sugar
2 cups water
1 tablespoon fresh lemon juice

Gently toss the berries together in a large bowl. Combine the sugar, water, and lemon juice in a saucepan and bring to a rapid simmer over medium-high heat, stirring occasionally to dissolve the sugar crystals. Remove from the heat, immediately pour over the berries, and allow to steep for 5 minutes. Serve warm, or cover and refrigerate until serving time. (If you are chilling an all-strawberry sauce, refrigerate the berries and the poaching liquid separately, to keep the strawberries from becoming unpleasantly soft.)

Seasonal Fruit Torte

SERVES 6

This is the master recipe for the simple fruit tortes we produce in the Hay Day bakeries. We bake them all year round, and they are particularly nice in the summer, made with any combination of soft summer fruits. The rich pastry rises up to cloak the fruit handsomely, and the whole thing comes easily out of the pan for serving.

1 cup unbleached all-purpose flour
¼ teaspoon salt
1 teaspoon baking powder
8 tablespoons (1 stick) unsalted butter,
at room temperature
¾ cup granulated sugar
2 eggs
1 teaspoon pure vanilla extract
1 teaspoon finely grated citrus zest
(see About Zest, page 229)
(lemon, lime, or orange according to
the juice used in the fruit topping)
Seasonal fruit combination of choice
(see box, facing page)

1. Preheat the oven to 350°F. Lightly butter and flour an 8-inch cake pan; pour out any excess flour.

2. In a small bowl, whisk together the flour, salt, and baking powder and set aside.

3. In another bowl, cream the butter and sugar together with an electric mixer on high speed until light and fluffy. Add the eggs one at a time, mixing well after each addition. Beat until smooth. Blend in the vanilla and zest. Add the reserved dry ingredients and mix to form a smooth, thick batter. Spread the batter evenly in the prepared cake pan.

4. Prepare the selected fruit topping: Toss the fruit with the specified citrus juice and sugar. Arrange the topping decoratively over the batter, using just enough fruit to cover the batter in a single overlapping layer. Sprinkle with the sugar and spices specified, and bake in the middle of the oven until lightly browned around the edges and just set in the middle, 30 to 35 minutes.

5. Remove from the oven and allow to cool in the pan for at least 20 minutes. Top with a flat plate and gently flip the plate and cake pan over, turning the cake out of the pan. Invert the cake once more, this time turning it right side up onto a serving dish. Slice and serve.

FRUIT TORTE TOPPINGS

Cranberry-Apple
1 Granny Smith apple, cored, peeled, and thinly sliced
¼ cup fresh cranberries, coarsely chopped
2 teaspoons fresh orange juice
2 teaspoons light brown sugar
2 teaspoons cinnamon sugar, for sprinkling

Summer Plum
2 plums, rinsed, pitted, and thinly sliced
2 teaspoons Grand Marnier or fresh orange juice
2 teaspoons cinnamon sugar
1 tablespoon granulated sugar, for sprinkling

Gingered Pear
1 ripe red-skin pear (unpeeled), rinsed, cored and thinly sliced
2 teaspoons fresh lemon juice
1 teaspoon light brown sugar
1 tablespoon minced crystallized ginger mixed with 2 teaspoons granulated sugar, for sprinkling

Strawberry-Mango
½ cup rinsed, hulled, sliced fresh ripe strawberries
1 ripe mango, peeled and cut into thin slices
2 teaspoons fresh lime juice
1 teaspoon granulated sugar
2 tablespoons unsweetened flaked coconut mixed with 2 teaspoons granulated sugar, for sprinkling

Peaches and Berries
1 ripe peach, pitted, peeled, and thinly sliced
Generous ½ cup stemmed fresh blueberries or raspberries, gently rinsed and drained
2 teaspoons fresh lemon juice
2 teaspoons granulated sugar
2 teaspoons cinnamon sugar, for sprinkling

Gingerbread-Peach Upside-Down Cake

SERVES 6

A variation on a traditional New England recipe, this is easy to make with chopped peaches (plums are wonderful, also). The fact that you turn it upside down for serving delights small children—and grownups, too.

◆◆◆◆◆◆

4 cups coarsely chopped, peeled ripe
*   peaches (about 4 large peaches)*
2 tablespoons light brown sugar
1 tablespoon fresh lemon juice
1½ cups unbleached all-purpose
*   flour*
2 teaspoons baking powder
½ teaspoon baking soda
½ teaspoon salt
2 teaspoons ground ginger
8 tablespoons (1 stick) unsalted butter,
*   at room temperature*
⅓ cup granulated sugar
1 egg, lightly beaten
⅓ cup molasses
½ cup buttermilk

◆◆◆◆◆◆

1. Preheat the oven to 350°F. Lightly butter a 9-inch round cake pan.

2. In a large bowl, toss the peaches with the brown sugar and the lemon juice. Spoon the mixture into the prepared cake pan, and spread it out in an even layer.

3. Whisk together the flour, baking powder, baking soda, salt, and ginger in a small bowl and set aside.

4. In a large bowl, cream the butter and granulated sugar together with an electric mixer on high speed until light and fluffy. Add the egg and molasses, and mix until smooth. Add the reserved dry ingredients alternately with the buttermilk, mixing to form a thick, smooth batter. Spread the batter evenly over the peaches.

5. Bake until the cake springs back when lightly touched, 35 to 40 minutes. Cool for 5 minutes; then invert the cake onto a large serving platter. Serve warm or at room temperature.

Pumpkin Cheesecake with Gingersnap Crust

SERVES 12

What do you do with gingersnaps that are too irregular or broken to sell in the stores? You crush them to make a crumb crust for pumpkin cheesecake, and it's so successful that you end up baking giant trays of gingersnaps purely for that purpose. The flavors go well together, obviously, and pressing the crumbs on after baking gives the crust a freshness that goes nicely with the mousse-like texture of the cheesecake.

A word to the wise: If you think the seal of your springform pan is anything less than perfect, wrap the pan in aluminum foil before immersing it in the water bath.

◆◆◆◆◆◆

1½ pounds (three 8-ounce packages) cream cheese, at room temperature
1 cup sugar
4 eggs
2 cups pumpkin purée (see About Pumpkin Purée, page 3)
Finely grated zest of 1 orange (see About Zest, page 229)
2 teaspoons pumpkin pie spice (see Note, page 2)
1 cup finely crushed gingersnap cookies (approximately 6 ounces cookies)
Crème Fraîche, for garnish (optional; page 255)
Bittersweet chocolate shavings, for garnish (optional)

◆◆◆◆◆◆

1. Preheat the oven to 275°F. Lightly butter a 9-inch springform pan.

2. Bring a large tea kettle of water to a boil.

3. Meanwhile, using an electric mixer, blend the cream cheese and sugar in a bowl on high speed until light and fluffy. Add the eggs one at a time, mixing well and scraping down the sides of the bowl as needed. Blend in the pumpkin purée, orange zest, and pumpkin pie spice, and mix until smooth. Pour into the prepared

A Black Tie Dessert Buffet

Atempting dessert buffet is an elegant and delicious way to entertain in the late evening. Invite friends over for a New Year's Eve toast or after a special night out at the theater. Prepare the desserts a day in advance, and then slice and arrange them shortly before serving. Finish the table with a tempting selection of seasonal fruits appropriate for eating out of hand.

Cranberry-Apple Fruit Torte

Pumpkin Cheesecake with Gingersnap Crust topped with Crème Fraîche and shavings of bittersweet chocolate

Lemon Sugar Snap Cookies

Chocolate-Hazelnut Biscotti

Forelle pears, fresh figs, clementines, and Champagne grapes

springform pan, and place the pan inside a large roasting pan.

4. Add enough boiling water to the roasting pan to reach halfway up the sides of the springform pan, and place the whole thing in the oven. Bake until firm and set, 1¾ hours.

5. Remove the roasting pan from the oven, and place the springform on a rack to cool to room temperature. Then cover and refrigerate for at least 4 hours. (The cheesecake can be prepared and refrigerated up to 3 days in advance.)

6. Just before serving, release the cake from the pan and firmly press the cookie crumbs around the sides. If you like, garnish the servings with crème fraîche and shavings of bittersweet chocolate.

Country Shortcake with Blackberries and Peaches

SERVES 6 TO 8

A generous dose of lemon adds lively flavor to this classic American dessert. Creating one large shortcake instead of individual servings is easier and makes for a more impressive presentation. Golden peaches tossed in a rosy blackberry purée are gorgeous tucked inside, but any combination of raspberries, strawberries, and/or blueberries works just as well (6 cups of fruit fill the biscuit nicely). Mascarpone is sumptuously rich, but freshly whipped cream works beautifully, too.

Fruit
12 ounces (about 3 cups) fresh blackberries, gently rinsed and drained
½ cup sugar
Juice of 1 lemon
3 large peaches, pitted, peeled, and thinly sliced

Shortcake
2½ cups unbleached all-purpose flour, plus more for dusting
1 tablespoon baking powder
½ teaspoon salt
3 tablespoons plus 2 teaspoons sugar
8 tablespoons (1 stick) unsalted butter, chilled, cut into large chunks
⅔ cup whole milk, chilled
1 egg
½ teaspoon pure lemon extract
Finely grated zest of 1 lemon (see About Zest, page 229)

8 ounces mascarpone cheese

1. Preheat the oven to 375°F. Lightly butter an 8-inch cake pan.

2. Prepare the fruit: In a blender, purée ¾ cup blackberries with the sugar and lemon juice. Toss the purée with the peaches and remaining berries, and set aside.

3. Prepare the shortcake: Whisk together the 2½ cups flour, baking powder, salt, and 3 tablespoons sugar in a large bowl. Cut the butter in until the mixture resembles coarse meal (this can be done in a food processor, with a hand-held pastry blender, or with two knives).

4. In a separate bowl, whisk the milk, egg, lemon extract, and zest together.

234

Add this to the dry ingredients, and stir gently to form a soft, slightly crumbly, biscuit-like dough. Press it together and turn it out onto a lightly floured work surface. Divide the dough in half, and using the heel of your hand, press it out to form two 8-inch rounds. Place the rounds in the prepared pan, one on top of the other, separating the two layers with a light dusting of flour. Press lightly to fit. Sprinkle with the remaining 2 teaspoons sugar, and bake until lightly browned and nearly doubled in height, 20 to 25 minutes. Remove from the oven, turn out of the pan, and allow to cool for at least 10 minutes before splitting. (The shortcake can be made up to a day in advance, then lightly warmed before splitting and filling.)

5. Just before serving, split the shortcake in half, gently prying the layers apart with your fingers. Place the bottom layer on a platter, and spread the mascarpone over it. Then spoon on the fruit and juices, and set the top layer over the fruit. Cut into wedges and serve.

Variations

◆ **Peaches and Strawberries** (sliced peaches tossed in strawberry sauce)

◆ **Peaches and Blueberries** (sliced peaches tossed in blueberry sauce)

◆ **Black and Blue Berries** (blueberries tossed in blackberry sauce)

◆ **Raspberries and Blueberries** (raspberries tossed in blueberry sauce)

Old-Fashioned Apple Crumb Cake

MAKES 2 CAKES; SERVES 12 TO 16

Serve this cake—especially warm, with cider alongside—to anybody getting off the school bus in the winter. Tart-sweet apples and creamy yogurt transform a simple crumb cake into a nourishing snack. The cake stays fresh for several days, so you can make one for a special Sunday meal and keep the other one to inspire term papers and lab reports.

◆◆◆◆◆◆

Cake
8 tablespoons (1 stick) unsalted butter,
  at room temperature
1 cup granulated sugar
2 eggs
1 teaspoon pure vanilla extract
2 cups unbleached all-purpose flour
2 teaspoons baking powder
½ teaspoon baking soda
¼ teaspoon salt
1 cup plain yogurt
2 large crisp baking apples, cored,
  peeled, and cut into small dice
  (2 cups diced)

Nut Topping
½ cup chopped pecans
½ cup (packed) light brown sugar
1 teaspoon ground cinnamon
2 tablespoons unsalted butter, melted

◆◆◆◆◆◆

1. Preheat the oven to 350°F. Butter and flour two 8-inch square cake pans. Pour out any excess flour.

2. In a large bowl, cream the butter and sugar with an electric mixer on high speed until light and fluffy. Add the eggs one at a time, blending well after each addition. Stir in the vanilla.

3. In another bowl, whisk together the flour, baking powder, baking soda, and salt. Add this to the creamed mixture in batches, alternating with the yogurt, and mix until fully incorporated. Stir in the apples. Then divide the batter evenly between the two prepared cake pans.

4. Combine the topping ingredients in a small bowl, and stir with a fork until combined. Sprinkle evenly over the two cakes, and bake until the tops are nicely browned and a toothpick inserted in the center comes out clean, about 35 minutes. Cool in the pans for at least 15 minutes. Then turn the cakes out onto a wire rack, and invert them again onto serving plates.

Lemon Sugar Snap Cookies

MAKES ABOUT 24 COOKIES

These cookies aren't just for kids. Crisp and lemony, they turn a cup of tea or a simple bowl of berries into an event, and they are incredibly good crumbled to form a crust for a cheesecake or fruit tart. We've sold literally tons of them over the years. You can make the dough on a quiet morning ahead of time—it will keep well for 2 or 3 weeks in the refrigerator.

◆◆◆◆◆◆

8 tablespoons (1 stick) unsalted butter, at room temperature
¾ cup superfine sugar
1 egg yolk
Finely grated zest of 1 lemon (see About Zest, page 229)
1 tablespoon pure lemon extract
¾ cup unbleached all-purpose flour
¼ teaspoon salt

◆◆◆◆◆◆

1. Preheat the oven to 350°F. Lightly butter two baking sheets.

2. In a large bowl, cream the butter and sugar together with an electric mixer on high speed until light and fluffy. Add the egg yolk, lemon zest, and lemon extract, and mix well.

3. Add the flour and salt, and blend on low speed until all the dry ingredients are moistened. Scrape down the sides of the bowl as needed, and blend to form a smooth, thick batter.

4. Drop heaping teaspoons of the dough, at least 2 inches apart, onto the prepared baking sheets. Bake, rotating the sheets once, until the cookies are very lightly colored around the edges, 12 to 15 minutes.

5. Remove the baking sheets from the oven and allow the cookies to cool for 5 minutes; then transfer them to a wire rack to cool completely.

Oatmeal Crisp Cookies

MAKES 24 COOKIES

It wasn't a deliberate policy, but somehow Hay Day never got onto the chewy-cookie bandwagon. We've always liked cookies with some snap and character, like these crisp versions of the oatmeal classic. We've learned through experience that a longer, slower baking time produces the crispest, most delicious oatmeal cookie. Of course they're great packed with raisins, but try dried cherries for a special occasion and you may never look back. (This recipe doubles easily.)

◆◆◆◆◆◆

8 tablespoons (1 stick) unsalted butter,
    at room temperature
½ cup granulated sugar
½ cup (firmly packed) dark brown sugar
1 egg
1 teaspoon pure vanilla extract
1 cup unbleached all-purpose flour
2 rounded teaspoons ground cinnamon
½ teaspoon salt
½ teaspoon baking soda
1½ cups old-fashioned rolled oats
¾ cup raisins, or 3½ ounces dried
    tart cherries

◆◆◆◆◆◆

1. Preheat the oven to 325°F. Lightly butter two baking sheets, or line them with parchment.

2. In a large bowl, cream the butter, sugars, and egg together with an electric mixer on high speed until light in color and fluffy, 2 to 3 minutes. Blend in the vanilla.

THE MAGIC OF COOKIES

Everybody loves cookies; for us they're an essential food group. We've been baking and shipping cookies since we opened our first bakery. We like to think that we have made a modest contribution to better scores on midterm exams and LSATs all over the U.S.

The quest for the truly outstanding cookie has led us to combinations and quantities that we are revealing in these pages for the first time. As you'll see, the magic is in the proportions and the quality of the ingredients, not in the machinery or the decoration—but it *is* magic. These cookies will transform teatime, or bring a smile to a neighbor's face, or make the sun come out for young ones coming home from school on a rainy afternoon. Honest.

3. Measure the flour, cinnamon, salt, and baking soda into another bowl, and whisk together. Using a large wooden spoon or a mixer set on low speed, stir the dry ingredients into the creamed mixture. Add the oats and raisins and blend well.

4. Drop large rounded tablespoons of the dough at least 2 inches apart onto the prepared baking sheets and bake, rotating the sheets once, until the cookies are lightly browned all over and still a bit soft at the center, 20 to 22 minutes. (The cookies will continue to crisp as they cool, so they should feel a bit soft emerging from the oven.) Remove the sheets from the oven and allow the cookies to cool for a couple of minutes before transferring them to a wire rack to cool completely.

Chocolate-Hazelnut Biscotti

MAKES ABOUT 48 BISCOTTI

This is a variation on the crunchy Italian twice-baked classic, prepared the traditional way but just a little softer than the original. These biscotti are surprisingly easy to make at home and wonderful with coffee or cocoa. Packed in big clamp-top jars, they make a wonderful present—especially when they're paired in a basket with a pound of really good coffee beans.

1⅓ cups whole hazelnuts (skins on or blanched)
8 tablespoons (1 stick) unsalted butter, at room temperature
1 cup sugar
2 eggs
1 teaspoon pure vanilla extract
2⅓ cups unbleached all-purpose flour
3 tablespoons unsweetened cocoa powder (see Note)
½ teaspoon baking soda
½ teaspoon baking powder
⅛ teaspoon salt

1. Preheat the oven to 325°F.

2. Scatter the nuts on a baking sheet and toast them in the oven until lightly browned and fragrant, 8 to 10 minutes.

3. Meanwhile, in a large bowl, cream the butter and sugar together with an electric mixer on high speed until light and fluffy. Add the eggs and vanilla, and mix until smooth and well incorporated,

SKINNING HAZELNUTS

Blanched hazelnuts have already been treated to remove their outer skin. If you're working with whole raw nuts (skins on), toast them in a 375°F oven until they are fragrant and the skins are splitting and beginning to flake off, about 8 minutes. Remove the nuts from the oven and immediately wrap them in a clean kitchen towel. Set them aside for a couple of minutes (the nuts will steam inside the towel, helping to separate the skins). Then vigorously roll the towel back and forth over the counter to rub off as much of the skins as possible.

scraping down the sides of the bowl as needed.

4. In another mixing bowl, whisk together the flour, cocoa, baking soda, baking powder, and salt. Add this to the creamed mixture, and blend on low speed just until a stiff dough forms and pulls away from the sides of the bowl.

5. Remove the hazelnuts from the oven; leave the oven on. Coarsely chop half of the toasted nuts, and stir both the chopped and the whole nuts into the dough. Divide the dough in half, and using lightly floured hands, form each half into a 12 × 3-inch flattened log. Place the logs, spaced at least 2 inches apart, on a large ungreased baking sheet. Bake until firm, lightly browned, and cracked on top, 25 to 30 minutes.

6. Remove the baking sheet from the oven and reduce the oven temperature to 300°F. Allow the logs to cool on the sheet for 10 minutes. Then loosen them with a large flat spatula and transfer them to a cutting board. Using a thin sharp knife, cut them into ½-inch-thick slices. Return the slices to the baking sheet, cut sides up, and return the baking sheet to the oven. Bake, rotating the pan once to ensure even browning, until the biscotti are firm and dry throughout, 20 to 25 minutes. (They will be slightly soft coming from the oven but will crisp up nicely as they cool.)

7. Allow the biscotti to cool completely on the baking sheet for at least 30 minutes. Then transfer them to the cookie jar or arrange them upright in clamp-top glass jars.

Note: Bensdorf, Droste, and Cocoa Barry are excellent baking cocoas; we use all of them in the bakeries and sell them in the stores. And if you can't find those, Hershey's will do perfectly well.

Cranberry-Almond Biscotti

MAKES ABOUT 48 BISCOTTI

At Christmastime quite a number of years ago, Hay Day transformed a rather traditional almond-based biscotti recipe by adding dried cranberries—and we've been making them that way ever since. The cookies are very pretty, and they keep well in an airtight container for a couple of weeks; pack them in glass jars or oversized coffee mugs for a terrific present.

◆◆◆◆◆◆

8 tablespoons (1 stick) unsalted
    butter, at room temperature
1 cup sugar
2 eggs
Finely grated zest of 1 orange
    (see About Zest, page 229)
¼ teaspoon pure almond extract
2¾ cups unbleached all-purpose flour
1 teaspoon baking powder
½ teaspoon salt
4 ounces (¾ cup) dried cranberries
1 cup slivered almonds

◆◆◆◆◆◆

1. Preheat the oven to 325°F.

2. In a large bowl, cream the butter and sugar together with an electric mixer on high speed until light and fluffy. Add the eggs, orange zest, and almond extract, and mix until smooth and well incorporated, scraping down the sides of the bowl as needed.

3. In another mixing bowl, whisk together the flour, baking powder, salt, and cranberries. Add this to the creamed mixture and blend on low speed just until a stiff dough forms and pulls away from the sides of the bowl. Then stir in the almonds.

4. Divide the dough in half, and using lightly floured hands, form each half into a 12 × 3-inch flattened log. Place the logs, spaced at least 2 inches apart, on a large ungreased baking sheet. Bake until firm, lightly browned, and cracked on top, 25 to 30 minutes.

5. Remove the baking sheet from the oven and reduce the oven temperature to 300°F. Allow the logs to cool on the sheet for 10 minutes. Then loosen them with a large flat spatula and transfer them to a cutting board. Using a thin sharp knife, cut them into ½-inch-thick slices. Return the slices to the baking sheet, cut sides up, and return the baking sheet to the oven. Bake, rotating the pan once to ensure even browning, until the biscotti are firm and dry throughout, 20 to 25 minutes. (They will be slightly soft coming from the oven but will crisp up nicely as they cool.)

6. Allow the biscotti to cool completely on the baking sheet for at least 30 minutes. Then transfer them to the cookie jar or arrange them upright in clamp-top glass jars.

Variation

◆ **Apricot-Pistachio Biscotti:** Once the holidays have passed, try this bright variation flecked with green pistachios. A small amount of whole-wheat flour adds an extra bit of nutty flavor.

Substitute the following:

- ◆ 1 cup shelled unsalted pistachios for the almonds
- ◆ 4 ounces dried unsulfured apricots, coarsely chopped (¾ cup chopped), for the cranberries
- ◆ ½ cup stone-ground whole-wheat flour for ½ cup of the unbleached all-purpose flour
- ◆ ½ teaspoon pure vanilla extract for the almond extract

Old-Fashioned Peanut Butter Cookies

MAKES 24 COOKIES

There's no question that peanut butter made from freshly ground roasted nuts gives cookies the most intense flavor. We've always been pretty fanatical about fresh peanut butter, for years making our own with a hand-cranked machine; now we buy it from natural-foods titans like Walnut Acres of Pennsylvania. You can always find freshly ground peanut butter in health-food stores, but these days most regular supermarkets have it too. (Note that not all peanut butter cookie recipes work with fresh-ground peanut butter, but this one definitely does.)

♦♦♦♦♦♦

8 tablespoons (1 stick) unsalted butter,
    at room temperature
½ cup (firmly packed) dark brown
    sugar
½ cup granulated sugar
1 teaspoon pure vanilla extract
1 egg
¾ cup fresh-ground peanut butter,
    chunky or smooth (see Note)
1½ cups unbleached all-purpose flour
¾ teaspoon baking soda
Cinnamon sugar, for topping
    (1½ tablespoons granulated sugar
    mixed with ½ teaspoon ground
    cinnamon; optional)

♦♦♦♦♦♦

1. Preheat the oven to 375°F.

2. In a large bowl, cream the butter and sugars together with an electric mixer on high speed until light and fluffy. Add the vanilla, egg, and peanut butter, and blend in until smooth and incorporated.

3. In another mixing bowl, whisk together the flour and baking soda. Add this to the creamed mixture and mix on low speed to form a stiff dough, scraping down the sides of the bowl as needed.

4. Drop rounded tablespoons of the dough, spaced 2 inches apart, onto ungreased baking sheets. Flatten the cookies with the back of a fork to make ridges first in one direction, then in another. Sprinkle each with a pinch of cinnamon sugar (if desired). Bake, rotating the sheets once, until lightly browned all over, 12 to 15 minutes. (The cookies will be soft coming from the oven but will crisp up as they cool.) Allow to cool on the baking sheets for at

COOKIE CRAZY?

For efficiency and uniform results, invest in a small hand-held cookie scoop. It looks and works just like an ice cream scoop and cuts your production time in half.

least 5 minutes before transferring to a wire rack to cool completely.

Note: Fresh-ground peanut butter often contains no added salt. If you use unsalted peanut butter, add ½ teaspoon salt when you mix the flour and baking soda.

Granola Chocolate-Chip Cookies

MAKES 36 COOKIES

We make these cookie-jar perennials with one of our own lightly toasted granolas that is full of raisins and sunflower seeds, but any good granola will do. The point is that when you add granola to classic Toll House cookies you can almost convince yourself they're the foundation of the food group pyramid!

♦♦♦♦♦♦

1½ cups granola cereal

2 cups unbleached all-purpose flour

1 teaspoon baking soda

1 teaspoon salt

1 cup (2 sticks) unsalted butter, at
room temperature

¾ cup granulated sugar

½ cup (firmly packed) light brown
sugar

1 teaspoon pure vanilla extract

2 eggs

1 cup bittersweet chocolate bits
(see Note)

½ cup pecans, preferably toasted
(see Toasting Nuts, page 55),
coarsely chopped (optional)

♦♦♦♦♦♦

1. Preheat the oven to 350°F. Lightly butter two baking sheets.

2. Stir the granola, flour, baking soda, and salt together in a mixing bowl.

3. In a large bowl, cream the butter and both sugars together with an electric mixer on high speed until light and fluffy. Add the vanilla and eggs, one at a time, mixing on low speed until well blended.

4. Blend the dry ingredients into the creamed mixture until they are moistened and incorporated. The dough should be stiff. Add the chocolate bits and pecans (if using), and stir in well.

5. Place heaping tablespoons of the dough, at least 2 inches apart, on the prepared baking sheets. Bake, rotating the sheets once, until nicely browned, 10 to 12 minutes. Allow to cool for 10 minutes on the baking sheets; then transfer to a wire rack to cool completely.

Note: For the best quality chocolate bits, start with good-quality baking chocolate and coarsely chop your own.

Variations

♦ For thicker, chewier cookies, chill the dough in the refrigerator, well wrapped, until firm, about 1 hour. Then bake 8 to 10 minutes.

♦ Use mini-morsels for smaller chunks of chocolate.

♦ Substitute peanuts or walnuts for the pecans.

Cookies to Go

Prepare this delicious assortment of sturdy favorites over the course of a few days. Then arrange them in jars, baskets, or tins to be shipped to a college dorm or hand-delivered to a potluck supper.

❦ ❦ ❦

Raspberry-Almond Thumbprints

Belgian Chocolate Brownies

Cranberry-Almond Biscotti

Oatmeal Crisp Cookies

Maple-Cashew Crisps

❦ ❦ ❦

Double Chocolate Espresso-Chip Cookies

MAKES 36 COOKIES

Chocolate-covered dark-roasted espresso beans are easy to find these days (sometimes you can even get them in bulk), and they make a very grown-up cookie. A great present for teachers and neighbors at holiday time.

◆◆◆◆◆◆

1 cup (2 sticks) unsalted butter, at
   room temperature
1 cup granulated sugar
½ cup (firmly packed) dark brown
   sugar
1 egg
1 teaspoon pure vanilla extract
1¾ cups unbleached all-purpose flour
¼ teaspoon baking soda
⅓ cup unsweetened cocoa powder
   (see Note, page 239)
8 ounces (1½ cups) chocolate-covered
   espresso beans

◆◆◆◆◆◆

1. Preheat the oven to 350°F.

2. In a large bowl, cream the butter and sugars together with an electric mixer on high speed until light and fluffy. Add the egg and vanilla, mixing until well blended.

3. In another mixing bowl, whisk together the flour, baking soda, and cocoa powder. Stir this into the creamed mixture on low speed just until combined. Add the espresso beans and stir them in until well blended.

4. Place rounded tablespoons of the dough, spaced 2 inches apart, on two ungreased or parchment-lined baking sheets. Bake, rotating the sheets once, until the cookies are just crisp around the edges but still a bit soft and puffed in the center, 12 to 15 minutes. Remove from the oven, allow to cool on the baking sheets for a couple of minutes, then transfer to a wire rack to cool completely.

Raspberry-Almond Thumbprints

MAKES 24 COOKIES

These festive American cookies are a wonderful Christmas project for kids. After all, how often are you *asked* to put your thumbs in the dough?

◆◆◆◆◆◆

8 tablespoons (1 stick) unsalted butter,
   at room temperature
⅓ cup sugar
½ teaspoon pure vanilla extract
¼ teaspoon salt
1 egg, separated
1 cup unbleached all-purpose flour
¾ cup slivered almonds
¼ cup red raspberry jam

◆◆◆◆◆◆

1. In a large bowl, cream the butter and sugar together with an electric mixer on high speed until well blended. Add the vanilla, salt, and egg yolk, and beat well until fluffy, scraping down the sides of the bowl as needed.

2. Add the flour and mix it in on low speed to form a stiff dough. Scrape the dough onto a large sheet of wax paper, and using floured hands, roll it back and forth to make a long rope about ¾ inch in diameter and 12 inches long. Roll it up tightly in the wax paper and refrigerate until firm, about 30 minutes. The dough for the cookies can be prepared to this point up to 3 days in advance; remove it from the refrigerator and allow it to rest for 10 minutes at room temperature (so that it's firm yet malleable) before proceeding.

3. Meanwhile, lightly beat the egg white in a small bowl and set aside. Coarsely chop the almonds and transfer them to a separate bowl.

4. Preheat the oven to 300°F.

5. Unwrap and slice the chilled cookie dough into ½-inch-thick pieces. Roll them into ball shapes. Dip each ball in the egg white, then roll it in the nuts until coated. Space the balls 1 inch apart on an ungreased baking sheet, and make a small indentation in the center of each one by pressing down on it with your thumb. Fill each hollow with a generous ¼ teaspoon of jam.

6. Bake, rotating the pan once, until *very* lightly browned, 18 to 20 minutes. Remove from the oven and allow to rest for at least 5 minutes on the baking sheet before transferring to wire racks to cool. Resist the temptation to eat these pretty cookies straight from the oven—hot jam burns tender tongues.

Maple-Cashew Crisps

MAKES 48 COOKIES

R eadily available by mail order or in specialty food stores, powdered maple sugar is wonderful stuff to have in the larder. It is great sprinkled on all sorts of baked goods and cereals, and you can even reconstitute it (3 parts maple sugar simmered in 1 part water) to create a maple syrup that is intensely flavored and often more economical than the kind in the crock. Here the maple sugar makes a wonderful combination with rich, buttery cashews.

◆◆◆◆◆◆

1 cup (2 sticks) unsalted butter, at
   room temperature
1 cup granulated sugar
1 egg
1 tablespoon pure vanilla extract
⅔ cup unsalted cashew nuts, finely
   chopped
2 cups unbleached all-purpose flour
⅓ cup maple sugar
48 cashew halves

◆◆◆◆◆◆

1. In a large bowl, cream the butter and sugar together with an electric mixer on high speed until light and fluffy. Add the egg and vanilla, and mix until well combined. Then blend in the chopped cashews on low speed.

2. Add the flour and blend in on low speed to form a soft dough. Cover and refrigerate until firm enough to handle, at least 30 minutes. The dough for the cookies can be prepared to this point up to 3 days in advance; remove it from the refrigerator and allow it to rest for 10 minutes at room temperature (so that it's firm yet malleable) before proceeding.

3. Preheat the oven to 325°F. Put the maple sugar in a shallow dish.

4. Form the chilled dough into 1-inch balls, and toss them in the maple sugar to coat. Place them on two ungreased baking sheets, and firmly press a cashew half into the top of each cookie.

5. Bake, rotating the sheets once, until very lightly browned at the edges, 12 to 15 minutes. Allow the cookies to cool on the baking sheets for a couple of minutes. Then transfer to a wire rack to cool completely.

Cherry-Apricot Crumb Bars

MAKES 12 BARS

We've always chosen unsulfured apricots for their clean, rich taste, but that can mean trading color for flavor; here we compensate by adding the cheery brightness of dried cherries. These great take-along bar cookies are wonderful for tailgating, and their simple press-in crust makes them a great project for kids. Dried cranberries make a good substitute for the cherries.

◆◆◆◆◆◆

Fruit
3 ounces (generous ½ cup) unsulfured dried apricots
3 ounces (generous ½ cup) dried tart cherries
⅔ cup fresh orange juice

Bar Crust
½ cup sliced or slivered almonds, coarsely chopped
½ cup flaked unsweetened coconut
1¼ cups plus 1 tablespoon unbleached all-purpose flour
¾ cup old-fashioned rolled oats
¾ cup (firmly packed) light brown sugar
1 teaspoon ground cinnamon
½ teaspoon salt
12 tablespoons (1½ sticks) unsalted butter, chilled, cut into small chunks

◆◆◆◆◆◆

1. Combine the apricots, cherries, and orange juice in a small saucepan and bring to a boil over medium-high heat. Reduce the heat, cover, and simmer gently until very tender, about 20 minutes. Using a fork or a potato masher, crush the fruit to form a thick paste. Set aside to cool.

2. Meanwhile, preheat the oven to 300°F.

3. Scatter the almonds and coconut on a baking sheet and toast in the oven until the coconut is nicely browned and the nuts are golden, 8 to 10 minutes. Remove and set aside to cool. Increase the oven temperature to 350°F.

4. Combine the 1¼ cups flour with the oats, brown sugar, cinnamon, and salt in the bowl of a heavy-duty mixer, and mix on low speed to stir and combine. Add the cooled coconut and almonds along with the butter, and mix on medium speed until the mixture pulls together into coarse crumbs, 3 to 5 minutes.

5. Set aside 1 scant cup of the coarse crumbs for the topping. Firmly press the remaining crumb mixture into the bottom of an 8-inch square baking pan. Spread the mashed fruit filling evenly on top, leaving a ⅛-inch border around the edge of the pan. Blend the remaining 1 tablespoon flour into the reserved crumbs, and scatter this evenly over the top; press down lightly.

6. Bake in the middle of the oven until lightly browned, 30 to 35 minutes. Remove from the oven, and cool completely in the pan before slicing into bars.

Pumpkin Date Bars

MAKES 16 BARS

These bar cookies are one of our favorite afternoon treats from the Hay Day bakery. When served with fresh cider for an after-school snack, they are said to do extraordinary things for math homework and piano practice. In this version we top them with raw pepitas—which are simply shelled pumpkin seeds. They give the bars a nice crunchy texture and visual appeal. Pepitas are readily available in health-food and specialty shops and in Mexican food stores.

◆◆◆◆◆◆

Bars
8 tablespoons (1 stick) unsalted butter, at room temperature
¾ cup granulated sugar
¾ cup (firmly packed) light brown sugar
1 cup pumpkin purée (see About Pumpkin Purée, page 3)
2 eggs, lightly beaten
⅓ cup buttermilk
1¾ cups unbleached all-purpose flour
1 teaspoon salt
1 teaspoon baking powder
1 teaspoon baking soda
1 tablespoon pumpkin pie spice (see Note, page 2)
½ cup pitted dates, coarsely chopped
½ cup unsalted raw pepitas

Glaze
1 cup confectioners' sugar
¼ cup fresh orange juice
Finely grated zest of 1 orange
◆◆◆◆◆◆

1. Preheat the oven to 350°F. Lightly butter and flour a 13 × 9-inch glass baking dish. Pour out any excess flour.

2. In a large bowl, cream the butter and sugars together with an electric mixer on high speed until light and fluffy. Blend in the pumpkin purée, eggs, and buttermilk.

3. In another mixing bowl, whisk together the flour, salt, baking powder, baking soda, and pumpkin pie spice. Add this to the pumpkin mixture, and blend until all the dry ingredients are moistened. Stir in the chopped dates.

4. Spread the batter in the prepared baking dish and sprinkle with the pepitas. Bake until the cake has risen and a toothpick inserted in the center comes out clean, 25 to 30 minutes. Remove from the oven and set on a wire rack to cool to room temperature.

5. Combine the ingredients for the glaze in a small bowl, and stir. Pour the glaze over the cooled cake, spreading it with a spatula or cake knife. Cut into 16 rectangular bars.

Mochaccino Brownie Wedges

MAKES 16 BITE-SIZE BROWNIES

Everyone should have a spectacular brownie recipe, and this is another one of ours. Finely ground coffee adds intense flavor to cookies and cakes; here it makes a brownie that is irresistible.

Dusting the pan with unsweetened cocoa just intensifies the experience.

About 3 tablespoons unsweetened cocoa powder, for dusting
3 ounces (a generous ½ cup) blanched hazelnuts (see Skinning Hazelnuts, page 238)
8 tablespoons (1 stick) unsalted butter
4 ounces semisweet chocolate, coarsely chopped
2 tablespoons finely ground dark-roast coffee
1½ teaspoons ground cinnamon
1 teaspoon pure vanilla extract
¾ cup sugar
2 large eggs
¾ cup unbleached all-purpose flour
¼ teaspoon salt

1. Preheat the oven to 350°F. Lightly butter an 8-inch square baking pan, and dust it with unsweetened cocoa powder. Set aside.

2. Scatter the hazelnuts in another small baking pan and toast them in the oven until lightly colored and fragrant, 5 to 7 minutes. Remove the nuts from the oven; leave the oven on. Coarsely chop the nuts and set them aside.

3. Melt the butter and chocolate in a small heavy-bottomed saucepan over low heat. Add the coffee, cinnamon, and vanilla, and stir until smooth and combined. Remove from the heat and stir in the sugar. Add the eggs, one at a time, stirring briskly after each addition. Stir until the mixture is thick and shiny. Then stir in the flour, salt, and all but 2 tablespoons of the hazelnuts.

4. Scrape the batter into the prepared baking pan and spread it out evenly. Sprinkle with the reserved 2 tablespoons nuts, pressing them in lightly with the back of a spoon or a spatula. Bake in the middle of the oven until the brownies are firm to the touch and a toothpick inserted in the center comes out with moist crumbs attached, 30 to 35 minutes. Remove from the oven and cool completely in the pan. Then cut into four squares, and cut each square into four bite-size triangular brownies.

Belgian Chocolate Brownies

MAKES 18 BROWNIES

There's no big mystery: to get the best brownie, use the best chocolate, and use a lot of it. This recipe yields a really serious brownie—an irresistibly rich, dark, fudgy confection with a crackly top. For going on twenty years our brownie has made it almost impossible for chocolate-lovers to drive past a Hay Day store without stopping.

◆◆◆◆◆◆

8 ounces unsweetened Belgian
*   chocolate, coarsely chopped (see Note)*
1 cup (2 sticks) unsalted butter
6 large eggs
1 tablespoon pure vanilla extract
½ teaspoon salt
3½ cups sugar
2 cups unbleached all-purpose flour
1 tablespoon milk

◆◆◆◆◆◆

1. Preheat the oven to 375°F. Lightly butter a 13 × 9-inch baking dish.

2. Melt the chocolate and butter together in a small heavy-bottomed saucepan over low heat. Stir to combine, and set aside to cool.

3. Combine the eggs, vanilla, salt, and sugar in a large bowl and stir together vigorously, using a large wooden spoon or the paddle attachment of a heavy-duty mixer, until light and fluffy.

4. Add the flour and the chocolate mixture, in alternating batches, to the egg mixture, stirring until it's a smooth thick batter. Spread the batter in the prepared pan, brush the milk evenly on top, and bake until risen and lightly cracked on top, and just set, 35 minutes. A toothpick inserted in the center should come out chocolate-coated. Remove from the oven and allow to cool completely in the pan before cutting.

Note: This recipe will work with any brand of baking chocolate, but we get the best results with a rich Belgian baking chocolate like Callebaut or with the extra-smooth, intense flavor of French Valrhona.

Variation

◆ **Chocolate-Walnut Brownies:** Stir 2 cups coarsely chopped walnuts into the batter.

The Pantry

Talk about giving away secrets! These recipes have made Hay Day's reputation, and paid our bills, since 1978. Why are we giving them away? Because we know our customers: They'll buy things from us when they're in a hurry, just as they always have, and they'll make them at home when there's time. They already know they love Dan's Mustard; now they can also have the satisfaction of making it themselves. And for those cooks who aren't able to visit our stores, what better way for us to make new friends than to share a few special secrets?

So these are the basics, the points of departure, the traditional stocks, vinaigrettes, and flavored mayonnaises plus newer salsas, barbecue sauces, and other up-to-the-minute condiments we've come to rely on. Stocks and salad dressings to use as building blocks for preparing delicious meals. Pasta and barbecue sauces for dressing up everything from spaghetti to ribs to swordfish steaks. Flaky pie crusts to combine with the freshest fruits for mouthwatering desserts.

You'll find "Bright Ideas" here too, for using condiments and dressings to liven up everything from grilled foods to salads, sandwiches, and canapés. This may be the last chapter, but as you can tell, the recipes are all number one with us!

Pesto

MAKES 2 CUPS

We have friends who insist that making pesto with a mortar and pestle (hence the name) produces a more interesting texture, but we're seduced by the ease of the blender or food processor. Pesto is not difficult— you just combine fresh basil leaves, pine nuts, olive oil, garlic, and freshly grated cheese—but quality counts. Use really good oil and freshly cut basil, and you'll know the difference. Pesto freezes well (try freezing small quantities in ice cube trays), as long as there's extra olive oil on the surface to seal out the air; if you do freeze it, omit the cheeses and stir them in just before serving.

◆◆◆◆◆

*2 generous cups (packed) fresh basil
    leaves, rinsed and patted dry*
*2 large cloves garlic, crushed with
    the side of a knife and peeled*
1 cup extra-virgin olive oil
*½ cup pine nuts, lightly toasted
    (see Toasting Pine Nuts)*
*6 tablespoons freshly grated Parmesan
    cheese (see Grating Cheeses, facing
    page)*
*6 tablespoons freshly grated Pecorino
    Romano cheese*

◆◆◆◆◆

1. Combine the basil, garlic, oil, and pine nuts in a blender or food processor, and blend to form a smooth paste.

2. Stir in the cheeses. The sauce will keep, covered tightly, for several days in the refrigerator. Allow it to come to room temperature before serving.

Bright Ideas

❦ Toss with warm boiled new potatoes or tender cooked green beans.

❦ Brush over hot ears of corn on the cob.

❦ Mix with a little plain yogurt or mayonnaise and serve as a dipping sauce for a platter of summer vegetable crudités.

❦ Drizzle over grilled fish fillets or sliced sweet summer tomatoes.

❦ Brush over focaccia or pizza crust before baking.

Sauce Verte

MAKES 1½ CUPS

This is a particularly good version of the classic blend of fresh herbs, an exceptional sauce for everything from seafood to beef. We use it in our Maryland Crab Cakes (page 175) and as the dressing for Confetti Lobster Salad (page 177).

TOASTING PINE NUTS

Pine nuts toast so quickly that you must not turn your back on them even for a minute. We find it easiest to keep an eye on them at the stove: Toast the nuts in a dry skillet over moderate heat, shaking or stirring frequently, until lightly colored, 2 to 3 minutes.

GRATING CHEESES

When we talk about Parmesan cheese, we mean Parmigiano-Reggiano, the king of imported grating cheeses, easily identified by the pin dots outlining its name on the rind. There simply is no substitute for this cheese in terms of flavor. For pesto we mix it with sheep's-milk Pecorino Romano, which has a slightly more assertive flavor. All aged grating cheeses are dry, so buy them in one piece, store them in the refrigerator, and grate them as needed; once grated, their essential oils begin to evaporate along with their flavor.

The best way to store these chunks of cheese is in tight-fitting plastic wrap in the refrigerator, where they will keep for several weeks. Each time you grate a bit of the cheese, rewrap it in a clean sheet of plastic wrap; re-used wrap won't cling closely enough to be airtight. Aluminum foil does terrible things to the surface and flavor of cheese.

◆◆◆◆◆◆

¼ cup coarsely chopped fresh Italian
   (flat-leaf) parsley
2 generous tablespoons coarsely
   chopped fresh tarragon
3 generous tablespoons coarsely
   chopped fresh dill
3 large scallions, white and light
   green parts coarsely chopped
1 tablespoon fresh lemon juice
1 teaspoon Dijon mustard
1 cup mayonnaise, preferably
   homemade
Freshly ground black pepper

◆◆◆◆◆◆

1. Place the chopped herbs, scallions, lemon juice, and mustard in a food processor. Process to form a slightly lumpy paste, scraping down the sides of the bowl as needed.

2. Add the mayonnaise and blend until the mixture turns celadon green, about 1 minute. Season to taste with pepper. Refrigerate until ready to use. Well covered, it will keep in the refrigerator for up to 2 weeks.

Bright Ideas

❦ Serve as an elegant dipping sauce for steamed artichokes, snow-crab claws, or shrimp or lobster cocktail.

❦ Serve as a condiment for cold poached salmon or sliced beef tenderloin.

❦ Use as a sauce for canapés topped with smoked salmon, smoked trout, or fresh shrimp.

❦ Use as a spread for turkey, roast beef, or tomato and cucumber sandwiches.

❦ Toss with chunks of cooked crabmeat, shrimp, or lobster for a spectacular seafood salad.

Country Remoulade

MAKES 1 GENEROUS CUP

Keep this classic French staple—which looks and tastes like a very fresh, fancy tartar sauce—on hand for dressing up everything from cold sliced meats to fish and shellfish.

♦♦♦♦♦♦

4 good-size cornichon pickles
1 tablespoon large capers, rinsed
  and drained
Large pinch of fresh dill
3/4 cup mayonnaise, preferably
  homemade
2 tablespoons sour cream
1 1/2 teaspoons prepared horseradish,
  drained
2 teaspoons medium-dry sherry
  (see About Sherry, page 82)
1 tablespoon fresh lemon juice

♦♦♦♦♦♦

1. Combine the cornichons, capers, and dill in a blender or food processor and chop to form a coarse paste.

2. Combine the remaining ingredients in a small mixing bowl. Stir in the cornichon mixture, cover, and refrigerate for a couple of hours to allow the flavors to develop. Remoulade will keep well for several days in the refrigerator.

Bright Ideas

❦ Use as a sauce for crab cakes and fish fries.

❦ Serve as a sauce for tuna or beef carpaccio, assembled on small baguette rounds for an elegant appetizer.

❦ Serve with cold poached salmon, or flake the salmon and toss it with whole capers and remoulade for a very special salad.

❦ Use as a spread for roast beef or turkey sandwiches.

Dan's Mustard

MAKES 2 CUPS

*In Bermuda, a mogul named Franz
Sat gloomily out on the sands.
He said, when asked why,
"I miss Hay Day nearby,
'Cause I simply can't do without Dan's!"*

We find new customers wandering around looking for it. "Where's that mustard?" they ask. "The stuff you put on the ham?" Dan's Mustard was one of the first things we made when the Westport store opened, and since then we have probably sold tons of it—enough to serve with all the salamis and ham sandwiches in southwestern Connecticut. The recipe, created by Sallie's brother Dan, has been in the Van Rensselaer family for years, and now we're sharing one of our oldest secrets with you.

♦♦♦♦♦♦

1 cup (loosely packed) dry mustard,
  preferably Colman's English Mustard
1 cup distilled white vinegar
2 large eggs
1 cup sugar
1/2 teaspoon coarse (kosher) salt

♦♦♦♦♦♦

1. In a mixing bowl, stir the mustard and 1/4 cup of the vinegar together to form a paste. Then gradually add the remaining 3/4 cup vinegar, whisking until smooth and thoroughly incorporated.

2. Beat the eggs in another mixing bowl. Add the sugar and salt, and blend with an electric mixer on high speed until thick and lemony in color. Add this to the mustard mixture and whisk to combine thoroughly.

3. Pour into the top of a double boiler, and cook over simmering water, whisking occasionally and scraping down the sides of the pan as needed, until smooth, glossy, and thickened to the consistency of a thin custard, about 30 minutes (the mustard will continue to thicken as it cools). Remove from the heat, allow to cool thoroughly, pour into a clean jar, and refrigerate until ready to use. Tightly covered, it will keep well for months in the refrigerator.

Bright Ideas

❧ Serve with grilled hot dogs, braised bratwurst, or sausages.

❧ Use as a sandwich spread. It's great with smoked turkey, almost any kind of cheese, and ham. (One of our best-selling sandwiches is Black Forest ham and sliced ripe brie on freshly baked rye smeared with a generous amount of Dan's Mustard.)

❧ Use as a finishing glaze for grilled chicken or swordfish steaks.

❧ Serve as a dip for hard salami and cheeses.

❧ Add to dressings for potato salads and coleslaw.

Oven-Baked Croutons

MAKES 4 CUPS

Croutons add just the right crunch to soups and salads. For the Mediterranean Crouton Salad (page 110), we prefer them unseasoned because they soak up the flavors in the dressing. But for other uses, you may want to toss in a tablespoon or two of your favorite fresh garden herbs—or a tablespoon or two of Parmesan cheese.

◆◆◆◆◆◆

1 small baguette, preferably day-old
2 tablespoons olive oil
Minced aromatic fresh herbs, such as
*   marjoram, oregano, dill, tarragon,*
*   or basil (optional)*
Freshly grated Parmesan cheese
*   (optional)*

◆◆◆◆◆◆

1. Preheat the oven to 325°F.

2. Using a large serrated knife, cut the bread into ½- to ¾-inch cubes (you should have about 4 cups). Transfer the bread cubes to a large bowl and drizzle with the oil, tossing to coat evenly. If you are using them, toss in the herbs or cheese.

3. Scatter the cubes on a large baking sheet and spread them out in a single layer. Bake until lightly browned and very crisp, 15 to 20 minutes. Remove from the oven and allow to cool completely. Use immediately or store in a plastic bag and refrigerate.

Bright Ideas

❦ Sprinkle a handful over any puréed soup. Two favorites to match with croutons are the Winter Squash Bisque (page 87) and the Fresh Tomato and Basil Soup (page 92).

❦ Crush the croutons with a rolling pin and use them as a savory topping on baked or broiled tomato halves, hearty casseroles, and gratins.

❦ Chicken tenders and mild-flavored fish fillets benefit, too, from a coating of crushed croutons. Use them as you would plain or seasoned bread crumbs.

❦ For a barbecue or patio party, make the croutons with herbs and cheese. They are perfect nibbles to serve alongside the more traditional finger foods, such as nuts, chips, and pretzel sticks.

Yogurt Cheese

MAKES 1³/₄ CUPS

Although this sounds trendy, it's actually a centuries-old Middle Eastern staple; we Westerners just took a while to catch on. It's a wonderful dip, spread, condiment, or substitute for sour cream or mayonnaise in dips and sauces. We use it in our Creamy Mustard Coleslaw (page 114) and with sliced summer tomatoes. The yogurt does take most of the day to drain, but it needs no help from the cook.

1 teaspoon coarse (kosher) salt
1 quart best-quality plain yogurt
    (see Note)

Stir the salt into the yogurt. Line a strainer with a double thickness of cheese-cloth and set it over a large bowl. Spoon the yogurt into the colander, cover with plastic wrap, and refrigerate. The yogurt cheese is ready when it has the consistency of a soft, velvety spreadable cheese, about 6 hours. Discard the drained liquid, spoon the yogurt cheese into a small clean bowl, cover tightly, and refrigerate until ready to use. It will keep for up to a week.

Note: Use fresh yogurt that contains no stabilizers or preservatives. Don't worry about the acidopholus, bifidus, and bulgaricus that may be listed on the label; they are healthful active cultures, not enemies. Cream-on-top yogurt offers excellent flavor and texture, but you can also use low-fat or nonfat yogurt.

Bright Ideas

❦ Blend in a small handful of minced fresh herbs and serve as a dip for wedges of fresh pita and crudité vegetables, or as a topping for a baked potato.

❦ Serve as a nutritious spread for breakfast toast—with or without a little honey.

❦ Pack into lightly oiled decorative molds and chill for a couple of hours. Turn out, drizzle with good olive oil, and serve as a fresh cheese for hors d'oeuvres.

❦ Serve as a cooling condiment with spicy fish or meats.

❦ Spread on toast and top with chopped olives. Cut into triangles and serve as a canapé.

Crème Fraîche

MAKES 1 CUP

Used in many instances where sour cream or heavy cream is called for, crème fraîche is wonderful on vegetables and fruit and makes heavenly sauces. We use it in a creamy sauce for Pasta and Snap Peas in Saffron Lemon Cream (page 179) and for Grilled Portobello Mushrooms in Mustard Sauce (page 189). Its great virtue is that (unlike sour cream) it does not curdle with heat, so you can just whisk it into pan juices as you would cream or butter. Crème fraîche is becoming more widely available in markets—we're partial to the one made by the Vermont Butter and Cheese Company—but it's also incredibly easy to make at home. The only hitch is that it won't work with ultrapasteurized heavy cream. Luckily there's so much good fresh cream being produced by small dairies these days that you shouldn't have a problem finding it.

◆◆◆◆◆◆

*1 cup non-ultrapasteurized
heavy cream
1½ tablespoons buttermilk*

◆◆◆◆◆◆

Combine the cream and buttermilk in a clean glass jar, cover, shake well, and set aside at room temperature (60° to 70°F) until the cream becomes very thick, 10 to

24 hours. (The warmer the room, the quicker it will thicken.) Then stir, cover, and refrigerate to prevent further fermentation. Crème fraîche will keep in the refrigerator for at least a week.

Note: Don't worry about the crème fraîche spoiling while it's sitting on the counter. The acid in the mixture prevents the bacterial disease associated with dairy products.

Bright Ideas

❦ Whisk crème fraîche into sauces calling for cream or butter; it will add extra body and a rich velvety texture.

❦ Use a dollop of crème fraîche as an elegant finish for fruit tarts and other pastries.

❦ Sweeten crème fraîche with a bit of honey and serve it over sliced fruit and berries.

❦ Serve at breakfast time as a creamy spread for toast, muffins, or scones.

Aunt Maud's Apple Cider Applesauce

MAKES 3 GENEROUS CUPS

In truth, Aunt Maud opted for more sugar and swirled in some sweet butter at the end; her applesauce tasted like the filling for a really good apple pie. But this version is true to Aunt Maud in every other way—it's a celebration of fall apples, using the natural sweetness of cider to intensify their flavor. We use it in the topping for our Cranberry-Applesauce

Crumb Cake (page 11). Adding cardamom to the classic cinnamon creates a sauce that is also excellent as a rich, aromatic accompaniment to game, roast poultry, potato panakes, baked ham, or fresh pork.

◆◆◆◆◆◆

5 cups fresh apple cider
6 large assorted cooking apples
    (see Note), peeled, cored, and cut
    into 1-inch chunks
½ teaspoon ground cinnamon
¼ teaspoon ground cardamom
3 tablespoons sugar, or to taste
    (optional)

◆◆◆◆◆◆

1. Bring the cider to a boil in a large heavy-bottomed saucepan. Reduce the heat and simmer rapidly, uncovered, over medium-high heat until reduced by half, 30 to 35 minutes.

2. Stir in the apples and return to a simmer. Cover and simmer gently, stirring from time to time, until the apples have softened completely and begun to break apart, 35 to 45 minutes. The applesauce should be thick and chunky; if there is too much liquid, remove the lid and simmer uncovered until thickened.

3. Stir in the cinnamon and cardamom. Taste, and add sugar as desired. Serve warm or cold.

Note: As with cider, the fullest-flavored sauces are made with a variety of seasonal cooking apples. A few great apples: Jonamac, Granny Smith, Greening, Empire, Winesap, Macoun, and McIntosh.

Bright Ideas

❦ Serve as a light spread with toast or hot fresh muffins.

❦ Stir into a bowl of plain yogurt for a nutritious snack.

❦ Use as a filling for puff-pastry turnovers.

❦ Fold into sweetened whipped cream or crème fraîche for a fool-style dessert.

Fresh Cranberry Sauce

MAKES 3 CUPS

The simplest cranberry sauces are usually the best; this one balances the tartness of the berries with just enough sugar, cinnamon, and brandy for a not-too-sweet flavor. Brief cooking gives the sauce a lovely whole-berry texture.

◆◆◆◆◆◆

½ cup brandy, preferably apple
¼ cup cranberry juice
1 bag (12 ounces) fresh cranberries,
    rinsed
1 cup sugar
¼ teaspoon ground cinnamon
1 whole (3-inch) cinnamon stick,
    broken in half
⅓ cup blanched hazelnuts, lightly
    toasted (see Toasting Nuts, page 55)

◆◆◆◆◆◆

Combine the brandy, cranberry juice, cranberries, sugar, ground cinnamon, and cinnamon stick in a saucepan. Stir to combine. Bring to a boil over high heat, stirring occasionally. Reduce the heat, stir in the hazelnuts, and simmer gently just until the berries begin to split and release their juices, about 10 minutes. Remove from the heat, pour into a serving dish, and allow to cool to room temperature. Remove the cinnamon stick before serving. The sauce will keep, covered, for several weeks in the refrigerator.

Bright Ideas

❦ Serve as a condiment for a platter of sliced smoked meats and cheeses.

❦ Pack into decorative jars and tie with ribbon and cinnamon sticks for holiday hostess gifts.

❦ Drop a few whole berries into a tall glass of Champagne and add a spoonful of the juices for a festive holiday cranberry kir royale.

Fresh Tomato Marinara Sauce

MAKES 1 GENEROUS QUART

When made with fresh summer tomatoes, this sauce is great. And if you make it in January with good canned plum tomatoes, it will break right through the gloom of midwinter. This recipe makes a very light sauce; if you like it thicker, just simmer it for a few minutes longer. We use it as a simple topping for our Vegetable-Pasta Frittata (page 180).

When summer tomatoes are at their peak, make a double batch and freeze half. You'll thank yourself later on.

◆◆◆◆◆◆

2½ pounds ripe fresh tomatoes, or
  5 cups good-quality canned plum
  tomatoes, drained
¼ cup extra-virgin olive oil
⅓ cup diced onion
⅓ cup diced red or yellow bell pepper
2 large cloves garlic, peeled and minced
¾ cup fruity medium-bodied red wine
  (such as Chianti, Merlot, or
  Cabernet)
Coarse (kosher) salt
2 tablespoons shredded fresh basil
1 tablespoon chopped fresh thyme
  or oregano
Freshly ground black pepper

◆◆◆◆◆◆

1. If you are using fresh tomatoes, core them (peeling is unnecessary). Cut the tomatoes into large chunks and pile them into a blender or food processor. Purée until smooth, in batches if necessary.

2. Heat the oil in a large heavy-bottomed saucepan over medium heat. Add the onion, bell pepper, and garlic, and sauté until tender and fragrant, 2 to 3 minutes.

3. Add the puréed tomatoes, wine, 1 teaspoon salt, and the basil and thyme; stir. Bring to a boil over medium-high heat. Reduce the heat and simmer gently, uncovered, stirring occasionally, until slightly thickened, about 20 minutes. Season to taste with salt and pepper. This sauce will keep well in the refrigerator for at least 1 week and freezes beautifully for up to 3 months.

Bright Ideas

❦ Use as a light fresh sauce for pizza.

❦ Serve as a dip for wedges of freshly baked focaccia.

❦ Spoon over grilled fillet of beef or chicken.

❦ Stir a bit of light cream or crème fraîche (for extra body) and some Parmesan cheese into the sauce to create a creamy tomato Alfredo sauce.

Classic Ratatouille

MAKES 7 CUPS

This classic French vegetable stew is a delight to prepare during the late summer and early autumn months, when the harvest is at its peak. As with other stews, its rich flavor is developed with long, slow cooking and seems to even improve the next day. So it makes sense to prepare a substantial batch; it will keep well in the refrigerator and the freezer. Ratatouille is a great sauce to have on

hand for a quick meal. Serve it over hot rice or pasta, topped with a bit of freshly grated Parmesan cheese.

♦♦♦♦♦♦

1 cup extra-virgin olive oil
1 large onion, peeled and thinly sliced (2 cups sliced)
3 large cloves garlic, peeled and minced
1 eggplant (about 1 pound), unpeeled, cut into ½-inch dice
1 large zucchini (about 1 pound), scrubbed and cut into ½-inch dice
1 red bell pepper, stemmed, seeded, and cut into ½-inch dice
1 green bell pepper, stemmed, seeded, and cut into ½-inch dice
1 teaspoon coarse (kosher) salt
4 large ripe tomatoes, peeled and coarsely chopped, or 4 cups good-quality canned plum tomatoes, drained and coarsely chopped
2 tablespoons red wine vinegar
½ teaspoon dried thyme
Tabasco or other hot sauce, to taste
3 tablespoons shredded fresh basil leaves
Freshly ground black pepper

♦♦♦♦♦♦

1. Heat the oil in a large heavy-bottomed saucepan over medium heat. Add the onion and garlic, and sauté until wilted and just beginning to color, about 5 minutes.

2. Add the eggplant, zucchini, and the bell peppers. Stir in the salt and sauté over medium-high heat until the vegetables have softened and cooked down by one-third, about 10 minutes.

3. Stir in the tomatoes, vinegar, thyme, and a couple of dashes of hot sauce. Bring to a gentle simmer over medium heat. Reduce the heat and cook, partially covered, until all the vegetables are very tender and the sauce is aromatic and slightly thickened, about 45 minutes. Stir in the basil, and season to taste with black pepper. Serve, or let cool and store, tightly covered, in the refrigerator for up to 1 week or in the freezer for up to 6 months.

Bright Ideas

❦ Serve as a topping on toasted bread rounds for ratatouille crostini appetizers.

❦ Use as a vegetable topping for pizza or a sauce for lasagne.

❦ Serve as a sauce with grilled tuna, swordfish, or sea bass.

Eggplant, Tomato, and Caper Sauce

MAKES 1½ QUARTS

Easily assembled and quickly cooked, this fragrant chunky sauce makes a substantial and very satisfying supper over a bowl of hot pasta. It's also scrumptious spooned over grilled sea bass, tuna, or swordfish steaks. Leave the skins on the fresh tomatoes; their texture is not a problem in a rustic sauce like this.

◆◆◆◆◆◆

⅓ cup extra-virgin olive oil
1 cup chopped onions
2 large cloves garlic, peeled
¼ cup dry red wine
1 eggplant (about 1 pound),
 peeled and cut into ½-inch dice
2½ to 3 pounds very ripe tomatoes,
 coarsely chopped, or 5 generous cups
 good-quality canned plum tomatoes,
 drained, coarsely chopped
⅓ cup large capers, rinsed and drained
⅓ cup Kalamata olives, pitted and
 coarsely chopped
¼ cup shredded fresh basil
Coarsely ground black pepper

◆◆◆◆◆◆

1. Heat the oil in a large heavy-bottomed saucepan over medium heat. Add the onions and garlic, and sauté until the onion is tender and transparent, 5 minutes. Add the wine and simmer briefly. Stir in the eggplant and cook, uncovered, over medium-high heat, stirring occasionally, until tender and cooked down, about 15 minutes.

2. Stir in the tomatoes, capers, and olives. Simmer gently until the tomatoes are very soft and the sauce is aromatic, about 20 minutes. Add the basil, stir, and season to taste with pepper. Serve, or let cool, then store, tightly covered, in the refrigerator for up to 1 week or in the freezer for up to 6 months.

Bright Ideas

❦ Serve over hot spaghetti squash for a light meal or for a vegetable side dish to accompany roast chicken.

❦ Use as a topping for crostini, finished with a little grated Parmesan cheese.

❦ Create a chunky vegetable lasagne by layering the sauce with cooked noodles and a blend of mozzarella and ricotta cheeses.

Tuscan Tomato and Bacon Sauce

MAKES 1 QUART

This rich, intensely flavored sauce makes a hearty meal when served over pasta. It's best prepared with thick-sliced smoked bacon and fresh Italian sausage (with or without fennel)—or you can substitute a fresh poultry sausage if you feel the need for something a little leaner.

◆◆◆◆◆◆

2 tablespoons olive oil
4 ounces fresh sweet Italian sausage,
   bulk or slipped out of its casing
4 strips thick-sliced smoked bacon, diced
1 large clove garlic, peeled and minced
½ cup coarsely chopped Spanish onion
½ cup port
2 pounds fresh plum tomatoes or 4 cups
   good-quality canned plum tomatoes,
   drained, coarsely chopped
½ teaspoon coarse (kosher) salt
½ teaspoon red pepper flakes
1 tablespoon shredded fresh basil,
   or more to taste

◆◆◆◆◆◆

1. Heat the oil in a large skillet over medium-high heat. Add the sausage and bacon, and sauté until the sausage is browned and the bacon is crisp, about 5 minutes. Drain the excess fat from the pan, add the garlic and onion, and continue to cook over medium-high heat until the onion is tender and lightly colored, 8 to 10 minutes.

2. Add the port and simmer for 1 minute, scraping up the browned bits from the bottom of the skillet. Stir in the tomatoes, salt, and red pepper flakes. Bring to a gentle simmer over medium-high heat and cook, uncovered, until the tomatoes are softened and cooked down, 20 to 25 minutes. Then stir in the basil and serve. Or let cool and store, tightly covered, in the refrigerator for up to 1 week or in the freezer for up to 3 months.

Bright Ideas

❦ Serve over a mound of hot linguine with a few warm grilled shrimp tucked on top.

❦ Use as a pizza topping, along with a bit of grated mozzarella cheese (smoked mozzarella is wonderful).

❦ Stir in a generous cup of tender cooked cannellini beans for a heartier sauce, and serve over bowls of hot penne or farfalle (bowties).

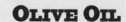

OLIVE OIL

Olive oil not only tastes sublime, it's now officially recognized as the good guy in the fat wars, the monounsaturated cholesterol-lowering champion of the heart-healthy Mediterranean diet. Which means, of course, that store shelves are lined with a dizzying array of seductively packaged oils from France, Italy, Spain, Greece, and California. But don't be intimidated. In today's burgeoning market all but the very greatest estate-bottled olive oils are reasonably priced, so it's easy to experiment.

How to choose? By color and flavor, to begin with. Intensely green oils are generally produced from early harvest (less mature) olives and have a pungent, grassy fruit flavor. Golden oils are pressed from later harvests and offer a smoother, mellower flavor. Both are equally prized; sample them on some bread cubes and savor the differences. Like wine, it's all a matter of taste.

Equally important is the way the oil will be used. There's no point in cooking with a costly cold-pressed oil because the heat will affect the flavor; so use a humbler pure or virgin oil for cooking and save the really great ones to use unheated—in salads and antipasto, brushed on bruschetta, or tossed with vegetables or seafood.

One of the purest ways to enjoy a really good cold-pressed extra-virgin oil is in a salad of fresh greens. Make the dressing in the empty salad bowl: Rub the bowl with a split clove of garlic (if you like), add 1 part lemon juice or vinegar to every 3 parts oil (the classic proportion), and season with salt and pepper to taste. You can add a drop of Dijon mustard or a bit of crumbled blue cheese too, but keep it simple—the flavor of the oil should dominate. Add clean dried greens to the bowl, and toss them in the dressing just before serving.

A word to the wise: Don't be misled by the term "light" on a label. Those oils contain just as many calories as the rest—they're only "light" on flavor.

Basil-Infused Olive Oil

MAKES 1½ CUPS

Blanched basil leaves keep their color and make this oil intensely green. To highlight the flavor of the herb, use an inexpensive light-flavored olive oil—you could even use equal quantities of olive and safflower oils. (The bold peppery flavor of an expensive Tuscan oil will overpower the basil.)

◆◆◆◆◆◆

Large pinch of coarse (kosher) salt
3 cups (packed) fresh basil leaves,
rinsed and patted dry
1 cup light–flavored olive oil

◆◆◆◆◆◆

1. Place a large pot of water on to boil. Meanwhile, fill a sink or large mixing bowl with cold water.

2. Once the water reaches a rolling boil, add the salt, return to a boil, and toss in the basil leaves all at once. Blanch just until the leaves are bright green, no more than 30 seconds. Then drain immediately and plunge the leaves into the cold water to stop the cooking and set their color.

3. Drain the basil, and using your hands, squeeze the leaves to extract as much moisture as possible. Place them in a blender, add the olive oil, and purée for about 1 minute. The oil should be bright green and fluid.

4. Pour the purée through a fine-mesh sieve into a clean bottle or jar, and seal tightly until ready to use. Store in the refrigerator for up to 2 weeks.

Bright Ideas

❦ Toss into hot pasta with chopped fresh tomato and freshly grated Parmesan cheese. Garnish the servings with a bit of shredded fresh basil.

❦ Drizzle over grilled fish steaks, shellfish, or crab cakes.

❦ Sprinkle over slices of fresh garden tomatoes.

❦ Pour over warm mashed potatoes.

❦ Serve as a dipping sauce for slices of country bread.

Olive Oil Vinaigrette

MAKES 1¼ CUPS

In general, the simpler the vinaigrette, the better the oil should be. A cold-pressed oil with rich, fruity flavor really shines in this elegant, uncomplicated dressing. Nowadays it's easy to find olive oil that's labeled "extra-virgin," but look for the words "cold-pressed" in addition. On a reputable label, it means the olives haven't been heated and will thus have the lowest acidity and the truest pure olive flavor.

If you're going to store this vinaigrette in the fridge, remember that olive oil congeals with cold and the dressing will thicken—so bring it back to room temperature several hours before serving. Or substitute a little safflower oil for some of the olive oil to prevent thickening.

◆◆◆◆◆◆

½ teaspoon herbes de Provence (see Note)
1 teaspoon Dijon mustard
⅓ cup sherry vinegar
¼ teaspoon coarse (kosher) salt
⅔ cup cold-pressed extra-virgin olive oil
Freshly ground black pepper

◆◆◆◆◆◆

1. Using a mortar and pestle, crush the herbes de Provence into a coarse powder. Or sandwich the herbs between two sheets of wax paper and crush them with a rolling pin.

2. In a small bowl, whisk together the crushed herbs, mustard, vinegar, and salt.

Add the oil in steady even stream, whisking continuously to form an emulsified dressing. Season to taste with pepper. Use immediately or store in a clean glass jar in the refrigerator for up to 3 weeks.

Note: Herbes de Provence, an aromatic blend of rosemary, sage, basil, fennel, lavender, thyme, and other herbs typically used in southern France, is available in specialty stores and in most good supermarkets. It's also delicous on roast chicken and in marinades for lamb.

Red Wine Vinaigrette

MAKES 1 GENEROUS CUP

This is about as basic as it gets, but if you use good ingredients, this vinaigrette is as civilized as it is effortless. Use it for simple weeknight salads or as a marinade for chicken and steak. Add a small handful of minced fresh herbs if you like. It will keep almost indefinitely in the door of the fridge (bring it to room temperature before using).

◆◆◆◆◆◆

1 tablespoon minced shallot
2 teaspoons Dijon mustard
6 tablespoons red wine vinegar
1 tablespoon minced fresh tarragon, oregano, parsley, chervil, or dill (optional)
¾ cup safflower, canola, or light-flavored olive oil
Pinch of coarse (kosher) salt
Freshly ground black pepper, to taste

◆◆◆◆◆◆

MARINATING WITH VINAIGRETTES

Many of our vinaigrettes make excellent marinades, but the timings are very different for fish and meats. Acids like vinegar and lemon juice are highly effective tenderizers, and while this is great for sturdy meats like lamb and beef, it can be murder for fish and shellfish. (Think of a scallop ceviche, after all, which is fully "cooked" in lime juice after about half an hour.) So while you should never marinate seafoods for more than an hour, lamb and even chicken will profit from being left in a marinade overnight. Always shake off excess marinade before grilling to avoid flare-ups, and fight the temptation to use the leftover marinade for anything but a basting sauce—once it's left at room temperature for any length of time, it can be a breeding ground for bacteria.

Whisk the shallot, mustard, and vinegar together in a small bowl. (If you are adding herbs, work them in at this point.) Add the oil in a slow thin steam, whisking continuously to form an emulsified dressing. Season with the salt and pepper. Store in the refrigerator in a tightly sealed glass jar. Shake before using.

Balsamic Vinaigrette

MAKES 1¼ CUPS

The real *aceto balsamico tradizionale* from Modena comes in a tiny bottle and costs a king's ransom, but a good-quality balsamic vinegar will make this vinaigrette truly exceptional. Its rich sweet-tart flavor goes well with peppery greens and makes an exceptional marinade for highly flavored meats like lamb, venison, and game birds. We use it over a dish of Wilted Radicchio with Gorgonzola and Walnuts (page 203) and as a marinade for Grilled Portobello Mushrooms in Mustard Sauce (page 189).

◆◆◆◆◆◆

1 small clove garlic, peeled and
   minced
1 tablespoon coarse-grain or
   beer-style mustard
½ cup balsamic vinegar
1 teaspoon minced fresh rosemary,
   thyme, or oregano
¾ cup extra-virgin olive oil
Freshly ground black pepper

◆◆◆◆◆◆

1. Whisk together the garlic, mustard, vinegar, and rosemary in a small bowl.

2. Slowly add the oil, whisking continuously until the mixture thickens slightly. Season to taste with pepper.

3. Allow the dressing to stand at room temperature for the flavors to develop, 30 minutes. Tightly covered, it will keep well for up to 3 weeks in the refrigerator.

Bright Ideas

❦ Sprinkle over a summer tomato salad.

❦ Toss with warm steamed asparagus.

❦ Use the dressing as a marinade for grilled lamb or poultry; marinate for up to 2 days for exceptional flavor.

Black Peppercorn Dressing

MAKES 1½ CUPS

This is another Hay Day basic. We offer samples in the produce department next to bowls of bright ripe tomato sections. One taste and it sells by the ton! Its assertive peppery flavor makes a spectacular dressing for a platter of sliced summer tomatoes, and it's the B in our favorite summer BLT: Black Peppercorn, Lettuce, and Tomato on Peasant Bread.

◆◆◆◆◆◆

8 ounces sour cream
¼ cup mayonnaise, preferably
   homemade
1 tablespoon Worcestershire sauce
2 tablespoons Browned Beef Stock
   (page 269), or 1 tablespoon demi-
   glace (see Note, page 134)
3 teaspoons freshly ground black
   pepper, or more to taste
1 teaspoon coarse (kosher) salt

◆◆◆◆◆◆

In a small bowl, whisk together the sour cream, mayonnaise, Worcestershire sauce, stock, and pepper. Season to taste with the salt, and additional pepper if desired. Cover and refrigerate. For the fullest flavor, allow the sauce to rest for a few hours before serving. It will keep well for several days in the refrigerator.

Bright Ideas

❦ Serve as a condiment with grilled steak or sliced beef tenderloin.

❦ Use as a spread for roast beef sandwiches.

❦ Serve as a topping for hamburgers.

❦ Toss with shredded cabbage and thinly sliced bell peppers for a great peppery slaw.

❦ Use as a dressing for green and potato salads.

Sun-Dried Tomato Vinaigrette

MAKES 1 GENEROUS CUP

Keep this vivid vinaigrette on hand (it stores well in the refrigerator for several weeks) to toss with peppery arugula or mesclun or to use as a marinade for fish, shellfish, or poultry.

◆◆◆◆◆◆

½ ounce dry-packed sun-dried
*   tomatoes (6 dried tomatoes)*
¾ cup hot water
2 tablespoons red wine vinegar
1 tablespoon balsamic vinegar
1 small clove garlic, peeled and
*   coarsely chopped*
3 large basil leaves, torn
½ cup extra-virgin olive oil

◆◆◆◆◆◆

1. In a small bowl, soak the tomatoes in the water until soft, about 30 minutes. Then drain, reserving the soaking liquid, and coarsely chop the tomatoes.

2. Combine the tomatoes, vinegars, garlic, and basil in a food processor or blender and pulse five or six times to make a slightly chunky mixture. With the machine running, add the reserved tomato soaking liquid, then the oil, in a slow thin stream. Blend until all the oil is incorporated to form a thin, fluid vinaigrette with small bits of tomatoes and basil. Tightly cover and refrigerate until ready to use.

Bright Ideas

❦ Use as the dressing for a light summer salad of pasta and steamed vegetables.

❦ Serve as a dipping sauce for brochettes of grilled chicken or shrimp.

❦ Drizzle over buttons of fresh goat cheese and serve with slices of warm French bread.

Lemon Vinaigrette

MAKES 1½ CUPS

Like fiddlehead ferns, this bright, lemony dressing is a springtime event in our stores. We recommend it as a sauce over snap peas or asparagus spears and as a dressing over mixed baby greens or California artichokes. We also use it over our Smoked Salmon and Spinach Rotollo (page 168). Its brilliant flavor clears the mind and the palate as surely as spring sunshine.

◆◆◆◆◆◆

1 egg (see Using Raw Eggs, page 174)
1 teaspoon Dijon mustard
2 tablespoons tarragon vinegar
Juice of 1 large lemon
1 teaspoon fresh thyme
1 cup light vegetable oil (canola or safflower)
Coarse (kosher) salt and freshly ground black pepper

◆◆◆◆◆◆

Combine the egg, mustard, vinegar, lemon juice, and thyme in a blender or food processor and blend for 1 minute. With the machine still running, slowly add the oil in a thin steady stream, blending until the dressing is smooth and thickened. Season to taste with salt and pepper. The dressing will remain emulsified and will keep well, tightly covered, in the refrigerator for several weeks.

Bright Ideas

❦ Fold a little crème fraîche into the dressing and serve it as a light spring sauce for grilled or poached salmon.

❦ Use as a dip for spring vegetable crudités.

❦ Serve as a dipping sauce for an elegant spring hors d'oeuvre made of small wedges of smoked salmon tucked into blanched snow pea pods.

Hickory-Smoked Barbecue Sauce

MAKES 1½ QUARTS

Of all the smoky eastern-style tomato-based barbecue sauces, this was the head-and-shoulders winner in a blind tasting by Hay Day staffers a couple of years ago. Thick, slow-simmered, and rich with tomatoes, it is a classic basting and finishing sauce for beef brisket, chicken, and shrimp on the grill—and it makes a great substitute for ketchup or steak sauce at the table. It also gives a lovely smoky flavor to thick slices of grilled onion, peppers, zucchini, and eggplant.

◆◆◆◆◆◆

⅓ cup vegetable oil
2 cups chopped onions
5 pounds ripe tomatoes, cored, peeled, and coarsely chopped
1½ cups cider vinegar
Coarse (kosher) salt
½ cup honey
1 teaspoon Tabasco or other hot sauce
1 fresh jalapeño pepper, deveined, seeded, and minced
1 can (6 ounces) tomato paste
2 tablespoons all-natural liquid smoke
Freshly ground black pepper, to taste

◆◆◆◆◆◆

1. Heat the oil in a large saucepan over medium heat. Add the onions and sauté until lightly colored, about 10 minutes. Add the tomatoes, vinegar, and 1 tablespoon salt. Bring to a simmer over medium-high heat, reduce the heat a bit, and simmer gently, partially covered,

BARBECUE SAUCES

Trying to make sense of all the barbecue sauces on the shelves can make a strong man weep. Briefly, there are *marinades* (to flavor and tenderize meats before cooking), *basting sauces* (the kind you brush on during grilling), and *finishing sauces* (to brush on cooked meat or serve as a condiment, like ketchup).

Marinades are generally thin and are made with a generous amount of acid (vinegar, wine, or citrus), which acts as a tenderizer. Chicken, meats, fish, and seafood all benefit from marinating before grilling. Chicken and meat can marinate overnight, but fish and seafood will begin to "cook" in the acid if they are left in a marinade for more than an hour.

Mopping and basting sauces, like marinades, are usually thin and acidic, although they may also contain a fair amount of tomatoes and sugar. They are applied repeatedly to meats during cooking to keep them moist.

Glazes or finishing sauces are thick and ketchupy and tend to be high in sugar. So they are applied only during the last 10 minutes or so of cooking to create a crisp glaze; if they are introduced too early, they will burn off, losing all their flavor and blackening the food.

until the tomatoes have cooked down to a thick sauce, about 1 hour.

2. Stir in the honey, hot pepper sauce, jalapeño, and tomato paste. Continue to simmer, uncovered, until the sauce is very thick, dark, and fragrant, another 50 to 60 minutes. Add the liquid smoke and stir it in well; then taste and season with salt and pepper as needed. Stored in a clean glass jar, this will keep for several weeks in the refrigerator.

Low-Country Barbecue Sauce

MAKES 2 CUPS

Traditional in western North Carolina, this nicely balanced, chunky finishing sauce is a sweet, tangy blend of tomatoes, onions, vinegar, lime juice, and fennel seed. It is superb on shredded pork barbecue (we use it on the pulled pork barbecue from our own smokers) and great on chicken, salmon steaks, and shrimp kebabs.

◆◆◆◆◆◆

6 tablespoons vegetable oil
2 generous cups chopped onions
1 large clove garlic, peeled and minced
1 teaspoon hot paprika
½ teaspoon fennel seeds
¼ teaspoon ground cumin
Coarse (kosher) salt and freshly ground black pepper
6 tablespoons white wine vinegar
3 tablespoons light brown sugar
2 tablespoons Worcestershire sauce
⅔ cup tomato ketchup
Juice of 1 large lime

◆◆◆◆◆◆

Heat the oil in a saucepan over medium-high heat. Add the onions and garlic, and sauté until very tender and just beginning to color, 5 to 7 minutes. Add the paprika, fennel seeds, cumin, 1 teaspoon salt, and 1 teaspoon pepper; sauté for another 2 to 3 minutes. Stir in all the remaining ingredients and simmer gently, uncovered, until slightly thickened and fragrant, 15 to 20 minutes. Season to taste with additional salt and pepper as needed. Transfer to a clean covered jar and store in the refrigerator. It will keep for several weeks; stir before using.

Bright Ideas

❦ Brush on grilled chicken, salmon steaks, and shrimp kebabs during the last few minutes of cooking.

❦ Serve as a condiment for oysters, either oven-roasted or grilled in their shells.

Helen's Honey Barbecue

MAKES 1½ CUPS

A lthough this is the only product that has her name on it, Helen Brody (the first Hay Day culinary director) developed many of the soups, dips, salads, and dressings that we sell today. This high-sugar finishing glaze was one of our first and is still one of our greatest sauces. It is spectacular brushed on roast chicken or grilled racks of ribs near the end of the cooking time, or for glazing grilled swordfish or tuna steaks.

◆◆◆◆◆◆

½ cup honey, preferably wildflower
¼ cup Dijon mustard
2 teaspoons fresh thyme, or ½ teaspoon dried
1 teaspoon Indian-style curry paste (see About Curry Paste, page 52)
½ teaspoon coarse (kosher) salt
¼ cup water
¼ cup vegetable oil

◆◆◆◆◆◆

Whisk the honey, mustard, thyme, curry paste, salt, and water together in a small saucepan. Bring to a low simmer over medium heat and drizzle the oil in slowly, whisking to incorporate. Pour into a clean jar, allow to cool thoroughly, then cover and refrigerate until ready to use. This will keep for several weeks refrigerated; stir or shake well before using.

Bright Ideas

❦ Brush on prosciutto-wrapped scallops, shrimp, ripe plantain slices, mushroom caps, or split ripe figs before grilling or broiling.

❦ Use as a finishing glaze for chicken, pork tenderloin, swordfish, or beef kebabs, or baby back ribs.

❦ Serve as a dipping sauce for grilled skewered chicken tenderloins or wings.

Savannah Barbecue Sauce

MAKES 2 CUPS

I n Georgia cooks add mustard to the classic thin vinegar-based barbecue sauce and call it a "three-way" sauce— because it's used for marinating, mopping (basting), and finishing. Its mustard flavor is particularly nice on poultry and pork tenderloin or chops. We use it as the sauce for our Southern Pulled Chicken Barbecue (page 148).

◆◆◆◆◆◆

½ cup ketchup
⅓ cup coarse-grain mustard
¼ cup white wine vinegar
1 clove garlic, peeled and minced
¼ cup finely chopped onion
1 teaspoon Worcestershire sauce
⅓ cup dark corn syrup
2 teaspoons fresh lemon juice
2 tablespoons sugar
4 or 5 dashes all-natural liquid smoke
Coarse (kosher) salt and freshly
    ground black pepper

◆◆◆◆◆◆

Combine all the ingredients except the salt and pepper in a saucepan and simmer gently, uncovered, for 30 minutes. Season to taste with salt and pepper. Transfer to a clean glass jar, let cool thoroughly, cover, and store in the refrigerator for several weeks. Shake or stir well before using.

Browned Beef Stock

MAKES 6 CUPS

Good butchers always keep a supply of fresh, meaty bones in the cooler, so don't be shy about asking for some. Roasting the bones with half of the vegetables pays huge dividends in this stock's color and depth of flavor. If you refrigerate the stock overnight, all the fat will rise obediently

to the surface, to be skimmed off and discarded in one layer in the morning.

◆◆◆◆◆◆

4 pounds meaty beef or veal bones
2 large carrots, scrubbed and coarsely
    chopped
2 large ribs celery, rinsed and coarsely
    chopped
1 large Spanish onion, peeled and
    quartered
2 large leeks, white parts only,
    well washed and coarsely chopped
Generous 1½ cups coarsely chopped
    or crushed fresh plum tomatoes
1 bouquet garni (see below)
6 black peppercorns
3 quarts water

◆◆◆◆◆◆

1. Preheat the oven to 450°F.

2. Place the bones in a large roasting pan along with half of the carrots, celery,

BOUQUET GARNI

When you come across packets of bouquet garni (mixtures of dried herbs like thyme, bay leaf, and parsley that are packaged for soups, stews, and sauces), don't hold back—buy half a dozen. They are a godsend because they are an easy way to add rich flavor to stocks, soups, and sauces. Or you can make your own by wrapping a couple of dried bay leaves, a small bunch of fresh thyme sprigs, and a couple of fresh parsley sprigs in a cheesecloth bag.

onion, and leeks. Roast until the vegetables are dark and caramelized, 30 to 40 minutes. Using a slotted spoon, transfer the bones and vegetables to a large stockpot.

3. Add the tomatoes, bouquet garni, peppercorns, and remaining vegetables to the stockpot. Add the water (or enough to cover) and bring to a boil. Reduce the heat and simmer gently, partially covered, stirring occasionally, until the liquid is reduced by half, 4 to 5 hours.

4. Pour the contents of the pot through a large fine-mesh sieve or a cheesecloth-lined colander into another container, pressing the vegetable solids with the back of a spoon to extract their juices. Discard the solids. Allow to cool to room temperature. Skim off the fat or cover and refrigerate the stock. Remove the solidified fat before using or freezing.

Chicken Stock

MAKES 5½ TO 6 CUPS

Of course you can boil the bones from last night's roast chicken, and we often do—but if you use the whole bird, you get a lot more flavor (and you also get the dividend of poached chicken meat for a pot pie, soup, pasta, or stir-fry). For that matter, you can make the stock with both cooked and uncooked chicken on the bone.

♦♦♦♦♦♦

4 to 5 pounds chicken parts or 1 whole chicken, cut into parts
2 quarts water
3 large carrots, scrubbed and cut into large pieces
4 large ribs celery, rinsed and cut into large pieces
1 large onion, peeled and quartered
2 leeks, white parts only, well washed and cut into large pieces
6 black peppercorns
1 bouquet garni (see page 269)

♦♦♦♦♦♦

1. Rinse the chicken well and place it in a large stockpot. Cover with the water and bring to a boil over high heat, skimming off any foam that rises to the surface. Reduce the heat to medium, add the vegetables, peppercorns, and bouquet garni, and return to a gentle simmer. Simmer gently, partially covered, over medium heat for 1 hour.

2. Remove the chicken parts and set them aside to cool, leaving the stock to continue cooking at a low simmer. Once the chicken is cool enough to handle, remove the meat and return the bones to the pot (save the meat for another use). Continue to simmer gently, partially covered, until reduced by nearly one-third, another 2 hours.

3. Pour the contents of the pot through a large fine-mesh sieve or a cheesecloth-lined colander into another container, pressing the vegetable solids with the back of a spoon to extract their juices. Discard the solids. Allow to cool to room temperature. Skim off the fat, or cover and refrigerate the stock. Remove the solidified fat before using or freezing.

Fish Stock

MAKES 2 QUARTS

Ask your fish market to save the bones and scraps from this morning's fillets. They will cost next to nothing, but after half an hour in the oven they will give you the basis for a magnificent, aromatic fish stock whose rich flavor will transform even the simplest sauce or chowder.

◆◆◆◆◆◆

2 tablespoons olive oil
1 large onion, peeled and coarsely
  chopped
4 carrots, scrubbed and coarsely
  chopped
3 large ribs celery, rinsed and coarsely
  chopped
2 pounds fish scraps (fresh filleted
  bones and heads)
1 bottle dry white wine
1 bouquet garni (see page 269)
6 black peppercorns
4 quarts water
Pinch of coarse (kosher) salt

◆◆◆◆◆◆

1. Preheat the oven to 350°F.

2. Toss the oil, onion, carrots, celery, and fish scraps in a large roasting pan. Roast until the vegetables are lightly colored, about 30 minutes.

3. Transfer the contents of the roasting pan to a large stockpot. Add the wine, bouquet garni, peppercorns, water, and a generous pinch of salt. Bring to a boil over medium-high heat. Reduce the heat and simmer gently, uncovered, stirring occasionally, until reduced by half, about 3 hours.

4. Pour the contents of the pot through a large fine-mesh sieve or a cheesecloth-lined colander into another container, pressing the vegetable solids with the back of a spoon to extract their juices. Discard the solids. Allow to cool to room temperature before refrigerating or freezing.

STORING STOCK

Fresh stock can be refrigerated for 3 or 4 days, and it keeps in the freezer for a couple of months. Freeze it in leftover plastic ice cream or yogurt containers. To freeze handy small amounts, pour the stock in ice-cube trays, then pop out the cubes and transfer them to freezer bags.

Vegetable Stock

MAKES 5 TO 6 CUPS

It doesn't take long to make a rich vegetable stock; the vegetables release their juices into the broth very quickly. You can make it from almost any combination of vegetables—parsnips, fennel, corncobs, mushrooms, bell peppers, and pea pods all add good flavor. You can even use vegetable scraps and trimmings, as long as they're clean and fresh, but resist the temptation to add the wizened survivors in the back of the vegetable bin—they have nothing to contribute. Avoid broccoli, artichokes, and members of the cabbage family as well, which will give the stock a strong, bitter flavor.

◆◆◆◆◆◆

1 large leek, white part only, well washed and cut into large pieces
2 large Spanish onions, peeled and quartered
3 carrots, scrubbed and cut into large pieces
4 ribs celery, rinsed and cut into large pieces
1 large clove garlic, peeled and cut in half
1 cup crushed fresh plum tomatoes
1 bouquet garni (see page 269)
Small bunch of parsley stems
2 quarts water

◆◆◆◆◆◆

1. Place all the ingredients in a large stockpot and bring to a boil over high heat. Reduce the heat to medium and simmer gently, partially covered, until the onions are translucent and the other vegetables are limp, about 1 hour. Remove from the heat and allow the vegetables to steep, covered, for another 30 minutes.

2. Pour the contents of the pot through a fine-mesh sieve or a cheesecloth-lined colander into another container, pressing the vegetable solids with the back of a spoon to extract their juices. Discard the solids. Allow to cool completely; then cover and refrigerate or freeze.

All-Purpose Pie Pastry

MAKES PASTRY FOR A 9-INCH
DOUBLE-CRUST PIE

This is a lightly sweetened classic pastry. Shortening and a bit of lemon juice make it tender and flaky. It's ideal for fruit pies, tarts, and turnovers. We use it for our Blueberry-Peach Crumb Pie (page 216) and our Bourbon-Apple-Walnut Pie (page 213). The recipe yields enough pastry for a double-crust pie, so if you're preparing a pie with a crumb topping, tuck away the other half for another creation. (Well wrapped in plastic wrap, the pastry will keep in the refrigerator for up to a week. For longer storage, roll the pastry out, press it into a pie plate, wrap, and freeze.) The next time company arrives, a great dessert will be halfway ready.

◆◆◆◆◆◆

2½ cups unbleached all-purpose flour
1 tablespoon sugar
½ teaspoon salt
½ cup unsalted butter, chilled, cut into chunks
⅓ cup solid vegetable shortening, chilled
3 to 5 tablespoons ice-cold water
1 tablespoon fresh lemon juice

◆◆◆◆◆◆

HOW TO ROLL OUT PIE CRUST

If you chill the dough for at least 30 minutes, it will be easier to manage. Any longer than that, however, and the dough may be so stiff that it should sit briefly at room temperature before rolling.

The easiest way to handle pie crust is to put the disk of dough between two large sheets of lightly floured wax paper and to roll it out from the center, flipping and turning the whole thing as needed. Peel off the paper occasionally, and sprinkle the pastry sparingly with addi-tional flour if necessary to keep it from fusing to the paper. Roll the pastry out to extend 2 inches beyond the diameter of the pie dish. Remove the top sheet of wax paper, invert the crust over the pie plate, and peel off the remaining sheet of wax paper. Press the pastry lightly into the dish.

If you will be using a top crust, roll it out in the same manner, then drape it over the filled pie. Follow the recipe directions for crimping and venting.

1. Whisk together the flour, sugar, and salt in a large bowl.

2. Using a pastry blender, cut the butter into the dry ingredients until the mixture resembles small grains of rice. Add the shortening and cut it in until the mixture resembles coarse meal. (Or you can use a food processor; see page 275).

3. In a small cup, combine 3 tablespoons of the cold water with the lemon juice. Sprinkle this over the flour mixture, 1 tablespoon at a time, working it in with the tines of a fork. Continue adding the water (up to a total of 5 tablespoons if necessary) until the dough, although somewhat crumbly, can be packed together with your hands. Knead the dough a couple of times in the bowl to form a solid mass.

4. Divide the dough in half, and using the heel of your hand, press each half out on a large sheet of wax paper to form an 8-inch round. Wrap each round well in wax paper or plastic wrap, and refrigerate for 30 minutes or until firm enough to roll and handle easily.

5. For rolling instructions, see How to Roll Out Pie Crust.

Whole-Wheat Pie Pastry

MAKES PASTRY FOR A 9-INCH DOUBLE-CRUST PIE

Whole-wheat flour is very low in gluten and therefore pro-duces flaky, delicate pastries. The rich nutty flavor of whole-wheat pastry is particularly well suited to spiced autumn fruits, as in our Pear and Apple Potpies (page 214).

273

◆◆◆◆◆◆

1¼ cups unbleached all-purpose
flour
1¼ cups stone-ground whole-wheat
flour
3 tablespoons sugar
½ teaspoon salt
8 tablespoons (1 stick) unsalted
butter, chilled, cut into large chunks
¼ cup solid vegetable shortening,
chilled
4 to 5 tablespoons apple juice
or water, chilled

◆◆◆◆◆◆

1. Whisk together the flours, sugar, and salt in a large bowl.

2. Using a pastry blender, cut the butter into the dry ingredients until the mixture resembles small grains of rice. Add the shortening and cut it in until the mixture resembles coarse meal. (Or you can use a food processor; see facing page.)

3. Sprinkle the liquid over the flour mixture 1 tablespoon at a time, working it in with the tines of a fork until the pastry is just moist enough to hold together without breaking and crumbling into bits. Knead the dough a couple of times right in the bowl to form a solid mass.

4. Divide the dough in half, and using the heel of your hand, press each half out on a large sheet of wax paper to form a 6-inch round. Wrap each round well in plastic or wax paper, and refrigerate for 30 minutes or until firm enough to roll and handle easily.

5. For rolling instructions, see How to Roll Out Pie Crust, page 273.

Sweet Butter Cornmeal Crust

MAKES PASTRY FOR A 9-INCH
DOUBLE-CRUST PIE

This is a *pâte brisée* made with cornmeal, which gives it lovely color and texture. We use it for our Strawberry-Apple Pie (page 212) and the Blackberry Mango Tart (page 217).

◆◆◆◆◆◆

1½ cups unbleached all-purpose flour
1 cup medium-grain stone-ground
cornmeal
3 tablespoons sugar
½ teaspoon salt
12 tablespoons (1½ sticks) unsalted
butter, chilled, sliced into small chunks
1 egg yolk
3 to 4 tablespoons ice-cold water

◆◆◆◆◆◆

1. Whisk together the flour, cornmeal, sugar, and salt in a large bowl.

2. Using a pastry blender, cut the butter into the dry ingredients until the mixture resembles coarse meal. (Or you can use a food processor; see facing page.)

3. In a small cup, whisk together the egg yolk and 3 tablespoons cold water. Sprinkle this over the cornmeal mixture, working it in with the tines of a fork until the dough, although somewhat crumbly,

can be packed together with your hands. If it is still dry, add the remaining 1 tablespoon water. Knead the dough a couple of times in the bowl to form a solid mass.

4. Divide the dough in half, and using the heel of your hand, press each half out on a large sheet of wax paper to form a 5-inch round. Wrap each round well in wax paper or plastic wrap, and refrigerate for 30 minutes or until firm enough to roll and handle easily.

5. For rolling instructions, see How to Roll Out Pie Crust, page 273.

PASTRY IN THE PROCESSOR

Measure the dry ingredients into a food processor and pulse five or six times to mix. Add the chilled butter and/or shortening, and pulse until the mixture resembles a coarse meal. Add the liquid through the feed tube, 1 tablespoon at a time, pulsing to incorporate. Continue adding liquid just until the dough begins to pull together.

Liquid Conversions

US	IMPERIAL	METRIC
2 tbs	1 fl oz	30 ml
3 tbs	1½ fl oz	45 ml
¼ cup	2 fl oz	60 ml
⅓ cup	2½ fl oz	75 ml
⅓ cup + 1 tbs	3 fl oz	90 ml
⅓ cup + 2 tbs	3½ fl oz	100 ml
½ cup	4 fl oz	125 ml
⅔ cup	5 fl oz	150 ml
¾ cup	6 fl oz	175 ml
¾ cup + 2 tbs	7 fl oz	200 ml
1 cup	8 fl oz	250 ml
1 cup + 2 tbs	9 fl oz	275 ml
1¼ cups	10 fl oz	300 ml
1⅓ cups	11 fl oz	325 ml
1½ cups	12 fl oz	350 ml
1⅔ cups	13 fl oz	375 ml
1¾ cups	14 fl oz	400 ml
1¾ cups + 2 tbs	15 fl oz	450 ml
1 pint (2 cups)	16 fl oz	500 ml
2½ cups	1 pint	600 ml
3¾ cups	1½ pints	900 ml
4 cups	1¾ pints	1 liter

Weight Conversions

US/UK	METRIC	US/UK	METRIC
½ oz	15 g	7 oz	200 g
1 oz	30 g	8 oz	250 g
1½ oz	45 g	9 oz	275 g
2 oz	60 g	10 oz	300 g
2½ oz	75 g	11 oz	325 g
3 oz	90 g	12 oz	350 g
3½ oz	100 g	13 oz	375 g
4 oz	125 g	14 oz	400 g
5 oz	150 g	15 oz	450 g
6 oz	175 g	1 lb	500 g

Oven Temperatures

FAHRENHEIT	GAS MARK	CELSIUS
250	½	120
275	1	140
300	2	150
325	3	160
350	4	180
375	5	190
400	6	200
425	7	220
450	8	230
475	9	240
500	10	260

Note: Reduce the temperature by 20°C (68°F) for fan-assisted ovens.

Approximate Equivalents

1 stick butter = 8 tbs = 4 oz = ½ cup
1 cup all-purpose presifted flour/dried bread crumbs = 5 oz
1 cup granulated sugar = 8 oz
1 cup (packed) brown sugar = 6 oz
1 cup confectioners' sugar = 4½ oz
1 cup honey/syrup = 11 oz
1 cup grated cheese = 4 oz
1 cup dried beans = 6 oz
1 large egg = 2 oz = about ¼ cup
1 egg yolk = about 1 tbs
1 egg white = about 2 tbs

Note: All the above conversions are approximate, but close enough to be useful when converting from one system to another.

Index